Raquel Fornieles
The Concept of News in Ancient Greek Literature

Trends in Classics – Supplementary Volumes

Edited by
Franco Montanari and Antonios Rengakos

Associate Editors
Stavros Frangoulidis · Fausto Montana · Lara Pagani
Serena Perrone · Evina Sistakou · Christos Tsagalis

Scientific Committee
Alberto Bernabé · Margarethe Billerbeck
Claude Calame · Kathleen Coleman · Jonas Grethlein
Philip R. Hardie · Stephen J. Harrison · Stephen Hinds
Richard Hunter · Giuseppe Mastromarco
Gregory Nagy · Theodore D. Papanghelis
Giusto Picone · Alessandro Schiesaro
Tim Whitmarsh · Bernhard Zimmermann

Volume 141

Raquel Fornieles

The Concept of News in Ancient Greek Literature

—

DE GRUYTER

ISBN 978-3-11-153682-8
e-ISBN (PDF) 978-3-11-102237-6
e-ISBN (EPUB) 978-3-11-102295-6
ISSN 1868-4785

Library of Congress Control Number: 2022946900

Bibliographic information published by the Deutsche Nationalbibliothek
The Deutsche Nationalbibliothek lists this publication in the Deutsche Nationalbibliografie; detailed bibliographic data are available on the Internet at http://dnb.dnb.de.

© 2024 Walter de Gruyter GmbH, Berlin/Boston
This volume is text- and page-identical with the hardback published in 2023.
Editorial Office: Alessia Ferreccio and Katerina Zianna
Logo: Christopher Schneider, Laufen

www.degruyter.com

Preface

In this book I aim to show that the concept of news that we have today is not a modern invention, but rather a social and cultural institution that has been passed down to us by the Ancient Greeks. This concept is only modified by the social, political and economic conditions that make our society different from theirs.

This book started out as my doctoral thesis, "The transmission of news in Ancient Greek Literature" (recognized with the Award of the Spanish Society for Classical Studies), which I wrote at the Universidad Autónoma de Madrid and submitted in 2015. I wish to express my sincere gratitude to my supervisor, Emilio Crespo, and thank the members of the committee before whom I defended my thesis: Marina Benedetti, Luz Conti, Óscar Loureda, Luis Macía and Rafael Martínez. I was fortunate enough to have been given valuable advice and useful suggestions from a number of colleagues, including Georgios Giannakis and Carmen Leal Soares, who also wrote the reports that were required for me to be awarded an International PhD.

It is very difficult to express in a few words the gratitude I feel towards my friends and my family. This book would not have been possible if it were not for the love of the most important people in my life: my parents, Matías and Antonia, my brother, Matías, and, of course, Roberto, whose unconditional support I felt at every stage of this journey.

This book is dedicated to all of them and, above all, to Adriana and Héctor.

Contents

Preface — **V**
List of Figures — **IX**

Introduction — **XI**
The approach from Anthropology — **XIV**
The concept of news today — **XVI**
The concept of news in Ancient Greek Literature — **XVII**
Using ἄγγελος and its derivatives to understand the concept of news — **XVII**
Etymology: ἄγγελος, a Greek creation — **XX**
Meanings — **XXI**

1 Homer: The *Iliad* and the *Odyssey* — **1**
Κήρυκες: heralds by profession — 2
Ἄγγελοι: anyone can be a messenger — 5
From the death of Patroclus to the return of Odysseus: bad and good news — 13
Final remarks — 32

2 Greek Lyric Poetry: Pindar and Bacchylides — **34**
Two practically identical figures — 35
The triumph is news — 38
Final remarks — 45

3 Tragedy — **47**
Κήρυκες: heralds by profession — 47
Ἄγγελοι: professional messengers — 58
Why messenger scenes? — 60
The presence of the chorus makes scene-shifts practically impossible — 60
A chorus cannot act crowd-scenes — 60
Miracles cannot be shown on stage — 61
Death on stage was not feasible — 61
Literary tradition — 62
Defining the tragic messenger — 62
Ἄγγελοι play an informative role — 65
Ἄγγελοι are eyewitnesses: the αὐτοψία — 66
Ἄγγελοι reinforce their speeches with statements from the main characters of the events they relate — 68

VIII — Contents

The news transmitted by ἄγγελοι is completely reliable —— 69
Criteria for classifying characters as ἄγγελοι —— 70
From war to suicides: a wide range of news —— 72
Final remarks —— 100

**4	Aristophanic Comedy —— 101**
Κήρυκες: heralds by profession —— 101
Ἄγγελοι: the parody of the tragic messenger —— 106
Absurd announcements: the mockery of tragic news —— 115
Final remarks —— 125

**5	Historians: Herodotus, Thucydides and Xenophon —— 127**
Ἄγγελοι and κήρυκες: professionals in diplomatic missions —— 129
Bearers of news —— 134
Spies looking for information from the enemy —— 139
Royal messengers —— 143
From news of war to legal terms —— 143
Final remarks —— 182

**6	Greek Oratory: Isocrates, Lysias, Aeschines and Demosthenes —— 185**
No news from the messenger —— 185
Public matters and legal language —— 187
Final remarks —— 213

**7	Fake News —— 215**
Derivatives of ἄγγελος: truth and falsehood —— 216
Fake news in Greek tragedy —— 219
Fake news in the works of historians —— 225
Final remarks —— 229

**8	Conclusions —— 230**

Bibliography —— 233
General Index —— 251
Index Locorum —— 255

List of Figures

Fig. 1: Ἄγγελος and its derivatives in Homer, Pindar, Bacchylides, Aeschylus, Sophocles, Euripides, Aristophanes, Herodotus, Thucydides, Xenophon, Lysias, Isocrates, Demosthenes and Aeschines. —— XVIII
Fig. 2: Ἄγγελος and its derivatives in the *Iliad*. —— 14
Fig. 3: Ἄγγελος and its derivatives in the *Odyssey*. —— 14
Fig. 4: Ἄγγελος and its derivatives in Pindar's Odes. —— 38
Fig. 5: Ἄγγελος and its derivatives in Bacchylides' Odes. —— 38
Fig. 6: Ἄγγελος and its derivatives in Aeschylus. —— 73
Fig. 7: Ἄγγελος and its derivatives in Sophocles. —— 73
Fig. 8: Ἄγγελος and its derivatives in Euripides. —— 74
Fig. 9: Ἄγγελος and its derivatives in Aristophanes' comedies. —— 115
Fig. 10: Ἄγγελος and its derivatives in Herodotus. —— 144
Fig. 11: Ἄγγελος and its derivatives in Thucydides. —— 145
Fig. 12: Ἄγγελος and its derivatives in Xenophon. —— 146
Fig. 13: Ἄγγελος and its derivatives in Lysias' speeches. —— 188
Fig. 14: Ἄγγελος and its derivatives in Isocrates' speeches. —— 188
Fig. 15: Ἄγγελος and its derivatives in Demosthenes' speeches. —— 189
Fig. 16: Ἄγγελος and its derivatives in Aeschines' speeches. —— 189

Introduction

> Corker looked at him sadly. 'You know, you've got a lot to learn about journalism. Look at it this way. News is what a chap who doesn't care much about anything wants to read. And it's only news until he's read it. After that it's dead. We're paid to supply news. If someone else has sent a story before us, our story isn't news'.
>
> <div align="right">Evelyn Waugh, <i>Scoop: a novel about journalists</i></div>

Our societies are constantly checking the news. Day in and day out, we read the news in newspapers and on websites, we watch it on the television, and we listen to it on the radio. We are given news by our neighbours and friends and we instantly learn everything — as it happens almost — through social networks. A pandemic is news, as are the movements of royalty, celebrities, presidents, political parties, and football teams. We are also told news about forthcoming weddings, divorces, deaths, and the births of celebrity children. Even the dresses and suits worn by actresses and actors at the Oscars (or any other gala) are in the news. We might even consider newsworthy the fact that a relative should win the lottery or that someone has broken into your neighbour's house. But is news for one person news for another? Not always.

We live surrounded by news. News makes us think; it is at the heart of many of our conversations and discussions and, on numerous occasions, we wait for it eagerly. However, do we really know what we mean when we are talking about news? The answer is, in my opinion, clear and simple: no, we do not. Defining news is an almost impossible task and the proof of this is that the different definitions given by dictionaries are imprecise (although they do provide us with some key concepts). The English term 'news' indicates that we are dealing with something new; something that we did not previously know. The *Cambridge Dictionary* states that it is "information or report about recent events" and the term is defined in the *Oxford English Dictionary* as follows:

> The report or account of recent (esp. important or interesting) events or occurrences brought or coming to one as new information; new occurrences as a subject of report or talk; tidings.

The French 'nouvelle' and the Spanish 'nueva' are synonyms to news, so the idea of novelty is something that we must bear in mind. On the other hand, in the *Diccionario de la lengua española* (*DLE*) it is highlighted that 'noticia' comes from the Latin *notitia*, which refers to something that is made known. *Notitia* is formed by adding the suffix *–itia* to *notus*, perfect participle of *nosco* ('to know') whose etymology is in the Indo-European root *$gneh_3$-* from which we also have the Greek terms γνῶσις ('knowledge') or γιγνώσκω ('know'). We can deduce, therefore, that news is something that was previously unknown but is no longer so. The *DLE* is also clear that the fact or event must be disclosed, and the announcement must be made publicly.

The proposals offered in journalism handbooks do not exactly shed light on the matter either. In 1934, Carl N. Warren published *Modern News Reporting*,[1] long regarded as the great reference manual both inside and outside the United States. Warren divided journalistic texts into 'straight news' and 'features'. The main objective of 'straight news' was to inform, to offer strictly informative stories about significant people, things or events. The purpose of 'features', on the contrary, was to entertain, amuse the reader and generate emotions in more literary style.[2] In addition, he listed the characteristics that, with few nuances, are still being proposed today. According to Warren, for an event to be considered news it must meet the following requirements:[3]

> a) Immediacy: referred to time. Although it seems to be obvious, Warren insists: "News, first of all, must be new". However, Warren specifies: "The immediacy rule does not apply to the time of occurrence, but only to the time of disclosure. No matter how old it is, the reporter may give an up-to-the-minute touch to his story by the simple process of pointing out that it has just become available for publication".

> b) Proximity: immediacy in space. Warren says that a person's life can be described as a series of concentric circles. The smallest, the one in the center, represents his / her own wants, needs and problems. Next would be his / her family, companions, neighbours or the neighborhood in which he / she lives. The next circle would be his / her city; then his / her country and so on.

---

[1] Ross (1911, 46–47) had already established a similar division. See also Martín Vivaldi (2006, 389), Grijelmo (2008) or Martínez Albertos (1972, 37; 2004 and 2007, 271–287), who classifies 'news' as one of the journalistic genres.

[2] In 1996, in his speech entitled "The best job in the world", Gabriel García Márquez stated that "print journalism is a literary genre". We cannot tackle the speech in this book, but it is interesting to bear in mind certain studies, such as that of Fernández Parrat (2006), who concludes that the boundaries between both disciplines are indeed there, although they are somewhat blurred. She adds that differences lie in the aims, commitment to real events and the truth, the medium, regularity, choice of content and the author's profession. See also Gargurevich (1982), Gomis (1989), Carandell Robusté (1997), Martínez Hernando (1998) and Padrón Barquín (2004). Also interesting are Coseriu (1992) and the Spanish translation of Coseriu/Loureda Lamas (2006), in which he focuses on the historical tale. The theory of the genres of journalism can be traced back to the tradition of literary genres, but its development does not depend so much on literature as on the evolution of mass media.

[3] See Warren (1934, 13–28).

c) Prominence: people, places, things or situations well known to the public based on the audience's position, wealth, notoriety or achievements arouse a strong interest. Everyone likes or dislikes heroes, politicians, singers or athletes.

d) Curiosity: what is strange, what arouses our curiosity, is news. In this respect, an old aphorism is always repeated: it is not news that a dog bites a man, but that a man bites a dog.

e) Conflict: Warren also points out that, for better or for worse, fights between men and armies, that of men against animals, that of one way of thinking against another or that of one power against another have always disturbed people. Journalists are aware that any fight for supremacy constitutes an element of journalistic interest and, therefore, they constantly use terms such as 'attack, 'challenge', 'duel', 'dispute', 'victim', 'defeat', 'failure', 'success' or 'triumph', 'victory'.

f) Oddity, emotion: the fact that the event affects our emotions, awakens our instincts. Warren considers that all emotions gathered make up 'human interest': ambition, hate or resentment but also love, desire, and so on. Closely linked to emotion, actuality and proximity is transcendence, that is, the significance or importance that a given fact has for the people (as individuals or in mass) who receive the news.

g) Suspense: news generates intrigue, and we want to know more. Uncertainty is one of the aspects that, in Warren's opinion, creates and expands the appeal of the news.

h) Consequences: How is the reported piece of news going to affect the audience? Future repercussions, positive or negative, that the event may entail. According to Warren, news has relevant consequences.

These are the 'ingredients' proposed by Warren, who also claims that they do not always all need to be present. Most of these requirements are reflected in the different definitions and interpretations I have offered, although it is striking that Warren does not mention such a determining factor as truthfulness. As we will see throughout this book, news must be true (and the source of information is useful to check that it is). If not, we are not dealing with news but with rumours or with false (*fake*) news.[4]

The various definitions of news offered so far have several elements in common. All of them highlight that news is something new and previously unknown. But it is worth asking now if we really view as news everything and anything that is communicated to us that we did not know before, because the answer is again negative. We are also told about the interest that the reported fact arouses in the receiver. However, not all of us have the same concerns, so it

---

4 See, among others, Vázquez Bermúdez (2006, 58).

is obvious that we will not always be interested in the same things as others. A series of pragmatic factors come into play in which the basic elements of any communicative act take part: the speaker (sender), the hearer (or receiver), the message and the context.

On the other hand, we cannot forget the importance of the mass media as a channel through which we receive news. This applies in the case of advanced societies in which press, radio, television and even social networks play a dominant role, but this has not always been the case and not all societies are like ours.

No matter how hard we try, we cannot answer the question: what is news? According to Loureda Lamas (2001, 133–138), the answer to questions like this lies in language itself:

> These are questions that refer to that which is usually common (general) in a class of things. Therefore, words and concepts are likely to be defined (for example, the concept of 'word', the concept of 'phrase', the concept of 'sentence', etc.), but objects are also identified, delimited, described and classified.

Loureda adds that what is empirically formed from object traits is not a concept but a prototype, a representation, or an abstract ideal model.

The approach from Anthropology

Nowadays, the concept of news is intrinsically linked to elements such as the mass media and, above all, social networks, and a mass audience. This applies, in my view, to current journalism models (a modern discipline subject to constant changes) and to those societies in which the mass media and social networks play such a significant role. However, I have asked myself the following questions: does the emergence of the concept of news expressly derive from the birth of journalism? Did news not exist before the emergence of journalism (as we know it today)? What happens in societies less advanced than ours or, quite simply, in those places where mass (media) culture does not even exist?

The answers to the two first questions are obvious: news was not conceived alongside journalism because the concept of news already existed before this discipline was born. In this respect, it should be noted that specifying the origins of journalism is not an easy task. The commonly accepted theory is the one that links them to the concepts of 'newspaper' and 'periodicity' and, therefore, back to 1605, when the first known weekly publication appeared in Strasbourg: *Relation*.[5]

Regarding what happens in other societies, we do not need to go back to classical antiquity or the origins of humanity. Just think of small rural villages where access to the media is virtually non-existent or in the tribes of hunter-gatherers who live completely isolated from what we mean by civilization. These peoples also feel the need to exchange news, as the anthropologist Raymond Firth tells us in his studies on Tikopia, a small island in the southwestern Pacific Ocean. The author lived there in 1928 and 1929 and quickly became aware of the eagerness of its inhabitants for news. Firth (1956)[6] says that the population travelled the coast and the island roads daily and the exchange of news (obviously based on word of mouth) was one of the foundations of social relations. However, contact was reduced among the different districts where the natives lived, and they hardly met unless there was a formal ceremony, such as some type of dance or religious festival. Of course, his contact with the outside world was practically non-existent. He only saw others on the few occasions that a ship reached the island or if they received a visit of some kind.

One of the anecdotes told by Raymond Firth is of great significance for our understanding of news. According to Firth, he lived on a hill in the Faea district and regularly went to greet the chief of another district. As soon as he saw him arrive, this man asked: "Any news from Faea?" and then, Firth informed him of possible developments in fishing and hunting, notified him if someone had fallen ill or passed away, and told him what the chief of Faea had been up to since his previous visit.

Some years later, specifically in 1952, when Firth returned to Tikopia, he met this man again, who was spending the night in Somosomo, in the island's

---

5 The complete name was *Relation aller Fürnemmen und gedenckwürdigen Historien*. Until relatively recently, the first weekly publication was considered to be *Avisa Relation oder Zeitung*, which was published in 1609 in Wolfenbüttel. However, the *World Association of Newspapers* recognized in 2005 that *Relation*, printed by the German Johann Carolus (1575–1634), began to be published four years earlier. Anyway, the first journalistic manifestations go much further back in time. Timoteo Álvarez (2004, 26–28) warns of the existence of certain "informational products" from the 13th and 14th centuries. The next pivotal moment in history was the development of the printing press in Mainz. According to Guillamet Lloveras (2008, 44–47), some scholars have attempted to establish a remote history of journalism in the written forms of circulation of private news in ancient Greece and Rome. They focused, above all, on the ways in which political and military events were recorded by Herodotus, Thucydides and Xenophon. Precedents have also been sought in Annals or in the *Acta Diurna* whose origin is attributed to Julius Caesar. On the latter, see also Boissier (1903, 239–278) or Frasca (2003, 80).
6 See also Firth (1966).

centre. The man asked a similar question: "Any news from the beach?". On this occasion, the anthropologist's answer was: "No", and his negative word greatly disappointed the interlocutor.

Firth clarifies that he translates as 'news' the word 'taranga', a term that refers to speech in general, which indicates the oral nature of communication in Tikopia. The source of information is very relevant for the people of Tikopia, but they do not make a distinction between verified news and unverified rumours. The only difference is, according to Firth, when they use the expressions 'taranga' or 'faoa', which means 'speech of the crowd' or 'speech of the people in general'.

In my opinion, examples like these are clear evidence of why we cannot give a definition of 'news'. The chief of Uta did not have access to the mass media that societies like ours have. His concept of news is not at all (*a priori*) similar to ours, but he and the rest of the inhabitants of the island also feel the need to receive news. We are still unable to define 'news' and we cannot do so because, unlike other terms (e.g. 'house', 'car', 'dog', etc.), 'news' is not a natural entity reflected in a word. In the same way as other words like wisdom, justice and so on, 'news' is a concept, a mental construction (Shoemaker 2006, 105), a complex cultural, social, and even economic construction that can only be understood by considering the historical, technological, political, social, and economic conditions that surround it (Harrison 2006, 11). News also enjoys a prestigious position in the hierarchy of our cultural scale of values (Hartley 1982, 9).

Of course, news also existed in ancient Greece, and this is why this volume does not aim to offer a definition of news per se, but simply aims to find out how the concept of news was created in ancient Greek literature, how it has been passed down to us, and whether it is the same as ours or is different.

The concept of news today

In an attempt to date the birth of the concept of news, Michael Schudson (1978, 4) claimed that it is an American invention of the nineteenth century — born during the term of Andrew Jackson (1829–1837) —, a product of the democratization of the political, social and economic life of the time. However, critical voices emerged later to prove that this was not the case.

According to scholars such as Hartley (1982), the historical account of news begins along with the birth of humanity and the development of language. On the other hand, Mitchell Stephens (1988) in his book, *A History of News: from the Drum to the Satellite*, fiercely criticized many historians of journalism. History itself, affirms Stephens, should provide us with the keys to understanding news.

For this reason, he proposed an approach to news in which history was taken into account to prove that we are not dealing with a modern discovery, but with a basic essential in all societies.⁷

The concept of news in Ancient Greek Literature

In *News and Society in the Greek Polis,* Sian Lewis (1996, 3) points out that news can only be interpreted as a specific type of information whose dissemination makes it important. According to Lewis, the fact that Sophocles wrote *Philoctetes* is just information; instead, it is news that he won the first prize at the Dyonisia with this tragedy. In Lewis' opinion, both news and the process of reporting news are inseparable. For this reason, whatever happens when a fact is reported should be considered news, and not the fact itself. Therefore, the term that would allow us to identify something as a news item is the verb ἀγγέλλω, the word that refers to the process.

In order to understand what was considered news by the Greeks in the period spanning from the second millennium BC to the end of the fourth BC, I asked myself how they represented their concept of news. The formation of the terms of this lexical family led me to start not with ἀγγελία (ἀγγελίη), the word used, in principle, to designate news — but with ἄγγελος, from which ἀγγελία derives. From the term ἄγγελος, I continued my study with the analysis of its derivatives documented in the works of the authors that comprise the corpus of this book.

Using ἄγγελος and its derivatives to understand the concept of news

The study of ἄγγελος and its derivatives led me to analyse a total of fifty-two terms, all of which are included in Figure 1.

---

7 Sociologists Molotch and Lester (1974, 109) argue that news comes as a result of the need that we all feel to be told what we have not seen, the possibility of filling in these empty spaces with the help of others but also the production work offered by the mass media. Stephens (1998, 9) seems to share their point of view. Shoemaker/Cohen (2006) assure us that news is motivated by the innate interest that human beings have in two types of information: that related to people, ideas or deviant events (both positively and negatively) and that linked to ideas or significant events for societies.

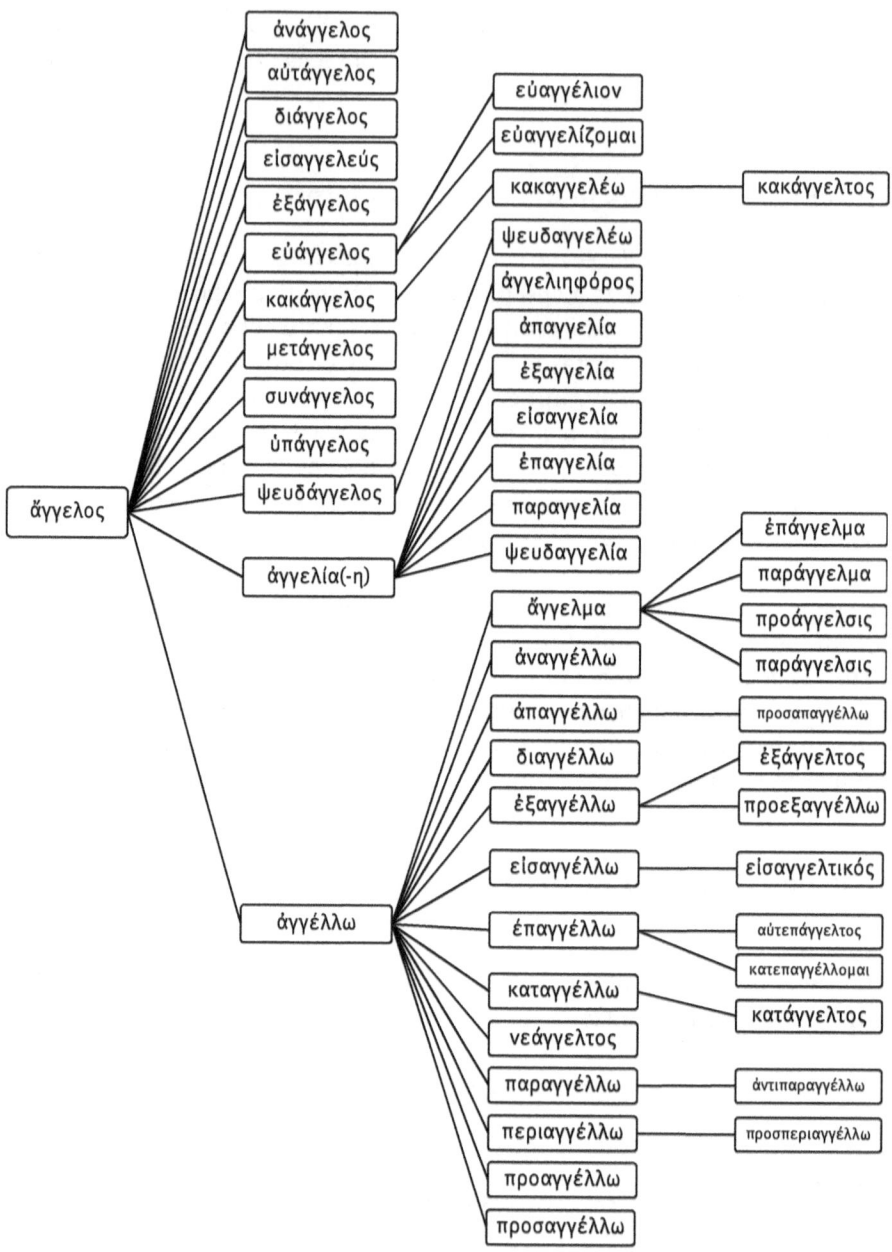

Fig. 1: Ἄγγελος and its derivatives in Homer, Pindar, Bacchylides, Aeschylus, Sophocles, Euripides, Aristophanes, Herodotus, Thucydides, Xenophon, Lysias, Isocrates, Demosthenes and Aeschines.

By examining all these terms, we can draw certain relevant conclusions regarding what was considered news in ancient Greece. I take as a starting point the fact that the ἄγγελος is traditionally considered to be the bearer of news par excellence, especially in Greek tragedy, a genre in which, as we will see, the terms derived from the primitive word become consolidated as technical terms associated with this specific figure. It should be noted, however, that not everything announced by means of ἄγγελος and its derivatives is news. However, in the vast majority of cases it is, and almost all the words studied refer to news at a certain moment.

Furthermore, the items of the lexical family derived from ἄγγελος share an essential feature: the fact that they all tend to imply a public announcement. Even so, that a public announcement is made does not necessarily mean that it is, in turn, something official. In ancient Greece, news was transmitted by word of mouth. This is somewhat inevitable, since the Greeks did not have any other (mass) media.[8] As Camp (1986, 99) rightly points out, so long before the existence of television, radio, newspapers, telephone, internet and Facebook, Twitter, Instagram and other social networks, constructions such as this one could be conceived as perfect media for the spread of official information, but neither this information nor the rest of state notifications were transmitted by using ἄγγελος and its derivatives.

The Greek language clearly differentiates the official proclamation (κήρυγμα) made by a herald (κῆρυξ), a kind of official, from the announcement made by an ἄγγελος, which is rarely linked to the State. We will also see that ἄγγελοι report news that has to do with something public or private insofar as the public or private element affects a public (or not) character, which explains how close the figures of the ἄγγελος and the κῆρυξ turn out to be.

The public character of ἄγγελος and its derivatives is also developed in some different scenarios — as verbal and extraverbal contexts reflect[9] — and this will also provide us with relevant data. For instance, public proclamations of victories in athletic competitions are announced using ἀγγελία, ἀγγέλλω, ἀπαγγέλλω and διαγγέλλω.

On the other hand, the tragic ἄγγελος is expected to (publicly) report both to the other characters and the spectators the news that cannot be represented on stage and, nevertheless, turns out to be crucial for the development of the action.

---

8 Ober (1989, 148) argues that precisely because of the lack of organized media, much of the information exchanged by Greeks depended on rumours.
9 On verbal and extraverbal context, see Coseriu (1982).

In times of war, in the works of historians, no one expects to be informed that a certain festival will be held, for instance. Public affairs are considered news, however; that is, everything that affects the community. This is usually linked to war and all that war entails: deaths, defeats, victories, truces, and so on.

In many of the speeches of Isocrates, Lysias, Demosthenes and Aeschines, on the other hand, there are also political problems and war-associated interests, and this is why news that interests people points in the same direction. However, the context is quite different. It is no longer a matter of the battlefield, but of the Assembly or the Council, where explanations are required and decisions that affect all citizens are made. For this reason, the words derived from ἄγγελος tend to appear in the speeches of ambassadors who are accountable for their actions as mediators in conflicts. Other aspects related to public life — such as crimes or offences committed by citizens — are also of interest. On rare occasions, the derivatives of ἄγγελος refer to the private sphere. They usually allude to the public sphere, however, because the offences affect the entire *polis*.[10]

Etymology: ἄγγελος, a Greek creation

The etymology of ἄγγελος is uncertain. Dictionaries[11] rule out a possible provenance from Sanskrit *áṅgiras-*, linked to mythical names, which would be based on the fact that intermediaries between gods and men would also be mentioned. Instead, it is proposed that it could be an oriental loanword, as in the case of ἄγγαρος, which designates the Persian royal mount described by Herodotus (Hdt., 8.98.2).[12]

We are told by Chantraine, Beekes and *DGE* that ἄγγελος could be documented in Mycenaean Greek in the form *a-ke-ro*, which occurs in four tablets: PY Cn 1287.1, PY Ea 136, PY Jo 438.20 and PY Vn 493.1.[13] In PY Vn 493 we find the phrase *a-ke-ro e-po a-ke-ra₂-te* and the interpretation of *a-ke-ro* will also influence how we understand *a-ke-ra₂-te*, the Mycenaean word for which a possible correspondence with the verb ἀγγέλλω (specifically with the participle ἀγγείλα-

---

10 In this respect, see Stephens (1988, 35).
11 See Chantraine (1974, 8), Frisk (1960, 8), Beekes (2010, 9) and *DGE*.
12 Cf. the example (10) in the chapter on historians. Remember also that ἄγγαρος occurs once in Greek tragedy. Cf. Aesch. *A*. 282, a passage given in example (8) in the chapter dealing with Greek tragedy.
13 For explanations on these, see Fornieles Sánchez (2015, 42–45).

ντες) has been proposed. Likewise, there is a third Mycenaean term that could be related to a derivative of ἄγγελος, in particular ἀγγέλλω. I am referring to *a-ke-ra-no*, an anthroponym only documented in KN Vc 205.

From my point of view, it is hard to believe that *a-ke-ro*, *a-ke-ra₂-te* and *a-ke-ra-no* do not allude to the mentioned terms on any of the tablets on which they appear. Therefore, it is very likely that the term ἄγγελος already existed in Mycenaean Greek and that we are not dealing with a loanword, but with a Greek creation (and the same goes for the verb ἀγγέλλω, which also seems to exist already in Mycenaean Greek).

Meanings

The ἄγγελος is defined in dictionaries as a 'messenger', 'envoy' and, on some occasions (especially in the works of historians), as equivalent to an 'ambassador'. The main function of an ἄγγελος is to announce or report[14] something and it is common for him to have an animate referent, although the term can be also used to designate objects that act as signals that reveal something hidden or unknown, such as dust (Aesch., *Supp.* 180: κόνιν, ἄναυδον ἄγγελον στρατοῦ·) or the tongue (Eur., *Supp.* 203: ἄγγελον γλῶσσαν λόγων).

In Homer, it is very common for the term to allude to gods like Iris and Hermes, messengers sent by other gods. However, heralds, omens and even some heroes are called ἄγγελοι. This leads us to conclude that in the *Iliad* and the *Odyssey* anyone who has something to report can be an ἄγγελος. The same goes for lyric choral poetry, but not for Greek tragedy, where the ἄγγελος — and the ἐξάγγελος — is a crucial character created to play a very specific role: to transmit news that cannot be represented on stage. In Aristophanic comedy, this figure will be continually parodied. On the other hand, in the works of historians the ἄγγελος carries out important diplomatic tasks. In the speeches of Isocrates, Lysias, Demosthenes and Aeschines, the term ἄγγελος is scarcely productive but that does not mean that there was no news to announce.

In the corpus studied in this volume, a total of fifty-two words formed by composition or derivation from the lexem ἀγγελ- are documented (Figure 1). All of these will be properly dealt with in the following chapters, but I want to draw attention to two now, the noun ἀγγελία and the verb ἀγγέλλω, to make some clarifications. If we turn to dictionaries again, we are told that ἀγγελία can be a 'message', an 'announcement' or 'proclamation', a 'news item' and an 'order'.

---

14 Cf. *LSJ* s.u. ἄγγελος: "generally, one that announces or tells".

Ἀγγέλλω, for its part, is a verb of saying whose basic meaning is 'to announce' and whose expected construction is that of ἀγγέλλω with three syntactic arguments: a subject, a second argument in the accusative (expressing result)[15] and a third argument in the dative (recipient). Thus, ἀγγέλλω implies the presence of a speaker who announces something to a hearer. The semantic content of the announcement inherent to the verb is not always easy to pin down. The different definitions given in dictionaries indicate that ἀγγέλλω means 'to report', 'bear a message or news', 'make a proclamation' or 'transmit orders'. There are examples of all these cases in the authors studied.

---

15 As we will see, it can also be a ὡς or ὅτι substantive clause, an AcI (*accusativus cum infinitivo*), or an AcP (*accusativus cum participio*) construction.

1 Homer: The *Iliad* and the *Odyssey*

Even casual readers of the *Iliad* and the *Odyssey* will have noted the constant presence of an expression associated with the communicative act: ἔπεα πτερόεντα (προσηύδα), 'winged words'. Words are endowed with wings in both poems, and this association also applies to news, which 'flies'. In the *Iliad*, how far away or ferocious a battle is has little impact on the spread of information, which flows successfully both among fellow warriors and between rival factions. In the *Odyssey*, the importance of news can be perceived from the very beginning of the poem: in light of the unsustainable situation caused by the suitors, Telemachus, Odysseus' son, is urged by Athena to undertake a journey in search of news of his father (the Telemachy).

Communicative effectiveness is taken for granted in the Homeric poems, and the formula 'winged words' is strong evidence of this, since it implies a very positive consideration of the process of communication. We can easily assume that the words of the speaker reach the receiver without having been modified (Durán López 1999, 10). However, all winged words cannot be labelled as news. An analysis of the word ἄγγελος and its derivatives can help us to understand what was considered 'news' by the members of the societies represented in the *Iliad* and the *Odyssey*.

The lexicon could be, *a priori*, a very useful tool for differentiating between those primarily responsible for the effective dissemination of information in the *Iliad* and the *Odyssey*. The Greek language makes a clear distinction between the messenger and the herald in the terms ἄγγελος and κῆρυξ. The ἄγγελος would be the person in charge of transmitting news, whereas the κῆρυξ would be responsible, among other things, for conveying official messages.[1] However, the difference is not always so evident in the Homeric poems,[2] especially when

---

[1] See Longo (1978, 72): "Quanto alla differenziazone fra la funzione di messagero e quella di araldo, va detto che, anche se esse comportano un'area abbastanza ampia di coincidenze, di norma l'*anghelos* è latore di una notizia, il *keryx* di una notifica. In altri termini: l'*anghelos* è portatore di una comunicazione informativa (che potrà essere 'attiva', quando vi sia transmissione di notizia dalla fonte al destinatario, o 'passiva', quando il messo venga spedito ad attingere la notizia ad una fonte, e destinatario, fruitore, ne sia il primo mittente), il *keryx* è portatore di una comunicazione ingiuntiva (che è sempre 'attiva')".

[2] Nor in Greek literature in general, as this study shall demonstrate. A *Suda*'s entry ("Κῆρυξ ἐν πολέμῳ, πρέσβυς ἐν εἰρήνῃ") offers an interesting solution proposing that the κῆρυξ performs his duties during wartime, whereas the πρέσβυς intercedes in peacetime (see Adler 1971). The grammarian Hesychius complicates the situation by defining the κῆρυξ as ἄγγελος, διάκονος,

we consider the fact that Homer refers to the heralds Talthybius, Eurybates and Idaeus as ἄγγελοι (cf. Hom., *Il.* 1.334 and Hom., *Il.* 7.274: κήρυκες Διὸς ἄγγελοι ἠδὲ καὶ ἀνδρῶν).

Κήρυκες: heralds by profession

The herald is remarkably present in Homer's poems. The term κῆρυξ occurs 87 times in total (43 in the *Iliad* and 44 in the *Odyssey*) and the poet attributes to this figure an essential feature to distinguish him from the ἄγγελος. Being a herald means practicing a profession:

(1) Hom., *Od.* 19.134–135

> τῶ οὔτε ξείνων ἐμπάζομαι οὔθ' ἱκετάων
> οὔτε τι **κηρύκων**, οἳ δημιοεργοὶ ἔασιν·

> Therefore, I pay no attention to strangers, nor to suppliants, nor yet to **heralds**, who are in the public service.[3]

The speaker is Penelope, who is explaining to Odysseus — disguised as a beggar — how much she misses her husband. The queen alludes to the heralds as δημιοεργοί (δημιουργοί), that is, as men who are in the public service. Previously, the swineherd Eumaeus had listed other trades under this term:

(2) Hom., *Od.* 17.382–385

> τίς γὰρ δὴ ξεῖνον καλεῖ ἄλλοθεν αὐτὸς ἐπελθὼν
> ἄλλον γ', εἰ μὴ τῶν, οἳ **δημιοεργοὶ** ἔασι;
> μάντιν ἢ ἰητῆρα κακῶν ἢ τέκτονα δούρων,
> ἢ καὶ θέσπιν ἀοιδόν, ὅ κεν τέρπῃσιν ἀείδων.

> For who goes visiting elsewhere so as to call in another stranger, unless he is **one who works for the people**, either a prophet, or a healer of sickness, or a skilled workman, or inspired singer, one who can give delight by his singing?

πρεσβυτής in the singular and by insisting on it in the plural: "οἱ ἄγγελοι, οἱ διάκονοι, οἱ τὰς ὑπηρετικὰς ἐπιτελοῦντες πράξεις" (see Latte 1953).
3 Translations of the *Odyssey* are taken from Lattimore (1965) with some modifications.

By referring to heralds also as δημιοεργοί, Penelope is highlighting their professional nature as individuals who were in public service. However, as we will show below, this official nature appears only in certain contexts.

Homeric heralds belong to a very specific social class: they are servants, θεράποντες,[4] as is evident in the mentions of Talthybius and Eurybates, "who were heralds and hard-working henchmen to him (Agamemnon)"[5] and Mulius, a herald from Dulichium, Amphinomus' henchman.[6] Moreover, with very few exceptions, the identity of the κήρυκες is well-known. In the *Iliad*, Talthybius, Eurybates, Odius and Thootes are the heralds of the Achaeans, whilst Idaeus is the herald of the Trojans. Eumedes (Dolon's father), Periphas and Epytos (his father) are also mentioned. In the *Odyssey*, Peisenor and Medon are heralds in Ithaca, whereas Pontonous belongs to Alcinous' house.

Thalmann (2011) states that heralds are blessed with the gift of ubiquity. In the public sphere, they often behave as town criers.[7] On the contrary, during wartime they summon the hosts to the assembly (Hom., *Il*. 2.50, 2.437, 9.10, 11.685 and Hom., *Od*. 2.6), demand silence (Hom., *Il*. 2.97, 2.280 or 18.503) and place the sceptre in the hands of the man who is going to speak (Hom., *Il*. 18.502, 23.567 and Hom., *Od*. 2.38). Heralds also oversee the lots (Hom., *Il*. 7.183), act as jurors (Hom., *Il*. 7.275–278), command warriors to attack (Hom., *Il*. 2.442) and order men on guard to stay alert (Hom., *Il*. 8.517). They also receive and act as guides to visitors (Hom., *Od*. 4.301 and 13.64), accompany those who go on embassies (Hom., *Il*. 9.170 and 24.282 and Hom., *Od*. 9.90, 10.59, 10.102 and 19.244) and deliver word-for-word messages, especially when it comes to passing on orders from others (Hom., *Il*. 4.190 or 12.342) or negotiating with the enemy, as in this passage:

---

[4] However, some of them seem to enjoy a high social position (Gil Fernández 1963, 430), as the epithets πολύχρυσος and πολύχαλκος ('a man of much gold and much bronze') attributed to Eumedes (Hom., *Il*. 10.315) suggest. On their role as servants, cf. Hesychius' definition: "οἱ τὰς ὑπηρετικὰς ἐπιτελοῦντες πράξεις".
[5] Cf. Hom., *Il*. 1.321: τώ οἱ ἔσαν κήρυκε καὶ ὀτρηρὼ θεράποντε.
[6] Cf. Hom., *Od*. 18.424: θεράπων δ' ἦν Ἀμφινόμοιο.
[7] On the figure and functions of the herald see, for instance, Oehler (1958–1980), Pallí Bonet (1956), Durán López (1999) and Barrett (2002, 57–69). Dickin (2009, 1), according to Mondi (1978), points out that one of the main differences between heralds and messengers is that the former tends to enjoy a higher social status and may even be entrusted by the king to act on his behalf.

(3) Hom., *Il.* 7.383–397

(...) αὐτὰρ ὃ τοῖσι
στὰς ἐν μέσσοισιν μετεφώνεεν ἠπύτα **κῆρυξ·**
Ἀτρεΐδη τε καὶ ἄλλοι ἀριστῆες Παναχαιῶν
ἠνώγει Πρίαμός τε καὶ ἄλλοι Τρῶες ἀγαυοὶ
εἰπεῖν, αἴ κέ περ ὔμμι φίλον καὶ ἡδὺ γένοιτο,
μῦθον Ἀλεξάνδροιο, τοῦ εἵνεκα νεῖκος ὄρωρε·
κτήματα μὲν ὅσ' Ἀλέξανδρος κοίλης ἐνὶ νηυσὶν
ἠγάγετο Τροίηνδ'· ὡς πρὶν ὤφελλ' ἀπολέσθαι·
πάντ' ἐθέλει δόμεναι καὶ οἴκοθεν ἄλλ' ἐπιθεῖναι·
κουριδίην δ' ἄλοχον Μενελάου κυδαλίμοιο
οὔ φησιν δώσειν· ἦ μὴν Τρῶές γε κέλονται.
καὶ δὲ τόδ' ἠνώγεον εἰπεῖν ἔπος αἴ κ' ἐθέλητε
παύσασθαι πολέμοιο δυσηχέος εἰς ὅ κε νεκροὺς
κήομεν· ὕστερον αὖτε μαχησόμεθ' εἰς ὅ κε δαίμων
ἄμμε διακρίνῃ, δώῃ δ' ἑτέροισί γε νίκην.

The **herald** with the great voice took his stand in their midst, and spoke to them: 'Son of Atreus, and you other great men of all the Achaeans, Priam and the rest of the haughty Trojans have bidden me give you, if this message be found to your pleasure and liking, the word of Alexander, for whose sake this strife has arisen. All those possessions that Alexander carried in his hollow ships to Troy, and I wish that he had perished before then, he is willing to give all back, and to add to these from his own goods. But the very wedded wife of glorious Menelaus he says that he will not give, though the Trojans would have him do it. They told me to give you this message also, if you are willing; to stop the sorrowful fighting until we can burn the bodies of our dead. We shall fight again afterwards, until the divinity chooses between us, and gives victory to one or the other.'[8]

The herald Idaeus is the man to pass Priam's message on to the Atreides.[9] Just beforehand (Hom., *Il.* 7.345–378), the Trojans were assembled and Antenor had suggested that the Atreides turn Helen over to end the fight. Alexander objected, but proposed handing over his wealth. Priam then ordered the herald to voice his son's proposal to the Achaeans as well as his request that the combat cease until the bodies had been burned. The obedient Idaeus did as he was

---

8 Translations of the *Iliad* are taken from Lattimore (1961) with slight modifications.
9 This passage is listed in the 22 "repeated messenger-speeches" identified by De Jong (1989, 180–185) in the *Iliad*. She explains them as follows: a character A orders a character B to transmit a message — it is usually an order (*instruction speech*) — and then B delivers it to a character C (*delivery speech*). B is often a professional herald. On other messenger scenes, see Coventry (1987). See also Cesca (2017, 2017b and 2022).

ordered. This scene also shows that loyalty[10] is one of the characteristics that best defines the Homeric κήρυκες, since it highlights the credit they enjoy from those who hold the authority and the trust that they place in them.

On the other hand, heralds play a relevant role in the celebration of institutional events, especially in libations and sacrifices (Hom., *Il.* 3.245, 3.265, 3.271, 9.174 and 23.39 and Hom., *Od.* 3.338, 20.276 and 21.270). As a result of their good work and loyalty, they are described as 'hard-working henchmen' (Hom., *Il.* 1.321 and Hom., *Od.* 1.109) and 'proud heralds' (Hom., *Il.* 3.268 and Hom., *Od.* 8.418). They are also 'sacred' heralds (Hom., *Il.* 4.192, 10.315 and 12.343)[11] and 'the heralds Zeus loves' (Hom., *Il.* 8.517).

As expected, the role of heralds in the public sphere is more evident in the *Iliad*. In the *Odyssey*, however, their presence in the domestic sphere is much more remarkable: they mix the wine and serve it (Hom., *Od.* 1.109, 1.143, 7.163, 7.178, 13.49, 17.335 and 18.424), provide assistance to the singers (Hom., *Od.* 1.153, 8.62, 8.69, 8.107, 8.261 and 8.471) and carry their masters' presents (Hom., *Od.* 8.399, 8.418 and 18.291).

Ἄγγελοι: anyone can be a messenger

The term ἄγγελος is less frequent than κῆρυξ in the Homeric poems — it occurs 34 times (25 in the *Iliad* and 9 in the *Odyssey*). Unlike the herald, the messenger is not included in the catalogue of δημιοεργοί or professionals. There is a long list of characters called ἄγγελοι in the *Iliad* and the *Odyssey*. Although the term

---

10 This fidelity is reciprocal, as we can see in the *Odyssey* (22.356–360), where Telemachus asks Odysseus to save Medon, who took care of him as a child. Another characteristic that defines the κήρυκες is their voice, an essential tool for their role as town criers. In this regard, the following epithets are attributed to them: 'clear-voiced' (λιγυφθόγγοισιν: Hom., *Il.* 2.50, 2.442, 9.10 and 23.39 and Hom., *Od.* 2.6), 'loud-voiced' (ἠπύτα: Hom., *Il.* 7.384), 'with a voice that sounds through air' (ἠεροφώνων: Hom., *Il.* 18.505), 'crier' (καλήτορα: Hom., *Il.* 24.577) and 'calling through the city' (ἀστυβοώτην: Hom., *Il.* 24.701). The denominative verb κηρύσσω ('make proclamation as a herald') also refers to the tasks carried out by heralds away from the domestic sphere. It occurs eight times and always with the noun κῆρυξ. In addition, some other verbs are related to the role of these heralds in the public sphere and evoke their status as spokesmen: βοάω ('shout': Hom., *Il.* 2.97) and λιγαίνω ('cry out with a loud, clear voice': Hom., *Il.* 11.685).
11 A god takes on the figure of a herald three times in order to merge in with the heroes: Apollo takes on both the appearance and the voice of Periphas to encourage Aeneas to fight (Hom., *Il.* 17.319–332) and Athena silences the host (Hom., *Il.* 279–282) and urges the Phaeacians to meet Odysseus, Alcinous' host (Hom., *Od.* 8.6–14).

ἄγγελος does not always designate the gods, the fact remains that the vast majority of Homeric ἄγγελοι are divinities.[12] The ἄγγελος par excellence in the *Iliad* is the goddess Iris. Although she is not mentioned once in the *Odyssey*, in the *Iliad* her name appears 40 times. Iris is labelled as ἄγγελος 7 times,[13] as μετάγγελος twice (Hom., *Il* 15.144 and 23.199) and in a single case as ψευδάγγελος (Hom., *Il*. 15.159).

Alongside Hermes, in the *Iliad* Iris is the goddess in charge of transmitting messages from the gods and is especially linked to Zeus.[14] An example of her role is found in the following passage, where Zeus sends her to order Poseidon to leave the battlefield:

(4) Hom., *Il*. 15.158–159

> Βάσκ' ἴθι Ἶρι ταχεῖα, Ποσειδάωνι ἄνακτι
> πάντα τάδ' **ἀγγεῖλαι**, μὴ δὲ **ψευδάγγελος** εἶναι.

'Go on your way now, swift Iris, to the lord Poseidon, and **give him all this message** nor be **a false messenger**.'

Immediately afterwards, Zeus tells Iris the message she must deliver (vv. 160–167) and she obeys:

(5) Hom., *Il*. 15.174–183

> **ἀγγελίην τινά** τοι γαιήοχε κυανοχαῖτα
> ἦλθον δεῦρο φέρουσα παραὶ Διὸς αἰγιόχοιο.
> παυσάμενόν σ' ἐκέλευσε μάχης ἠδὲ πτολέμοιο
> ἔρχεσθαι μετὰ φῦλα θεῶν ἢ εἰς ἅλα δῖαν.
> εἰ δέ οἱ οὐκ ἐπέεσσ' ἐπιπείσεαι, ἀλλ' ἀλογήσεις,
> ἠπείλει καὶ κεῖνος ἐναντίβιον πολεμίξων
> ἐνθάδ' ἐλεύσεσθαι· σὲ δ' ὑπεξαλέασθαι ἄνωγε
> χεῖρας, ἐπεὶ σέο φησὶ βίῃ πολὺ φέρτερος εἶναι
> καὶ γενεῇ πρότερος· σὸν δ' οὐκ ὄθεται φίλον ἦτορ
> ἶσόν οἱ φάσθαι, τόν τε στυγέουσι καὶ ἄλλοι.

---

12 Cf. Chantraine (1974, 8): "ἄγγελος, -ου: m. 'messager' (Hom. Où le mot se dit souvent des messagers des dieux, notamment d'Iris)".
13 Cf. Hom., *Il*. 2.786, 3.121, 15.207, 18.167, 18.182, 24.169 and 24.173.
14 Iris is also under the order of Hera. In book 18, Zeus' wife sends the winged goddess as a messenger to order Achilles to arm himself to defend Patroclus' corpse (cf. Hom., *Il*. 18.170–180).

'I have **a certain message** for you, dark-haired, earth-encircler, and came here to bring it to you from Zeus of the aegis. His order is that you quit the war and the fighting, and go back among the generations of gods, or into the bright sea. And if you will not obey his words, or think nothing of them, his threat is that he himself will come to fight with you here, strength against strength, but warns you to keep from under his hands, since he says he is far greater than you are in strength, and elder born. Yet your inward heart shrinks not from calling yourself the equal of him, though others shudder before him.'

In these two passages there are three terms that belong to the lexical family of ἄγγελος: ἀγγεῖλαι, ψευδάγγελος and ἀγγελίη, although we are unable to interpret the transmission of one piece of news. As stated above, the content of the announcement implied in the verb ἀγγέλλω can be a piece of news, but also a message or an order. The context, the intention of the speaker (reflected through the illocutionary speech act) and the status of both the speaker and the hearer are the factors that determine what is announced. In this case, although Zeus, Iris and Poseidon are gods, they have different positions in the social hierarchy. Is not uncommon for Zeus to turn to Iris as an intermediary for her to convey an order from him to Poseidon. However, it would be inconceivable for Iris to give the order and for Zeus and Poseidon to obey it. In this way, here we see an example of human institutions — in this case the messengers — being mirrored in the social organization of the gods. This is a common occurrence in Greek culture, since myths reflect the society in which they appear or live together.

As we can see, the role played by Iris in (5) is that of the heralds,[15] since she merely reproduces the order *verbatim*. In the following example, however, the winged divinity announces a painful piece of news. In the first place, Iris is described as an ἄγγελος:

(6) Hom., *Il.* 2.786–787

Τρωσὶν δ' **ἄγγελος** ἦλθε ποδήνεμος ὠκέα Ἶρις
πὰρ Διὸς αἰγιόχοιο σὺν **ἀγγελίῃ** ἀλεγεινῇ·

Now to the Trojans came as **messenger** wind-footed Iris, in her speed, with the dark **message** from Zeus of the aegis.

Soon afterwards, the goddess announces the outbreak of war:

---

15 Examples similar to this are located in Hom., *Il.* 7.413–424, 11.200–209, 15.146–148, 18.170–180, 23.205–210, 24.88 and 24.171–187).

(7) Hom., *Il.* 2.796–806

> ὦ γέρον αἰεί τοι μῦθοι φίλοι ἄκριτοί εἰσιν,
> ὥς ποτ' ἐπ' εἰρήνης· πόλεμος δ' ἀλίαστος ὄρωρεν.
> ἤδη μὲν μάλα πολλὰ μάχας εἰσήλυθον ἀνδρῶν,
> ἀλλ' οὔ πω τοιόνδε τοσόνδέ τε λαὸν ὄπωπα·
> λίην γὰρ φύλλοισιν ἐοικότες ἢ ψαμάθοισιν
> ἔρχονται πεδίοιο μαχησόμενοι προτὶ ἄστυ.
> Ἕκτορ σοὶ δὲ μάλιστ' ἐπιτέλλομαι, ὧδε δὲ ῥέξαι·
> πολλοὶ γὰρ κατὰ ἄστυ μέγα Πριάμου ἐπίκουροι,
> ἄλλη δ' ἄλλων γλῶσσα πολυσπερέων ἀνθρώπων·
> τοῖσιν ἕκαστος ἀνὴρ σημαινέτω οἷσί περ ἄρχει,
> τῶν δ' ἐξηγείσθω κοσμησάμενος πολιήτας.

'Old sir, dear to you forever are words beyond number as once, when there was peace; but stintless war has arisen. In my time I have gone into many battles among men, yet never have I seen a host like this, not one so numerous. These look terribly like leaves, or the sands of the sea-shore, as they advance across the plain to fight by the city. Hector, on you beyond all I urge this, to do as I tell you: all about the great city of Priam are many companions, but multitudinous is the speech of the scattered nations: let each man who is their leader give orders to these men, and let each set his citizens in order, and lead them.'

The passage is located after the Catalogue of Ships, and for this reason Iris declares never to have seen such a large host before. The Trojans were assembled, and Iris arrives with the imminent purpose of announcing the painful piece of news (σὺν ἀγγελίῃ ἀλεγεινῇ, v. 787): the war has started, and multiple warriors are on their way there to fight. To make the announcement, Iris adopts the figure and the voice of Polites, son of Priam. For this reason no one doubts the veracity of such words. In any case, the goddess highlights her position as an eyewitness (as discussed below, αὐτοψία or the action of seeing something with one's own eyes is essential in the transmission of news) by using the perfect ὄπωπα (v. 799). Once the piece of news has been reported, Iris takes the opportunity to advise Hector on how to organize the troops so that the Trojans are ready to fight when the enemies arrive.

In addition to Iris, there are also anonymous messengers in the *Iliad* (Hom., *Il.* 12.73 and 22.438). Labelled as ἄγγελοι are the heralds Talthybius and Eurybates, mentioned above, the divinities Athena (Hom., *Il.* 11.715), Dream (Hom., *Il.* 2.26 and 2.63), Rumour (Hom., *Il.* 2.94) and Thetis (Hom., *Il.* 24.133 and 24.561), the omen of birds (Hom., *Il.* 24.292, 24.296 and 24.310) some heroes, like Tydeus (Hom., *Il.* 10.286), Patroclus (Hom., *Il.* 11.652) and, as we will see below, Antilochus. Apparently, in the *Iliad* the term ἄγγελος is used to refer to anyone who reports something, and this function does not require any qualification: anyone can be the subject of ἀγγέλλω (Durán López 1999, 30).

The same thing happens in the *Odyssey*. In addition to various anonymous messengers (Hom., *Od.* 15.458 and 24.405), the following ἄγγελοι are identified: a falcon, the swift messenger of Apollo (Hom., *Od.* 15.526), Hermes (Hom., *Od.* 5.29), Rumour (Hom., *Od.* 24.413), Helios (Hom., *Od.* 8.270) and Lampetia, his daughter (Hom., *Od.* 12.374), Eumaeus (Hom., *Od.* 16.138) and the herald who gets ahead of him when he tries to inform Penelope of Telemachus' return, as the swineherd confesses to the son of Odysseus:

(8) Hom., *Od.* 16.465–469

οὐκ ἔμελέν μοι ταῦτα μεταλλῆσαι καὶ ἐρέσθαι
ἄστυ καταβλώσκοντα· τάχιστά με θυμὸς ἀνώγει
ἀγγελίην εἰπόντα πάλιν δεῦρ' ἀπονέεσθαι.
ὡμήρησε δέ μοι παρ' ἑταίρων **ἄγγελος** ὠκύς,
κῆρυξ, ὃς δὴ πρῶτος ἔπος σῇ μητρὶ ἔειπεν.

'It was not on my mind to go down through the city, nor to ask, nor try to find out; rather the will was urgent within me to speak my message with all speed and be on my way back here. But one of your fellows as a swift **messenger** joined my company, the herald; he was the first who told the word to your mother.'

The situation had developed in this way:

(9) Hom., *Od.* 16. 333–337

τὼ δὲ συναντήτην κῆρυξ καὶ δῖος ὑφορβὸς
τῆς αὐτῆς ἕνεκ' **ἀγγελίης**, ἐρέοντε γυναικί.
ἀλλ' ὅτε δή ῥ' ἵκοντο δόμον θείου βασιλῆος,
κῆρυξ μέν ῥα μέσῃσι μετὰ δμῳῇσιν ἔειπεν·
'ἤδη τοι, βασίλεια, φίλος πάϊς εἰλήλουθε.'

The two of them met, the herald and the noble swineherd, going by reason of the same message, to bear **tidings** to the lady. But when they had come to the house of the sacred king, the herald stood in the midst of the serving maids and delivered his message: 'Now, O queen, your beloved son is back in this country.'

The piece of news is identified again by the lexicon. Eumaeus refers to the herald as an ἄγγελος ὠκύς who had come before Penelope to report the news (ἀγγελίης): that is, Telemachus, who had set out in search of news concerning his father had already returned to Ithaca.

Another distinctive feature of Homeric ἄγγελοι is that they act on demand to transmit newsworthy items. One of the characters labelled as ἄγγελος in the *Iliad* is Antilochus, the man in charge of transmitting, from my point of view, the most important piece of news in the whole poem: the death of Patroclus. Homer introduces him as an ἄγγελος when he is about to inform Achilles:

(10) Hom., *Il.* 18.1–2

> Ὣς οἳ μὲν μάρναντο δέμας πυρὸς αἰθομένοιο,
> Ἀντίλοχος δ' Ἀχιλῆϊ πόδας ταχὺς **ἄγγελος** ἦλθε.
>
> So these fought in the likeness of blazing fire. Meanwhile, Antilochus came, a swift-footed **messenger**, to Achilles.

Homer's ἄγγελοι do not act on their own initiative as the tragic ἄγγελοι do, but on other people's orders, as the examples that precede the arrival of Antilochus before Achilles show.[16] In (11) Hector has already killed Patroclus, and Telamonian Ajax addresses Menelaus in the following way:

(11) Hom., *Il.* 17.640–642

> εἴη δ' ὅς τις ἑταῖρος ἀπαγγείλειε τάχιστα
> Πηλεΐδῃ, ἐπεὶ οὔ μιν ὀΐομαι οὐδὲ πεπύσθαι
> **λυγρῆς ἀγγελίης**, ὅτι οἱ φίλος ὤλεθ' ἑταῖρος.
>
> 'But there should be some companion who could carry the message quickly to Peleus' son, since I think he has not yet heard **the ghastly news**, how his beloved companion has fallen.'

The son of Atreus goes in search of Nestor's son and encourages him:

(12) Hom., *Il.* 17.685–693

> Ἀντίλοχ' εἰ δ' ἄγε δεῦρο διοτρεφὲς ὄφρα πύθηαι
> **λυγρῆς ἀγγελίης**, ἣ μὴ ὤφελλε γενέσθαι.
> ἤδη μὲν σὲ καὶ αὐτὸν ὀΐομαι εἰσορόωντα
> γιγνώσκειν ὅτι πῆμα θεὸς Δαναοῖσι κυλίνδει,
> νίκη δὲ Τρώων· πέφαται δ' ὥριστος Ἀχαιῶν
> Πάτροκλος, μεγάλη δὲ ποθὴ Δαναοῖσι τέτυκται.
> ἀλλὰ σύ γ' αἶψ' Ἀχιλῆϊ θέων ἐπὶ νῆας Ἀχαιῶν
> εἰπεῖν, αἴ κε τάχιστα νέκυν ἐπὶ νῆα σαώσῃ
> γυμνόν· ἀτὰρ τά γε τεύχε' ἔχει κορυθαίολος Ἕκτωρ.

---

16 This can also be observed in example (8), in which the ἄγγελος who gets ahead of Eumaeus comes from Telemachus' comrades.

'Antilochus, turn this way, illustrious, and hear from me **the ghastly news** of a thing I wish never had happened. You can see for yourself, I think, already, from watching, how the god is wheeling disaster against the Danaans and how the Trojans are winning. The best of the Achaeans has fallen, Patroclus, and a huge loss is inflicted upon the Danaans. Run then quickly to Achilles, by the ships of the Achaeans, and tell him. He might in speed win back to his ship the dead body, which is naked. Hector of the shining helm has taken his armour.'

Antilochus, devastated, resolves to fulfil his mission:

(13) Hom., *Il.* 17.700–701

Τὸν μὲν δάκρυ χέοντα πόδες φέρον ἐκ πολέμοιο
Πηλεΐδῃ Ἀχιλῆϊ **κακὸν ἔπος ἀγγελέοντα**.

His feet carried him, weeping, out of the battle **to carry the bad news** to Achilles, son of Peleus.

And, finally, the son of Nestor delivers the awful piece of news:

(14) Hom., *Il.* 18.18–21

ὤ μοι Πηλέος υἱὲ δαΐφρονος ἦ μάλα **λυγρῆς**
πεύσεαι **ἀγγελίης**, ἣ μὴ ὤφελλε γενέσθαι.
κεῖται Πάτροκλος, νέκυος δὲ δὴ ἀμφιμάχονται
γυμνοῦ· ἀτὰρ τά γε τεύχε' ἔχει κορυθαίολος Ἕκτωρ.

'Ah me, son of valiant Peleus; you must hear from me **the ghastly news** of a thing I wish never had happened. Patroclus has fallen, and now they are fighting over his body, which is naked. Hector of the shining helm has taken his armour.'

The news' relevance is undeniable, as is evidenced by the fact that the consequences are immediate: as soon as he is informed, Achilles makes a decision. The son of Peleus gives up his anger and becomes involved in the fighting, which changes the course of the war.

As we can see, some terms are key for our understanding of the concept of news. Ajax utters ἀπαγγέλλω, Homer clarifies Antilochus' purpose with ἀγγέλλω and introduces him as an ἄγγελος when he is in the presence of Achilles to give him the ghastly news (λυγρῆς ἀγγελίης). This passage is also interesting from another point of view, however: there is no term from the lexical family studied in this volume to designate bad news in the Homeric poems.[17] The negative nuance is given by adjectives such as λυγρός ('ghastly' or 'mournful')[18] and ἀλεγεινός ('painful')[19] or the phrase κακὸν ἔπος functioning as the direct object of the verb ἀγγέλλω in example (13).[20] To designate good news, however, we see the term εὐαγγέλιον, which I will examine later.

It should also be noted that Homeric ἄγγελοι stand out for their speed, as most of the epithets assigned to the goddess Iris show: ποδήνεμος ὠκέα ('wind-footed, swift Iris'),[21] πόδας ὠκέα ('swift-running', 'Iris of the swift feet'),[22] ὠκέα ('swift'),[23] ταχεῖα ('quick'),[24] ἀελλόπος ('storm-footed, storm-swift'),[25] θεά ('divine')[26] and χρυσόπτερον ('with wings of gold').[27] The other messengers are also characterized by their celerity: in the *Iliad*, Antilochus is named πόδας ταχύς ('swift-footed') – see example (10) – and an omen is ταχύς ('quick');[28] in the *Odyssey* the falcon messenger of Apollo is ταχύς [29] and the herald who gets ahead of him, Eumaeus, is ὠκύς ('swift'), as we see in example (8).

Lastly, Homeric ἄγγελοι are considered to be completely trustworthy. This is evidenced by the adjective ἐτήτυμος, which describes the ἄγγελος of the next passage:

---

17 And they barely appear in the other authors in this corpus. As we will see, Aeschylus' *Agamemnon* has κακάγγελος (Aesch., *Ag.* 636) and Sophocles' *Antigone* documents κακαγγέλτος ('caused by ill tidings'. Cf. Soph., *Ant.* 1286). Demosthenes' speech *On the Crown* has one example of κακαγγελεῖν (Dem., *De cor.* 267), the infinitive of κακαγγελέω ('bring evil tidings').
18 Always in the genitive (λυγρῆς ἀγγελίης: Hom., *Il.* 17.642, *Il.* 17.686 and *Il.* 18.19) or in the accusative (λυγρὴν ἀγγελίην: Hom., *Il.* 19.337).
19 In the dative (ἀγγελίῃ ἀλεγεινῇ: Hom., *Il.* 2.787) or in the accusative (ἀγγελίην ἀλεγεινήν: Hom., *Il.* 18.17).
20 This construction only occurs in this passage. In Hom., *Il.* 24.767 the verb is ἀκούω (ἄκουσα κακὸν ἔπος), not in reference to news but to insults (rude words).
21 Cf. Hom., *Il.* 2.786, 5.368, 11.195, 15.168, 15.200, 18.166, 18.183, 18.196 and 24.95. Only ποδήνεμος in Hom., *Il.* 5.353.
22 Cf. Hom., *Il* 2.790, 2.795, 3.129, 8.425, 11.210, 18.202, 24.87 and 24.188.
23 Cf. Hom., *Il.* 15.172.
24 Cf. Hom., *Il.* 11.186, 15.158 and 24.144. The three examples, all in the vocative, are uttered by Zeus. The god orders Iris to take a message on his behalf and the name of the goddess and her epithet are preceded by βάσκ' ἴθι.
25 Cf. Hom., *Il.* 8.409, 24.77 and 24.159. In the three cases, the hexameter is the same: Ὣς ἔφατ', ὦρτο δὲ Ἶρις ἀελλόπος ἀγγελέουσα.
26 Cf. Hom., *Il.* 15.206 and 18.82.
27 Cf. Hom., *Il.* 8.398 and 11.185. In both cases the hexameter is the same: Ἶριν δ' ὄτρυνε χρυσόπτερον ἀγγελέουσαν·.
28 Cf. Hom., *Il.* 24.292 and 24.310.
29 Cf. Hom., *Od.* 15.526.

(15) Hom., *Il.* 22.437–439

Ὣς ἔφατο κλαίουσ', ἄλοχος δ' οὔ πώ τι πέπυστο
Ἕκτορος· οὐ γάρ οἵ τις **ἐτήτυμος ἄγγελος** ἐλθὼν
ἤγγειλ' ὅττί ῥά οἱ πόσις ἔκτοθι μίμνε πυλάων.

So she spoke in tears but the wife of Hector had not yet heard: for no **sure messenger** had come to her and told her how her husband had held his ground there outside the gates.

The woman crying is Hecuba. Inside the palace is Andromache, unaware that her husband, Hector, has been killed by Achilles since, as the poet points out, no messenger had come before her to announce (ἤγγειλ') this piece of news. The adjective ἐτήτυμος[30] reflects that the ἄγγελος has full credibility. This fact also suggests that this character is considered a very reliable source of information in the *Iliad* and the *Odyssey*. This is also one of the main traits that define the tragic ἄγγελοι, as eyewitnesses of the reported events.

From the death of Patroclus to the return of Odysseus: bad and good news

As we shall see from now on, the nature of both poems justifies the predominance of bad news in the *Iliad* and the greater presence of good news in the *Odyssey*. The analysis of the term ἄγγελος has allowed me to approach the concept of news in the Homeric poems, but the range of possibilities is wider. In the *Iliad* (see Figure 2), in addition to ἄγγελος, μετάγγελος and ψευδάγγελος — discussed in the previous section —, we have the noun ἀγγελίη, the verb ἀγγέλλω, and the derivative verbs ἀπαγγέλλω and ἐξαγγέλλω. The terms ἀγγελίη, εὐαγγέλιον, ἀγγέλλω and ἀπαγγέλλω occur in the *Odyssey* (Figure 3).

---

[30] An expressive form of the adjective ἔτυμος and derivative of ἐτεός. See Chantraine (1974: 381): "Forme expressive à redoublement et allongement de la seconde syllabe, ἐτήτυμος 'véritable'".

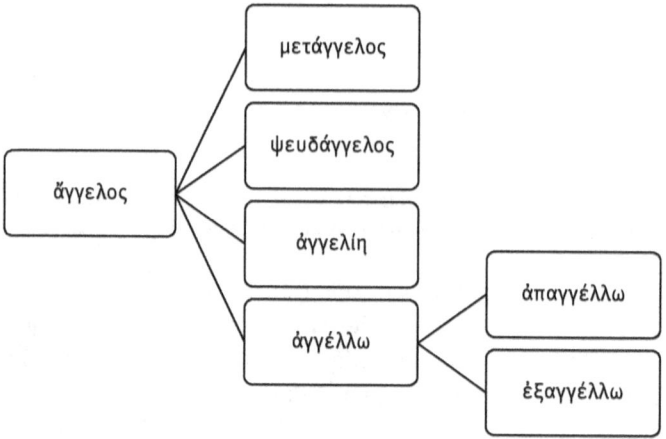

Fig. 2: Ἄγγελος and its derivatives in the *Iliad*.

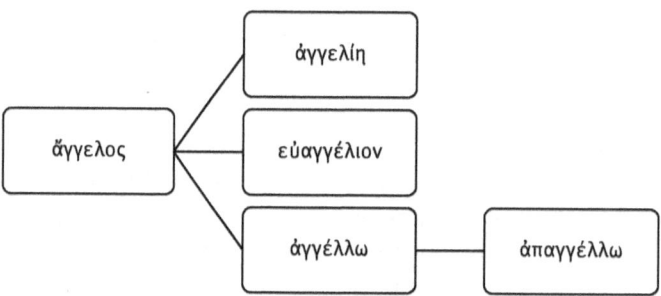

Fig. 3: Ἄγγελος and its derivatives in the *Odyssey*.

The term ἀγγελίη is documented relatively frequently in Homer's poems (17 times in the *Iliad* and 20 in the *Odyssey*). It is very common for ἀγγελίη to be the complement of a verb of saying. Some examples have already been explored in this chapter, for instance, with the death of Patroclus (Hom., *Il.* 18.17: φάτο δ' ἀγγελίην) or Telemachus' return to Ithaca (Hom., *Od.* 16.334: τῆς αὐτῆς ἕνεκ' ἀγγελίης ἐρέοντε), also referred to by ἀγγελίη in the accusative as a direct object (Hom., *Od.* 15.41: ἀγγελίην ἐρέοντα, 16.329: ἀγγελίην ἐρέοντα and 16.467: ἀγγελίην εἰπόντα). Another return mentioned in the same way is that of Odysseus (Hom., *Od.* 15.314: ἀγγελίην εἴποιμι). The same applies to Hera's plan (Hom., *Il.* 14.355: ἀγγελίην ἐρέων) and the fate of Odysseus' comrades, turned into pigs by Circe (Hom., *Od.* 10.245: ἀγγελίην ἑτάρων ἐρέων καὶ ἀδευκέα πότμον). On the other hand, the term ἀγγελίη refers to the messages delivered by those who are sent in embassy, as in Hom., *Il.* 7.416 (ἀγγελίην ἀπέειπε), Hom., *Il.* 9.422 (ἀγγελίην ἀπόφασθε) and in the following passage:

(16) Hom., *Il.* 9.649–655

> ἀλλ' ὑμεῖς ἔρχεσθε καὶ **ἀγγελίην** ἀπόφασθε·
> οὐ γὰρ πρὶν πολέμοιο μεδήσομαι αἱματόεντος
> πρίν γ' υἱὸν Πριάμοιο δαΐφρονος Ἕκτορα δῖον
> Μυρμιδόνων ἐπί τε κλισίας καὶ νῆας ἱκέσθαι
> κτείνοντ' Ἀργείους, κατά τε σμῦξαι πυρὶ νῆας.
> ἀμφὶ δέ τοι τῇ ἐμῇ κλισίῃ καὶ νηΐ μελαίνῃ
> Ἕκτορα καὶ μεμαῶτα μάχης σχήσεσθαι ὀΐω.

> 'Do you then go back to him and take him **this message**: that I shall not think again of the bloody fighting until such time as the son of wise Priam, Hector the brilliant, comes all the way to the ships of the Myrmidons, and their shelters, slaughtering the Argives, and shall darken with fire our vessels. But around my own shelter, I think, and beside my black ship Hector will be held, though he be very hungry for battle.'

The speaker is Achilles, who has received Ajax, Odysseus and Phoenix, sent in embassy by Agamemnon and accompanied by two heralds to try to convince him to accept some presents — among them, Briseis —, set aside his anger and take part in the war.

Ἀγγελίη often is the complement of a verb of perception, like πυνθάνομαι. An example of this in the *Iliad* alludes to the death of Patroclus (Hom., *Il.* 17.641–642: πεπύσθαι λυγρῆς ἀγγελίης, 17.685–686: πύθηαι λυγρῆς ἀγγελίης and 18.18–19: λυγρῆς πεύσεαι ἀγγελίης). Moreover, Achilles claims to be convinced that, if he is still alive, his father must feel overwhelmed waiting to learn the fateful news of the death of his own son (Hom., *Il.* 19.337: λυγρὴν ἀγγελίην, ὅτ' ἀποφθιμένοιο πύθηται). In the *Odyssey*, one of the suitors reflects on the possible departure of Telemachus and suggests that if no one convinces Odysseus' son to undertake the journey in search of news from his father, he will have to settle for those rumours he hears in Ithaca (Hom., *Od.* 2.255–256: ἀγγελιάων πεύσεται). On one occasion, the verb is πείθω, in the middle voice, which is used by Telemachus to confirm that he has already given up hope that Odysseus might return (Hom., *Od.* 1.414: οὔτ' οὖν ἀγγελίῃ ἔτι πείθομαι, εἴ ποθεν ἔλθοι).

Furthermore, it is also usual for ἀγγελίη to complement verbs of hearing, like ἀΐω and the derivatives of κλύω. With the former, the soul of Agamemnon explains to the soul of Achilles in Hades that Thetis had already heard the news of his death (Hom., *Od.* 24.48: ἀγγελίης ἀΐουσα). Mention of a command is made using other verbs: Hermes, sent by Zeus, commands Calypso to allow Odysseus to leave (Hom., *Od.* 5.150: ἐπέκλυεν ἀγγελιάων).[31] Likewise, the suitors wonder whether Telemachus has received news of the return of Odysseus' host (Hom., *Od.* 2.30: ἠέ τιν' ἀγγελίην στρατοῦ ἔκλυεν ἐρχομένοιο), the hero's son replies that he has not received this news (Hom., *Od.* 2.42: οὔτε τιν' ἀγγελίην στρατοῦ ἔκλυον ἐρχομένοιο) and Achilles, who finds Patroclus sobbing, wants to know what has happened to him:

(17) Hom., *Il.* 16.7–16

τίπτε δεδάκρυσαι Πατρόκλεες, ἠΰτε κούρη
νηπίη, ἥ θ' ἅμα μητρὶ θέουσ' ἀνελέσθαι ἀνώγει
εἰανοῦ ἁπτομένη, καί τ' ἐσσυμένην κατερύκει,
δακρυόεσσα δέ μιν ποτιδέρκεται, ὄφρ' ἀνέληται·
τῇ ἴκελος Πάτροκλε τέρεν κατὰ δάκρυον εἴβεις.
ἠέ τι Μυρμιδόνεσσι πιφαύσκεαι, ἢ ἐμοὶ αὐτῷ,
ἦέ **τιν' ἀγγελίην** Φθίης ἐξέκλυες οἶος;
ζώειν μὰν ἔτι φασὶ Μενοίτιον Ἄκτορος υἱόν,
ζώει δ' Αἰακίδης Πηλεὺς μετὰ Μυρμιδόνεσσι;
τῶν κε μάλ' ἀμφοτέρων ἀκαχοίμεθα τεθνηώτων.

'Why then are you crying like some poor little girl, Patroclus, who runs after her mother and begs to be picked up and carried, and clings to her dress, and holds her back when she tries to hurry, and gazes tearfully into her face, until she is picked up? You are like such a one, Patroclus, dropping these soft tears. Could you have some news to tell, for me or the Myrmidons? Have you, and nobody else, received **some news** from Phthia? Yet they tell me Actor's son Menoetius lives still and Aeacus' son Peleus lives still among the Myrmidons. If either of these died we should take it hard.'

The passage is interesting because Achilles mentions the possibility that some of their loved ones — in this case their parents — may have died. Patroclus, however, has some very different news to announce:

(18) Hom., *Il.* 16.21–29

ὦ Ἀχιλεῦ Πηλῆος υἱὲ μέγα φέρτατ' Ἀχαιῶν
μὴ νεμέσα· τοῖον γὰρ ἄχος βεβίηκεν Ἀχαιούς.
οἳ μὲν γὰρ δὴ πάντες, ὅσοι πάρος ἦσαν ἄριστοι,
ἐν νηυσὶν κέαται βεβλημένοι οὐτάμενοί τε.
βέβληται μὲν ὁ Τυδεΐδης κρατερὸς Διομήδης,

---

31 At the court of Alcinous, Odysseus relates that Calypso let him go and that he did not know if it had been because of an order he had received from Zeus (Hom., *Od.* 7.263: Ζηνὸς ὑπ' ἀγγελίης).

οὔτασται δ' Ὀδυσεὺς δουρικλυτὸς ἠδ' Ἀγαμέμνων,
βέβληται δὲ καὶ Εὐρύπυλος κατὰ μηρὸν ὀϊστῷ.
τοὺς μέν τ' ἰητροὶ πολυφάρμακοι ἀμφιπένονται
ἕλκε' ἀκειόμενοι· σὺ δ' ἀμήχανος ἔπλευ Ἀχιλλεῦ.

'Son of Peleus, far greatest of the Achaeans, Achilles, do not be angry; such grief has fallen upon the Achaeans. For all those who were before the bravest in battle are lying up among the ships with arrow or spear wounds. The son of Tydeus, strong Diomedes, was hit by an arrow, and Odysseus has a pike wound, and Agamemnon the spear-famed, and Eurypylus has been wounded in the thigh with an arrow. And over these the healers skilled in medicine are working to cure their wounds. But you, Achilles; who can do anything with you?'

The term ἀγγελίη also functions as the complement of verbs of sending. In the *Odyssey*, for instance, the suitors complain about Penelope's behaviour and blame her for making false promises to them through confusing messages that give them false hopes of marrying her (Hom., *Od.* 2.92 and 13.381: ἀγγελίας προϊεῖσα).

On the other hand, when the suitors hear of Telemachus' return to Ithaca, they realize that their plan to kill him has failed and consider telling those who were awaiting his arrival to murder him. To that end, Eurymachus suggests that they should launch a black ship to order them to abandon their watch posts. However, Amphinomus, convinced that they know that Odysseus' son is at home (Hom., *Od.* 16.355: μή τιν' ἔτ' ἀγγελίην ὀτρύνομεν· οἴδε γὰρ ἔνδον) and that they have already left, dissuades him.

Finally, almost at the end of the poem, Laertes says he fears that the men of Ithaca, informed of the slaughter of the suitors, will come against him and his son Odysseus and send messages to the cities of the Cephallenians asking for help (Hom., *Od.* 24.354-355: ἀγγελίας δὲ πάντῃ ἐποτρύνωσι Κεφαλλήνων πολίεσσι). Thus, when ἀγγελίη is the complement of verbs of sending in Homer, it never alludes to the transmission of news but rather orders or messages.

Moreover, ἀγγελίη functions as the complement of the verb φέρω in two passages. The first one has been already presented above — the example shown in (5): Zeus orders Iris to demand that Poseidon leave the battlefield —; in the second one the suitor Eurymachus wants to know the identity of the stranger who has already arrived in Ithaca and what his intentions are:

(19) Hom., *Od.* 1.405-409

ἀλλ' ἐθέλω σε, φέριστε, περὶ ξείνοιο ἐρέσθαι,
ὁππόθεν οὗτος ἀνήρ· ποίης δ' ἐξ εὔχεται εἶναι
γαίης; ποῦ δέ νύ οἱ γενεὴ καὶ πατρὶς ἄρουρα;

ἠέ **τιν' ἀγγελίην** πατρὸς φέρει ἐρχομένοιο,
ἦ ἑὸν αὐτοῦ χρεῖος ἐελδόμενος τόδ' ἱκάνει;

'But, best of men, I wish to ask you about this stranger, where he came from, what country he announces as being his own, where lies his parent stock, and the fields of his fathers. Has he brought **some news** from your father who is on his way here?'

In two examples from the *Odyssey*, ἀγγελίη appears as the subject of a verb of movement (ἔρχομαι and ἱκνέομαι). In one of these, Eumaeus tells Odysseus how he met Laertes: it was thanks to a Phoenician servant who wanted to escape with a group of sailors. In order for her plan to work out, she asked the sailors to send someone to tell her when the ship was loaded with goods (Hom., *Od.* 15.447: ἀγγελίη μοι ἔπειτα θοῶς πρὸς δώμαθ' ἱκέσθω). In the other passage, Eumaeus explains to Odysseus how his daily life runs:

(20) Hom., *Od.* 14.372–374

αὐτὰρ ἐγὼ παρ' ὕεσσιν ἀπότροπος· οὐδὲ πόλινδε
ἔρχομαι, εἰ μή πού τι περίφρων Πηνελόπεια
ἐλθέμεν ὀτρύνῃσιν, ὅτ' **ἀγγελίη** ποθὲν ἔλθῃ;

'But I keep away and with my pigs, and I do not go now to the city, unless circumspect Penelope for some reason ask me to go, when **word** comes in from one place or another.'

Finally, attention should be paid to five occurrences of the term ἀγγελίη, which are difficult to interpret. Three of these have been understood as the possible nominative singular of a masculine noun ὁ ἀγγελίης, -ου that would designate the 'messenger'[32] instead of as the genitive singular of ἡ ἀγγελίη, -ης. The first can be found in the Teichoscopy. Priam is talking to Helen:

(21) Hom., *Il.* 3.205–206

ἤδη γὰρ καὶ δεῦρό ποτ' ἤλυθε δῖος Ὀδυσσεὺς
σεῦ ἕνεκ' **ἀγγελίης** σὺν ἀρηϊφίλῳ Μενελάῳ·

---

[32] The controversy arises from a passage in Hesiod's *Theogony* in which ἀγγελίη appears associated with Iris (cf. Hes., *Th.* 781). The problem comes from the fact that according to one scholiast the term must be interpreted as 'messenger' in that case. Based on this proposal, it is difficult to know whether ἀγγελίη can be interpreted in the same way in some passages of the Homeric poems (see Leumann (*HW*) and *LfgrE*). For explanations on the term, see also Ebeling (1885), Bailly, *LSJ*, *DGE*, Leaf (1900), Benner (1903), Seymour (1891), Frisk (1960), Leaf/Bayfield (1962), Willcock (1970), Chantraine (1974), Kirk (1985) or Forssman (1994).

'Once in the days before now brilliant Odysseus came here with warlike Menelaus because of **some news** about you.'

Those who interpret it as the nominative understand it as a predicative and the translation would reflect that Odysseus arrived 'as a messenger'. Nevertheless, from my point of view ἀγγελίης must be interpreted, in this case, as the genitive of the feminine noun ἀγγελίη; the nominal constituent in the genitive that accompanies the preposition ἕνεκα.

A similar case can be found in the passage shown in (9), where the news is related to Telemachus' return. Below are the two hexameters of interest for this discussion:

(22) Hom., *Od.* 16.333–334

τὼ δὲ συναντήτην κῆρυξ καὶ δῖος ὑφορβὸς
τῆς αὐτῆς ἕνεκ' **ἀγγελίης**, ἐρέοντε γυναικί.

The two of them met, the herald and the noble swineherd, going by reason of the same message, to bear **tidings** to the lady.

The following passage places us in the heat of the battle. Idomeneus notices the presence of Meriones and addresses him in the following terms:

(23) Hom., *Il.* 13.249–252

Μηριόνη Μόλου υἱὲ πόδας ταχὺ φίλταθ' ἑταίρων
τίπτ' ἦλθες πόλεμόν τε λιπὼν καὶ δηϊοτῆτα;
ἠέ τι βέβληαι, βέλεος δέ σε τείρει ἀκωκή,
ἦέ τευ **ἀγγελίης** μετ' ἔμ' ἤλυθες; (…).

'Meriones, son of Molos, swift-footed, dearest beloved companion, why have you come back and left the battle and fighting? Have you been hit somewhere? Does pain of a spear's head afflict you? Have you come back with **news** for me?'

Meriones' answer is not clear, since he tells him that his spear was broken when he was fighting, and he is on his way to find another one. In my opinion, ἀγγελίης must again be interpreted as the genitive of the feminine ἀγγελίη. The reason for this is that, in this context, it is the complement of the verb μετέρχομαι and the preverb (μετά) is separated from the verb by tmesis. Dictionaries explain both examples as genitives denoting purpose with verbs of movement and include in the same list the following example:

(24) Hom., *Il.* 15.636–640

(...) ὣς τότ' Ἀχαιοὶ
θεσπεσίως ἐφόβηθεν ὑφ' Ἕκτορι καὶ Διὶ πατρὶ
πάντες, ὁ δ' οἶον ἔπεφνε Μυκηναῖον Περιφήτην,
Κοπρῆος φίλον υἱόν, ὃς Εὐρυσθῆος ἄνακτος
ἀγγελίης οἴχνεσκε βίῃ Ἡρακληείῃ.

So now the Achaeans fled in unearthly terror before father Zeus and Hector, all, but he got one only, Periphetes of Mycenae, beloved son of Copreus, who for the lord Eurystheus had gone often with **messages** to powerful Heracles.

Finally, in two other contexts that have also been discussed by scholars, the term is in the accusative. In the first of these, Agamemnon reproaches Diomedes for his cowardly behaviour and exemplifies the courage shown by his father on previous occasions:

(25) Hom., *Il.* 4.382–384

οἳ δ' ἐπεὶ οὖν ᾤχοντο ἰδὲ πρὸ ὁδοῦ ἐγένοντο,
Ἀσωπὸν δ' ἵκοντο βαθύσχοινον λεχεποίην,
ἔνθ' αὖτ' **ἀγγελίην** ἐπὶ Τυδῆ στεῖλαν Ἀχαιοί.

Now as these went forward and were well on their way, and came to the river Asopus, and the meadows of grass and the deep rushes, from there the Achaeans sent Tydeus ahead on a **message-bearing** mission.

I follow, in this case, the proposal put forward by Kirk (1985)[33] and accept the meaning of 'embassy' given by the lexicons.[34] As far as I can judge, the term acquires the same meaning in (26), framed in this Agamemnon's reproof of Peisander and Hippolochus:[35]

(26) Hom., *Il.* 11.138–142

εἰ μὲν δὴ Ἀντιμάχοιο δαΐφρονος υἱέες ἐστόν,
ὅς ποτ' ἐνὶ Τρώων ἀγορῇ Μενέλαον ἄνωγεν

---

[33] "ἀγγελίην, 'on a message-bearing mission'". See also Macía Aparicio/García Blanco (1998).
[34] Cf. Bailly (1973): "députation, à l'acc. adv. ἀγγελίην". In *DGE* it is interpreted as an accusative dependent on the verb of movement ἐπιστέλλω, although a possible reading as a predicative complement of the masculine noun ὁ ἀγγελίης is not ruled out.
[35] Kirk (1993) has no doubts in this case: "ἀγγελίην is clearly an internal accusative, as at 4.384".

> ἀγγελίην ἐλθόντα σὺν ἀντιθέῳ Ὀδυσῆϊ
> αὖθι κατακτεῖναι μηδ' ἐξέμεν ἂψ ἐς Ἀχαιούς,
> νῦν μὲν δὴ τοῦ πατρὸς ἀεικέα τίσετε λώβην.

> 'If in truth you are the sons of wise Antimachus, that man who once among the Trojans assembled advised them that Menelaus, who **came as envoy** with godlike Odysseus, should be murdered on the spot nor let go back to the Achaeans, so now your mutilation shall punish the shame of your father.'

The analysis of ἄγγελος and its derivatives suggests that the term εὐαγγέλιον — the basis for all the 'Evangel-' terms and from where the Spanish term 'Evangelio' ('good news') derives — appears for the first time in Greek literature in the *Odyssey* (two times) to refer to the return of Odysseus, arguably the most important news in the poem.

Let us now turn to book 14. The swineherd Eumaeus, overcome by uncertainty, talks to Odysseus (who is disguised as a beggar) and assures him that he no longer trusts that the long-awaited return of the hero will take place, as he is convinced that he has died. Odysseus, not yet willing to reveal his real identity in order to prevent his plan from failing, tries then to encourage him with these words:

(27) Hom., *Od*.14.149–153

> ὦ φίλ', ἐπεὶ δὴ πάμπαν ἀναίνεαι οὐδ' ἔτι φῇσθα
> κεῖνον ἐλεύσεσθαι, θυμὸς δέ τοι αἰὲν ἄπιστος·
> ἀλλ' ἐγὼ οὐκ αὔτως μυθήσομαι, ἀλλὰ σὺν ὅρκῳ,
> ὡς νεῖται Ὀδυσεύς· **εὐαγγέλιον**[36] δέ μοι ἔστω
> αὐτίκ', ἐπεί κεν κεῖνος ἰὼν τὰ ἃ δώμαθ' ἵκηται·

> 'Dear friend, since you are altogether full of denial, you do not think he will come, and your heart is ever untrusting; but I will not speak in the same manner, but on my oath tell you Odysseus is on his way home. Let me have **my reward for good news** then, as soon as he is come back and enters his own home.'

In fact, the good news has already come true. Although Eumaeus is not yet aware, he is talking to Odysseus. The swineherd uses the same term immediately afterwards when responding to the hero sceptically:

---

[36] On the term, cf. *LfgrE*, *LSJ* o Bailly. See also Merry (1907). On the root εὐαγγελ-, see Dickson (2005). On this passage, De Jong (2001, 351).

(28) Hom., *Od.* 14.166–167

ὦ γέρον, οὔτ' ἄρ' ἐγὼν **εὐαγγέλιον** τόδε τείσω
οὔτ' Ὀδυσεὺς ἔτι οἶκον ἐλεύσεται· (...)

'Old sir, I will never pay you **that gift for good news**, nor will Odysseus come to this house again.'

Εὐαγγέλιον is not attested either in the *Iliad* or in tragedy, but it does appear in Aristophanes' comedy, in Xenophon's *Hellenica*, and in some speeches in Greek oratory. As we shall see in subsequent chapters, the sense of 'reward for good tidings' only emerges in the Homeric poems. In plays by other authors this nuance is not so evident and εὐαγγέλιον seems to designate just the good news itself. On this note, mention must be made of the New Testament, although we cannot tackle it in any more detail in this book unfortunately.[37]

In my view, although we have not received this term directly from the *Odyssey* but from later tradition, the fact that εὐαγγέλιον is already attested in this Homeric poem and in some other texts of Classical Period with the same sense that we attribute to it nowadays, reinforces my hypothesis: the concept of news that we have today is not a modern invention, but an inheritance: a legacy that we preserve from the Greeks.

Let us now examine the verbs derived from ἄγγελος attested in the Homeric poems: ἀγγέλλω, ἀπαγγέλλω and ἐξαγγέλλω. The former two are well-documented in both poems; the latter, however, occurs only once in the *Iliad*.

The verb ἀγγέλλω ('announce, report') appears 27 times in Homer (13 in the *Iliad* and 14 in the *Odyssey*). As a verb of saying, it is common for ἀγγέλλω to take three arguments. In addition to the subject, ἀγγέλλω is expected to take an accusative (the object) and a dative (recipient) that usually designates human beings. This construction occurs in two passages from the *Iliad* presented above, examples (4) and (13). In (4) Iris is sent by Zeus to give an order (referred to in the accusative πάντα τάδ') to the lord Poseidon (Ποσειδάωνι ἄνακτι). In (13) Antilochus is about to report the bad news (κακὸν ἔπος, that is, the death of Patroclus) to Peleus' son, Achilles (Πηλεΐδῃ Ἀχιλῆϊ).

In five other contexts, the dative is omitted and only the accusative is present. In three examples, the accusative is a direct object that has an inanimate referent, as shown in (29):

---

37 See Léon-Dufour (1977), Delgado Jara (2006) or García Santos (2011).

(29) Hom., *Od.* 13.93–95

εὖτ' ἀστὴρ ὑπερέσχε φαάντατος, ὅς τε μάλιστα
ἔρχεται **ἀγγέλλων** φάος Ἠοῦς ἠριγενείης,
τῆμος δὴ νήσῳ προσεπίλνατο ποντοπόρος νηῦς.

At the time when shines that brightest star, which beyond others comes with **announcement** of the light of the young Dawn goddess, then was the time the sea-faring ship put it in to the island.

In the example given below, the complement in the accusative is the neuter of the demonstrative pronoun οὗτος in the plural:

(30) Hom., *Od.* 23.20–24

ἀλλ' ἄγε νῦν κατάβηθι καὶ ἂψ ἔρχευ μεγαρόνδε.
εἰ γάρ τίς μ' ἄλλη γε γυναικῶν, αἵ μοι ἔασι,
ταῦτ' ἐλθοῦσ' **ἤγγειλε** καὶ ἐξ ὕπνου ἀνέγειρε,
τῷ κε τάχα στυγερῶς μιν ἐγὼν ἀπέπεμψα νέεσθαι
αὖτις ἔσω μέγαρον· σὲ δὲ τοῦτό γε γῆρας ὀνήσει.

'But go down now and take yourself back into the palace. If any of those other women, who are here with me, **had come with news** like yours, and wakened me from my slumber, I would have sent her back on her way to the hall in a hateful fashion for doing it. It shall be your age that saves you.'

The speaker is a sceptical Penelope who is urging Eurycleia to leave as soon as she has announced the most important piece of news of the poem: Odysseus' return. The pronoun ταῦτα refers to the following words of the wet nurse:

(31) Hom., *Od.* 23.5–9

ἔγρεο, Πηνελόπεια, φίλον τέκος, ὄφρα ἴδηαι
ὀφθαλμοῖσι τεοῖσι τά τ' ἔλδεαι ἤματα πάντα.
ἦλθ' Ὀδυσεὺς καὶ οἶκον ἱκάνεται, ὀψέ περ ἐλθών·
μνηστῆρας δ' ἔκτεινεν ἀγήνορας, οἵ θ' ἑὸν οἶκον
κήδεσκον καὶ κτήματ' ἔδον βιόωντό τε παῖδα.

'Wake, Penelope, dear child, so that, with your own eyes, you can see what all your days you have been longing for. Odysseus is here, he is in the house, though late in his coming, and he has killed the haughty suitors, who were afflicting his house, and using force on his son, and eating his property.'

The following example places us in the Doloneia. The Achaeans have captured Dolon, who had come to spy on them for the Trojans. However, Dolon is discovered, and Diomedes announces that he is going to kill him:

(32) Hom., *Il.* 10.447–448

> μὴ δή μοι φύξίν γε Δόλων ἐμβάλλεο θυμῷ·
> ἐσθλά περ **ἀγγείλας**, ἐπεὶ ἵκεο χεῖρας ἐς ἁμάς.

> 'Do not, Dolon, have in your mind any thought of escape now you have got in our hands, though you **brought** us excellent **tidings**.'

Obviously, Dolon will not manage to escape alive. But what useful news is Diomedes alluding to with the adjective ἐσθλά? Shortly beforehand, as soon as Dolon had been captured by his enemies, Odysseus had interrogated him with the intention of obtaining as much information as possible about the Trojans. "Where did you leave Hector when you came here? Where is his gear of war lying? Where are his horses?", he asks him, "How are the rest of the Trojans disposed, the guards and the sleepers? What do they deliberate among themselves? Do they purpose to stay where they are, close to the ships? Or else to withdraw back into the city, now that they have beaten the Achaeans?"[38] The prisoner responds immediately:

(33) Hom., *Il.* 10.413–422

> τοὶ γὰρ ἐγώ τοι ταῦτα μάλ' ἀτρεκέως καταλέξω.
> Ἕκτωρ μὲν μετὰ τοῖσιν, ὅσοι βουληφόροι εἰσί,
> βουλὰς βουλεύει θείου παρὰ σήματι Ἴλου
> νόσφιν ἀπὸ φλοίσβου· φυλακὰς δ' ἃς εἴρεαι ἥρως
> οὔ τις κεκριμένη ῥύεται στρατὸν οὐδὲ φυλάσσει.
> ὅσσαι μὲν Τρώων πυρὸς ἐσχάραι, οἷσιν ἀνάγκη
> οἱ δ' ἐγρηγόρθασι φυλασσέμεναί τε κέλονται
> ἀλλήλοις· ἀτὰρ αὖτε πολύκλητοι ἐπίκουροι
> εὕδουσι· Τρωσὶν γὰρ ἐπιτραπέουσι φυλάσσειν·
> οὐ γάρ σφιν παῖδες σχεδὸν εἵαται οὐδὲ γυναῖκες.

> 'See, I will accurately recite all these things to you. Hector is now among those who are the men of counsel and they hold their deliberations by the barrow of godlike Ilus apart from the confusion. But those guards that you ask of, hero, there is no detail that protects the army and guards it. As for the watchfire hearths of the Trojans, those who must do it

---

38 Cf. Hom., *Il.* 10.405–411.

keep awake by the fires and pass on the picket duty to each other, but their far-assembled companions in battle are sleeping and pass on to the Trojans the duty of watching, since their own children do not lie nearby, nor their women.'

Odysseus, dissatisfied with the answer he had received from Dolon, continues with his interrogation (Hom., *Il.* 10.424–425) until he gets Dolon to answer:

(34) Hom., *Il.* 10.427–441

> τοὶ γὰρ ἐγὼ καὶ ταῦτα μάλ' ἀτρεκέως καταλέξω.
> πρὸς μὲν ἁλὸς Κᾶρες καὶ Παίονες ἀγκυλότοξοι
> καὶ Λέλεγες καὶ Καύκωνες δῖοί τε Πελασγοί,
> πρὸς Θύμβρης δ' ἔλαχον Λύκιοι Μυσοί τ' ἀγέρωχοι
> καὶ Φρύγες ἱππόμαχοι καὶ Μῄονες ἱπποκορυσταί.
> ἀλλὰ τί ἢ ἐμὲ ταῦτα διεξερέεσθε ἕκαστα;
> εἰ γὰρ δὴ μέματον Τρώων καταδῦναι ὅμιλον
> Θρήϊκες οἵδ' ἀπάνευθε νεήλυδες ἔσχατοι ἄλλων·
> ἐν δέ σφιν Ῥῆσος βασιλεὺς πάϊς Ἠϊονῆος.
> τοῦ δὴ καλλίστους ἵππους ἴδον ἠδὲ μεγίστους·
> λευκότεροι χιόνος, θείειν δ' ἀνέμοισιν ὁμοῖοι·
> ἅρμα δέ οἱ χρυσῷ τε καὶ ἀργύρῳ εὖ ἤσκηται·
> τεύχεα δὲ χρύσεια πελώρια θαῦμα ἰδέσθαι
> ἤλυθ' ἔχων· τὰ μὲν οὔ τι καταθνητοῖσιν ἔοικεν
> ἀνδρέσσιν φορέειν, ἀλλ' ἀθανάτοισι θεοῖσιν.

'See, I will accurately recite all these things to you. Next the sea are the Carians, and Paeonians with their curved bows, the Leleges and Caucones and the brilliant Pelasgians. By Thymbre are stationed the Lycians and the proud Mysians with the Phrygians who fight from horses, and Maeonians, lords of chariots. But why do you question me on all this, each thing in detail? For if you are minded to get among the mass of the Trojans, here are the Thracians, new come, separate, beyond all others in place, and among them Rhesus their king, the son of Eioneus. And his are the finest horses I ever saw, and the biggest; they are whiter than snow, and their speed of foot is the wind's speed; his chariot is fairly ornate with gold and with silver, and the armour is golden and gigantic, a wonder to look on, that he brought here with him. It is not like armour for mortal men to carry but for the immortal gods.'

Dolon's statements are very useful to the Achaeans, since they provide them with valuable information concerning their enemies. Immediately afterwards, Diomedes, keeping his word, cuts off the informer's head. Although he failed in his attempt, Dolon had been sent on a spy mission. In this regard, as we will see in the chapter on historians, this type of task is commonplace in times of war.

In (35) the role of recipient is not encoded by the dative case but by the accusative.³⁹ The passage belongs to the *Odyssey*.⁴⁰ The animate accusative μιν refers to Eumaeus, who converses with Odysseus, still disguised as a beggar. The hero asks the swineherd to tell him about his king:

(35) Hom., *Od.* 14.118–120

> εἰπέ μοι, αἴ κέ ποθι γνώω τοιοῦτον ἐόντα.
> Ζεὺς γάρ που τό γε οἶδε καὶ ἀθάνατοι θεοὶ ἄλλοι,
> εἴ κέ μιν **ἀγγείλαιμι** ἰδών· (...).

'Then tell me, and perhaps I might know him if he was such a man, for Zeus knows as do the other immortal gods, if I might have seen him and **have some news** to give you.'

In eight passages from the *Odyssey*, the accusative is omitted and only the dative recipient appears, indicating who is the person to receive the announcement. The example given in (36)⁴¹ is again related to espionage. Telemachus was in Sparta listening to Menelaus' report. In the meantime, the suitors were hatching a plan against him, and Penelope will be soon informed of the men's intentions:

(36) Hom., *Od.* 4.675–679

> οὐδ' ἄρα Πηνελόπεια πολὺν χρόνον ἦεν ἄπυστος
> μύθων, οὓς μνηστῆρες ἐνὶ φρεσὶ βυσσοδόμευον.
> κῆρυξ γάρ οἱ ἔειπε Μέδων, ὃς ἐπεύθετο βουλὰς
> αὐλῆς ἐκτὸς ἐών· οἱ δ' ἔνδοθι μῆτιν ὕφαινον.
> βῆ δ' ἴμεν **ἀγγελέων** διὰ δώματα Πηνελοπείῃ.

Nor did Penelope go for a long time without knowing of the counsels which the suitors had been secretly planning, for Medon the herald told her, having overheard their counsels. He had been standing outside the court while they plotted inside it, and he went on his way **with the piece of news** into the house of Penelope.

Medon the herald had eavesdropped on the conversation between the suitors and is now telling Penelope what was happening:

---

39 This construction is typical of some verbs of saying and is used in alternation with the dative. Cf. Crespo *et al.* (2003, 120).
40 Cf. also Hom., *Il.* 19.120: ἀγγελέουσα Δία Κρονίωνα.
41 Cf. also. Hom., *Od.* 4.528.

(37) Hom., *Od.* 4.697–702

'εἰ γὰρ δή, βασίλεια, τόδε πλεῖστον κακὸν εἴη.
ἀλλὰ πολὺ μεῖζόν τε καὶ ἀργαλεώτερον ἄλλο
μνηστῆρες φράζονται, ὃ μὴ τελέσειε Κρονίων·
Τηλέμαχον μεμάασι κατακτάμεν ὀξέϊ χαλκῷ
οἴκαδε νισόμενον· ὁ δ' ἔβη μετὰ πατρὸς ἀκουὴν
ἐς Πύλον ἠγαθέην ἠδ' ἐς Λακεδαίμονα δῖαν'.

'If only, my queen, that could be the worst of the evil. But the suitors now are devising another thing that is much worse and harder to bear. May the son of Cronos not see it accomplished. Now they are minded to kill Telemachus with the sharp bronze on his way home. He went in quest of news of his father to Pylos the sacrosanct and to glorious Lacedaemon.'

In some other examples, the form of ἀγγέλλω used is the future participle, which is dependent on a verb of moving and expresses purpose. It is not news but orders that are announced, as illustrated in (38). Before asking Eurycleia to go in search of Penelope so that she finally finds out about his return, Odysseus wants to punish the twelve maids who he believed were disloyal to him. The hero commands Eurycleia to bring the servants to him and she sets out to obey:[42]

(38) Hom., *Od.* 22.431–434

'μή πω τήν γ' ἐπέγειρε· σὺ δ' ἐνθάδε εἰπὲ γυναιξὶν
ἐλθέμεν, αἵ περ πρόσθεν ἀεικέα μηχανόωντο'.
ὣς ἄρ' ἔφη, γρηῢς δὲ διὲκ μεγάροιο βεβήκει
ἀγγελέουσα γυναιξὶ καὶ ὀτρυνέουσα νέεσθαι.

'Do not wake her yet but tell those women who have been shameful in their devisings to come here to my presence'. So, he spoke, and the old woman went through the palace, **bringing the message** to the women and urging them onward.

Finally, sometimes it is simply a character's arrival that is announced in Homer's poems.[43]

Ἀγγέλλω is used twice as a verb of commanding alongside the infinitive and the dative.[44] In (39) Zeus commands Iris to urge Priam to rescue Hector's corpse and give him the funeral he deserves:

---

[42] Cf. also Hom., *Od.* 22.496. There is a third passage which details an order for the housewife Eurynome to give to one of the maids (cf. Hom., *Od.* 18.185–189).
[43] Cf. Hom., *Od.* 4.24. Or the intention to do something, as in Hom., *Od.* 6.50 and 15.458.

(39) Hom., *Il.* 24.144–148

> Βάσκ' ἴθι Ἶρι ταχεῖα λιποῦσ' ἕδος Οὐλύμποιο
> **ἄγγειλον** Πριάμῳ μεγαλήτορι Ἴλιον εἴσω
> λύσασθαι φίλον υἱὸν ἰόντ' ἐπὶ νῆας Ἀχαιῶν,
> δῶρα δ' Ἀχιλλῆϊ φερέμεν τά κε θυμὸν ἰήνῃ
> οἶον, μὴ δέ τις ἄλλος ἅμα Τρώων ἴτω ἀνήρ.

> 'Go forth, Iris the swift, leaving your place on Olympus, and go to Priam of the great heart within Ilion, **tell** him to ransom his dear son, going down to the ships of the Achaeans and bringing gifts to Achilles which might soften his anger: alone, let no other man of the Trojans go with him.'

On just one occasion, the complement of ἀγγέλλω is an accusative with the infinitive (AcI) construction.[45] The example is from *Iliad* book 8. At nightfall, Hector calls a meeting to give the Trojans some orders, including the following:

(40) Hom., *Il.* 8.517–519

> κήρυκες δ' ἀνὰ ἄστυ Διῒ φίλοι **ἀγγελλόντων**
> παῖδας πρωθήβας πολιοκροτάφους τε γέροντας
> λέξασθαι περὶ ἄστυ θεοδμήτων ἐπὶ πύργων·

> 'And let the heralds Zeus loves **give orders** about the city for the boys who are in their first youth and the grey-browed elders to take stations on the god-founded bastions that circle the city.'

As we can see, the semantic content of the verb seems closer in this context to that of an order than that of a news announcement. The fact that ἀγγελλόντων is an imperative favours this interpretation. The context also helps, since this is just one more in a series of instructions given by Hector to the Trojans.

Finally, we should also take into consideration those passages in which ἀγγέλλω appears with an absolute use. One of them is in *Iliad* book 9, when the embassy sent by Agamemnon to convince Achilles to accept his gifts arrives. Peleus' son addresses Phoenix, a member of the embassy, in these terms:

---

44 On this typical construction of verbs of commanding, cf. Crespo (1984). A good example of this type of verb belongs precisely to the lexical family that we are studying here and is παραγγέλλω. This verb is not documented in Homer but does appear in tragedy, Aristophanes, the works of the historians and in oratory.

45 In Homer, this construction alternates only once with a ὅττι substantive clause, as illustrated in (15). As we will see in subsequent chapters of this volume, this type of construction in alternation with ὡς clauses is very common in Greek literature, especially in Attic prose.

(41) Hom., *Il.* 9.617–618

οὗτοι δ' **ἀγγελέουσι**, σὺ δ' αὐτόθι λέξεο μίμνων
εὐνῇ ἔνι μαλακῇ· (...)

'These men will **carry back the message**; you stay here and sleep here in a soft bed.'

Although a complement is not referred to explicitly, once again the context allows us to understand that the addressee of the message to be reported back is Agamemnon. Likewise, what will be announced to him is Achilles' refusal to accept his proposals.[46]

Ἀπαγγέλλω occurs 10 times in Homer (3 times in the *Iliad* and 7 in the *Odyssey*). Like ἀγγέλλω, ἀπαγγέλλω is a verb of saying ('announce or report from')[47] and is also expected to be accompanied by three arguments: the subject in the nominative, a complement in the accusative (the object), and a dative (recipient). In the Homeric poems, these complements are explicitly expressed twice. One example can be found in (42),[48] a passage located shortly before Antilochus announces Patroclus' death to Achilles. Hector has already killed Patroclus, but Peleus' son still does not know. Not even his own mother has told him:

(42) Hom., *Il.* 17.408–411

πολλάκι γὰρ τό γε μητρὸς ἐπεύθετο νόσφιν ἀκούων,
ἥ οἱ **ἀπαγγέλλεσκε** Διὸς μεγάλοιο νόημα.
δὴ τότε γ' οὔ οἱ ἔειπε κακὸν τόσον ὅσσον ἐτύχθη
μήτηρ, ὅττί ῥά οἱ πολὺ φίλτατος ὤλεθ' ἑταῖρος.

---

[46] Besides, as shown in the example given in (16) shortly afterwards Achilles himself asks them to go back to Agamemnon and take him his message: (Hom., *Il.* 9.649: ἀγγελίην ἀπόφασθε). On the other examples, cf. Hom., *Il.* 8.397, Hom., *Il.* 9.85, Hom., *Il.* 8.409, Hom., *Il.* 24.77, Hom., *Od.* 14.123 (Odysseus, disguised as a beggar, wants to bring news to Penelope, but Eumaeus tells him that no one will believe the tidings of a beggar) and Hom., *Od.* 16.150.
[47] Cf. Crespo et al. (2003, 167) on the preverb.
[48] The other example also belongs to the *Iliad*. Cf., Hom., *Il.* 9.626–627. In this case ἀπαγγέλλω accompanies the impersonal verb χρή and both the object in the accusative (μῦθον) and the recipient in the dative (Δαναοῖσι) are explicitly referred to. The term μῦθος is of enormous complexity and we cannot tackle it in this work, unfortunately. Nevertheless, we must not overlook the fact that the dictionaries include the following among their many meanings, some of which are related to the transmission of news (cf. *LSJ*, Bailly, Ebeling, HW, *LgfrE*). Martin (1989, 10–26) argues that in the Homeric poems μῦθος, as opposed to other terms such as ἔπος, usually refers to an authoritarian expression. See also Lincoln (1999, 19–46).

For often he had word from his mother, not known to mortals; she **was ever telling** him what was the will of great Zeus; but this time his mother did not tell Achilles of all the evil that had been done, nor how his dearest companion had perished.

In Homer, it is very common for ἀπαγγέλλω to only take the dative recipient (in four of the ten passages in which this verb is used). In the *Iliad* there is only one example, which is shown in (11) concerning the death of Patroclus. Ajax tells Menelaus that he wishes there were someone to announce (ἀπαγγείλειε) the bad news to Peleus' son (Πηλεΐδη). The remaining examples are taken from the *Odyssey*. In (43), Telemachus asks Nestor's son to let him leave the ship and not to force him to appear before Nestor, because he fears that Nestor will not allow him to leave:

(43) Hom., *Od.* 15.209–210

'σπουδῇ νῦν ἀνάβαινε κέλευέ τε πάντας ἑταίρους,
πρὶν ἐμὲ οἴκαδ' ἱκέσθαι **ἀπαγγεῖλαί** τε γέροντι'.[49]

'Go aboard now in haste, and urge on all your companions to go, before I reach home and **take the news** to the old man.'

The last excerpt is related to Odysseus' final homecoming (Hom., *Od.* 16.458–459). The hero is in conversation with his son, Telemachus, and Eumaeus heads straight for them. At that moment, Athena gives Odysseus the appearance of a beggar again, fearing that the swineherd will recognize the hero and, full of emotions, go and spread the news (ἀπαγγέλλων) to Penelope (Πηνελοπείη).

Finally, ἀπαγγέλλω appears with an absolute use. In (44) the suitors are hatching a plan to kill Telemachus when he arrives at Ithaca. Some of them boast about their — from their point of view — great cleverness, but Antinous warns them:

(44) Hom., *Od.* 4.774–775

'δαιμόνιοι, μύθους μὲν ὑπερφιάλους ἀλέασθε
πάντες ὁμῶς, μή πού τις **ἀπαγγείλῃσι** καὶ εἴσω'.

'You are all mad. Keep clear of all this kind of disorderly talk, for fear somebody may go inside and **report** us.'

---

49 Cf. also Hom., *Od.* 16.153.

Antinous' warning, however, is too late: Medon has already heard everything and informed Penolope.

In the second example, the verb is an infinitive and functions as a complement of ἐθέλω. Odysseus is describing his experience with the Lotus–eaters and explains that once his comrades had tasted the fruit they were given, they did not want to return to Ithaca with the news (Hom., *Od.* 9.95: οὐκέτ' ἀπαγγεῖλαι πάλιν ἤθελεν οὐδὲ νέεσθαι); they were eager to stay in that strange place.

The absolute use of ἀπαγγέλλω is also seen in the description of the beggar Arnaeus (Hom., *Od.* 18.1–7), who is called Irus by all the young men because he used to run on errands when anyone asked him (ἀπαγγέλλεσκε).

Finally, in (45) the participle ἀπαγγείλας leads as to a relevant piece of news. Penelope must know that Telemachus has returned and so the son of Odysseus asks Eumaeus:

(45) Hom., *Od.* 16.130–134

'ἄττα, σὺ δ' ἔρχεο θᾶσσον, ἐχέφρονι Πηνελοπείῃ
εἴφ', ὅτι οἱ σῶς εἰμι καὶ ἐκ Πύλου εἰλήλουθα.
αὐτὰρ ἐγὼν αὐτοῦ μενέω, σὺ δὲ δεῦρο νέεσθαι
οἴη **ἀπαγγείλας**· τῶν δ' ἄλλων μή τις Ἀχαιῶν
πευθέσθω· πολλοὶ γὰρ ἐμοὶ κακὰ μηχανόωνται'.

'Father Eumaeus, go quickly now, and tell the circumspect Penelope that I am safe and have come from Pylos. I will stay here. You go there quickly, and **give this news** to her alone, and let no other Achaean hear it; for there are many there who are plotting against me.'

The other derivative verb of ἀγγέλλω documented in the Homeric poems is ἐξαγγέλλω.[50] It occurs only once, in the *Iliad*, in a digression that Gaisser (1969, 6) called Dione's Catalogue. Aphrodite has been wounded in the battle and Iris has brought her to Dione, who tells her that she is not the only goddess who has suffered because of men. On one occasion beforehand, Ares was bound by Otus and Ephialtes and spent thirteen months locked in a bronze jar. According to Dione's report, Ares would have died if it had not been for Penelope, who reported the news to Hermes. Hermes, as soon as he heard what happened, went to Ares' aid:

---

50 Let us not forget the presence of the ἐξάγγελος in tragedy, which differs from the ἄγγελος precisely in the fact that the ἐξάγγελος comes from inside the palace to report what has happened inside. This verb is often used by historians to allude to those who are sent on a spy mission. We will see also in the corresponding chapter that this is a technical term in oratory.

(46) Hom., *Il.* 5.388–391

> καί νύ κεν ἔνθ' ἀπόλοιτο Ἄρης ἆτος πολέμοιο,
> εἰ μὴ μητρυιὴ περικαλλὴς Ἠερίβοια
> Ἑρμέᾳ **ἐξήγγειλεν**· ὃ δ' ἐξέκλεψεν Ἄρηα
> ἤδη τειρόμενον, χαλεπὸς δέ ἑ δεσμὸς ἐδάμνα.

And now might Ares, insatiable of fighting, have perished, had not Eeriboea, their stepmother, the surpassingly lovely, **brought tidings** to Hermes, who stole Ares away out of it as he was growing faint, and the hard bondage was breaking him.

Final remarks

It is clear that the concept of news already existed in the Homeric poems, and the analysis of ἄγγελος and its derivatives allows us to observe its development. Unlike the herald, the ἄγγελος is not a professional but anyone who has an announcement to make. He does not act on his own initiative, like the tragic ἄγγελος, but relates news because someone asks him to do so. In addition, celerity is one of the defining characteristics of the Homeric ἄγγελος and the news he transmits is totally reliable.

One of the main conclusions drawn so far is that for the members of the society reflected in the *Iliad*, everything linked to war was considered news. In this regard, as shown, Iris announces to the Trojans that the war has broken out, Dolon gives the Achaeans relevant information about the situation of the Trojans, and Patroclus tells Achilles about their comrades' critical condition after they have been wounded in combat. When Patroclus dies at the hands of Hector, Antilochus tells Achilles this piece of news that will change the outcome of the war.

Although there is no term in the lexical family derived from ἄγγελος that expressly designates bad news, the fact is that in the *Iliad* the vast majority of news is negative. This is evident in the adjectives ἀλεγεινός and λυγρός that accompany the term ἀγγελίη or the phrase κακὸν ἔπος, which functions as the complement of the verb ἀγγέλλω in reference to the death of Patroclus.

In the *Odyssey*, the situation is remarkably different, however. On the one hand, the lexicon derived from ἄγγελος reflects that for the individuals portrayed in the poem everything related to the heroes' return home was newsworthy (such as that of Agamemnon, that of Telemachus and, above all, that of Odysseus). There is only one context in which death is referred to as news: that of Achilles in Hom., *Od.* 24.48. Although the suitors plot to assassinate Telemachus when he returns home (as announced to Penelope by the herald Medon), their plan will not succeed. On the other hand, the term ἀγγελίη is never accompanied in the *Odyssey* by an adjective that allows us to distinguish whether the news is good or bad. However, from the context we know that almost all the news reported in this poem is good news. Besides, the noun εὐαγγέλιον is documented for the first time in and refers to the most important piece of news of the *Odyssey*: the return of Odysseus.

The very nature of both poems justifies the predominance of bad news in the *Iliad* and the greater presence of good news in the *Odyssey*. According to López Eire (2000, 53), the *Iliad* is a war poem with a pessimistic background that begins with Achilles' anger and ends with Hector's funeral pyre. Conversely, as Clarke (1989, 29) points out, the *Odyssey* is an optimistic poem (perhaps too easily optimistic in its vision of a world where the good and the bad get their due).

In other developments, in Homer the term ἀγγελίη can designate not only a piece of news, but also a message or an order. Syntactic constructions make the distinction easier, although some other factors such as the receiver's social status or extraverbal context provide us with definitive clues. For example, most of the time ἀγγελίη is the complement of verbs of saying or verbs of perception. In such cases, it can almost always be interpreted as news. When it comes to a complement of verbs of sending, however, it has to be understood as a message. On the other hand, in those passages in which ἀγγελίη appears as the subject of a verb of movement or as the complement of φέρω, only the context and the social position of the sender and the receiver enable us to classify it as news or not. Nevertheless, this problem does not arise when it comes to the noun εὐαγγέλιον. This term is documented for the first time in the *Odyssey* and in neither of the two passages in which it appears is there any room for doubt: both allude to the most important piece of news of the poem, namely Odysseus' return to Ithaca.

In addition to the above, the analysis of the verbs derived from ἄγγελος (ἀγγέλλω, ἀπαγγέλλω and ἐξαγγέλλω) in this chapter has been useful to outline the concept of news prevalent in the societies represented in Homer.

All things considered, the news reported in both the *Iliad* and the *Odyssey* has several points in common: it is always relevant to the development of the plot, related to the main characters (and affects them), and has major consequences. Patroclus' death in the *Iliad*, for example, is Achilles' only motive for setting aside his anger so as to return to battle and this piece of news completely changes the course of the Trojan War. The situation is similar in the *Odyssey*, where all of Ithaca's inhabitants await the return of Odysseus except the suitors, who will die when the hero eventually returns.

2 Greek Lyric Poetry: Pindar and Bacchylides

This chapter does not aim to offer an overview of Greek lyric poetry as a whole, as it is not relevant to our overall aims. Instead, I will examine the concept of news in two of the three greatest authors of choral poetry (Pindar and Bacchylides) and in two genres: the epinicion and the dithyramb.[1] Here I will focus on the eminently public nature[2] of both types of composition, which is arguably their most interesting characteristic feature. Pindar's Odes have enjoyed greater renown, and it is important to remember the historical and social contexts in which these odes were written. Pindar was born (*ca.* 518 BC) in Cynoscephalae, although he soon moved to Athens and witnessed a crucial moment in the history of Greek: the decline of the aristocratic system in favour of the growth and consolidation of the new democratic regime. The 6th and the 5th centuries BC saw tyrannies begin to fall, except in cities like Cyrene and in Sicily, and many of Pindar's Odes celebrate the tyrants who ruled in the latter (especially in Gela, Syracuse and Agrigento). As we will see in the examples below, the athletic victories celebrated in Pindar's epinicia are only a pretext that pursues a very specific goal: the praise of the ἀρετή, the excellence of the exalted aristocratic society.

In *The Aggelia in Pindar*, Laura Nash[3] alludes to ἀγγελία as a literary *topos*, a convention of the genre that is, from her point of view, the basis of the epinicion:

> Pindar has at hand at least one fixed outline for determining the facts relevant to the victory and for giving them a structural foundation in the ode: the *aggelia*. Like the herald's proclamation at the festival, the epinician *aggelia* announces the victor's name, father and city. The exact point at which the *aggelia* was pronounced in the games is unclear, but it is most likely to have been recited at the end of each event and / or the final crowning of the victor.

---

[1] Most notably absent is Simonides and his absence is justified by the scarcity of material that we have. It should be noted, however, that one of the most beautiful and famous epigrams of all that we preserve (the epigram devoted to those who fell at the Thermopylae) is attributed to him. On the use of the infinitive ἀγγέλλειν in this epigram, see Fornieles Sánchez (2015, 133–148).

[2] Let us remember that these choral compositions were performed in two contexts: in local and national public festivals and in the private houses of nobility and tyrants. The most noteworthy are the epinicia: choral compositions that were composed to celebrate an athletic triumph, a victory. They were commissioned by the winner or his relatives.

[3] See Nash (1990, 15).

Thus, in Pindar's Odes at least, the ἀγγελία is a type of discourse associated with athletic competitions and involves the formal and public announcement of the triumph. It includes the proclamation of the winner's name, that of his father, and that of the festival.

Two practically identical figures

Despite the fact that the terms ἄγγελος and κῆρυξ are little documented in the odes of Pindar and Bacchylides, an analysis of both nouns allows us to draw some interesting conclusions. As we will see below, the κῆρυξ has a very defined role in athletic competitions, and almost identical functions are attributed to the ἄγγελος, to the extent that both roles seem to be the same.[4]

It is not clear when athletic competitions began to be linked with the solemn announcement of the winner by a κῆρυξ.[5] According to Homer in the *Iliad*, heralds were present at the Funeral Games in honour of Patroclus, but their function was not to announce the competitors.[6] It is well known, however, that (at least in Olympia) heralds invited those who wanted to participate in the competitions and announced the events (Wolicki 2002, 74). Pindar is the first author to mention the task attributed to the κήρυκες in *Olympian Ode* 13, which celebrates the double Olympic victory (stadion and penthatlon) of Xenophon of Corinth:

(1) Pind., *Ol.* 13.97–100

>   Ἰσθμοῖ τά τ' ἐν Νεμέᾳ παύρῳ ἔπει
>   θήσω φανέρ' ἀθρό', ἀλαθής τέ μοι
>   ἔξορκος ἐπέσσεται ἐξηκοντάκι δὴ ἀμφοτέρωθεν
>   ἀδύγλωσσος βοὰ **κάρυκος** ἐσλοῦ.

---

4 In fact, some authors, like Schadewaldt (1928, 274 ff.), emphasize that Pindar aims to imitate the performance of the herald at the festival in his use of some forms of both ἀγγελ- and of καρυξ-.
5 Besides the examples given in (1) and (2), the term occurs in Pind., *Ol.* 6.78 (in reference to Hermes, the herald of the gods) and Pind., *Pyth.* 4.170 (in allusion to some heralds who Jason ordered to spread news of the Argonaut's journey). In the case of Bacchylides, the context is quite different: κῆρυξ occurs twice, not in the epinicia but in the dithyrambs. Cf. Bacchyl., *Dith.* 15.40 ("Then heralds rushed through the broad town and brought together the ranks of the Trojans into the assembly-place of the army") and Bacchyl., *Dith.* 18.17 (Aegeus claims that a herald is trumpeting the exploits of Theseus).
6 Cf. Hom., *Il.* 23.566–569 and Hom., *Il.* 23.896–897. On the role of heralds in athletic competitions, see Crowther (1994).

I shall make their many victories at the Isthmus and at Nemea manifest in a few words; and, as a truthful witness under oath, the sweet-tongued cry of the noble **herald**, who announced their victories sixty times at both places, will confirm my words.[7]

The action performed by the herald is also expressed using the verb κηρύσσω.[8] Nevertheless, in Pindar's *Pythian Ode* 1 the κῆρυξ announces Hieron's win using ἀγγέλλω:

(2) Pind., *Pyth.* 1.28–33

εἴη, Ζεῦ, τὶν εἴη ἁνδάνειν,
ὃς τοῦτ' ἐφέπεις ὄρος, εὐκάρποιο γαί-
ας μέτωπον, τοῦ μὲν ἐπωνυμίαν
κλεινὸς οἰκιστὴρ ἐκύδανεν πόλιν
γείτονα, Πυθιάδος δ' ἐν δρόμῳ **κά-**
ρυξ ἀνέειπέ νιν **ἀγγέλ-**
λων Ἱέρωνος ὑπὲρ καλλινίκου
ἅρμασι. (...).

Grant that we may be pleasing to you, Zeus, you who frequent this mountain, this brow of the fruitful earth, whose namesake city near at hand was glorified by its renowned founder, when **the herald** at the Pythian racecourse proclaimed the name of Aetna, **announcing** Hieron's triumph with the chariot.

From what we can gather, the subject of ἀγγέλλω can be anyone — even a herald, who is supposed to proclaim the winner by using the verb κηρύσσω. In this way, Pindar is similar to Homer in his use of this verb. However, in what follows I shall show how victories are the main announcements in the odes analysed and these triumphs are reported using ἀγγέλλω. This fact suggests that already in the Archaic period, terms derived from ἄγγελος begin to specialize as technical terms related to the transmission of news.

It is also worth noting here that the preliminary Olympic events began a few months earlier, when three official heralds — the so-called σπονδοφόροι[9] ('those who bring proposals for a truce') — toured the Greek cities in order to announce

---

7 Translations of the Pindar's *Odes* are borrowed from Svarlien (1991) with some slight modifications.
8 Cf. Pind., *Ol.* 5.8, Pind., *Isthm.* 3–4.43 or Bacchyl., *Ep.* 13.98.
9 Heralds are designated using this term in Pind., *Isthm.* 2.23 (σπονδοφόροι Κρονίδα Ζηνός). As we will see in the chapter on Greek historians, negotiations and proclamations of truces are one of the main functions attributed to both ἄγγελοι and heralds during wartime.

that the competitions were about to take place and to proclaim the sacred truce (ἐκεχειρία) between rivals.

Let us pay attention now to the ἄγγελος. The term occurs only 4 times in Pindar's Odes and twice in those of Bacchylides. Given its relatively infrequent use, we can conclude that ἄγγελος is only used to refer to the following: Hermes, messenger of Zeus (Bacchyl., *Dith.* 19.30: ποδαρκέ' ἄγγελο[ν Διὸς), an eagle — also related to Zeus — (Bacchyl., *Ep.* 5.19–20: αἰετὸς εὐρυάνακτος ἄγγελος | Ζηνὸς), and Aeneas, who behaved 'correctly' (Pind., *Ol.* 6.90: ἄγγελος ὀρθός), as well as those brave messengers mentioned by Homer (Pind., *Pyth.* 4.277–278: ἄγγελον ἐσλὸν ἔφα τι- | μὰν μεγίσταν πράγματι παντὶ φέρειν).[10] According to Pindar, the ἄγγελοι also delivered speeches (Pind., *Nem.* 1.59: ἀγγέλων ῥῆσιν) and were in charge of proclaiming the triumphs, as we can conclude from this passage from the *Nemean Ode* 6, which celebrates Alcimidas of Aegina's victory in boys' wrestling:

(3) Pind., *Nem.* 6.56–61

> (...) ἑκόντι δ' ἐγὼ νώ-
> τῳ μεθέπων δίδυμον ἄχθος
> **ἄγγελος** ἔβαν,
> πέμπτον ἐπὶ εἴκοσι τοῦτο γαρύων
> εὖχος ἀγώνων ἄπο, τοὺς ἐνέποισιν ἱερούς,
> Ἀλκίμιδα, σέ γ' ἐπαρκέσαι
> κλειτᾷ γενεᾷ (...).

I came **as a messenger**, willingly bearing on my back a double burden, to proclaim that this twenty-fifth boast of victory from the games which men call sacred, Alcimidas, has been provided by you for your glorious family.

As we can see in this example, there does not seem to be a clear distinction between κήρυκες and ἄγγελοι in Greek lyric poetry either. In this case, Pindar also identifies himself with an ἄγγελος, as in examples (11) and (12), which document the verb ἀγγέλλω.

---

10 Pindar mentions Homer in what seems to be a literal reference. The most similar hexameter is in the *Iliad* (Hom., *Il.* 15.207: ἐσθλὸν καὶ τὸ τέτυκται ὅτ' ἄγγελος αἴσιμα εἰδῇ). As we can see, Pindar's verse only resembles the one that the poet presents as Homeric in the term that alludes to the messenger and the quality assigned to him. Commentators attribute this error to the fact that 'Homer' was a very broad term in antiquity and that Pindar could have a bad memory. See Gildersleeve (1885) and Braswell (1988).

The triumph is news

In addition to ἄγγελος, Pindar and Bacchylides also document the noun ἀγγελία, which has special connotations in their odes. As I have pointed out above, the ἀγγελία is here associated with athletic competitions and involves the public announcement of the triumph. On the other hand, the verbs ἀγγέλλω, ἀπαγγέλλω, διαγγέλλω and ἐπαγγέλλω only occur in Pindar's epinicia.

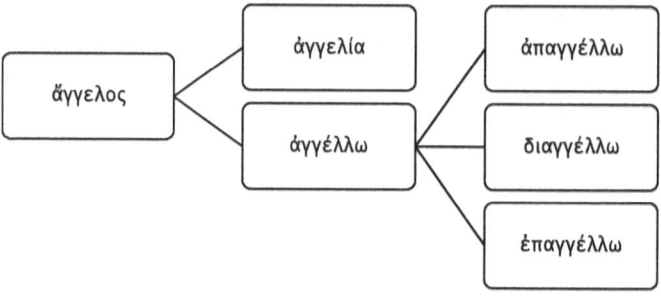

Fig. 4: Ἄγγελος and its derivatives in Pindar's Odes.

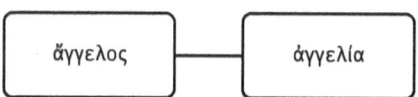

Fig. 5: Ἄγγελος and its derivatives in Bacchylides' Odes.

The term ἀγγελία occurs 12 times in the two authors studied here: 10 in Pindar's Odes and twice in those of Bacchylides. In Bacchylides *Ode* 16, ἀγγελία is the complement of the verb πυνθάνομαι. This dithyramb deals with a well-known myth related to Heracles. The king Eurytus of Oechalia had promised to marry his daughter Iole to whomever managed to beat him and his children in an archery contest. Heracles won, but the king broke his promise by claiming that the hero might kill the children he might have with Iole in another attack of madness. Later, when he was already married to Deianeira, Heracles came back to Oechalia, plundered the city, and took Iole with him. Then, Deianeira, desperate and jealous, made use of a supposed love potion that the centaur Nessus had given her a long time ago. The remedy, however, turned out to be a poison and had catastrophic consequences. The passage in which the noun ἀγγελία occurs refers to the moment in which Deianeira finds out that she has a rival:

(4) Bacchyl., *Dith.* 16.23–29

> Τότ' ἄμαχος δαίμων
> Δαϊανείρᾳ πολύδακρυν ὕφανε
> μῆτιν ἐπίφρον', ἐπεὶ
> πύθετ' **ἀγγελίαν** ταλαπενθέα,
> Ἰόλαν ὅτι λευκώλενον
> Διὸς υἱὸς ἀταρβομάχας
> ἄλοχον λιπαρὸ[ν π]οτὶ δόμον πέμποι.

Then a god, useless to fight against, wove for Deianeira, to her great sorrow, a clever scheme, when she heard the bitter **news** that the son of Zeus, fearless in battle, was sending white-armed Iole to his splendid house to be his bride.[11]

This example is also interesting because it is the only case in which the announced ἀγγελία is negative, as illustrated by the adjective ταλαπενθέα ('bearing great griefs').[12] I should also highlight the fact that this is the only passage in a dithyramb in which the term appears. In the epinicia, as expected, the situation is quite different: what is celebrated is victory and the ἀγγελία is qualified as 'glorious' (Pind., *Ol.* 14.21: κλυτάν), 'of gracious import' (Bacchyl., *Ep.* 2.2–3: χαριτώνυμον) and 'sweet' (Pind., *Ol.* 4.5: γλυκεῖαν).

In Pindar's *Olympian Ode* 9, which celebrates Epharmostus of Opus, the wrestling winner, ἀγγελία is the complement of a verb of sending, πέμπω. The poet is about to praise the remote past of the Opuntian Locrians and assures he will spread his message (Pind., *Ol.* 9.25: ἀγγελίαν πέμψω ταύταν) everywhere (παντᾷ) so that their glory will be known all over the world.

In three other contexts, ἀγγελία is the complement of φέρω.[13] Pindar's *Olympian Ode* 14 celebrates Asopichus of Orchomenus, winner in the stade-race. At the end of this brief composition, Pindar invokes Echo.[14] The poet's aim is to get the Echo to descend into Hades and tell the winner's father some news that will please him, even if he does not receive it whilst alive:

---

11 Translations are taken from Svarlien (1991b) with some slight modifications.
12 As already stated in the previous chapter, there are no terms to designate bad news in Homer. The adjectives attributed to the noun provide the negative nuance. As we will see, the same is true in later literature, with very few exceptions.
13 According to Verdenius (1979, 34) this is a literary trope that highlights the strong bond between father and son.
14 Apparently, there was no cult dedicated to Echo. The personification of this term, which must be interpreted as 'Echo' and not as 'rumour', is assumed to be an invention of Pindar. See Rumpel (1883, 83), Verdenius (1979, 34) and Segal (1998, 142). Fernández-Galiano (1994, 333) points out that it is difficult not to think of Echo, Narcissus' lover, here.

(5) Pind., *Ol.* 14.20–25

> (...) μελαντειχέα νῦν δόμον
> Φερσεφόνας ἔλθ', Ἀ-
> χοῖ, πατρὶ κλυτὰν φέροισ' **ἀγγελίαν**,
> Κλ<εό>δαμον ὄφρ' ἰδοῖσ', υἰὸν εἴπῃς ὅτι οἱ νέαν
> κόλποις παρ' εὐδόξοις Πίσας
> ἐστεφάνωσε κυδίμων ἀέθλων πτεροῖσι χαίταν.

> Now go, Echo, to the dark-walled home of Persephone and bring the glorious **piece of news** to his father; when you see Cleodamus, tell him that his son, by the famous valley of Pisa, has wreathed his youthful hair with the wings of the renowned games.

In Pindar's *Pythian Ode* 2, the celebrated tyrant is Hieron of Syracuse. At the beginning of the poem, the poet addresses the city and declares that he has arrived bringing (φέρων) a song (μέλος): the news of the earth-shaking four-horse race (Pind., *Pyth.* 2.4: ἀγγελίαν τετραορίας ἐλελίχθονος), in which Hieron was victor. Despite the fact that the term is usually translated as 'message' in this passage, I propose interpreting it as 'news'. In my opinion, as in other cases, the bearer of the news is aware of the interest that his ode will arouse in the receivers and that it can be therefore interpreted as news.

In the passage given in (6), Fame is the one who must transmit the good news on the island:

(6) Bacchyl., *Ep.* 2.1–5

> Ἄ[ϊξον, ὦ] σεμνοδότειρα Φήμα,
> ἐς Κ[έον ἱ]εράν, χαριτώ-
> νυμον φέρουσ' **ἀγγελίαν**,
> ὅτι μ[ά]χας θρασύχειρ<ος> Ἀρ-
> γείο[ς ἄ]ρατο νίκαν.

> Fame, whose gifts are revered, speed to holy Ceos bringing **the piece of news** of gracious import: that Argeius won the victory in the battle of bold hands.

Let us now turn to Pindar's *Isthmian Ode* 8, which celebrates Cleandros of Aegina, winner in the boy's pankration. The term ἀγγελία appears in the central part of the poem, in the narration of a myth that, on this occasion, deals with the dispute between Zeus and Poseidon for the heart of Thetis. However, neither was victorious in that battle, since fate had determined that Thetis would give birth to a boy more powerful than his own father. The mediator was Themis, who urged the two gods to set aside their hostilities. Themis also foresaw that if Thetis eventually married a mortal, she would see her son die in war. Finally, she concludes that Peleus would be best chosen for this marriage. Themis' intervention ends as follows:

(7) Pind., *Isthm.* 8.40–47

> 'ἰόντων δ' ἐς ἄφθιτον ἄν-
> τρον εὐθὺς Χίρωνος αὐτίκ' **ἀγγελίαι**
> μηδὲ Νηρέος θυγάτηρ νεικέων πέταλα
> δὶς ἐγγυαλιζέτω
> ἄμμιν· ἐν διχομηνίδεσ-
> σιν δὲ ἑσπέραις ἐρατόν
> λύοι κεν χαλινὸν ὑφ' ἥ-
> ρωϊ παρθενίας' (...).

'Let **the message** be sent at once to Cheiron's immortal cave, right away, and let the daughter of Nereus never again place the leaves of strife in our hands. On the evening of the full moon let her loosen the lovely bridle of her virginity for that hero.'

This passage cannot be interpreted as the transmission of news as such, but of messages similar to those that Iris delivers from Zeus, as shown in the previous chapter. Themis' judgment is a message, but the pleas made to the gods to end their struggle and to Thetis to stick with her decision should be understood as orders to be obeyed. Once again, the status of both the speaker and the hearer are crucial in order to establish a distinction, especially in the case of Thetis. She is a nymph, and it would be inconceivable for her to disobey the commands given to her by Themis.

In (8) ἀγγελία is the complement of the verb ἀναδέκομαι (Attic ἀναδέχομαι) in Pindar's *Pythian Ode* 2. This time the myth is about Ixion, king of the Lapiths who, in love with Hera, tried to rape her. Zeus learned of his intentions, made a cloud in the shape of Hera, and allowed Ixion to lie with her. As a result, the race of the centaurs was conceived and Zeus decided to punish Ixion, binding him to a winged fiery wheel that was always spinning:

(8) Pind., *Pyth.* 2.40–41

> (...) ἐν δ' ἀφύκτοισι γυιοπέδαις
> πεσὼν τὰν πολύκοινον ἀνδέξατ' **ἀγγελίαν**.

He fell into inescapable bonds and received **the message** that warns the whole world.

In this case, Zeus' message is a piece of advice addressed to all mortals; a warning that shows the fate of those who dare to meddle in Zeus' affairs.[15]

In (9) ἀγγελία is the complement in the dative of the verb ἐνέχω. The passage belongs to the Pindar's *Pythian Ode* 8, in which the victor is Aristomenes of Aegina, whose glory is compared by Pindar to that of Alcmaeon. In addition, in the central part of the ode, which is dedicated to the myth, the poet mentions a prophecy that encouraged Adrastus, the only one who did not lose his life in the Seven against Thebes' campaign:

(9) Pind., *Pyth.* 8.48–51

> ὁ δὲ καμὼν προτέρᾳ πάθᾳ
> νῦν ἀρείονος ἐνέχεται
> ὄρνιχος **ἀγγελίᾳ**
> Ἄδραστος ἥρως· (…)
>
> And he who suffered in the earlier disaster, the hero Adrastus, now has **the tidings** of a better bird of omen.

We see ἀγγελία as an optional constituent in three of Pindar's Odes. In one, the term appears in a noun phrase in the dative expressing cause and referring to the commands (the twelve labours) issued to Heracles by Eurystheus (Pind., *Ol.* 3.28: ἀγγελίαις Εὐρυσθέος). In the other two passages, the noun also occurs in prepositional phrases that also express cause: the correct message with which the Muse is exalted (Pind., *Pyth.* 4.278: δι' ἀγγελίας ὀρθᾶς) or the sweet piece of news that delights the friends of those who succeed far away (Pind., *Ol.* 4.5: ἀγγελίαν ποτὶ γλυκεῖαν).

In the last example, the news relates to the personification of a divinity, the alleged daughter of Hermes:

(10) Pind., *Ol.* 8.81–84

> Ἑρμᾶ δὲ θυγατρὸς ἀκούσαις Ἰφίων
> **Ἀγγελίας**, ἐνέποι κεν Καλλιμάχῳ λιπαρὸν
> κόσμον Ὀλυμπίᾳ, ὅν σφι Ζεὺς γένει
> ὤπασεν. (…).

---

15 See Gildersleeve (1885): "ἀνδέξατ'": he received the message and delivered it, not in words, but by whirling on the wheel".

Having heard the voice of Hermes' daughter, **Angelia**, Iphion might tell Callimachus of the splendid adornment at Olympia, which Zeus gave to their race.

The poem celebrates Alcimedon of Aegina, the victor in boy's wrestling. When Ἀγγελία reports the news to Iphion, the winner's uncle, he will go on to announce it to his father Callimachus, who is also dead.

We have no record of Hermes having a daughter called Ἀγγελία. The personification of this figure, as well as that of Echo, has been assumed to be an invention of Pindar.[16]

Let us pay attention now to the other derivatives. In Bacchylides' Odes, there are no verbs derived from ἄγγελος. In Pindar's Odes, however, ἀγγέλλω, ἀπαγγέλλω, διαγγέλλω and ἐπαγγέλλω are documented. The verb ἀγγέλλω only appears in three passages of Pindar's epinicia and in all three cases as the present participle ἀγγέλλων. One of these has been already noted in example (2), in which Pindar mentions a κῆρυξ who announces the triumph of Hieron of Syracuse. In the other two passages, the subject is the poet himself. According to dictionaries and commentaries,[17] in Pindar's Odes ἀγγέλλω involves a public announcement, and this is also reflected in this study. The *Olympian Ode* 7 celebrates Diagoras of Rhodes, winner in boxing, and Pindar introduces the myth with ἀγγέλλω:

(11) Pind., *Ol.* 7.20–23

ἐθελήσω τοῖσιν ἐξ ἀρχᾶς ἀπὸ Τλαπολέμου
ξυνὸν **ἀγγέλλων** διορθῶσαι λόγον,
Ἡρακλέος
εὐρυσθενεῖ γέννᾳ (...).

I shall want to **proclaim my message** for them, the widely powerful race of Heracles, and tell correctly from the beginning, from Tlepolemus, the story that concerns all.

In *Pythian Ode* 9, however, the implied announcement is the triumph of Telesicrates of Cyrene, winner in the hoplite race:

---

16 Fernández-Galiano (1994, 248) offers an explanation based on the fact that it comes to an εἰδωλοποιία, that is, an image formed in the poet's mind, and not a genealogical one, as in the case of Echo in Pind., *Ol.* 14.21. On Ἀγγελία see also Rumpel (1883, 3), Gildersleeve (1885), Slater (1969, 3), Verdenius (1979, 34) and Segal (1998, 142).
17 Cf. *DGE*, Rumpel (1883, 3), Gildersleeve (1885), Slater (1969, 3), Verdenius (1987, 57), Fernández-Galiano (1994, 220), Willcock (1995, 118) or Wells (2009, 77).

(12) Pind., *Pyth.* 9.1–4

> Ἐθέλω χαλκάσπιδα Πυθιονίκαν
> σὺν βαθυζώνοισιν **ἀγγέλλων**
> Τελεσικράτη Χαρίτεσσι γεγωνεῖν
> ὄλβιον ἄνδρα διωξίππου στεφάνωμα Κυράνας·

With the help of the deep-waisted Graces I want to shout aloud **proclaiming** the Pythian victory with the bronze shield of Telesicrates, a prosperous man, the crowning glory of chariot-driving Cyrene.

When commenting on the presence of ἀγγέλλω, Suárez de la Torre (1984, 207) points out that here the poet is an ἄγγελος, almost a κῆρυξ, in his proclamation of Telesicrates' glory.

Ἀπαγγέλλω only occurs on Pindar's *Pythian Ode* 6, which celebrates Xenocrates of Acragas, winner in the chariot race, although represented by his son Thrasybulus. The verb takes a complement in the accusative that refers to the victory:

(13) Pind., *Pyth.* 6.14–17

> (...) φάει δὲ πρόσωπον ἐν καθαρῷ
> πατρὶ τεῷ, Θρασύβουλε, κοινάν τε γενεᾷ
> λόγοισι θνατῶν εὔδοξον ἅρματι νίκαν
> Κρισαίαις ἐνὶ πτυχαῖς **ἀπαγγελεῖ**.

Its facade, shining in pure light, **will announce** your chariot victory to the speech of men and make it famous—the victory you share with your father and your race, Thrasybulus, won in the vales of Crisa.

Διαγγέλλω also occurs once, in the proem of the *Nemean Ode* 5, for Pytheas of Aegina, winner in the boy's pancratium. Διαγγέλλω is complemented by a ὅτι clause:

(14) Pind., *Nem.* 5.2–5

> (...) ἀλλ' ἐπὶ πάσας
> ὁλκάδος ἔν τ' ἀκάτῳ, γλυκεῖ' ἀοιδά,
> στεῖχ' ἀπ' Αἰγίνας **διαγγέλλοισ'**, ὅτι
> Λάμπωνος υἱὸς Πυθέας εὐρυσθενής
> νίκη Νεμείοις παγκρατίου στέφανον.

Sweet song, go on every merchant–ship and rowboat that leaves Aegina, and **announce** that Lampon's powerful son Pytheas won the victory garland for the pancratium at the Nemean game.

The preverb δια- brings added value to the verb, since it implies the announcement of the triumph to be spread all over the world (Pfeijffer 1999, 103).[18]

The verb ἐπαγγέλλω only appears in Pindar's *Pythian Ode 4*, in honour of Arcesilaus of Cyrene, victor in the chariot race. One of the meanings given in lexicons is 'to offer', and it is this sense that it carries in the example,[19] inserted again into the portion of the ode devoted to a mythical event:

(15) Pind. *Pyth.* 4.29–31

> (...) φιλίων δ' ἐπέων
> ἄρχετο, ξείνοις ἅ τ' ἐλθόντεσσιν εὐεργέται
> δεῖπν' **ἐπαγγέλλοντι** πρῶτον.

He began to speak friendly words, such as beneficent hosts use when they first **invite** arriving strangers to a meal.

In this case, the announcement implied by the verb is that of the meal itself. However, as we will see in subsequent chapters, ἐπαγγέλλω indicates the presence of news in certain contexts of other corpora.

Final remarks

The ἄγγελος plays a crucial role in the epinicia of Pindar and Bacchylides, since he is the person in charge of the public proclamation of victors in athletic competitions. Although, in principle, there is a professional (the κῆρυξ) to whom this function is attributed, the truth is that the figures of both the κῆρυξ and the ἄγγελος are practically identical.

The terms derived from ἄγγελος are core elements in these compositions, especially in Pindar's Odes. The poet uses ἀγγελία, ἀγγέλλω, ἀπαγγέλλω and

---

18 See Rumpel (1883: "nuntio divulgans"), Slater (1969: "proclaim abroad") or *LSJ* ("noise abroad"). On διά cf. also Crespo *et al.* (2003, 168). Διαγγέλλω is not documented in Homer's poems, but appears in the plays of Euripides, Thucydides, Xenophon and Aeschines.
19 Cf. *LSJ* and Bailly in general. For the specific case of Pindar, see Rumpel (1883), Slater (1969) or Braswell (1988, 10): "Offer. Since in this use of the verb there is often a connotation that the offer is made of one's own free will and without a previous request, the middle is more usual".

διαγγέλλω to describe the epinicion itself as the action of publicly proclaiming the victory of the poet (Wells 2009, 77), a triumph that must also be spread in other cities and that, after all, is a mere pretext. According to Jaeger (1962, 202), Pindar gazes at the man who has achieved the victory, and that victory means ἀρετή, the highest human excellence reflected in the aristocratic society that he describes in his compositions. For this reason, except on rare occasions, the ἀγγελία is in this context a piece of news: the sweet (Pind., *Ol.* 4.5: γλυκεῖαν) and glorious (Pind., *Ol.* 14.21: κλυτάν) public announcement of the glory symbolized by the conquest of the prize and by the epinicion itself.

3 Tragedy

The study of the concept of news in Greek tragedy is undoubtedly linked to the ἄγγελος as the news 'reporter'. This figure, which can be anyone who announces something and requires no specialization, acquires an undeniable relevance in ancient Greek drama to the point that his performance becomes a key element of the genre. I am referring, of course, to the messenger scene, which we shall analyse in the following pages.

In Greek tragedy, the ἄγγελος is a specialized character with a very specific role. His function is to transmit news in a specific way that, in turn, constitutes a fundamental part of the drama. He is the person in charge of announcing news that cannot be represented on the stage but which is necessary for the development of the dramatic action.[1] As we shall see, unlike in Homer, in Greek drama the ἄγγελος and the subject of ἀγγέλλω is no longer just anybody: the main subject of ἀγγέλλω is the ἄγγελος, who will expand on the news he transmits with a long narrative: the ἀγγελικὴ ῥῆσις. Besides the ἄγγελος, other characters can report the news. However, as this chapter is intended to show, almost all of these other characters choose to adopt both the lexicon and the conventions used by the ἄγγελοι to successfully complete their informative task. As will be noted, their choice is by no means a coincidence.

At first glance, one might perhaps view Greek tragedy as the genre in which the two figures with the greatest role in the transmission of news, the κῆρυξ and the ἄγγελος, can most easily be distinguished. However, the following pages prove that this differentiation is not always clear.

Κήρυκες: heralds by profession

The term κῆρυξ is well documented in Greek tragedy, since it occurs 42 times (9 in Aeschylus' plays, 7 in those of Sophocles and 26 in Euripides). Most of these heralds are anonymous,[2] although the identity of some — such as the heralds Talthybius (*Agamemnon*) or Lichas (*The Women of Trachis*) — are made known. As for the gods, the most characteristic κῆρυξ is Hermes who, as illustrated in

---

[1] The importance of the ἄγγελος goes beyond the relevance that the character has in the dramatic action. As Julia Caverno points out (1917, 263), the actor who plays the role of a messenger is not just any old actor, but a star. In this regard, cf. Plut. *Lys.* 23.4. See also Gaisford (1972, 132).
[2] See Yoon (2012).

(1) where a herald invokes the god when he appears on the scene, was considered a sort of patron of the guild; the quintessential κῆρυξ and the pride of the heralds themselves (Pallí Bonet 1956, 345):

(1) Aesch., *Ag.* 513–515

> (...) τούς τ' ἀγωνίους θεοὺς
> πάντας προσαυδῶ, τόν τ' ἐμὸν τιμάορον
> Ἑρμῆν, φίλον **κήρυκα**, κηρύκων σέβας.

> And I address all the Assembled Gods, and especially the protector of my own office, Hermes, the **Herald**.[3]

Homer's κήρυκες, as seen above, are characterized by their diligence and loyalty. In tragedy, however, the herald is perceived differently. Tragic heralds strive to give an appearance of loyalty and confidence. They try to brand themselves as very efficient when it comes to their tasks, as this herald makes clear:

(2) Aesch., *Supp.* 930–933

> ἀλλ' ὡς ἂν εἰδὼς ἐννέπω σαφέστερον –
> καὶ γὰρ πρέπει **κήρυκ' ἀπαγγέλλειν**[4] τορῶς
> ἕκαστα — πῶς φῶ, πρὸς τίνος τ' ἀφαιρεθεὶς
> ἥκειν γυναικῶν αὐτανέψιον στόλον;

> Well, so that I can speak to them with more definite knowledge — for it is right that **a herald** should **bring back a** full and clear **report** — when I go back without this band of women who are their close cousins, by whom and by what right should I say I was deprived of possession of them?

By contrast, the other characters do not always have a good image of the κήρυκες. Philoctetes refers to them as liars, using the term ψευδοκήρυκας[5] (Soph., *Phil.* 1306). Furthermore, in several passages of Euripides' tragedies these individuals are attributed with negative traits and behaviours that do nothing in their favour. In *The Children of Heracles*, for instance, Demophon threatens a

---

[3] Translations of Aeschylus' tragedies are taken from Sommerstein (2009).
[4] Although the denominative verb that refers to the action carried out by the κῆρυξ is κηρύσσω, the presence of ἀπαγγέλλω (expected to be used by an ἄγγελος) should be noted.
[5] In his commentaries on *Philoctetes*, Jebb (1932) maintains that in Attic tragedy the figure of the κῆρυξ was especially tied to unsuccessful boastings, as is seen, for instance, in Eur., *Heracl.* 55 ff. or in Soph., *Phil.* 1293 ff.). See also Hogan (1991, 353) and Kamerbeek (1963b, 173–174).

herald with a beating if he does not learn to be prudent (Eur., *Heracl.* 272: εἰ μὴ γ' ὁ κῆρυξ σωφρονεῖν μαθήσεται) and the chorus states that heralds tend to build up a tale twice as large as the truth (Eur., *Heracl.* 292–293: πᾶσι γὰρ οὗτος κήρυξι νόμος, | δὶς τόσα πυργοῦν τῶν γιγνομένων). The messenger of *Orestes* also defines them as follows:

(3) Eur., *Or.* 895–897

> τὸ γὰρ γένος τοιοῦτον· ἐπὶ τὸν εὐτυχῆ
> πηδῶσ' ἀεὶ **κήρυκες**⁶ ὅδε δ' αὐτοῖς φίλος,
> ὃς ἂν δύνηται πόλεος ἔν τ' ἀρχαῖσιν ᾖ.⁷
>
> But that's your **herald** for you — always jumping for the winning side, the friend of any man with influence or power.

On the other hand, although Aeschylus, Sophocles and Euripides do not refer to them as δημιουργοί, in tragedies heralds maintain the same professional character as in Homer as men who are in the public service. This should come as no surprise if we bear in mind that one of the main tragic κήρυκες is Talthybius, one of Agamemnon's heralds in the *Iliad*.

Just as in Homer, tragic heralds are servants who are subordinated to a master,⁸ but who never appear in the domestic sphere. In this way, their functions are much closer to those performed by the heralds of the *Iliad* than to those carried out by the heralds of the *Odyssey*.⁹ Thus, tragic κήρυκες are in charge of summoning assembly (Eur., *Hec.* 146), inviting people to speak (Eur., *Or.* 885), ordering people to remain silent (Aesch., *Eum.* 566, Eur., *Supp.* 668, Eur., *Hec.* 530 or Eur., *Phoen.* 1631) and encouraging soldiers or citizens (Eur., *El.* 707). They also accompany those who go on embassy (Soph., *OT.* 753) and lead the

---

6 According to Benedetto (1965, 178), the full expression was ἐπὶ τὸν εὐτυχῆ τοῖχον χωρεῖν, but the speaker is even more sarcastic by using πηδάω. See also Willink (1986, 230).
7 Translations of *Orestes* are borrowed from Arrowsmith (2013).
8 In addition to Talthybius and Lichas, heralds of Agamemnon and Heracles, reference is made to some of Eurystheus' heralds (Eur., *Heracl.* 49), a herald of Theseus (Eur., *Supp.* 668) or even to the heralds of Hermes (Eur., *Supp.* 121).
9 To define the functions, I have analysed both those passages in which the term κῆρυξ occurs and those in which we see the verb κηρύσσω 'to be a herald', documented 6 times in Aeschylus, 11 in Sophocles and 16 in Euripides. The derivatives ἀνακηρύσσω (Soph., *OT.* 450), ἀντικηρύσσω (Eur., *Supp.* 673), εἰσκηρύσσω (Soph., *El.* 690), ἐκκηρύσσω (Soph., *Ant.* 27, Soph., *Ant.* 203 and Soph., *OC.* 430), ἐπικηρύσσω (Aesch., *Sept.* 634) and προκηρύσσω (Soph., *El.* 684, Soph., *Ant.* 34, Soph., *Ant.* 461 and Eur., *Or.* 1541) are also documented and have been examined.

expedition (Aesch., *Supp.* 727), make public announcements of the trials in athletic competitions and introduce some contests (e.g. the contest over the arms of Achilles in Soph., *Aj.* 1240). They also transmit messages on behalf of others (Eur., *Supp.* 467–475). In addition, heralds carry out a task that is not referred to in the *Iliad*: proclaiming official decrees.[10] These figures must also be considered when studying the transmission of news. It is here that we can truly appreciate the greatest similarities between the herald and the messenger.

The tragic κῆρυξ frequently uses the words derived from ἄγγελος which, as we shall see throughout this chapter, become consolidated in tragedy as technical terms tied to the ἄγγελος and closely related to the transmission of news. The fact that κήρυκες utter these terms instead of their specific lexicon (κηρύσσω, κήρυγμα, and so on) is clear evidence of this specialization. For instance, in *Oedipus at Colonus*, Oedipus himself assures Theseus that he is aware he is about to die because the gods, as heralds, report the news to him (Soph., *OC.* 1511: αὐτοὶ θεοὶ κήρυκες ἀγγέλλουσί μοι). In *Hecuba*, the chorus tells Priam's wife that he is a herald of sorrow because he has laden himself with heavy news (Eur., *Hec.* 105–106: ἀλλ' ἀγγελίας βάρος ἀραμένη | μέγα σοί τε, γύναι, κῆρυξ ἀχέων). Finally, in *Heracles*, Megara confesses to the hero that she is scared because Eurystheus' heralds have reported a terrible piece of news to her (Eur., *HF.* 553: Εὐρυσθέως κήρυκες ἤγγελλον τάδε): that a plan to kill her and her children is being hatched. Furthermore, this is the way Theseus addresses Creon's herald in Euripides' *The Suppliant Women*:

(4) Eur., *Supp.* 459–462

> (...) τὸν γὰρ ἄγγελον χρεών
> λέξανθ' ὅσ' ἂν τάξηι τις ὡς τάχος πάλιν
> χωρεῖν. τὸ λοιπὸν δ' εἰς ἐμὴν πόλιν Κρέων
> ἧσσον λάλον σου πεμπέτω τιν' **ἄγγελον**.[11]

> Messengers should state their mission promptly, then depart. I hope that henceforth, to my city, Creon sends a less wordy **messenger** than you.

Although the character on the scene is a κῆρυξ, Theseus refers to him twice as an ἄγγελος. However, he then performs a task typical of his profession, since he delivers a literal message: an official announcement from Creon (Eur., *Supp.* 467–475). Even so, it can be said that in Greek tragedy, despite the confusion

---

10 Cf., for instance, the intervention of the herald in Aesch., *Sept.* 1005ff.
11 Translations of *The Suppliant Women* are borrowed from Jones (2013).

that seems to exist in certain contexts regarding the roles of κήρυκες and ἄγγελοι, the former also play an interesting role when it comes to the transmission of news. When heralds are involved in the transmission of relevant news, they then adopt the conventions of the ἄγγελοι and behave like real messengers. For this reason, three tragic κήρυκες are included in the list of characters that, from my point of view, should be taken into consideration along with those labelled as ἄγγελοι. I am referring to the κῆρυξ of Agamemnon — although his identity is not specified, it is not difficult to assume that he is Talthybius[12] — in Aeschylus' *Agamemnon*, Lichas in Sophocles' *The Women of Trachis* and Talthybius in Euripides' *Hecuba*. None of the three characters behaves as a herald would be expected to, but as an ἄγγελος: they burst onto the scene to report news that cannot be represented on stage, use the lexicon typical of the ἄγγελοι, and give every detail in the ἀγγελικὴ ῥῆσις, the messenger speech.

The entrance of the first of these three characters is announced by the chorus, which notices that a herald crowned with boughs of olive (a sign of good tidings apparently) is approaching from the shore (Aesch., *Ag.* 493–494: κῆρυκ' ἀπ' ἀκτῆς τόνδ' ὁρῶ κατάσκιον | κλάδοις ἐλαίας·).[13] This κῆρυξ is coming to report both bad and good news. The first news he announces is good:

(5) Aesch., *Ag.* 522–526

> ἥκει γὰρ ὑμῖν φῶς ἐν εὐφρόνῃ φέρων
> καὶ τοῖσδ' ἅπασι κοινὸν Ἀγαμέμνων ἄναξ.
> ἀλλ' εὖ νιν ἀσπάσασθε, καὶ γὰρ οὖν πρέπει,
> Τροίαν κατασκάψαντα τοῦ δικηφόρου
> Διὸς μακέλλῃ, τῇ κατείργασται πέδον.
>
> For he has come, bringing light out of darkness to you and to all these people — King Agamemnon! Give him a noble welcome, for that is truly proper, when he has dug up Troy with the mattock of Zeus the Avenger, with which the ground has been worked over and the seed of the whole country destroyed.

Thus, the κῆρυξ delivers a hitherto unknown piece of news: Agamemnon's return home. Despite this, both the public and the chorus are already aware that the Achaeans have won the Trojan War and that the city has been ravaged. Let us see how the lexicon allows us to easily identify the item of news. In the prologue, a watchman explains that he is waiting for the arrival of the fire with its glad tidings (Aesch., *Ag.* 19: εὐαγγέλου πυρός), a sign that would indicate to

---

12 On Talthybius, see Dyson/Lee (2000).
13 See Perea Morales (1993, 392).

him that Troy has been conquered. Immediately afterwards, the watchman cries out for joy because, in fact, he is already watching the much-desired flame. He utters ἀγγέλλω to refer to the piece of news:

(6) Aesch., *Ag.* 26–30

> Ἀγαμέμνονος γυναικὶ σημαίνω τορῶς
> εὐνῆς ἐπαντείλασαν ὡς τάχος δόμοις
> ὀλολυγμὸν εὐφημοῦντα τῇδε λαμπάδι
> ἐπορθιάζειν, εἴπερ Ἰλίου πόλις
> ἑάλωκεν, ὡς ὁ φρυκτὸς **ἀγγέλλων** πρέπει·

> I proclaim plainly to the wife of Agamemnon that she should raise herself from her bed, as quickly as may be, and on behalf of the house raise a shrill, auspicious cry of triumph over this beacon, if indeed the city of Ilium has been taken as the fire-signal vividly **declares**.

The signal reaches Clytemnestra and, when the queen leaves the palace, the chorus asks her what news he has come to report (Aesch., *Ag.* 86: τίνος ἀγγελίας). After the chorus recounts the background about the war (Aesch., *Ag.* 40–257), Agamemnon's wife speaks to the chorus leader and he assures her that whether the news she is about to announce is good (Aesch., *Ag.* 262: εὐαγγέλοισιν) or bad, he wishes to hear it. Then, the queen delivers the favourable piece of news:

(7) Aesch., *Ag.* 264–267

> **εὐάγγελος** μέν, ὥσπερ ἡ παροιμία,
> ἕως γένοιτο μητρὸς εὐφρόνης πάρα.
> πεύσῃ δὲ χάρμα μεῖζον ἐλπίδος κλύειν·
> Πριάμου γὰρ ᾑρήκασιν Ἀργεῖοι πόλιν.

> In accordance with the proverb,[14] may a morning of **good news** be born from the womb of this night of auspicious. You are about to learn of a joy greater than one could hope to hear: the Argives have captured the city of Priam!

The chorus then enquires about the source of information and which messenger could have been so swift in delivering the news (Aesch., *Ag.* 280: καὶ τίς τόδ' ἐξίκοιτ' ἂν ἀγγέλων τάχος;) and she answers:

---

14 See Coleridge (1938, 31, n. 59): "The precise tenor of the proverb referred to is unknown; it may merely be the familiar generalization "like breeds like" or something more specific, e.g. about a tendency for one piece of good news to follow rapidly after another".

(8) Aesch., *Ag.* 281–283

> Ἥφαιστος Ἴδης λαμπρὸν ἐκπέμπων σέλας.
> φρυκτὸς δὲ φρυκτὸν δεῦρ' **ἀπ' ἀγγάρου**[15] **πυρὸς**
> ἔπεμπεν· (...).

> Hephaestus, sending a bright blaze on its way from Mount Ida; and then from that **courier-fire** beacon sent on beacon all the way here.

In her later account, the queen explains how the news spread. She relates how the pinewood torch reported the news to watchmen of mount Macistus (Aesch., *Ag.* 289: παραγγείλασα Μακίστου σκοπαῖς) who then, fulfilling their role as messengers (Aesch., *Ag.* 291: ἀγγέλου μέρος), passed it onto the watchmen on Messapion. The latter then made an announcement (Aesch., *Ag.* 294: παρήγγειλαν)[16] by setting fire to a heap of withered heather. In this way, they sped up the message. The following comes at the end of Clytemnestra's speech:

(9) Aesch., *Ag.* 315–316

> τέκμαρ τοιοῦτον σύμβολόν τε σοὶ λέγω
> ἀνδρὸς **παραγγείλαντος** ἐκ Τροίας ἐμοί.

> Such, I tell you, is the evidence and the token that my husband has **transmitted** to me from Troy.

In her report, παραγγέλλω occurs three times. As we note below, in the works of historians this verb goes on to become a military term referring to the transmission of orders through ranks of warriors. In this context, however, it must be understood that the announcement implied by the presence of this verb has nothing to do with commands but with Agamemnon's return home, that is, with the relevant piece of news transmitted by means of fire. The words of the κῆρυξ, therefore, confirm the excellent tidings that Clytemnestra had reported before.

---

15 The term ἄγγαρος refers to the Persian mounted courier in charge of carrying royal dispatches and is also documented in Herodotus' *Histories* (cf. Hdt. 5.95). In the second volume of his commentaries on *Agamemnon*, Fraenkel (1962, 153–154) relates this passage to that of Herodotus; he suggests that the most important role of an ἄγγαρος is the transmission of messages in turns, which makes this expression very appropriate in the description offered in this tragedy.

16 On the importance of fire and light signals in the transmission of news, see Riepl (1913, 48–98), who deals with these passages from *Agamemnon*.

The queen herself highlights this fact when the herald concludes the first part of his account:

(10) Aesch., *Ag.* 587–589

> ἀνωλόλυξα μὲν πάλαι χαρᾶς ὕπο,
> ὅτ' ἦλθ' ὁ πρῶτος νύχιος **ἄγγελος πυρός**,
> φράζων ἅλωσιν Ἰλίου τ' ἀνάστασιν.

> I raised a cry of triumphant joy long ago, when the first nocturnal **fire-messenger** came, telling of the capture and destruction of Ilium.

Throughout this sequence, there are five terms from the lexical family tackled in this study: ἄγγελος, εὐάγγελος, ἀγγελία, ἀγγέλλω and παραγγέλλω. All refer to one of the most important items of news: the victory in the Trojan War. In any case, the κῆρυξ must still announce the bad news. Once the herald has finished his report of the hardships they suffered during their journey home, the chorus asks him for Menelaus, and he replies:

(11) Aesch., *Ag.* 624–625

> ἀνὴρ ἄφαντος ἐξ Ἀχαιικοῦ στρατοῦ,
> αὐτός τε καὶ τὸ πλοῖον. οὐ ψευδῆ λέγω.

> The man has vanished from the Achaean armada, himself and his ship. I tell you no lie.

The chorus insists: "Did the general voice of other voyagers bring news of him as alive or dead?". The herald assures that nobody, except the sun, could clearly report this news (Aesch., *Ag.* 632: ἀπαγγεῖλαι τορῶς). At the beginning of the second part of his report, the κῆρυξ regrets having to deliver such disparate news. His reflection is interesting in terms of the vocabulary he uses:

(12) Aesch., *Ag.* 636–649

> εὔφημον ἦμαρ οὐ πρέπει **κακαγγέλῳ**
> γλώσσῃ μιαίνειν· χωρὶς ἡ τιμὴ θεῶν.
> ὅταν δ' ἀπευκτὰ πήματ' **ἄγγελος** πόλει
> στυγνῷ προσώπῳ πτωσίμου στρατοῦ φέρῃ,
> πόλει μὲν ἕλκος ἓν τὸ δήμιον τυχεῖν,
> πολλοὺς δὲ πολλῶν ἐξαγισθέντας δόμων
> ἄνδρας διπλῇ μάστιγι, τὴν Ἄρης φιλεῖ,
> δίλογχον ἄτην, φοινίαν ξυνωρίδα·
> τοιῶνδε μέντοι πημάτων σεσαγμένον

πρέπει λέγειν παιᾶνα τόνδ' Ἐρινύων.
σωτηρίων δὲ πραγμάτων **εὐάγγελον**
ἥκοντα πρὸς χαίρουσαν εὐεστοῖ πόλιν –
πῶς κεδνὰ τοῖς κακοῖσι συμμείξω, λέγων
χειμῶν' Ἀχαιῶν οὐκ ἀμήνιτον θεοῖς;

It is not proper to defile a day of good omen by the uttering of **bad news**: the honour due to the gods stands apart from that. When a grim-faced **messenger** brings a city the painful news of an army lost, news it had prayed not to receive — that the city has suffered one wound collectively, while many men have been taken from many houses as sacrificial victims, by the double whip that Ares loves, in a two-pronged ruin, in gory double harness — well, when someone is loaded down with that kind of misery, it is fitting to sing this paean to the Furies. But when one is coming with **good tidings** of success to a city rejoicing in prosperity — how can I mix together good and evil, by telling of the storm that showed no lack of divine anger against the Achaeans?

Let us not forget that the speaker here is a herald (a κῆρυξ), who would be expected to deliver a message from someone or, at best, proclaim an official decree. Nevertheless, this herald behaves just like a tragic ἄγγελος: he appears to report news and stars in a typical messenger scene. He complains about the difficult task that messengers are supposed to perform and then talks about sharing bad news (κακαγγέλῳ γλώσσῃ) and how negative the arrival of a grim-faced ἄγγελος to report a dire disaster can be. On the other hand, the situation he experienced beforehand was quite different, since he has been a messenger in charge of bringing good tidings of success (σωτηρίων δὲ πραγμάτων εὐάγγελον). From the fact that a herald uses this vocabulary we can gather that, unlike in Homer, in tragedy not just anyone can be an ἄγγελος. That is to say that if a herald or any other character does play the role of an ἄγγελος he or she complies with the conventions of the ἄγγελοι, using the same vocabulary and performing scenes identical to those the ἄγγελοι would perform.

This passage is therefore evidence that, already in Aeschylus tragedies, ἄγγελος and its derivatives are becoming technical terms linked to the transmission of news and connected with the ἄγγελος, the news-bearer par excellence in Greek tragedy.

The case of Lichas, the herald of Heracles, in Sophocles' *The Women of Trachis* is quite different. He appears to give Deianeira news concerning her husband. When she asks Lichas whether the hero is still alive or not, the herald exclaims with joy: "I certainly left him alive and well" (Soph., *Trach.* 232–235). Then Deianeira requests more details and Lichas expands the information in a messenger speech in which he explains that the hero has conquered the city.

Besides, he says that the women who accompany him (including Iole) are part of the spoils of war. However, the herald is not telling the truth here.[17] As soon as he leaves, he is betrayed by an ἄγγελος who confesses to Deianeira that Heracles is hopelessly in love with Iole. This is how the ἄγγελος refers to Lichas:

(13) Soph., *Trach.* 346–348

> Ἀνὴρ ὅδ' οὐδὲν ὧν ἔλεξεν ἀρτίως
> φωνεῖ δίκης ἐς ὀρθόν, ἀλλ' ἢ νῦν κακός,[18]
> ἢ πρόσθεν οὐ δίκαιος **ἄγγελος** παρῆν.

> Nothing that man has just been telling you was spoken in strict honesty. Either he is a liar now, or he was no honest **messenger** before.[19]

As we well know, Lichas is a κῆρυξ, and yet he clearly uses conventions typical of ἄγγελοι even to tell lies. No one doubts the reliability of an ἄγγελος, and other characters take advantage of that when they want to report false news. Deianeira trusts him, and he is betrayed by a real ἄγγελος, who refers to him not as κῆρυξ but as a dishonest ἄγγελος.

In the case of Talthybius in *Hecuba*, we can identify this character as an ἄγγελος, not because of the text's lexicon, but because of his behaviour. It is well known that Talthybius was Agamemnon's herald in the *Iliad*, and in this role he enters the scene to take Hecuba under the king's orders (Eur., *Hec.* 503–504). Hecuba eventually manages to find out the news the herald has come to announce: her daughter Polyxena has died (Eur., *Hec.* 508–510). Talthybius is clear that he has not arrived before Priam's wife on his own initiative, but to obey Agamemnon's orders. However, when Hecuba asks Talthybius how they ended her daughter's life, he expands on the information by delivering an extensive speech (Eur., *Hec.* 519–608) just like any of the best ἄγγελοι.

It is also interesting to consider Talthybius' role in another tragedy by Euripides: *The Trojan Women*. Here, he also enters the scene as a herald who has been entrusted to take the slaves away. He introduces himself as a κῆρυξ:

---

17 The speech delivered by Lichas is a *deception speech*, that is, an invented testimony.
18 See Kamerbeek (1970, 95): "The meaning of κακός ('dishonest') is brought out by οὐ δίκαιος; δίκη itself meaning in this context 'honesty', 'uprightness'". See also Easterling (1982, 121).
19 Translations of *The Women of Trachis* are borrowed from Jameson (2013).

(14) Eur., *Tro.* 235–238

> Ἑκάβη, πυκνὰς γὰρ οἶσθά μ' ἐς Τροίαν ὁδοὺς
> ἐλθόντα **κήρυκ'** ἐξ Ἀχαιικοῦ στρατοῦ,
> ἐγνωσμένος δὴ καὶ πάροιθέ σοι, γύναι,
> Ταλθύβιος ἥκω καινὸν **ἀγγελῶν** λόγον.

> Hecuba, incessantly my ways have led me to Troy as **the herald** of all the Achaean armament. You know me from the old days, my lady; I am sent, Talthybius **with news** for you to hear.[20]

Despite the fact that he himself affirms that he arrives as a κῆρυξ, Talthybius uses the verb ἀγγέλλω. As we shall see in what follows, this verb became consolidated in Greek tragedy as a technical term related to the transmission of news. By using it, the herald makes it clear that he will report relevant news before fulfilling the task entrusted to him. Directly afterwards, Talthybius tells Hecuba that the fates of the slaves have already been decided (Eur., *Tro.* 240). The herald then points out to Hecuba the heroes to which each of the women has been assigned. Later, Talthybius will appear again, and Hecuba announces his arrival, referring to him as an ἄγγελος and not a κῆρυξ:

(15) Eur., *Tro.* 707–708

> τίν' αὖ δέδορκα τόνδ' Ἀχαιικὸν λάτριν
> στείχοντα καινῶν **ἄγγελον** βουλευμάτων;

> Who is this Achaean servant I see coming here again (*as a messenger*), sent to tell us of some new design?[21]

Talthybius does not address Hecuba but Andromache, and once again uses the verb ἀγγέλλω (as well as the action noun ἄγγελμα) to make his purpose clear:[22]

(16) Eur., *Tro.* 709–713

> {Τα.} Φρυγῶν ἀρίστου πρίν ποθ' Ἕκτορος δάμαρ,
> μή με στυγήσῃς· οὐχ ἑκὼν γὰρ **ἀγγελῶ**

---

20 This translation is taken from Lattimore (2013) with slight modifications.
21 The translation of this passage and the following are taken from Coleridge (1891). Italics are mine.
22 In the example, besides the language used, there is another convention typical of ἄγγελοι: the fact that, when entering the scene, they apologize for the bad news they have come to give or refer to them in some way as a preamble to their story (Mastronarde 1979, 69).

> Δαναῶν τε κοινὰ Πελοπιδῶν τ' **ἀγγέλματα**.
> {Ἀν.} τί δ' ἔστιν; ὥς μοι φροιμίων ἄρχῃ κακῶν.
> {Ta.} ἔδοξε τόνδε παῖδα ... πῶς εἴπω λόγον;

> TALTHYBIUS. — You that once were the wife of Hector, bravest of the Phrygians, do not hate me, for **I am not a willing messenger**. The Danaids and sons of Pelops both command...
> ANDROMACHE. — What is it? Your prelude bodes evil **news**.
> TALTHYBIUS. — It is decreed your son is—how can I tell my news?

Frightened, Andromache now wants to know what is happening and, after some hesitation, Talthybius says: "They mean to slay your son; there is my hateful piece of news to you" (Eur., *Tro.* 719). This piece of news is not only relevant for Andromache, but also for the other women. With this announcement, the Trojans say goodbye to their final hope that the son of Hector and Andromache would grow up to avenge the death of his father and the defeat of Troy.[23]

Ἄγγελοι: professional messengers

In Euripides' *Electra*, Agamemnon's daughter, who has planned the murder along with her brother Orestes to avenge their father's homicide, is waiting for news with the chorus and begins to despair at the lack of information. Death cries are heard in the background and Electra, distressed, talks in this meaningful way to the chorus leader:

(17) Eur., *El.* 757–760

> {Ηλ.} σφαγὴν αὐτεῖς τῇδέ μοι· τί μέλλομεν;
> {Χο.} ἔπισχε, τρανῶς ὡς μάθῃς τύχας σέθεν.
> {Ηλ.} οὐκ ἔστι· νικώμεσθα· ποῦ γὰρ **ἄγγελοι**;
> {Χο.} ἥξουσιν· οὔτοι βασιλέα φαῦλον κτανεῖν.

> ELECTRA. — So you announce my death by sword. Why am I slow?
> CHORUS. — Lady, hold back until you learn the outcome clearly.
> ELECTRA. — Not possible. We are beaten. Where are the **messengers**?
> CHORUS. — They will come soon. To kill a king is not quick or light.[24]

---

23 See Barlow (1986, 194).
24 Translations of *Electra* are taken from Vermeule (2013).

Immediately afterwards, a hasty ἄγγελος bursts onto the scene[25] to announce (ἀγγέλλω) to Electra and the chorus the much-desired news. Orestes has killed Aegisthus:

(18) Eur., *El.* 761–763

> ὦ καλλίνικοι παρθένοι Μυκηνίδες,
> νικῶντ' Ὀρέστην πᾶσιν **ἀγγέλλω** φίλοις,
> Ἀγαμέμνονος δὲ φονέα κείμενον πέδωι
> Αἴγισθον· (...)

> Hail maidens of Mycenae, glorious in triumph! Orestes is victor! I **proclaim** it to all who love him. The murderer of Agamemnon lies on the earth crumpled in blood, Aegisthus.

Besides clearly intensifying the dramatic tension (Cropp 1988, 153), these passages highlight the importance of the figure of the messenger in Greek tragedy. The main characters themselves — represented in this case by Electra and the chorus leader, who also takes for granted that this will happen — assume that death must be reported by an ἄγγελος.[26] But this is only the prelude to what will come next: an extensive messenger speech to describe how Orestes deceived Aegisthus and killed him.

The messenger's performance is far from accidental. This character was already considered a typical figure in Greek tragedies and his intervention in the so-called messenger scene is a very important part of the play. The news reported by ἄγγελοι is not trivial. Indeed, it serves to increase the *dramatic pathos* and responds to the need to introduce information that cannot be staged[27] for the different reasons set out below.

Thus, the role of the messenger is purely informative and has several addressees: the characters on stage and the audience, since an ἄγγελος never

---

[25] Cf. Denniston (1968, 145): "The messenger does, in fact, arrive with remarkable speed, close on the heels of the cries, without even an intervening choral ode to gloss over the lack of realism".

[26] To the same effect, cf. Aesch., *Pers.* 14. In the prologue the chorus awaits news, but has not yet noticed the presence of any messenger or horseman (κοὔτε τις ἄγγελος οὔτε τις ἱππεύς) who comes to bring it to them. In Eur., *Heracl.* 751 the chorus invokes the earth and the moon and begs for the good news of the victory of the Athenian army. Shortly afterwards, the messenger enters the scene to announce the triumph.

[27] Monaco refers to the messenger scene as *scena allargata* because it seeks to broaden the spectator's vision. See Monaco (2004, 8): "Ma spesso la convenzione, quali risulta dai testi teatrali antichi, comporta anche un allargamento ad altri spazi, interni ed esterni, nei quali si svolge l'azione e che l'occhio dello spettatore non può raggiungere".

reports back on anything that the audience has witnessed. But what kind of events could not be staged? Let us now take a look.

Why messenger scenes?

In *Why Messenger Speeches?*, an exhaustive study on this character of Attic drama, J.M. Bremer suggests that important events are never shown and acted, but reported,[28] and proposes a number of reasons to justify messenger scenes.

The presence of the chorus makes scene-shifts practically impossible
Attic tragedy dealt with heroes, and it was inconceivable that those heroes would remain in their respective palaces without moving around. Let us recall, for example, the expedition to Troy or Heracles' journeys. Greek tragedians ran into a problem in representing these shifts: the main characters' movement was directly opposed to the static nature of the chorus which, once on stage, remained permanently in the *orchestra*.[29] With the physical presence of the chorus, the location was fixed at one point and scene-shifts were practically impossible. The entrance of an ἄγγελος to report what happened at another location was an effective way to get around the problem.

A chorus cannot act crowd-scenes
The tragic chorus, with very few exceptions,[30] remained static. The tradition of the genre apparently did not allow the chorus to have an active role in the heroic action of the play itself. Therefore, when the authors wanted to stage crowd-scenes they were faced with an obstacle. Since the chorus could not be used, the best solution was for a character who had witnessed the events to report those episodes in which crowds of people were involved.[31] Once again, the intervention of an ἄγγελος solved the problem.

---

28 See Bremer (1976, 29).
29 There are only five exceptions in which the chorus leaves the *orchestra*: in Aesch., *Eum.*, in Soph., *Aj.*, in Eur., *Alc.*, in Eur., *Hel.* and in Eur., *Rhes*. See Bremer (1976, 30–31).
30 Cf., for instance, the cases of the Danaides in Aesch., *Supp*. or the Furies in Aesch., *Eum*.
31 Bremer (1976, 34) identifies some battle scenes (Aesch., *Pers.* 290–531, Aesch., *Sept.* 375–652 and 792–821 and Aesch., *Ag.* 503–537; Soph., *Aj.* 719–732; Eur., *Heracl.* 800–867, Eur., *Andr.* 1085–1166, Eur., *Supp.* 650–730, Eur., *IT* 260–340, Eur., *Hel.* 1526–1619, Eur., *Phoen.* 1090–1479, Eur., *Or.* 1395–1503 and Eur., *Bacch.* 677–775 and 1085–1147). He also mentions two cases in which a peaceful assembly is reported (Eur., *Ion* 1122–1229 and Eur., *Or.* 866–957).

Miracles cannot be shown on stage

In Euripides' *Hippolytus*, an ἄγγελος tells us how he and his fellow travellers came to a deserted place when accompanying Hippolytus in exile. Suddenly, he says, the earth began to roar and a huge wave emerged from the sea and rolled towards them. Miraculously, a bull roared out of the wave and chased Theseus' son, frightening his horses, which dashed his chariot among the rocks. Hippolytus, dragged along by his own horses, almost died. However, he managed to free himself and fell to the ground, out of breath. Finally, the horses and the terrible bull disappeared as if by magic.

The issues that arose from staging these situations are perfectly understandable: in the 5th century BC authors lacked the theatrical mechanisms that would allow them to show any kind of special effect. However, the events described in such passages could not be ignored. The introduction of an ἄγγελος was once again the best solution: if the messenger, a direct witness of the events, reported them in a spectacular way, the problem would be solved.[32]

Death on stage was not feasible

It cannot go unnoticed that, although death is present in almost every Greek tragedy (in one way or another), the three tragedians avoided staging it. A variety of explanations have been suggested for this. As Bremer (1976, 37–42) explains so well, there was a probability that playwrights avoided death on stage because one of their three actors would be immobilized on stage for the rest of the play (there was no curtain between the episodes). It has been argued, however, that there are three instances in which a *dramatis persona* (Ajax, Alcestis and Hippolytus) do in fact die on stage.[33] Another hypothesis suggests that it would have been quite normal for an audience to be offended or pained by a bloody spectacle. Others explain it with reference to the religious taboo concerning death in the *temenos* of Dionysus, where the tragedy was staged.[34]

---

32 Cf. also Soph., *OC*. 1587–1666 (the mysterious disappearance of Oedipus), Eur., *Hel*. 605–616 (the ascent into heaven of Helen's ghost), Eur., *Bacch*. 604–641 (the earthquake at the palace of Pentheus), Eur., *Bacch*. 680–860 (the miracles performed by the maenads), Eur., *Med*. 1137–1221 (the effects of the magical gift on Glauce and Creon) or Eur., *Or*. 1493–1498 (the mysterious escape and consequent deification of Helen). Bremer (1976, 35–36) omits the miraculous rescue of Iphigenia.
33 For a comprehensive analysis of all of these, see Bremer (1976, 38–39). On Ajax's suicide in particular and on death on stage in general, see Arnott (1962, 131–139).
34 Lines 1437–1438 of *Hippolytus* could support this hypothesis. The speaker is the goddess Artemis, who leaves the scene before Hippolytus dies: "Farewell: it is not lawful for me to look upon the dead or to defile my sight with the last breath of the dying".

Whatever the case, even the characters themselves assume that death has to be reported by a messenger.

Literary tradition

Messenger speeches are clearly narrative in nature, and this narrative character is directly related to the orality of archaic literature.[35] The most obvious sign of its transcendence is that of all the tragedies that are still complete, only two tragedies by Aeschylus (*Eumenides* and *Prometheus Bound*) lack a messenger scene. Some have two or even three.

Defining the tragic messenger

Manuscripts indicate the presence of numerous ἄγγελοι who do not carry out secondary tasks but, as we will show in this chapter, play an important role in the development of the plot. Along with these ἄγγελοι, another character with an identical informative role stands out: the ἐξάγγελος.[36] The difference between the two[37] lies in the fact that the ἄγγελος brings news from afar but the ἐξάγγελος reports events that occur within the palace walls or behind the scenes. Nevertheless, both characters have to pass information on to the rest of the characters and the audience about certain events that, due to the reasons listed above, could not be staged.

Apart from the ἄγγελοι named in the manuscripts, fifty-two occurrences of ἄγγελος are documented in Greek tragedy[38] as well as two of αὐτάγγελος,[39] eight

---

[35] On the influence of the epic on the messenger's speech, see Bassi (1899), Bergson (1959), Segal (1986) or Barrett (2002, 23–55). On bards, heralds, and messengers in Homer, Durán López (1999).
[36] Setting aside the references to these characters in the manuscripts, the term ἐξάγγελος does not appear in Greek tragedy. It does occur, however, in Thucydides, as we shall see in the corresponding chapter.
[37] See Di Gregorio (1967, 3 and 54), who refers to a passage from Philostratus. Cf. Philostr. *VS* 1.9.
[38] This number refers to the times that the term occurs within the text, excluding those occasions in which the manuscripts indicate the intervention of an ἄγγελος. Thus, the term appears seventeen times in Aeschylus, twelve in Sophocles, and twenty-three in Euripides.
[39] The term αὐτάγγελος only occurs in Sophocles (Soph., *Phil.* 568 and Soph., *OC.* 333) and refers to the character who brings news of what he/she himself/herself has seen. In *Philoctetes* it is used to refer to Ulysses; in *Oedipus at Colonus*, to Ismene.

of εὐάγγελος,⁴⁰ one of κακάγγελος⁴¹ and one of ὑπάγγελος.⁴² The verbal adjectives κακάγγελτος,⁴³ αὐτεπάγγελτος⁴⁴ and νεάγγελτος can also be found.⁴⁵

Most of the ἄγγελοι or ἐξάγγελοι⁴⁶ in the tragedies of Aeschylus, Sophocles and Euripides have a point in common with the Homeric messenger: they are almost all anonymous. However, we have much more information about them. We know, for instance, that almost all of them are servants, like the κήρυκες in the *Odyssey*. In Aeschylus' tragedies, the manuscripts mention a spy messenger (κατάσκοπος) in *Seven against Thebes* and an anonymous κῆρυξ in *Agamemnon*. Sophocles' plays have a guard (φύλαξ) in *Antigone*, a nurse (τροφός) in *The Women of Trachis*, a merchant (ἔμπορος) in *Philoctetes* and a pedagogue (παιδαγωγός) in *Electra*. Finally, in the works of Euripides, reference is made to a handmaid (θεράπαινα) in *Alcestis*, a servant (θεράπων) in *Ion*, a herdsman (βουκόλος) in *Iphigenia among the Taurians*, a Phrygian slave (Φρύξ) in *Orestes*, and a charioteer (ἡνίοχος) in *Rhesus*. Some of the characters that we understand to be anonymous ἄγγελοι expressly refer to their profession. One of many examples would be the aforementioned messenger in Euripides' *Electra*. He himself explains to Agamemnon's daughter that he is a servant of Orestes:⁴⁷

(19) Eur., *El.* 765–766

{ΗΛ.} τίς δ' εἶ σύ; πῶς μοι πιστὰ σημαίνεις τάδε;
{Αγ.} οὐκ οἶσθ' ἀδελφοῦ μ' εἰσορῶσα πρόσπολον;

ELECTRA. — Who are you? Why should I think your message is the truth?
MESSENGER. — You do not know you're looking on your brother's servant?

---

40 'Messenger of good news'. Occurs five times in Aeschylus (Aesch., *Ag.* 21, Aesch., *Ag.* 262, Aesch., *Ag.* 264, Aesch., *Ag.* 475 and Aesch., *Ag.* 646) and three times in Euripides (Eur., *Phoen.* 1217, Eur., *Med.* 975 and Eur., *Med.* 1010).
41 'Messenger of ill tidings'. Cf. Aesch., *Ag.* 636.
42 'Summoned by a messenger'. Cf. Aesch., *Cho.* 838.
43 Cf. Soph., *Ant.* 1286. It refers to the pain caused by ill tidings. Creon uses this term when an ἐξάγγελος tells him his wife (Eurydice) has died.
44 'Offering of oneself, of one's free will'. Cf. Eur., *HF.* 706: αὐτεπάγγελτοι θανεῖν.
45 Cf. Aesch. *Cho.*, 736: τὴν νεάγγελτον φάτιν, alluding to the false report of the death of Orestes.
46 I mean most of them because, as illustrated by the cases of Talthybius and Lichas, there are some other characters who behave as ἄγγελοι.
47 There are some other characters named as ἄγγελοι in the manuscripts. However, we know their occupation because they or their interlocutors reveal it: the ἄγγελος of *The Children of Heracles* (a servant of Alcmene), the ἄγγελος of *Hippolytus* (an attendant of Theseus' son), the ἄγγελος of *Medea* (a servant of Jason) and the ἄγγελος of *Rhesus* (a shepherd).

If loyalty is a characteristic of the heralds in the Homeric poems, in tragedy this trait is associated to the ἄγγελοι, who are described as 'faithful' (Aesch., *PV*. 969: πιστόν) and 'true' (Aesch., *Sept*. 82: ἔτυμος). Nobody doubts the absolute reliability of the news they bring, even if some of it is not true. Besides, they have a 'kind voice' (Aesch., *Cho*. 195: φωνὴν ἔμφρον'), and only the dust is a 'voiceless messenger' (Aesch., *Supp*. 180: ἄναυδον), but even it transmits clear signals.

Speed is another of the characteristics they share with Homer's ἄγγελοι, since they are 'quick' (Aesch., *Ag*. 280: τάχος) and 'hasty' (Aesch., *Sept*. 285: σπερχνούς). When they have bad news to share, they come on stage 'with gloomy countenance' (Aesch., *Ag*. 639: στυγνῷ προσώπῳ) or with a 'gloomy look and face' (Eur., *Phoen*. 1333: σκυθρωπὸν ὄμμα καὶ πρόσωπον ἀγγέλου). Considering that most of the time the news they report is not good, such situations are very common.

When the herald of *Agamemnon* bursts onto the stage to complete his task, he exclaims that it is not proper to defile a day of good omen by uttering bad news (Aesch., *Ag*. 636: κακαγγέλῳ γλώσσῃ).[48] Likewise, some characters refer to these bearers of news as messengers of bad news (Soph., *Ant*. 277: ἄγγελον κακῶν ἐπῶν).[49] Nevertheless, on some occasions the news they transmit is good and, as a result, they are called εὐάγγελοι. In many of these cases, they themselves reassure their interlocutors after coming on stage. To give an example, the ἄγγελος of *Rhesus* does this when he addresses Hector with these words: "I bring joyful news to you".[50] He goes on to report that Rhesus is on his way to join Hector as his friend and ally of Troy.

With regard to the gods, only Hermes, acting on Zeus' orders, is referred to as ἄγγελος in Greek tragedy (Aesch., *PV*. 969, Eur., *El*. 461 and Eur., *IA*. 1301).[51] Additionally, the fire (Aesch., *Ag*. 291 and Aesch., *Ag*. 588: πῦρ), the dust (Aesch., *Sept*. 82 and Aesch., *Supp*. 180: κόνις), the tongue (Eur., *Supp*. 203: γλῶσσα), the shout (Eur., *Heracl*. 656: βοή) and a bird (Soph., *El*. 149: ὄρνις) are described as ἄγγελοι.

Furthermore, unlike the Homeric ἄγγελοι, tragic messengers do not act on behalf of another person but spontaneously, on their own initiative. It is precisely the informative task they perform that makes them interesting from the point of view of the transmission of news. Di Gregorio (1967, 33) refers to the ἄγγελος di-

---

48 See example (12).
49 Cf. also. Eur., *Or*. 856.
50 Cf. Eur., *Rhes*. 272: φέρω κεδνοὺς λόγους.
51 Hermes is also described as "courier of Zeus" (Aesch., *PV*. 941: τὸν Διὸς τρόχιν).

rectly as an 'informatore', and Barrett (2001, 377) expresses a similar view.[52] Perris (2011, 3), for his part, maintains that "ἄγγελος makes at least as much — if not more — sense, in this context, as 'reporter'" than as 'messenger'.[53] I share these views and present below the particular characteristics of the tragic ἄγγελοι that lead me to argue that these characters can be considered a kind of primary 'reporter' in Greek tragedy.[54]

Ἄγγελοι play an informative role

In most of their interventions, the ἄγγελοι define themselves and make it clear that their only task is to transmit news. This can be illustrated in the entrance of an ἄγγελος in *Ajax*:

(20) Soph., *Aj.* 718–721

> Ἄνδρες φίλοι, τὸ πρῶτον[55] **ἀγγεῖλαι** θέλω·
> Τεῦκρος πάρεστιν ἄρτι Μυσίων ἀπὸ
> κρημνῶν· μέσον δὲ προσμολὼν στρατήγιον
> κυδάζεται τοῖς πᾶσιν Ἀργείοις ὁμοῦ.

> Friends, I would **deliver this news** first to you: Teucer has just come back from rugged Mysia. No sooner did he reach headquarters than the whole Greek army gathered to abuse him.

On some other occasions, the messengers do not need to justify their entrance because other characters do it for them, as shown in (21). Dionysus notices the

---

52 "The ἄγγελος of the mss. is their regular designation for any minor character whose sole dramatic function is to report events that have taken place off the stage. The conventional translation 'messenger' is unfortunate: the ἄγγελος brings not a message but news".
53 "Generally speaking, moreover, ἀγγέλλειν is to report, not merely (although sometimes) to bring a message from someone. [...]. Even 'news-bringer', moreover, tends to imply a news-sender, so to speak. I propose that ἄγγελος makes at least as much — if not more — sense, in this context, as 'reporter', and that we would do well to describe as a reporter any character who reports".
54 For a first approach to this topic, see Fornieles Sánchez (2013b). See also Leal Soares (2007, 108).
55 The eagerness of the ἄγγελος to be the first to report the news is recurrent in tragedy. On this passage from *Ajax*, see Kamerbeek (1963): "τὸ πρῶτον: "in the first place". The asyndetic statement in direct speech following ἀγγεῖλαι does not mark the messenger as a man of the common people but is suggestive of the haste with which he wishes to bring his message". See also Finglass (2011, 350–351) and Hogan (1991, 207). Translations of *Ajax* are borrowed from Moore (2013).

arrival of a messenger who has come from the mountain to bring some news (the horrible[56] miracles performed by the Bacchae):[57]

(21) Eur., *Bacch.* 657–658

> κείνου δ' ἀκούσας πρῶτα τοὺς λόγους μάθε,
> ὃς ἐξ ὄρους πάρεστιν **ἀγγελῶν** τί σοι.

> But hear this messenger who **brings you news** from the mountain Cithaeron.[58]

Ἄγγελοι are eyewitnesses: the αὐτοψία

Consider now how the messenger of *Persians* comes on stage to report that the whole army has been destroyed. Neither the chorus nor the queen doubts the truth of this statement, because he claims he witnessed the events himself:[59]

(22) Aesch., *Pers.* 265–266

> καὶ μὴν παρών γε κοὺ λόγους ἄλλων κλύων,
> Πέρσαι, φράσαιμ' ἂν οἷ' ἐπορσύνθη κακά.

> And I can also tell you, Persians, what kinds of horrors came to pass; I was there myself, I did not merely hear the reports of others.

According to Garvie (2009, 143), the ἄγγελος gives authority to his narrative by stressing that he was an eyewitness of the events he describes. Besides, although it would be impossible to determine where he was at each point in the narrative and how he is able to report the details, the audience has no difficulty in accepting the conventional omniscience of the messenger. The same applies to (23):

---

56 See Dodds (1966, 159): "The messenger scene is essential to the psychological dynamics of the play, since it effect is to divert Pentheus' rage from the audience what could not be shown on the strange working of the Dionysiac madness upon the women, as it appeared in all its beauty and horror to a simple-minded observer".
57 On this announcement made by Dionysus and the attitude of this god, see Taplin (1978, 57). On the subsequent speech, Rijksbaron (1991): "This messenger speech is of the type that opens with a main clause, which gives time and place of the events described in the story proper".
58 Translations of *The Bacchae* are taken from Arrowsmith (2013).
59 On the messenger and αὐτοψία in tragedy, see Fornieles Sánchez (2018). This case is special because, as we all know, Aeschylus himself took part in the battle of Salamis and, therefore, may well be reporting the events as an eyewitness.

(23) Aesch. *Sept.* 40–41

> ἥκω σαφῆ τἀκεῖθεν ἐκ στρατοῦ φέρων,
> αὐτὸς κατόπτης δ' εἴμ' ἐγὼ τῶν πραγμάτων·[60]

> I come bringing definite news from the army out there; I was myself an eyewitness of what they were doing.

As rightly pointed out by De Jong (1991, 9–11), almost all the messengers refer explicitly to their position of eyewitnesses. From De Jong's point of view, the ἄγγελοι do this because they are fully aware that they are the only reliable source of information for those to whom they are reporting the news.[61] There are also some contexts in which it is not necessary for the ἄγγελοι to highlight their position as eyewitnesses, since the addressee takes it for granted. This is, for instance, the case seen in example (24). The speaker is the leader of the chorus:

(24) Eur., *Supp.* 647–649

> πῶς γὰρ τροπαῖα Ζηνὸς Αἰγέως τόκος
> ἔστησεν οἵ τε συμμετασχόντες δορός;
> λέξον· παρὼν γὰρ οὐ παρόντας εὐφρανεῖς·

> How did the son of Aegeus and his comrades gain victory? Tell us now. You saw it happen; you can give joy to those who were not there.

On numerous occasions, the messenger has not been a mere spectator of the events but has actually participated in them. This is pointed out, for example, by Jocasta in Euripides' *The Phoenician Women*:

(25) Eur., *Phoen.* 1072–1076

> ὦ φίλτατ', οὔ που ξυμφορὰν ἥκεις φέρων
> Ἐτεοκλέους θανόντος, οὗ παρ' ἀσπίδα
> βέβηκας αἰεὶ πολεμίων εἴργων βέλη;

---

[60] Hutchinson (1985, 48) emphasizes that the fact that messengers tend to make it clear that they have witnessed the events themselves implies that the news they transmit is true. He also points out that it is sometimes used as a resource to increase *dramatic pathos*, as applies to *The Children of Heracles* and to Sophocles' *Electra*. See also Leal Soares (2007, 123–124 and 1999, 63ff.).

[61] "This emphasis reflects the traditional topos of 'autopsy being a more reliable source of information than hearsay', which goes back to Homer and Herodotus". See also Allen-Hornblower (2016, 94–246).

τί μοί ποθ' ἥκεις καινὸν **ἀγγελῶν** ἔπος;
τέθνηκεν ἢ ζῆι παῖς ἐμός; σήμαινέ μοι.

Dear friend, you haven't come to tell disaster, Eteocles' death, you who march by his shield, constantly keeping off the enemy shafts? What is the **new word that you bring** to me? Is my son alive or dead? Now tell me true.[62]

Ἄγγελοι reinforce their speeches with statements from the main characters of the events they relate

This is a very frequent resource in messenger speeches and is a direct consequence of the position of these characters as witnesses. The ἄγγελος, in his informative role, does not just introduce himself as an eyewitness but usually includes in his speech statements made by the main characters of the events they are reporting on. To give an example, consider the following passage from *Medea*. Word by word, the messenger reproduces Jason's intervention:

(26) Eur., *Med.* 1149–1155

> (...) πόσις δὲ σὸς
> ὀργάς τ' ἀφήιρει καὶ χόλον νεάνιδος,
> λέγων τάδ'· Οὐ μὴ δυσμενὴς ἔσηι φίλοις,
> παύσηι δὲ θυμοῦ καὶ πάλιν στρέψεις κάρα,
> φίλους νομίζουσ' οὕσπερ ἂν πόσις σέθεν,
> δέξηι δὲ δῶρα καὶ παραιτήσηι πατρὸς
> φυγὰς ἀφεῖναι παισὶ τοῖσδ' ἐμὴν χάριν;

> Your husband then set out to mollify the woman's angry mood by saying: "You should not be unfriendly to your own; give up this anger and turn back your face. Consider as your own, your dear ones, those your husband does. Why not accept these presents and entreat your father to release the children from their banishment, please, for my sake?".[63]

Attention has been drawn to this technique by scholars who have dealt with the study of messenger speeches. It is attributed to the influence of epic poetry and is more frequent in the tragedies of Euripides than in those of Aeschylus and Sophocles. De Jong (1991, 131–139) points out that the presence of direct testimonies in Euripides' messenger speeches meets five criteria. Firstly, the messenger introduces direct speech when he himself is affected by his own words or those of his companions.[64] Secondly, they appear when they want to introduce

---

62 The translations of *The Phoenician Women* are borrowed from Wyckoff (2013).
63 The translations of *Medea* are borrowed from Taplin (2013).
64 For instance, Talthybius reproduces his own words in Eur., *Hec.* 532–533.

military exhortations or similar conventional speeches.⁶⁵ Thirdly, the messenger quotes speeches that contain information that is essential to correctly understand the development of the action.⁶⁶ Fourthly, they are used to increase the *dramatic pathos*, as in the case of the example given in (26). Finally, the messenger includes quotations from main characters of events when the quoted speech emphasizes the message or the news he wants to report.⁶⁷ It is obvious, therefore, that it is a convention within the ἀγγελικὴ ῥῆσις delivered in the frame of the messenger scene.⁶⁸

The news transmitted by ἄγγελοι is completely reliable

Another consequence of having witnessed the events they relate in person is the fact that no one doubts the credibility of the messengers. This is confirmed by the solemnity with which the rest of characters refer to them, since they are aware that, good or bad, the news transmitted by the ἄγγελοι is true. Let us consider the following passage from *Seven against Thebes*.⁶⁹ Previously, a messenger has reported the names of each of the seven captains that lead the Argive army against the seven gates of Thebes to Eteocles (Aesch., *Sept.* 375–652).⁷⁰ Having served his purpose, the messenger leaves the scene, but he will be back soon. No one will announce his arrival, but he addresses the chorus to report that everything is going well in six of the seven gates, but not in the seventh (Aesch., *Sept.* 791–802). Then, the chorus leader asks him to expand on this information and the messenger ends up giving the news: Eteocles and Polynices have killed each other (Aesch., *Sept.* 811). Once again, having accomplished his mission, the ἄγγελος leaves the stage and the chorus continues to lament the misfortunes. The members of the chorus have not seen the events reported by the messenger, but everyone knows for certain that what he has told is true, as we can deduce from their own words:

---

65 Cf., for instance, Eur., *Heracl.* 839–840.
66 Cf. Eur., *Andr.* 1092–1095.
67 As in the case of *Hippolytus* when the ἄγγελος reproduces Hippolytus' words.
68 Aeschylus only makes use of this resource in *Agamemnon*. Sophocles, for his part, includes it in all messenger speeches except in these cases: when Antigone's guard comes on stage for the second time, when Lichas intervenes in *The Women of Trachis*, when the merchant of *Philoctetes* delivers a deception speech, and when the performance of the ἐξάγγελος takes place in *Oedipus the King*. In Euripides' tragedies there are only two exceptions, both in *Rhesus*.
69 Cf. also Eur., *Phoen.* 1332–1334.
70 The first intervention of this character occurs in the prologue. He is a scout (ἄγγελος κατάσκοπος) who claims to be a watchman to be trusted (cf. Aesch., *Sept.* 66: πιστὸν ἡμεροσκόπον).

(27) Aesch., *Sept*. 848–850

> Τάδ' αὐτόδηλα, προῦπτος⁷¹ **ἀγγέλου λόγος·**
> διπλαῖ μέριμναι, διδύμα δ' ἀνορέα·
> κἀκ' αὐτοφόνα δίμοιρα τέλεα τάδε πάθη.

> Here it is, plain to see; **the messenger's words** are visible reality; with double lamentation I now behold this twin disaster; the sad event is fulfilled, a double death by kindred hands.

Sometimes it is the messenger himself who assures that he is telling the truth, as we see, for example, in *Agamemnon*: "Having heard this much, be assured that you have heard the truth".[72]

Nevertheless, an analysis of the words derived from ἄγγελος reveals some exceptions that cannot be overlooked. These exceptions occur when character reports false (*fake*) news by adopting the conventions of the ἄγγελος. All of these will be dealt with in the corresponding chapter.

Criteria for classifying characters as ἄγγελοι

Although the messenger scene is more than a consolidated convention, scholars who have dealt with its analysis have yet to reach a common consensus establishing a general catalogue of such scenes. In fact, there is intense discussion over the characters to be classified as ἄγγελοι and those who should be excluded from that classification. This matter has been the subject of methodological reviews. I am not going to dwell too much on it here, since I have addressed this issue in my article "On the tragic messenger: a proposal for classification".[73] I shall, therefore, limit myself simply to listing the criteria I propose in this article:

1. The character must perform a clearly informative function. In other words, he must transmit relevant news for the characters on the stage and for the audience. Moreover, this news must be important for the development of the dramatic action.

---

[71] On προῦπτος, see Hutchinson (1985, 188): "προοράω is used at Thuc. 7.44.2 and Xen., *Hell*. 4.3.23. Of seeing what is in front of one's eyes. Elsewhere προῦπτος is connected with the more common temporal sense of the verb."
[72] Cf. Aesch., *Ag*. 680: τοσαῦτ' ἀκούσας ἴσθι τἀληθῆ κλυών.
[73] See Fornieles Sánchez (2018b). In this paper all the specific references are given.

2. The ensuing messenger scene must have a tripartite structure.[74] That is, the news is expanded with the narration he reports first-hand (ἀγγελικὴ ῥῆσις). This narrative report is preceded by a conversation with the chorus or another character on stage (the *stichomythic prologue*)[75] and the scene ends with an epilogue. Occasionally, as in the case of *Hippolytus*, before leaving the stage, the ἄγγελος has a brief conversation with other characters.
3. The messenger's role as an informer must be indicated at some point in the scene by ἄγγελος or its derivatives. Unsurprisingly, this tends to happen when the messenger comes on stage. This may occur in two ways. In a number of tragedies, the arrival of the ἄγγελος is announced by a *dramatis persona* or the chorus leader. In the event that the messenger's arrival goes unannounced, he usually asks for the person to whom the news is addressed or just bursts onto the stage, making his purpose clear, as in the case of the ἄγγελος of *Ajax* given in example (20) or in the following:

(28) Aesch., *Pers.* 249–255

> ὦ γῆς ἀπάσης Ἀσιάδος πολίσματα,
> ὦ Περσὶς αἶα καὶ πολὺς πλούτου λιμήν,
> ὡς ἐν μιᾷ πληγῇ κατέφθαρται πολὺς
> ὄλβος, τὸ Περσῶν δ' ἄνθος οἴχεται πεσόν.
> ὤμοι, κακὸν μὲν πρῶτον **ἀγγέλλειν** κακά·
> ὅμως δ' ἀνάγκη πᾶν ἀναπτύξαι πάθος,
> Πέρσαι· στρατὸς γὰρ πᾶς ὄλωλε βαρβάρων.

> O you cities of the whole land of Asia! O land of Persia, Repository of great wealth! How all your great prosperity has been destroyed in a single blow, and the flower of the Persians are fallen and departed. Ah me, it is terrible to be the first to **announce** terrible news, but I have no choice but to reveal the whole sad tale, Persians: the whole of the oriental army has been destroyed!

As soon as the news has been reported, the ἄγγελος converses with the chorus leader or a *dramatis persona*. This conversation, which precedes the messenger speech, has two major functions: to increase tension and to expand on the news by providing all the details. This dialogue concludes with a Π-question with which the addressee invites the messenger to offer a detailed description of the events or with an imperative. The only exception occurs in *Rhesus*, where the chorus leader

---

[74] For a more in-depth treatment of the structure of messenger scenes, see Fornieles Sánchez (2018b, 33–36), which also covers the considerable amount of literature on this topic.
[75] On this convention, see Perris (2011a, 4), Halleran (2005, 14), Mills (1981, 132) or Strohm (1959, 267). Only *Seven against Thebes* lacks it, although the report is not prototypical either.

does not address the charioteer with a *Π-question* or an imperative. Instead, he draws the following conclusion before hearing the messenger speech:

(29) Eur., *Rhes.* 754–755

> τάδ' οὐκ ἐν αἰνιγμοῖσι σημαίνει κακά·
> σαφῶς γὰρ αὐδᾶι συμμάχους ὀλωλότας.
>
> There is no mystery in the ill news he reports now; it is plain to see that our allies are killed.[76]

This passage allows me to introduce another relevant point. On very few occasions there are no ἄγγελος derivatives in the interventions of the characters I have classified as ἄγγελοι. One of these few examples can be seen in (29), in which the chorus leader does not use ἀγγέλλω but σημαίνει κακά. In all of these cases, the characters utter other expressions that, according to Hutchinson (1985, 48), are a standardized formula to introduce the subsequent messenger speeches. One example would be the verb ἥκω followed by φέρω and the accusative giving rise to locutions such as ἥκω σαφῆ φέρων (Aesch., *Sept.* 40 or Eur., *Hel.* 1200), ἥκω καὶ φέρω καινοὺς λόγους (Aesch., *Cho.* 659), φέρω κεδνοὺς λόγους (Eur., *Rhes.* 272), etc. It is also common for the ἄγγελος to mention his informative role by means of the accusatives καινόν or νέον as complements of ἀγγέλλω or of some other verbs of saying (e.g. λέγω or σημαίνω)[77] or perception (e.g. ἀκούω[78] or μανθάνω).[79]

From war to suicides: a wide range of news

The results of the study of the tragic messenger provides us with an initial approach to ἄγγελος and its derivatives in Greek tragedy. As I have already highlighted, these derivatives can be considered as technical terms coined to denote the informative role of the tragic ἄγγελος. From now on, I will focus on a more detailed analysis of the terms from this lexical family to find out what was considered to be news by the members of the societies reflected in Greek drama.

---

76 Translations of *Rhesus* are borrowed from Lattimore (2013).
77 My proposal is in line with that of Mastronarde (2002, 352) regarding the passage from *Medea* shown in example (40): "καινόν: news from a messenger-figure is often anticipated by reference to revealing (σημαίνειν) or reporting (ἀγγέλλειν, λέγειν) something καινόν or νεόν: e.g. *PV.* 943, *Tro.* 238, *Phoen.* 1075, *Hec.* 217, *IT.* 237, *Bacch.* 1029".
78 Cf., for example, Eur., *Alc.* 731: τίνα τύχην ἀκούσομαι;
79 Cf. Eur., *Bacch.* 657: τοὺς λόγους μάθε.

From war to suicides: a wide range of news — 73

The figures below show the derivatives of ἄγγελος that appear in the plays of the three tragedians.

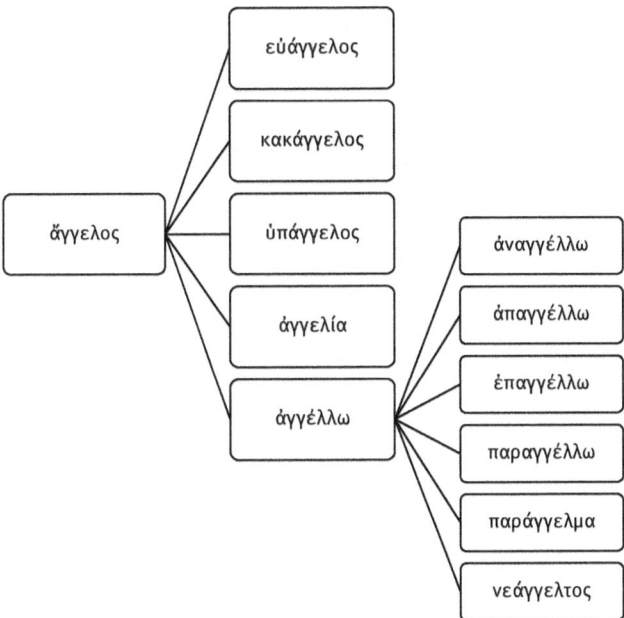

Fig. 6: Ἄγγελος and its derivatives in Aeschylus.

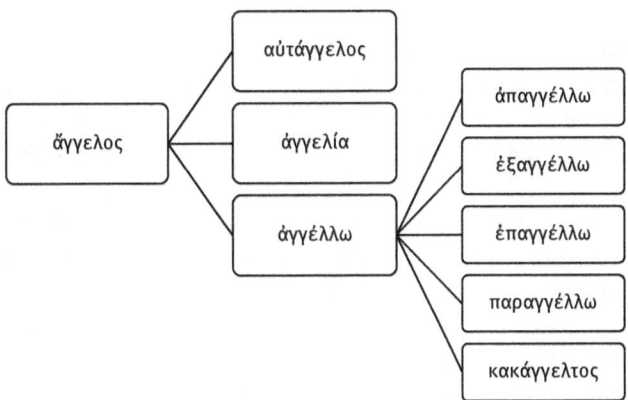

Fig. 7: Ἄγγελος and its derivatives in Sophocles.

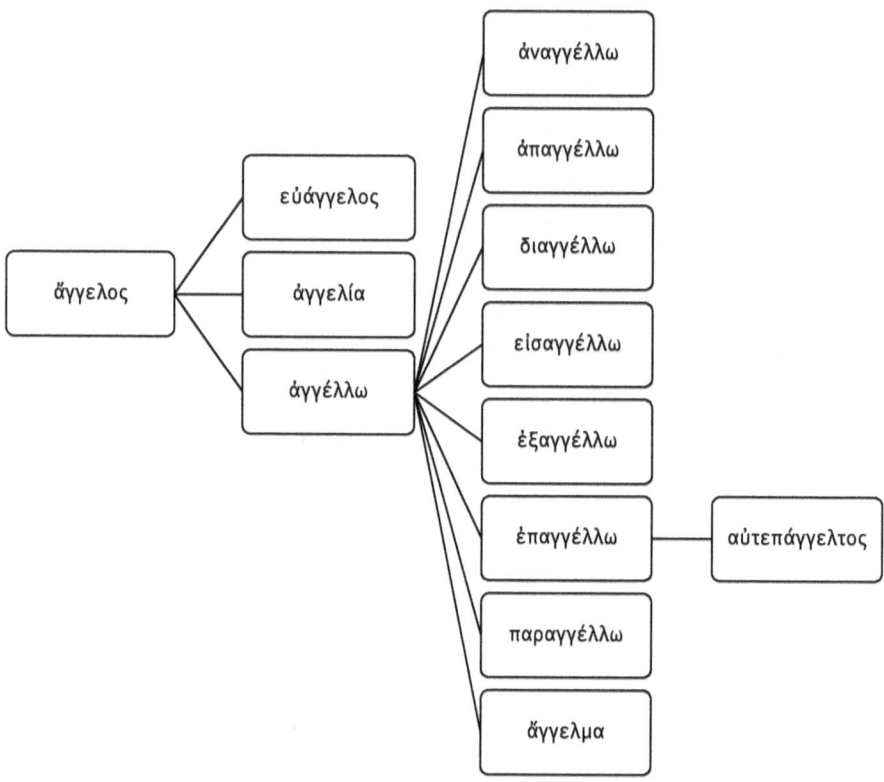

Fig. 8: Ἄγγελος and its derivatives in Euripides.

Contrary to what we might expect, the term ἀγγελία is hardly documented in Greek tragedy. It occurs only twice in Aeschylus's plays, twice in Sophocles, and eight times in Euripides. In eight of these twelve occasions, the term is uttered by an ἄγγελος or by another character when referring to the news reported by the ἄγγελος.

In two passages from Euripides, ἀγγελία is the complement of two verbs of saying: λάσκω and κηρύσσω. In both, it should be interpreted as a piece of news. In *Iphigenia among the Taurians*, a herdsman who acts as an ἄγγελος announces to Iphigenia that two foreigners have been captured (Orestes and Pylades). When prisoners enter the scene, the chorus refers to the truthful nature of the messenger's words: "The herdsman did not deliver false news".[80]

---

[80] Cf. Eur., *IT*. 461: οὐδ' ἀγγελίας ψευδεῖς ἔλακεν.

In *Helen*, the chorus calls upon the birds to spread the news (Menelaus is going to return):

(30) Eur., *Hel.* 1487-1494

> ὦ πταναὶ δολιχαύχενες,
> σύννομοι νεφέων δρόμωι,
> βᾶτε Πλειάδας ὑπὸ μέσας
> Ὠρίωνά τ' ἐννύχιον,
> καρύξατ' ἀγγελίαν
> Εὐρώταν ἐφεζόμεναι,
> Μενέλεως ὅτι Δαρδάνου
> πόλιν ἑλὼν δόμον ἥξει.

> O flying birds with the long throats, who share the course of the racing clouds, go to the midmost Pleiades. Go to Orion of the night, **proclaim like heralds your piece of news** as you light down on Eurotas, that Menelaus has taken the town of Dardanus and will come home.[81]

In this case, ἀγγελία is also the complement of a verb of saying, but this time of κηρύσσω, a special verb that denotes the specific function of a κῆρυξ[82] (not of an ἄγγελος).

In four other contexts ἀγγελία is the direct object of a verb of perception whose subject is an animate entity. In example (31) the verb is οἶδα:

(31) Aesch., *PV.* 1040-1041

> εἰδότι τοί μοι **τάσδ' ἀγγελίας**
> ὅδ' ἐθώυξεν (...).

> I already knew **these orders** that this has yelled at me.

The context leads us to interpret that the term does not refer to news, but to Zeus' orders, which are given to Prometheus by Hermes. Despite the fact that the titan is convinced that the god has come to bring him some news, (Aesch., *PV.* 943: πάντως τι καινὸν[83] ἀγγελῶν ἐλήλυθεν), the truth is that this is not the

---

81 The translations of *Helen* are taken from Lattimore (2013) with some modifications.
82 Allan (2008, 325) seems to have deemed the verb as a synonym of ἀγγέλλω and translates it as 'announce'.
83 It is common for τι καινόν to appear as the complement of ἀγγέλλω, as in the example given in (40). The adjective καινός ('new') by itself favours the content of the announcement implied by ἀγγέλλω as an item of news as opposed to a message or an order.

case. Zeus commanded Hermes to demand that Prometheus tell him who is threatening to overthrow him.[84]

The situation is a different one in *The Phoenician Women*, where Antigone tells Oedipus of the death of his sons (Eteocles and Polynices) and his wife (Jocasta):

(32) Eur., *Phoen.* 1546–1550

> δυστυχὲς ἀγγελίας ἔπος[85] εἴσῃ,
> πάτερ· οὐκέτι σοι τέκνα λεύσσει
> φάος οὐδ' ἄλοχος, παραβάκτροις
> ἃ πόδα σὸν τυφλόπουν θεραπεύμασιν αἰὲν ἐμόχθει,
> ὦ πάτερ, ὤμοι.

> You must hear the telling of **dreadful news**. Father, your sons are dead. And so is the wife who tended and guided your stumbling steps. O Father, woe is me.

In addition to this, ἀγγελία is the complement of the verbs of perception μανθάνω and δηλόω. In *Ion*, the chorus leader reveals that Xuthus is the (secret) father of Ion:

(33) Eur., *Ion.* 769–775

> {Πρ.} μήπω στενάξῃς {Κρ.} ἀλλὰ πάρεισι γόοι.
> {Πρ.} πρὶν ἂν μάθωμεν {Κρ.} **ἀγγελίαν** τίνα μοι;
> {Πρ.} εἰ ταὐτὰ πράσσων δεσπότης τῆς συμφορᾶς
> κοινωνός ἐστιν ἢ μόνη σὺ δυστυχεῖς.
> {Χο.} κείνωι μέν, ὦ γεραιέ, παῖδα Λοξίας
> ἔδωκεν, ἰδίαι δ' εὐτυχεῖ ταύτης δίχα.

> OLD MAN. — Mourn no more...
> CREUSA. — I have reason enough.
> OLD MAN. — ... until we now...
> CREUSA. — **What news** for me?
> OLD MAN. — ... If you alone have this misfortune, or my master too must share the same distress.

---

84 Cf. Aesch., *PV.* 947-948. Hermes says to Prometheus: "The Father orders you to state what this union".

85 It should be noted that ἀγγελίας accompanies ἔπος within the noun phrase δυστυχὲς ἀγγελίας ἔπος. According to Mastronarde (1994, 581), ἀγγελίας ἔπος is a poetic periphrasis equivalent to ἔπος ἀγγέλλειν, as in Soph., *OC.* 302: τοὔπος ἀγγελῶν.

CHORUS LEADER. — To him Apollo gave a son, but this good luck is his alone; his wife has nothing.[86]

In *Ajax* the bearer of news is Tecmessa, who acts as an ἐξάγγελος and tells of Ajax's fit of madness from within the palace. The item of news is reported in the *stichomythic prologue* of the ensuing messenger scene, and once the chorus has heard it laments: "What report of the fiery warrior have you revealed to us, unbearable, nor yet escapable".[87]

In another two passages, ἀγγελία is the complement of verbs of motion. As I will show in due course, in the plays of the historians this construction usually involves the transmission of messages and orders, but rarely news.[88] In tragedy, however, this is not the case. In (34), the news referred to by the term ἀγγελία (as the complement of the verb φέρω) is hypothetical, since the chorus is simply voicing the desire to receive favourable news (Eur., *Heracl.* 751: ἀγγελίαν μοι ἐνέγκαι). A moment later, this wish comes true. Suddenly, an ἄγγελος bursts onto the stage to report good tidings:

(34) Eur., *Heracl.* 784–792

{Αγ.}   δέσποινα, μύθους σοί τε συντομωτάτους
        κλύειν ἐμοί τε τῶιδε καλλίστους φέρω·
        νικῶμεν ἐχθροὺς καὶ τροπαῖ' ἱδρύεται
        παντευχίαν ἔχοντα πολεμίων σέθεν.
{Αλ.}   ὦ φίλταθ', ἥδε σ' ἡμέρα διήλασεν·
        ἠλευθέρωσαι τοῖσδε τοῖς ἀγγέλμασιν.
        μιᾶς δ' ἔμ' οὔπω συμφορᾶς ἐλευθεροῖς·
        φόβος γὰρ εἴ μοι ζῶσιν οὓς ἐγὼ θέλω.
{Αγ.}   ζῶσιν, μέγιστόν γ' εὐκλεεῖς κατὰ στρατόν.

MESSENGER. — Mistress, the report I bring is most beautiful for you to hear, and short for me to tell: We've won! Victory trophies are being set up bearing your enemies' captured weaponry.
ALCMENE. — My dearest friend, to you this day's a blessing: **for this report** I hereby set you free! But me — from one concern you've not yet freed me: my fear, whether those I most want are still alive.
MESSENGER. — They live — most glorious too in all the army.

---

86 The translations of *Ion* are taken from Willetts (2013) with slight modifications.
87 Cf. Soph., *Aj.* 221–223: "Οἵαν ἐδήλωσας | ἀνέρος αἴθονος ἀγγελίαν | ἄτλατον οὐδὲ φευκτάν".
88 Let us remember that in the Homeric poems the term occurs within the same context twice. In one of the cases, ἀγγελία denotes an order; in the other, the term refers to an item of news. In Greek lyric poetry, on the other hand, the term is always used to refer to news.

This passage is also interesting for two other reasons. Firstly, due to the presence of φέρω and the accusative in one of the tragic messenger's pieces of news instead of the verb ἀγγέλλω. On this occasion, the complement of φέρω is the accusative μύθους,[89] which is likely to be translated as news in contexts like this. Secondly, because Alcmene refers to the news by means of ἄγγελμα, a derivative of ἄγγελος that is not documented in the Homeric poems, in Greek lyric poetry, or in the plays of Aeschylus and Sophocles.

Ἀγγελία is also the complement of the verb ἀείρω. The passage belongs to *Hecuba*. The chorus of slave women informs Priam's wife of the destiny that awaits her daughter Polyxena:

(35) Eur., *Hec.* 104–109

οὐδὲν παθέων ἀποκουφίζουσ'
ἀλλ' **ἀγγελίας** βάρος ἀραμένη
μέγα σοί τε, γύναι, κῆρυξ ἀχέων.
ἐν γὰρ Ἀχαιῶν πλήρει ξυνόδωι
λέγεται δόξαι σὴν παῖδ' Ἀχιλεῖ
σφάγιον θέσθαι. (...).

I bring you painful **news**. I cannot lighten your load. I bring you worse to bear. Just now, in full assembly, the Greek decree came down. They voted your daughter must die ... to be slaughtered alive for Achilles![90]

On the other hand, ἀγγελία is the complement of the verb of reception δέχομαι and refers to a hypothetical item of news in *Iphigenia among the Taurians*. A herdsman has just told Iphigenia that the two foreigners have been captured. When this ἄγγελος ends the messenger speech, the chorus says: "What sweet news I should receive if a sailor came from Hellas, to put an end to my miserable slavery!".[91]

In another passage from *Orestes*, the term is the complement of the verb implying reception δίδωμι and is accompanied by a second complement in the dative (recipient). Electra wants to sneak out of the palace and asks the chorus to update her about the situation: "Give me good news, if the space before the front of the house is deserted".[92]

---

89 On the term μῦθος, cf. n. 48 in the chapter devoted to Homer.
90 Translation taken from Arrowsmith (2013).
91 Cf. Eur., *IT.* 447–451: ἥδιστ' ἂν δ' ἀγγελίαν | δεξαίμεσθ', Ἑλλάδος ἐκ γᾶς | πλωτήρων εἴ τις ἔβα | δουλείας ἐμέθεν | δειλαίας παυσίπονος·
92 Cf. Eur., *Or.* 1276–1278: δὸς ἀγγελίαν ἀγαθάν τιν', | εἰ τάδ' ἔρημα τὰ πρόσθ' αὐλᾶς.

In (36) ἀγγελία is the complement of the verb of generic motion ἔρχομαι. The spectators already know that Orestes is plotting to enter the palace and kill Aegisthus. Electra is desperately grieving, though, because she has no news from her brother:

(36) Soph., *El.* 168–172

> (...) ὁ δὲ λάθεται
> ὧν τ' ἔπαθ' ὧν τ' ἐδάη· τί γὰρ οὐκ ἐμοὶ
> ἔρχεται **ἀγγελίας**[93] ἀπατώμενον;
> ἀεὶ μὲν γὰρ ποθεῖ,
> ποθῶν δ' οὐκ ἀξιοῖ φανῆναι.

> But he has forgotten what he has suffered, what he has known. What kind of **news** comes from him to me that does not turn out false? Yes, he is always longing to come, but he does not choose to come, for all his longing.[94]

What Agamemnon's daughter does not know is that she is about to receive another untrue piece of news and that she will manage to avenge her father along with her brother.[95]

Finally, the most important item of news in *Agamemnon* is the imminent return of the king having won in the Trojan War.[96] The announcement is made by a herald. On this occasion, ἀγγελία is not the complement of a verb, but a dative of cause.[97] When Clytemnestra (who already was already aware of the news) leaves the palace, euphoric, the chorus begs her to share her joy:

(37) Aesch., *Ag.* 83–87

> σὺ δέ, Τυνδάρεω
> θύγατερ, βασίλεια Κλυταιμήστρα,
> τί χρέος; τί νέον; τί δ' ἐπαισθομένη
> **τίνος ἀγγελίας**
> πειθοῖ περίπεμπτα θυοσκεῖς;

---

93 See Jebb (1894): "τί γὰρ ... ἀγγελίας: cp. *Ant.* 1229: «ἐν τῷ συμφορᾶς»".
94 Translations of Sophocles' *Electra* are taken for Grene (2013) with slight modifications.
95 See the chapter devoted to *fake* news.
96 Cf. examples (6), (7), (8) and (9).
97 See Linwood (1843, 263) or Verrall (1889, 8): "πειθοῖ: literally 'from conviction of what report?', i.e. *by what report convinced?*".

But, daughter of Tyndareos, queen Clytemnestra, what has happened? What is the news? On what intelligence and convinced by **what report** do you send about your messengers to command sacrifice?

Let us continue our examination of the derivatives of ἄγγελος by analysing the verbs documented in the plays of the three tragedians: ἀγγέλλω, ἀναγγέλλω, ἀπαγγέλλω, διαγγέλλω, εἰσαγγέλλω, ἐξαγγέλλω, ἐπαγγέλλω and παραγγέλλω. In addition to these verbs, we also find ἄγγελμα and the derivative παράγγελμα.

The verb ἀγγέλλω appears 90 times (nine in Aeschylus, twenty in Sophocles and sixty-one in Euripides) and in Greek drama it is closely associated with the figure of the ἄγγελος. In fact, in tragedy ἀγγέλλω is uttered either by an ἄγγελος or by any character referring to the news he has come to announce in approximately 60% of cases.[98] In the remaining contexts, as the following examples will show, it is very common for ἀγγέλλω to be uttered by another character who is not labelled as an ἄγγελος but is also in charge of transmitting news. In my opinion, this provides evidence that suggests that ἀγγέλλω — as well as other derivatives of ἄγγελος — can be considered a technical term coined for the transmission of news. In this regard, we should bear in mind that these words, which are indicative of the informative role of the tragic messenger, also come from other characters performing as ἄγγελοι despite not being explicitly labelled as such.

As far as syntactic constructions are concerned, the three-argument construction with ἀγγέλλω that we would expect is relatively frequent (there are fifteen examples) in Greek drama. In the examples provided below, ἀγγέλλω — in addition to the subject — has a complement with an inanimate referent in the accusative (result) and a complement with an animate referent in the dative (recipient). Thus, in example (38) the accusative reflects the content of the announcement:[99]

---

98 This applies to nine of the twelve occurrences documented in Aeschylus, twelve of the twenty examples attested in Sophocles and thirty-two of the sixty-one in Euripides.
99 In Soph., *Aj.* 567 what must be announced is an injunction from Ajax (ἐμὴν ἐντολήν); in *Oedipus the King*, a true report of the oracle (Soph., *OT.* 604: τὰ χρησθέντ'); in *Oedipus at Colonus*, Oedipus' own words for Theseus to receive him (Soph., *OC.* 302: τοῦτο τοὔπος); in Euripides' *Electra*, the misfortunes of her sister are to be announced to Orestes (Eur., *El.* 303: τἀμὰ κἀκείνου κακά); in *The Trojan Women*, Menelaus superiority over Paris (Eur., *Tro.* 1004: τὰ τοῦδε κρείσσον') and, in *Orestes*, Menelaus refers to a false rumour he has heard from a man scared to death (Eur., *Or.* 1558: κενὴν βάξιν). Cf. also example (25) in this chapter (Eur., *Phoen.* 1075: τί καινὸν ἔπος).

(38) Soph., *Aj.* 845–849

> Σὺ δ', ὦ τὸν αἰπὺν οὐρανὸν διφρηλατῶν
> Ἥλιε, πατρῴαν τὴν ἐμὴν ὅταν χθόνα
> ἴδῃς, ἐπισχὼν χρυσόνωτον ἡνίαν
> **ἄγγειλον** ἄτας τὰς ἐμὰς μόρον τ' ἐμὸν
> γέροντι πατρὶ τῇ τε δυστήνῳ τροφῷ.

> And you that drive your chariot up steep heaven, lord Helios, when you next shall see my own dear country, hold in check your golden reins, and **announce** my death and downfall to my old father and to her that nursed me.

These words are uttered by Ajax as he bends over his sword before committing suicide by falling onto it. Whilst making the final preparations for his death, the hero invokes Helios to announce (ἄγγειλον) his death and his downfall (ἄτας τὰς ἐμὰς μόρον τ' ἐμόν) to both his father and his mother (γέροντι πατρὶ τῇ τε δυστήνῳ τροφῷ).

In other passages, the accusative of the inanimate referent is the neuter plural demonstrative pronoun τάδε,[100] the neuter singular indefinite pronoun (τι)[101] or an adjective in the neuter plural, as in (39). Orestes orders the pedagogue to enter the palace to tell him what is happening inside:

(39) Soph., *El.* 38–41

> Ὅτ' οὖν τοιόνδε χρησμὸν εἰσηκούσαμεν,
> σὺ μὲν μολών, ὅταν σε καιρὸς εἰσάγῃ
> δόμων ἔσω τῶνδ', ἴσθι πᾶν τὸ δρώμενον,
> ὅπως ἂν εἰδὼς ἡμὶν **ἀγγείλῃς** σαφῆ·

> Now since this was the oracle we heard, go you into this house when occasion calls you. Know all that is done there, and, knowing, **report** clear news to us.

On the other hand, it is also interesting to note that ἀγγέλλω begins to be reported in Greek drama in reference to prophetic predictions, with oracles (see Eur., *Ion* 180–181: τοὺς θεῶν ἀγγέλλοντας φήμας θνατοῖς).

The most frequent construction of ἀγγέλλω (thirty-six instances) is the one in which only the argument in the accusative expressing result is explicitly uttered. The complement in the dative is omitted, but it is easy to interpret within the context. In (40), for instance, Medea announces the entrance of an ἄγγελος:

---

100 Cf. Soph., *Trach.* 190.
101 Cf. Eur., *Bacch.* 658 given in (21), Eur., *IT.* 582, Eur., *IT.* 1182 and Eur., *IA.* 1447.

(40) Eur., *Med.* 1118–1120

καὶ δὴ δέδορκα τόνδε τῶν Ἰάσονος
στείχοντ' ὀπαδῶν· πνεῦμα δ' ἠρεθισμένον
δείκνυσιν ὥς τι καινὸν **ἀγγελεῖ** κακόν.

At last I see this man of Jason's coming; his labored breathing shows he **brings** grave news.

At this point in the drama, the on-stage characters are Medea and the chorus, who are about to be told by one of Jason's servants (an ἄγγελος) that princess Glauce and her father Creon have just been killed by Medea's poison.

In tragedy, the object in the accusative always has an inanimate referent that allows us to easily identify the content of the announcement implied by ἀγγέλλω.[102] In passages such as the one quoted above, several reasons lead me to suggest that we are dealing with a piece of news. Firstly, because the excerpt belongs to a typical messenger scene and the informative role of the ἄγγελος is already well-known. Secondly, because the adjective καινός ('new', 'fresh') indicates that the misfortune to be announced is exactly like that: new, recent, fresh. This is one of the defining features of news by nature. In fact, when it comes to ἀγγέλλω, we find καινός — in alternation with its synonym νέος, as in Eur., *Rhes.* 39 (τί νέον) — used relatively frequently to modify the head of the noun phrase in the accusative.[103]

Ἀγγέλλω with the accusative is also used to report someone's arrival, as we see in the speech of the maid in *Alcestis*: "But I will go and announce your arrival".[104] The complement in the accusative can also be the neuter plural demonstrative pronoun τάδε,[105] the interrogative pronoun in the neuter singular (τί),[106]

---

102 Cf. also κοινὰ ἀγγέλματα in example (16), Eur., *Andr.* 1070 (οἵας τύχας), Eur., *Phoen.* 1334 (πᾶν τὸ δρώμενον), Eur., *Rhes.* 34 (τὰ δείματ'), Eur., *Rhes.* 52 (φόβον), Eur., *Hel.* 448 (τοὺς σοὺς λόγους), Eur., *Heracl.* 798 (ἀγῶνα), Eur., *Med.* 1009 (τιν' ... τύχην), Eur., *Med.* 1011 (οἷ' ἤγγειλας), Eur., *Or.* 618 (ὄνειδος), Eur., *Supp.* 399 (λόγους), Eur., *Supp.* 638 (νίκην), Eur., *Supp.* 641 (νόστον) and Eur., *Supp.* 643 (πάντ' [...] φίλα).
103 Cf. καινὸν λόγον in example (14), καινῶν βουλευμάτων in (15), καινὸν ἔπος in (25) or Aesch., *PV.* 944 (τι καινόν), Eur., *IT.* 1306 (καινῶν κακῶν) and Eur., *Tro.* 55 (καινὸν ἔπος).
104 Cf. Eur., *Alc.* 209: ἀλλ' εἶμι καὶ σὴν ἀγγελῶ παρουσίαν.
105 Cf. Aesch., *Cho.* 709, Eur., *Or.* 1539 and Eur., *Hel.* 1617.
106 Cf. Eur., *Hec.* 187 and Eur., *Hel.* 604.

the pronoun οὗτος in the neuter plural (ταῦτα)[107] or an adjective also in the neuter plural.[108]

On five occasions, the omitted complement of ἀγγέλλω is the one in the accusative, and only the third argument with an animate referent in the dative (recipient) is expressed. The semantic content of the announcement that we expect is about to be uttered in the accusative can be easily inferred from the context, as in (41).[109] Iphigenia and Orestes are about to recognise each other but, just beforehand, she orders Pylades to leave and deliver her brother a tablet with a message from her:

(41) Eur., *IT*. 769–771

> ἄγγελλ' Ὀρέστηι, παιδὶ τἀγαμέμνονος·
> Ἡ 'ν Αὐλίι σφαγεῖσ' ἐπιστέλλει τάδε
> ζῶσ' Ἰφιγένεια, τοῖς ἐκεῖ δ' οὐ ζῶσ' ἔτι.

> **Give the message** to Orestes, son of Agamemnon: "The one slaughtered at Aulis sends you word, Iphigenia, who is alive although at Argos they think otherwise."[110]

In (42) Orestes, pretending to be a foreigner, asks a servant to report the arrival of the two visitors (he and Pylades) to those inside the palace:

(42) Aesch., *Cho*. 658–659

> ἄγγελλε τοῖσι κυρίοισι δωμάτων,
> πρὸς οὕσπερ ἥκω καὶ φέρω καινοὺς λόγους·[111]

> **Announce** us to the masters of the house. I've come with news for them.

---

107 Cf. Aesch., *Cho*. 770.
108 In Aesch., *Pers*. 253 — example (28) —, Eur., *Heracl*. 54 and Eur., *HF*. 1136, the accusative is the adjective κακός in the neuter plural (κακά). In Eur., *El*. 230, however, it is its antonym in the neuter plural ἀγαθός (τἀγάθ'). In Eur., *El*. 418 we have the adjective πικρός ('sharp') in the accusative plural (πικράς). Cf. also Soph., *OC*. 1429: Οὐδ' ἀγγελοῦμεν φλαῦρ'.
109 Cf. also Soph., *OC*. 1511 (Oedipus says that the gods have announced his own death), Eur., *Rhes*. 522 (Hector has just given Rhesus the password he must say before the Thracian army) or Eur., *Hel*. 447 (Menelaus asks a maid to report his misfortunes).
110 The translations of *Iphigenia among the Taurians* are taken from Carson (2013).
111 The item of news to be reported is the false death of Orestes.

As we can see, in this case ἀγγέλλω has two complements with an animate referent and both the patient (τοῖσι) and the recipient (κυρίοισι) are expressed by the dative case.[112]

The third construction with ἀγγέλλω in the dative is explicitly referred to just once, but the second argument in this case is an infinitive (instead of an accusative complement). This construction is documented twice in Homer's poems, but there is a significant difference. In the latter, the verb is in the active voice and the announcement implied by the presence of ἀγγέλλω is clearly an order. Instead, in the following example the verb is used in the middle voice and does not express a command.[113] These words are spoken by Odysseus:

(43) Soph. *Aj.* 1376–1377

Καὶ νῦν γε Τεύκρῳ τἀπὸ τοῦδ' **ἀγγέλλομαι**,
ὅσον τότ' ἐχθρὸς ἦ, τοσόνδ' εἶναι φίλος·

And now **I have a promise**, Teucer, **to make** to you. From now on, I shall be as much a friend as I was once an enemy.

The scene is from the exodus of Sophocles' *Ajax*. Teucer, with the help of Odysseus, has managed to convince Agamemnon to surrender so that Ajax can have a decent burial. Laertes' son, in turn, offers him his friendship. In his commentary on this tragedy, Jebb highlights the fact that this use of the simple verb does not occur elsewhere,[114] since the term ἐπαγγέλλομαι[115] fits the context better.

Sometimes ἀγγέλλω is accompanied by a complement in the dative (recipient) and an accusative with participle (AcP) construction (result). An example has been given in (18), a passage from Sophocles' *Electra* in which the ἄγγελος bursts onto the stage to report (ἀγγέλλω) to all his friends (πᾶσιν φίλοις) that

---

112 Unlike in some other cases, such as Eur., *Alc.* 209, where we have the accusative with an inanimate referent (σὴν παρουσίαν).
113 Cf. also Eur., *Rhes.* 91–92.
114 Although, as we see below, it does fit with ἐξαγγέλλω.
115 See also Kamerbeek (1963): "ἀγγέλλομαι in the sense of ἐπαγγέλλομαι"; Stanford (1963, 230): "Τεύκρῳ ... ἀγγέλλομαι (this Middle voice of the uncompounded verb occurs only here, but cf. LS at ἐπ- and ἐξαγγέλλω) etc.: 'I proclaim to Teucer that from this time forward [τἀπὸ τοῦδ', sc. χρόνου] I am as much his friend as I was formerly his enemy'. Odysseus thinks it best not to address Teucer directly at first, but makes a general proclamation as if he were a herald" and Finglass (2011, 515–516): "The simplex ἀγγέλλομαι (a unique middle) is used for ἐπαγγέλλομαι (ἀγγέλλω elsewhere means 'bring news' from or about someone or somewhere else); for this as a feature of the high style cf. *OC* 738".

Orestes has been victorious (νικῶντ' Ὀρέστην).[116] The dative complement can be omitted, as in Soph., *El.* 1452 or in Eur., *Heracl.* 659.

An accusative with the infinitive (AcI) construction can also be found. The dative recipient can be omitted or not, as in (44). Agamemnon rebukes Hecuba:

(44) Eur., *Hec.* 726–728

> Ἑκάβη, τί μέλλεις παῖδα σὴν κρύπτειν τάφωι
> ἐλθοῦσ' ἐφ' οἷσπερ Ταλθύβιος **ἤγγειλέ** μοι
> μὴ θιγγάνειν σῆς μηδέν' Ἀργείων κόρης;

> Why this delay of yours, Hecuba, in burying your daughter? I **received your message** from Talthybius that none of our men should touch her.

The only possible interpretation is, in my opinion, that ἀγγέλλω denotes an order (not a piece of news) that the herald Talthybius has passed on to Menelaus from Hecuba. Several factors support my point of view. Firstly, the fact that Hecuba, using some imperatives, had recently (Eur., *Hec.* 604–606) ordered Talthybius to go (ἐλθέ) and tell (σήμηνον) the Argives that they should not touch her daughter's body but keep the crowd away (μὴ θιγγάνειν μοι μηδέν' ἀλλ' εἴργειν ὄχλον | τῆς παιδός). Secondly, because in accusative and infinitive constructions we find οὐ whenever their content is declarative and μή when their content is impressive (Crespo *et al.* 2003, 397). In addition to this, an AcI construction does admit the impressive value that ὅτι or ὡς substantive clauses cannot express.

These constructions with ἀγγέλλω alternate between ὅτι in (45) and (46), ὡς[117] substantive clauses as in (47), and indirect interrogative clauses. In (45) Heracles curses Deianeira (the reason of his misfortunes) and the recipient in the dative is explicitly expressed (πᾶσιν):

(45) Soph., *Trach.* 1109–1111

> (...) προσμόλοι μόνον,
> ἵν' ἐκδιδαχθῇ πᾶσιν **ἀγγέλλειν** ὅτι
> καὶ ζῶν κακούς γε καὶ θανὼν ἐτεισάμην.

> Only let her come who has done this to me. These hands will teach her, and she can **tell the word** to all the world: alive I punished the evil, and I punish them in death.

---

116 Cf. also Soph., *El.* 1442–1444 and Eur., *Rhes.* 267–268.
117 Also Soph., *El.* 1341, Eur., *Hel.* 618–619 and Eur., *IT.* 704.

In (46), on the other hand, the dative is elided and only the ὅτι substantive clause is uttered:

(46) Eur., *El.* 169–174

> ἔμολέ τις ἔμολεν γαλακτοπότας ἀνὴρ
> Μυκηναῖος οὐριβάτας·
> **ἀγγέλλει** δ' ὅτι νῦν τριται–
> αν καρύσσουσιν θυσίαν
> Ἀργεῖοι, πᾶσαι δὲ παρ' Ἥ–
> ραν μέλλουσιν παρθενικαὶ στείχειν.

There came, came a man bred on the milk of the hills. A Mycenaean mountaineer who **gave me word** that two days from now the Argives proclaim at large a holy feast, when all the maidens will pass in procession up to the temple of Hera.

In (47) an ἄγγελος has come with very important news for Oedipus, as Jocasta explains:

(47) Soph., *OT.* 954–956

> {ΟΙ.} Οὗτος δὲ τίς ποτ' ἐστί, καὶ τί μοι λέγει;
> {ΙΟ.} Ἐκ τῆς Κορίνθου, πατέρα τὸν σὸν **ἀγγελῶν**
>   ὡς οὐκέτ' ὄντα Πόλυβον, ἀλλ' ὀλωλότα.

OEDIPUS. — Who is he? What is his message for me?
JOCASTA. — He comes from Corinth and **tells** you that your father Polybus is no more, but dead and gone.[118]

As we can see, then, the dative is not uttered here, but we can infer from the context that Oedipus is the recipient of the tidings.

In (48) Menelaus asks a messenger to tell his friends some good news:

(48) Eur., *Hel.* 736–738

> καὶ νῦν μετασχὼν τῆς ἐμῆς εὐπραξίας
> **ἄγγειλον** ἐλθὼν τοῖς λελειμμένοις φίλοις
> τάδ' ὡς ἔχονθ' ηὕρηκας οὗ τ' ἐσμὲν τύχης.

Share now the blessings of my fortune too, and go to **take the news back** to those friends I left behind: how you have found our state here, how our luck holds now.

---

118 Translations of *Oedipus the King* are borrowed from Grene (2013).

Sometimes, the omitted element is the infinitive of the verb εἰμί,[119] as illustrated in (49). Polyxena has just asked her mother what she wants her to say to Hector on her behalf, and Hecuba replies:

(49) Eur., *Hec.* 423

ἄγγελλε πασῶν ἀθλιωτάτην ἐμέ.

Announce them this: I am the queen of sorrow.

Finally, I will refer to the contexts in which ἀγγέλλω displays an absolute use.[120] It is common to find the verb in its infinitive or participle forms,[121] as we see in the following example, with the entrance of an ἄγγελος[122] in *The Women of Trachis*. The messenger has good news to report to Deianeira:

(50) Soph., *Trach.* 180–183

Δέσποινα Δηάνειρα, πρῶτος **ἀγγέλων**
ὄκνου σε λύσω· τὸν γὰρ Ἀλκμήνης τόκον
καὶ ζῶντ' ἐπίστω καὶ κρατοῦντα κἀκ μάχης
ἄγοντ' ἀπαρχὰς θεοῖσι τοῖς ἐγχωρίοις.

O Deianeira, my mistress, I am **the first messenger** to free you from your uncertainty. You should know that Alcmene's son lives and is victorious and brings from battle first fruits for the gods of the land.

The verb ἀναγγέλλω is not documented in the Homeric poems nor in Greek lyric poetry, but it does appear once in Greek drama. The speaker is Io, who is telling the story of her metamorphosis into a cow:

---

119 Cf. also Aesch., *Cho.* 741, Eur., *IT.* 739–740, Eur., *Hec.* 591 and Eur., *Hec.* 734–735. In Soph., *Trach.* 73, the verb is in the middle voice. Once again, we can infer this from the context because the passage occurs in a conversation about Heracles between Deianeira and her son Hyllus.
120 Some examples are those shown in (6) or (21).
121 Cf. also Aesch., *Cho.* 774, Soph., *El.* 1111, Eur., *IT.* 588 or Eur., *Andr.* 821.
122 On the expression πρῶτος ἀγγέλων, cf. Ringer (1998, 55): "The messenger announces himself as 'the first messenger [πρῶτος ἀγγέλων] to free [Deianeira] from fear'. There is a degree of artistic self-consciousness in the messenger's use of ἄγγελος, which describes his actual role within the tragedy, an effect similar to the use of the word in Ajax (719) and Electra (47, 1443)".

(51) Aesch., *PV.* 658–662

ὁ δ' ἔς τε Πυθὼ κἀπὶ Δωδώνης πυκνοὺς
θεοπρόπους ἴαλλεν, ὡς μάθοι τί χρὴ
δρῶντ' ἢ λέγοντα δαίμοσιν πράσσειν φίλα.
ἧκον δ' **ἀναγγέλλοντες** αἰολοστόμους
χρησμοὺς ἀσήμους δυσκρίτως τ' εἰρημένους.

And he sent messengers repeatedly to Pytho and Dodona to consult the oracles, so that he could learn what he should do or say so as to act in a manner pleasing to the gods: they returned **reporting** ambiguous responses, their expression obscure and hard to interpret.

The participle of ἀναγγέλλω depends on the verb ἥκω and its second argument is the accusative with an inanimate referent (αἰολοστόμους χρησμοὺς ἀσήμους) which elucidates the content of the announcement (the ambiguous responses). As noted above, in Greek drama ἀγγέλλω is to be associated with prophetic predictions related to oracles. As we can see in this example, the same applies to the compound verb formed with the preverb ἀνά-, whose basic spatial meaning is 'up', 'from bottom to top' (Crespo *et al.* 2003, 164).[123]

Ἀπαγγέλλω, documented in both Homer and Pindar's Odes, appears 18 times in Greek tragedy (7 times in Aeschylus, once in Sophocles, and 10 times in Euripides). The expected construction of ἀπαγγέλλω with a second argument in the accusative expressing the result and a third argument in the dative expressing the recipient occurs only twice. In *Agamemnon*, the accusative is the neuter plural demonstrative ταῦτα. Clytemnestra addresses a herald who has come to bring news concerning Agamemnon:

(52) Aesch., *Ag.* 604–605

(...) ταῦτ' **ἀπάγγειλον** πόσει·
ἥκειν ὅπως τάχιστ' ἐράσμιον πόλει·

Order this to my husband: tell him to come with all speed, for this city passionately desires him.

Greek lexicons do not provide a definition of ἀπαγγέλλω as 'to order' or 'to command.'[124] However, from the context here we infer not the announcement of

---

[123] Cf. *LSJ*: "Carry back tidings of, report, τι Aesch. *PV.* 661)" or Bailly (1973, 49): "Revenir annoncer".
[124] And neither does Linwood (1843), who gives only the definition "to announce" when dealing with this term in his lexicon on Aeschylus. Cf. also Eur., *El.* 420–421.

a piece of news but an order. The key is given, in my opinion, by ἥκειν, which should be interpreted as an imperatival infinitive.[125]

In Greek drama we often find that the third argument of ἀπαγγέλλω is omitted (this construction occurs eight times). The second argument in the accusative with an inanimate referent clarifies what is being announced. This accusative can be a noun phrase,[126] as in (53). The Delphians have just killed Neoptolemus and Thetis orders Peleus to act as follows:

(53) Eur., *Andr.* 1239–1242

τὸν μὲν θανόντα τόνδ' Ἀχιλλέως γόνον
θάψον πορεύσας Πυθικὴν πρὸς ἐσχάραν,
Δελφοῖς ὄνειδος, ὡς **ἀπαγγέλληι** τάφος
φόνον βίαιον τῆς Ὀρεστείας χερός·

Take this dead man, Achilles' son, and make your way to the Pythian hearth, and bury him there, a reproach to the Delphians: the tomb will **tell** his violent murder by Orestes' hand.[127]

This excerpt happens to be one of the few examples (the other is the one offered just below) in which a derivative of ἄγγελος is used in relation to writing in Greek tragedy. It is also the only one in which the grave is referred to as the eternal messenger of the memory of the deceased.

In the following passage, ἀπαγγέλλω refers to the content of a tablet written by Iphigenia. She wants her relatives to receive her written message, which will inform them that she is alive:

(54) Eur., *IT.* 639–642

ἴσως ἄελπτα τῶν ἐμῶν φίλων τινὶ
πέμψω πρὸς Ἄργος, ὃν μάλιστ' ἐγὼ φιλῶ,
καὶ δέλτος αὐτῶι ζῶντας οὓς δοκεῖ θανεῖν
λέγουσ' ἀπίστους ἡδονὰς **ἀπαγγελεῖ**.[128]

---

125 Cf. also the second volume of Fraenkel (1962, 300): "What precedes she has said to the herald without describing it as message or commission; at the end she adds: 'tell him that!' and goes on immediately with vigour, as if what follows had just occurred to her in an afterthought: 'and he had better hurry about being here'". See also Denniston/Page (1957, 126): "ταῦτ' ἀπάγγειλον: 'Report back what I have just said'; ἥκειν is dependent on the idea of 'telling' in ἀπάγγειλον, 'report this back to him (and tell him) to come'".
126 Cf. also Eur., *Bacch.* 1109.
127 The translations of *Andromache* are taken from Roberts (2013).

Perhaps I will send unexpected news to one of my friends, whom I especially love, in Argos; and the tablet, in telling him that those whom he thought dead are alive, **will report** a joy that can be believed.

The complement in the accusative can also be the neuter plural demonstrative pronoun τάδε[129] or an adjective also in the neuter plural.[130]

The example given in (55) is from *Oedipus the King* and the form of ἀπαγγέλλω is uttered by an ἄγγελος who has some news to transmit. Let us remember the example given in (47), in which Jocasta tells Oedipus that the men have come to tell (ἀγγελῶν) him that his father Polybus is no longer alive. Subsequently, Oedipus asks him to corroborate the information:

(55) Soph., *OT*. 957–959

{ΟΙ.} Τί φῄς, ξέν'; αὐτός μοι σὺ σημήνας γενοῦ.
{ΑΓ.} Εἰ τοῦτο πρῶτον δεῖ μ' **ἀπαγγεῖλαι** σαφῶς,
εὖ ἴσθ' ἐκεῖνον θανάσιμον βεβηκότα.

---

128 This passage is troublesome. Dictionaries include it as an example of ἀναγγέλλω, not of ἀπαγγέλλω (cf. *LSJ* or *DGE*). I am following Murray's edition (1913), in which ἀπαγγέλλω is the chosen form. Kyriakou (2006, 216) explains this example of ἀπαγγελεῖ compared to the verse 901 of this tragedy. In this case, the chorus leader, enthusiastic because of Iphigenia meeting Orestes, affirms that the situation is exceeding any expectations, since he himself has been an eyewitness (τάδ' εἶδον αὐτὴ κοὐ κλύουσ' ἀπ' ἀγγέλων). On the piece of news written on the tablet, cf. Cropp (2000, 216): "Iphigenia expresses her hopes cryptically, without identifying her relatives in Argos, thus avoiding over-confidence and the possibility that some divine power will be tempted to thwart her wishes. This makes another dramatic irony, since she does not know just how unexpected and incredible the delivery of the news will be".
129 Cf. Aesch., *Cho*. 266 and Eur., *El*. 332.
130 Cf. also Aesch., *Sept*. 1005, Aesch., *Supp*. 931 o Aesch., *Pers*. 330. On this verse from *Persians*, see Broadhead (1960, 113): "329–330. These lines have been suspected (bracketed by Paley as an interpolation), unjustly, I think. We expect the speech to be rounded off, as Messenger's speeches commonly are, by a few words which show that the speaker has done with the theme (cf. dismissal clauses with μέν): πάντ' ἔχεις λόγον (*Ag*. 582): τοσαῦτ' ἀκούσας ἴσθι (*ibid*. 680); τοιαῦτά σοι ταῦτ' ἐστίν (Soph. *El*. 761), etc. With 330, which forms a suitable conclusion to the tale of woe already unfolded, compare 513–514 and 470 f.". Garvie (2009, 171) believes that the verse we are dealing with is an alternative to the usual formulae with which the ἄγγελος ends the messenger speech and which include pronouns such as τοιόσδε, τοσοῦτος, etc.: "Here the idea that he could say much more (implying that the individual deaths which he has reported are only a tiny fraction of the whole). In a different formula the speaker sums up by saying that the recipient has heard the whole story, or the truth".

OEDIPUS. — What's this you say, stranger? Tell me yourself.
MESSENGER. — If this is what you first **want** clearly **told**: be sure, Polybus has gone down to death.

In this case, the complement in the accusative is the anaphoric pronoun τοῦτο, which refers to the words previously uttered by Jocasta (Soph., *OT*. 955–956: Ἐκ τῆς Κορίνθου, πατέρα τὸν σὸν ἀγγελῶν | ὡς οὐκέτ' ὄντα Πόλυβον, ἀλλ' ὀλωλότα).

On just one occasion the omitted complement is the one in the accusative (the content of the announcement is referred to in the AcI construction depending on ἀπειλέω) and only the dative recipient is expressed. In this excerpt, Creon rebukes Medea:

(56) Eur., *Med.* 287–289

κλύω δ' ἀπειλεῖν σ', ὡς **ἀπαγγέλλουσί**[131] μοι,
τὸν δόντα καὶ γήμαντα καὶ γαμουμένην
δράσειν τι. (…).

And I have heard — **so people say** — you're threatening some act against the giver in this marriage and the taker and the given bride.

In the next example, ἀπαγγέλλω takes an AcP construction and the dative recipient is elided. Electra needs her mother, Clytemnestra, and instructs an old man as follows:

(57) Eur., *El.* 650–652

{Πρ.} ἔσται τάδ'· εὑρίσκεις δὲ μητρὶ πῶς φόνον;
{Ηλ.} λέγ', ὦ γεραιέ, τάδε Κλυταιμήστραι μολὼν
λεχώ μ' **ἀπάγγειλ'** οὖσαν ἄρσενος τόκωι.

OLD MAN. — It shall be done. What death have you decided for her?
ELECTRA. — Old uncle, you must go to Clytemnestra; tell her that I am kept in bed after bearing a son.

---

131 See Page (1938, 94): "Here ὡς ἀπαγγ. is emphatic, not redundant: - 'it is not mere hearsay; I have had an accurate report'". Mastronarde (2002, 287) explains that ὡς ἀπαγγέλλουσί μοι refers to events that took place before the play began but fit the knowledge previously acquired by the spectators.

In (58) Theseus is interrogating Adrastus and assures him that he is not going to ask him about the enemies:

(58) Eur., *Supp.* 849–852

> κενοὶ γὰρ οὗτοι τῶν τ' ἀκουόντων λόγοι
> καὶ τοῦ λέγοντος, ὅστις ἐν μάχηι βεβὼς
> λόγχης ἰούσης πρόσθεν ὀμμάτων πυκνῆς
> σαφῶς **ἀπήγγειλ'** ὅστις ἐστὶν ἀγαθός.

> Vain to tell or hear such tales — as if a man in the thick of combat, with a storm of spears before his eyes, ever **brought back** sure **news** on who was a hero.

As we can see, in this case the result is expressed by the ὅστις interrogative clause. It is also interesting to note the importance given to the position of the eyewitness, an aspect that gives credibility to the news transmitted by the ἄγγελοι.[132]

Finally, ἀπαγγέλλω also displays an absolute use on two occasions. In the messenger scene of *Agamemnon,* a herald is reporting the misfortunes suffered by Menelaus during his return home after winning the Trojan War. The chorus interrupts him to ask for more details and the herald says that he cannot tell them whether Menelaus is alive or dead: "none knows to give clear report of this (ὥστ' ἀπαγγεῖλαι τορῶς)."[133]

In (59) the verb is in the passive voice. The example is from *Hecuba*, when Priam's wife is reprimanding a maid who is carrying Polyxena, his daughter's, corpse:

(59) Eur., *Hec.* 671–673

> ἀτὰρ τί νεκρὸν τόνδε μοι Πολυξένης
> ἥκεις κομίζουσ', ἧς **ἀπηγγέλθη** τάφος
> πάντων Ἀχαιῶν διὰ χερὸς σπουδὴν ἔχειν;

> But why have you brought here to me the corpse of Polyxena, on whose burial Achaean's army **was reported** to be busily engaged?

Διαγγέλλω is not documented in Homer but does occur in the proem of *Nemean Ode* 5, for Pytheas of Aegina, winner in the boy's pancratium. Greek tragedy documents this verb twice, both in the Euripides' plays.

---

[132] On the contrast between ἀκουόντων and λέγοντος, see Collard (1975, 322).
[133] Cf. Aesch., *Ag.* 632.

In *Helen*, Menelaus has just reached Egypt, where he will be reunited with his wife. When he is in front of the palace, he shouts for someone to come out and welcome him:

(60) Eur., *Hel.* 435–436

> ὠή· τίς ἂν πυλωρὸς ἐκ δόμων μόλοι,
> ὅστις **διαγγείλειε** τἄμ' ἔσω κακά;
>
> O-ay! Who is the reporter here? Will he come out and **take the message** of my griefs to those inside?

As we can see, the third argument in the dative is omitted and only the second argument in the accusative (on this particular occasion, the adjective in the neuter plural κακά) is explicitly referred to.

In the other occurrence of διαγγέλλω, the verb is accompanied by an infinitive (ἀφιέναι) instead of a complement in the accusative expressing result. In the example below we see one of the reproaches addressed to Agamemnon by his brother Menelaus:

(61) Eur., *IA.* 352–353

> (...) Δαναΐδαι δ' ἀφιέναι
> ναῦς **διήγγελλον**, μάτην δὲ μὴ πονεῖν ἐν Αὐλίδι.
>
> So the Danaans **urged** that you send back all the ships and at Aulis put an end to this toil without meaning.[134]

This construction of διαγγέλλω with the infinitive leads us to deduce that the content of the announcement is not a message or piece of news, but rather an order, as is indicated by the infinitive itself.[135]

Εἰσαγγέλλω is not attested in Homer or Greek lyric poetry as a whole. In Greek tragedy this verb occurs only once in *The Bacchae* and is accompanied by a ὅτι substantive clause expressing result. Tiresias is at the doorstep of the palace and asks for someone to announce inside that he is looking for the king:

---

[134] The translation is taken from Walker (2013).
[135] And as explained also in *LSJ* and Bailly. That is not the case with *DGE*.

(62) Eur., *Bacch.* 173–174

> ἴτω τις, **εἰσάγγελλε** Τειρεσίας ὅτι
> ζητεῖ νιν· (...).
>
> Let someone go and **announce** that Tiresias is looking for him.

In principle, εἰσαγγέλλω is the usual verb to indicate that someone enters somewhere to make an announcement,[136] in this case the arrival or the presence of someone. The idea of motion is given by the verbal prefix εἰσ-, whose basic meaning is 'into' (Crespo *et al.* 2003, 170). As will be shown in subsequent chapters, Aristophanes and Greek historians use εἰσαγγέλλω to refer to the transmission of news. In the judicial sphere, however, both this verb and the noun εἰσαγγελία become consolidated as technical terms to refer to an impeachment.

Ἐξαγγέλλω is not documented in Greek lyric poetry and is attested only once in the *Iliad*. It does not occur in any of Aechylus' tragedies, but does appear in two of Sophocles' plays, and in four of those by Euripides.

The arguments in the accusative (result) and in the dative (recipient) are explicitly expressed only in the following example from *Ion*. The passage is located at the end of the tragedy in the speech of the goddess Athena, introduced as *deus ex machina* to announce that Ion will be the king of Athens and that Xuthus and Creusa will have children together. Before ending her speech, the goddess says:

(63) Eur., *Ion.* 1605–1606

> (...) ἐκ γὰρ τῆσδ' ἀναψυχῆς πόνων
> εὐδαίμον' ὑμῖν πότμον **ἐξαγγέλλομαι**.
>
> After this relief from your sufferings, **I promise** you a happy destiny.

The verb is uttered in the middle voice and *DGE* explains this case as a special one in which ἐξαγγέλλω implies a personal or particular interest that I fail to notice. From my point of view, according to Owen,[137] the announcement has to do with a promise or simply with a prophecy that will come true and that is well known by the spectator, because the myth is familiar to them.

---

136 Cf. *LSJ*: "Go in and announce", Bailly: "entrer en annonçant (qqn) ou introduire (qqn) en l'annonçant" or *DGE*: "Anunciar la presencia de, introducir".
137 See Owen (1963): "ἐξαγγέλλομαι, 'promise', a use which W. M. says is confined to Soph. and Eur. In *Heracl.* 531–532 it has an infin. instead of a direct object in acc. as here".

In the example given in (64) the verb is in the middle voice and also makes reference to promises. Oedipus has sent Creon to consult the oracle to seek advice to save the city from the plague ravaging Thebes. When Creon returns, he reports that the plague is the result of religious pollution and that the only possible solution would be to catch the murderer of Laius, their former king. In what follows, Oedipus vows to find this man and a priest exclaims:

(64) Soph., *OT*. 147–148

> (...) τῶνδε γὰρ χάριν
> καὶ δεῦρ' ἔβημεν ὧν ὅδ' **ἐξαγγέλλεται**.[138]
>
> It was this we came to seek, which of himself the king now **promises** us!

In (65) the accusative is omitted and only the dative (recipient) appears. On his return home, Menelaus received some bad news himself, as he explains in *Orestes*:

(65) Eur., *Or*. 360–367

> Ἀγαμέμνονος μὲν γὰρ τύχας ἠπιστάμην
> καὶ θάνατον οἵωι πρὸς δάμαρτος ὤλετο,
> Μαλέαι προσίσχων πρῶιραν· ἐκ δὲ κυμάτων
> ὁ ναυτίλοισι μάντις **ἐξήγγειλέ** μοι
> Νηρέως προφήτης Γλαῦκος, ἀψευδὴς θεός,
> ὅς μοι τόδ' εἶπεν ἐμφανῶς κατασταθείς·
> Μενέλαε, κεῖται σὸς κασίγνητος θανών,
> λουτροῖσιν ἀλόχου περιπεσὼν πανυστάτοις.
>
> I was putting in to shore near Cape Malea when I first heard the news of Agamemnon's murder at the hands of his wife. For Glaucus, the god of sailors and a prophet who does not lie, suddenly rose from the sea in clear view, and he **cried out**: "Menelaus, your brother lies dying in his bath, the last bath his wife will ever give him."

---

138 Cf. Bailly: "Moy. Annoncer ‖ proclamer ‖ promettre". *LSJ* only considers the announcement of promises when the verb is accompanied by an infinitive. Ellendt (1841) takes into account these nuances: "to announce publicly, to proclaim". Jebb (1885) does understand that the verb denotes "promises unasked". Cf. also Jebb (1907): "In *O. T.* 148 'ἐξαγγέλλεται' (with acc.) = to offer a thing spontaneously. The ordinary word in this sense was 'ἐπαγγέλλομαι'". On the verb in the middle voice, see Kamerbeek (1967): "ἐξαγγέλλεται: not different from ἐπαγγέλλεται (cf. ἀγγέλλομαι *Aj.* 1376); the middle stresses Oedipus' personal readiness".

Menelaus reproduces exactly the same words which he heard from the mouth of the god and has never questioned, since Glaucus, according to Menelaus himself, is a truthful god (ἀψευδὴς θεός). It is worth noting the presence of the verbal prefix ἐξ- (ἐκ-), whose basic meaning is 'from inside' (Crespo et al. 2003, 171).[139] This nuance of motion from inside to outside is perfectly reflected in the passage, since Glaucus comes out from the waves (ἐκ δὲ κυμάτων) to report the news to Menelaus.

In the following excerpt from *The Children of Heracles*, ἐξαγγέλλω appears with the infinitive. The passage is reminiscent of one in Sophocles' *Ajax* given in the example (43), in which Odysseus reports, or rather promises (ἀγγέλλομαι + dative + infinitive), that Teucer will be his friend. In (66) the verb is also in the middle voice and the speaker is Macaria, who has volunteered herself for the sacrifice:[140]

(66) Eur., *Heracl.* 530–532

> νικᾶτε δ' ἐχθρούς· ἥδε γὰρ ψυχὴ πάρα
> ἑκοῦσα κοὐκ ἄκουσα, **κἀξαγγέλλομαι**
> θνῄσκειν ἀδελφῶν τῶνδε κἀμαυτῆς ὕπερ.

> Conquer your foes! My life's here at your service, ready and willing. **I offer** to be put to death on my brothers' behalf and on my own.

LSJ includes this example of ἐξαγγέλλω with the infinitive and suggests this translation: "promise to do". However, I agree with Jebb's proposal here.[141]

Finally, on only one occasion ἐξαγγέλλω displays an absolute use. The excerpt is from the *Medea*. A pedagogue has just informed Jason's wife that Glauce has received the mortal gifts she has sent her with great pleasure. To the old man's surprise, Medea is not happy to hear such news:

---

139 Let us remember the figure of the ἐξάγγελος in Greek drama. Besides, as we will see, historians often use this verb to refer to spies.
140 Remember that an oracle had told Demophon that only the sacrifice of a noble woman to Persephone could guarantee an Athenian victory.
141 Cf. Jebb (1907): "Eur. *Heracl.* 531 "κἀξαγγέλλομαι θνῄσκειν", 'offer to die'". See also Wilkins (1993, 119): "κἀξαγγέλλομαι: 'promise of one's own accord', for the more common ἐπαγγέλλομαι Soph. *El.* 1018, Eur. *Med.* 721; for the simple verb Soph. *Aj.* 1376".

(67) Eur., *Med.* 1007–1111

{Μη.} αἰαῖ.
{Πα.} τάδ' οὐ ξυνωιδὰ τοῖσιν ἐξηγγελμένοις.[142]
{Μη.} αἰαῖ μάλ' αὖθις. {Πα.} μῶν τιν' **ἀγγέλλων** τύχην
οὐκ οἶδα, δόξης δ' ἐσφάλην εὐαγγέλου;
{Μη.} ἤγγειλας οἶ' ἤγγειλας· οὐ σὲ μέμφομαι.

MEDEA. — Ah me!
PEDAGOGUE. — This tune is not in harmony with my report.
MEDEA. — Ah me, again!
PEDAGOGUE. — Can I be **bringing news** of some misfortune I don't know about, mistaken in believing my report is good?
MEDEA. — The news you've given is the news that you have given. I don't hold that against you.

In this case, from the context we can infer that the verb is referring to a piece of news, since it mentions words just uttered by the man, intended to be good news for Medea. The passage is also interesting because it shows two other derivatives of ἄγγελος. Both the pedagogue and Medea utter ἀγγέλλω up to three times and the old man expresses his regret for having believed himself to be a messenger of good news, that is, an εὐάγγελος.[143]

Greek drama shows instances of ἐπαγγέλλω (a verb that is not documented in Homer and is attested only once in Pindar) in three tragedies. The term is never used to refer to the transmission of news.

The construction of ἐπαγγέλλω with the accusative and the dative occurs only in a passage from Aeschylus. Orestes addresses her sister Electra in this way: "Pray for success, since you offer to the gods prayers that have been fulfilled (τοῖς θεοῖς τελεσφόρους εὐχὰς ἐπαγγέλλουσα)".[144]

The third argument in the dative is absent on two occasions. In Euripides' *Hippolytus*, the complement in the accusative is the adjective in the neuter plural κακά and appears in a speech made by the chorus, reproaching Theseus for not being ashamed of asking for disgusting things (ἐπαγγέλλειν κακά).[145] In this case, the context leads us to translate ἐπαγγέλλω as 'ask for'. In the *Medea*, nevertheless, only the interpretation of the allusion to a promise fits the context.

---

[142] Cf. *LSJ uu.ss.* ἐξαγγέλλω: "Pass., to be reported".
[143] On this passage, see Mastronarde (2002, 332): "δόξης δ' ἐσφάλην εὐαγγέλου: 'and have I been deceived in my expectation that I was bringing good news?'". See also Page (1938, 146).
[144] Aesc., *Cho.* 212–213. Cf. *LSJ*, Bailly: "Eschl. adresser des vœux aux dieux" and Linwood (1843): "Preferring prayers to the gods".
[145] Eur., *Hipp.* 998.

She is asking Aegeus to take her into his palace and she had previously promised him that she will put an end to his childlessness. Aegeus claims to be eager to grant her this favour for many reasons. Firstly, for the sake of the gods and, then: "for the children you promise I will beget (ἔπειτα παίδων ὧν ἐπαγγέλληι γονάς)".[146]

Lastly, in *Heracles* Theseus asks for Amphitryon to be quiet and he replies: "You order it to those who do not want (βουλομένοισιν ἐπαγγέλληι)".[147]

Παραγγέλλω is not attested in either Homer or in Greek lyric poetry. Greek tragedy documents nine occurrences of παραγγέλλω, a technical term from military language to refer to the issuing of commands.[148] Nonetheless, in a passage from *Agamemnon*, παραγγέλλω (in an absolute use) refers to news from Troy. The watchmen on Messapion have just received the signal bearing the news and now they have to inform the others:

(68) Aesch., *Ag.* 294–295

οἱ δ' ἀντέλαμψαν καὶ **παρήγγειλαν** πρόσω
γραίας ἐρείκης θωμὸν ἄψαντες πυρί.

And they flashed the signals in response and **transmitted** them **away**, setting on fire a pile of dry brush.

Now, I will focus on ἄγγελμα and the derivative παράγγελμα. Only Euripides uses the noun ἄγγελμα, and we find this five times in his works. The term always refers to news and in four of the five contexts in which it appears it refers to news reported by an ἄγγελος.

On one occasion — see the example shown in (16) from the *The Trojan Women* (Eur., *Tro.* 711) — ἄγγελμα is the complement in the accusative of ἀγγέλλω, its internal object. Talthybius comes on stage to announce terrible news to Andromache: his son Neoptolemus is about to be killed.

---

146 Eur., *Med.* 719–721.
147 Eur., *HF.* 1185. As we will show in the corresponding chapter, ἐπαγγέλλω is one of the derivatives of ἄγγελος used as military terms in the plays of Greek historians.
148 As we will see, the term is very well documented in the works of historians. In Greek tragedy cf. Eur., *Heracl.* 907-909 and Eur., *Supp.* 1169–1173 (παραγγέλλω + accusative), Aesch., *Pers.* 468–470, Aesch., *Ag.* 289 and 316; Eur., *Heracl.* 824–825 (παραγγέλλω + dative) and Eur., *Rhes.* 70–71 and Soph., *Phil.* 1178–1179 (παραγγέλλω + dative + infinitive, a typical construction of verbs to order. See Crespo [1984]).

In two other contexts, the verb is the subject or the object of verbs (or nouns)¹⁴⁹ of feeling. In (69), for instance, ἄγγελμα is the complement in the dative of χαίρω. The example belongs to *The Children of Heracles*. A servant of Hyllus has good news to transmit to Iolaus: Hyllus has arrived safe and without harm. Immediately afterwards, Iolaus makes the announcement to Alcmene:¹⁵⁰

(69) Eur., *Heracl.* 658–660

{Αλ.}   οὐκ ἴσμεν ἡμεῖς ταῦτα· τίς γάρ ἐσθ' ὅδε;
{Ιο.}   ἥκοντα παῖδα παιδὸς **ἀγγέλλει** σέθεν.
{Αλ.}   ὦ χαῖρε καὶ σὺ **τοῖσδε τοῖς ἀγγέλμασιν.**

ALCMENE. — I do not understand. Who's this man here?
IOLAUS. — He **brings news**: your grandson is here.
ALCMENE. — Greetings to you for **this news**!

In Aeschylus' *Agamemnon* the noun παράγγελμα is also documented. Once again, we are dealing with a military term to issue commands. The example given below is included in *LSJ*, where the suggested translation is this one: "message transmitted by beacons". In my opinion, however, only the allusion to a piece of news can be inferred here. The term undoubtedly refers to the most important and expected piece of news of the play: the aforementioned imminent return of the king after winning the Trojan War illustrated by examples (6), (7), (8), (9) and (37). In addition to this, the presence of the adjective νέοις reinforces my proposal. The following words are spoken by the chorus:

(70) Aesch., *Ag.* 479–482

τίς ὦδε παιδνὸς ἢ φρενῶν κεκομμένος,
φλογὸς **παραγγέλμασιν**
νέοις πυρωθέντα καρδίαν ἔπειτ'
ἀλλαγᾷ λόγου καμεῖν;

Who is so childish or so stricken out of his sense, once he has let his heart be fired by sudden **news** of a beacon fire to despair if the story changes?

---

149 Cf. Eur., *IT*. 1184: ἡδοναῖς ἀγγελμάτων.
150 Cf. also Eur., *Or.* 875–876, in which ἄγγελμα is the subject of ἀναπτερόω.

Final remarks

The concept of news is undoubtedly present in Greek tragedy, and the following conclusions can be drawn from the study of ἄγγελος and its derivative terms. In Greek drama, unlike in Homer, both the ἄγγελος and the subject of ἀγγέλλω is no longer just anybody: the news bearer par excellence is the ἄγγελος himself. The ἄγγελος is a professional with a purely informative role, a character created expressly to report news that cannot be represented on stage. This ἄγγελος usually comes on stage on his own initiative (not acting on the orders of other characters, like Homer's ἄγγελοι). He/she has also been an eyewitness and no one doubts his or her reliability. In addition, the ἄγγελοι have their own scene on stage, the so-called messenger scene, a more-than-consolidated convention that is a fundamental element of the drama, especially in the case of Euripides.

The research findings of this study have provided evidence that ἄγγελος and its derivatives (especially ἀγγελία, ἄγγελμα and ἀγγέλλω) have become specialized technical terms for the transmission of news, and we have several examples to prove this is the case. As I have shown, in a large percentage of the contexts is which these terms appear — at the rates of approximately 70% in the case of ἀγγελία, 80% in the case of ἄγγελμα and 60% in the case of ἀγγέλλω — they appear in the speech of an ἄγγελος or of another character referring to the news reported by an ἄγγελος. In the remaining contexts, as illustrated in this chapter, it is very common for ἀγγέλλω to be uttered by another character who is not labelled as an ἄγγελος but who is also in charge of transmitting news and adopts both the lexicon and the established conventions for this character.

The analysis of the syntactic constructions displayed for each term from the lexical family studied here (in addition to some other aspects, such as context and even the social status both of the speaker and the hearer), enable us to distinguish whether the announcement implied by these words has to do with news or with another type of notification, such as an order.

Having identified these differences, we can also infer what was considered to be news by the members of the societies reflected in Greek drama. In this regard, a study of vocabulary also tells us that in the plays of the three tragedians, news is always related to the main characters, is relevant, and has significant consequences. In Aeschylus, news on war is predominant, as is news on the return home of characters; in Sophocles, news on suicides appears most frequently, and in Euripides, news tends to refer to miracles, murders, and escapes.

4 Aristophanic Comedy

It is a well-known fact that in Aristophanes' plays, comedy and paratragedy can override the need to provide the audience with additional information. This comes as no surprise to us, especially if we consider the overall interpretation of political comedy, including the plays analysed in this study. Aristophanic comedy offers a critique of established power and this is just a sign of the times (Melero 2000, 438). However, the political leaders of Athens were not the only ones to be criticized. As highlighted by Slater (2002, 9):

> On one level tragedy is simply an important part of contemporary culture, calling for either praise or (more often) blame from the comic poet: Dikaiopolis is hoping to see Aeschylus when he goes to the theater (*Acharnians* 10), but tragedians as Morsimus (*Knights* 401, *Peace* 802–807), Agathon (*Thesmophoriazusae passim* and Aristophanes fr. 592 K–A., lines 33–35), and above all Euripides regularly arouse Aristophanes' scorn.

In this context, as we shall see, neither the ἄγγελος nor the typical messenger scene of Greek tragedy escape the parody.

On the other hand, in the chapter on Greek tragedy, I provided some evidence supporting the argument that the ἄγγελος is the news 'reporter' par excellence in drama. However, the scenario is remarkably different in Aristophanic comedy. According to Brioso Sánchez (2006, 111), Aristophanes only took advantage of those characters already present in Greek tragedy. Di Gregorio (1967, 27) argues that the comic ἄγγελος does not have such an important role to play in the drama, since comedy (which is less conservative and more fond of change in general), does not need a figure like that of the tragic messenger. The κῆρυξ is also present in Aristophanes, however, and I will examine this character in more detail in the following pages. In addition to ἄγγελοι and κήρυκες, as we shall see, other characters give news and behave like real, but comic, ἄγγελοι.

Κήρυκες: heralds by profession

Aristophanic comedies provide 12 instances of the noun κῆρυξ. All the heralds alluded to by this term are anonymous, with the exception of the public crier mentioned by Hiero in *Assembly-Women* and by Hermes in *Wealth*.[1] Just as in

---

[1] In *Women at the Thesmophoria* the traces made by a stylus are called κήρυκες (cf. Ar., *Thesm.* 780). The denominative verb κηρύσσω occurs 4 times (Ar., *Ach.* 623 and 748, Ar., *Eccl.*

Homer and in Greek tragedy, these characters are men in the public service who are tasked with introducing those who want to speak during an assembly (Ar., *Vesp.* 754). They also publicly proclaim decrees (Ar., *Ach.* 1000–1004) and negotiate truces (Ar., *Eq.* 668–669 or Ar., *Lys.* 983–984). In addition, the presence of four κήρυκες is indicated in the manuscripts, one of which is really interesting, since she is female. Let us examine *Assembly-Women*. Praxagora — whose plan has proved to be a success, since she has managed to put women at the head of the government — is considering holding a banquet and needs some help:

(1) Ar., *Eccl.* 711–713

> βαδιστέον τἄρ' ἐστὶν εἰς ἀγορὰν ἐμοί,
> ἵν' ἀποδέχωμαι τὰ προσιόντα χρήματα,
> λαβοῦσα **κηρύκαιναν** εὔφωνόν τινα.
>
> Well, I'm now needed in the Agora, to receive all property that's brought along; I'll take a fine-voiced **heraldess** with me.²

The term uttered by Praxagora to refer to this woman is κηρύκαινα, a ἅπαξ λεγόμενον (Chantraine 1974, 527)³ and, just as with Homer's heralds, she has a very particular voice⁴ with which she will summon all citizens to a common banquet (Ar., *Eccl.* 834–852).

In *Acharnians*, the intervention of the κῆρυξ turns out to be brief. The herald comes before Dikaiopolis and the chorus only to urge them to drain their glasses and offer the first to do so a wine-skin as round and plump as Ctesiphon's belly (Ar., *Ach.* 1000–1003). On the other hand, in *Lysistrata* a Spartan herald comes on stage to negotiate a truce. His entrance is reminiscent of that of a tragic ἄγγελος who asks for the addressees of the news:

---

684 and Ar., *Ran.* 1172) and ἀνακηρύσσω (only in Ar., *Plut.* 585) and εἰσκηρύσσω (only in Ar., *Ach.* 135) are also attested.

2 Translations of *Birds*, *Lysistrata*, *Assembly-Women* and *Wealth* are taken from Halliwell (1998). Those of *Clouds*, *Women at the Thesmophoria* and *Frogs* are borrowed from Halliwell (2016).

3 See also Rogers (1902), Van Leeuwen (1905), Sanxay (1974) or Todd (1962). Sommerstein (1998, 201) argues that both the term and the figure of a woman who works as a herald are creations that arise as a product of fantasy.

4 The term εὔφωνος is not documented in the Homeric poems, but there we do find ἠερόφωνος ('sounding through air, loud-voiced'). Ussher (1973, 176) maintains that this woman had not been chosen for having a beautiful voice, but for having a very powerful one.

(2) Ar., *Lys.* 980–981

Πᾶ τᾶν Ἀσανᾶν ἐστιν ἁ γερωχία
ἢ τοὶ πρυτάνιες; Λῶ τι μυσίξαι νέον.

Can you tell me where to find the Athenian Elders,
Or the Council committee? I've got some news for them.

The character on stage is Kinesias, who asks him for more information:

(3) Ar., *Lys.* 992–1001

{ΚΙ.}   Εἴπερ γε, χαὔτη 'στὶ σκυτάλη Λακωνική.
        Ἀλλ' ὡς πρὸς εἰδότ' ἐμὲ σὺ τἀληθῆ λέγε.
        Τί τὰ πράγμαθ' ὑμῖν ἐστι τὰν Λακεδαίμονι;
{ΚΗ.}   Ὀρσὰ Λακεδαίμων πᾶα καὶ τοὶ σύμμαχοι
        ἅπαντες ἐστύκαντι· τὰν πελλὰν δὲ δεῖ.
{ΚΙ.}   Ἀπὸ τοῦ δὲ τουτὶ τὸ κακὸν ὑμῖν ἐνέπεσεν;
        Ἀπὸ Πανός;
{ΚΗ.}   Οὔκ, ἀλλ' ἄρχε μέν, οἰῶ, Λαμπιτώ,
        ἔπειτα τἄλλαι ταὶ κατὰ Σπάρταν ἁμᾶ
        γυναῖκες ἅπερ ἀπὸ μιᾶς ὑσπλαγίδος
        ἀπήλααν τὼς ἄνδρας ἀπὸ τῶν ὑσσάκων.
{ΚΙ.}   Πῶς οὖν ἔχετε;

KINESIAS. — Well, if that's so, I've got one here myself! You can speak the truth to one who understands. Now, what's the situation back in Sparta?
HERALD. — The whole of Sparta's up in — well, just up. Our allies too. They've all got hards. It's dire.
KINESIAS. — But what's the cause of all your tribulation? A curse from Pan?
HERALD. — No, Lampito led the way, and all the other Spartan women joined her. They reached agreement when to hatch their plot, then banned their husbands from their entrances.
KINESIAS. — What did you do?

As is often the case in the *stichomythic prologues* of the tragic messenger scenes, the dialogue ends with a *Π-question* (πῶς). On this occasion, however, the κῆρυξ does not expand the information by means of an ἀγγελικὴ ῥῆσις. Instead, he makes his purpose clear by uttering (briefly) the piece of news he previously stated that he had come to give (τι νέον):

(4) Ar., *Lys.* 1002–1006

> {ΚΗ.} Μογίομες· ἂν γὰρ τὰν πόλιν
> ἅπερ λυχνοφορίοντες ὑποκεκύφαμες.
> Ταὶ γὰρ γυναῖκες οὐδὲ τῶ μύρτω σιγῆν
> ἐῶντι, πρίν χ' ἅπαντες ἐξ ἑνὸς λόγω
> σπονδὰς ποιηώμεσθα καττὰν Ἑλλάδα.

> HERALD. — Of course, we can't. We walk bent over, as though we're screening lamps, to keep them lit. Our wives won't let us touch their bushy plants until we all, by common accord, decide to make a peace that binds the whole of Greece.

The example of the κῆρυξ in *Birds* is quite a different one, since this one does star in a complete messenger scene similar to that of a tragic ἄγγελος. The context is as follows: Peisetairos, who has just founded the city in the air, had commanded that a herald be sent to the gods and another herald be sent to the humans to learn about the new city. In this part of the play, he is concerned because the man who had addressed the humans has not returned:

(5) Ar., *Av.* 1269–1270

> Δεινόν γε τὸν **κήρυκα** τὸν παρὰ τοὺς βροτοὺς
> οἰχόμενον, εἰ μηδέποτε νοστήσει πάλιν.

> There's something wrong if the **herald** we sent to earth doesn't come back here to make report to me.

Parody begins even before the scene occurs. Peisetairos gets distressed in a way reminiscent of the passage given in example (17) in the previous chapter. Remember that in this passage from Euripides' *Electra*, Agamemnon's daughter is waiting for news from his brother Orestes and begins to despair. As soon as Electra is silent, an ἄγγελος enters the scene to announce that Orestes has killed Aegisthus. The scenario is similar to one in *Birds*, when Peisetairos awaits the return of the κῆρυξ with news, but his delay begins to worry him. As soon as Peisetairos is silent, the κῆρυξ makes his entrance. Immediately afterwards, a *stichomythic prologue* identical to that of the tragedy takes place (vv. 1270–1275). The herald's sudden and hurried burst onto the stage is also an imitation of the solemn style of the tragic messenger. The ἄγγελος of Greek tragedy utters interjections and vocatives, and this herald does just the same, but in a complex and exaggerated way:

(6) Ar., *Av.* 1271–1273

> Ὦ Πισθέταιρ', ὦ μακάρι', ὦ σοφώτατε,
> ὦ κλεινότατ', ὦ σοφώτατ', ὦ γλαφυρώτατε,
> ὦ τρισμακάρι', ὦ — κατακέλευσον.

> O Peisetairos! Blessed! O wisest of men! Illustrious! Most wise! Most brilliant too! O three-times-blessed! What's next?

If we continue to focus on Euripides' *Electra*, we can observe that the ἄγγελος appears before Agamemnon's daughter and the chorus and exclaims with the utmost seriousness: "Hail maidens of Mycenae, glorious in triumph! Orestes is victor! I proclaim it to all who love him. The murderer of Agamemnon lies on the earth crumpled in blood, Aegisthus" (Eur., *El.* 761–763). To capture the attention of the addressees of his news, the Euripidean ἄγγελος pronounces a vocative with the interjection ὦ (ὦ καλλίνικοι παρθένοι Μυκηνίδες). Nonetheless, the herald in *Birds* does not utter just one (solemn) exclamation, but accumulates seven vocatives, including up to four superlative adjectives addressed to Peisetairos (σοφώτατε, κλεινότατ', σοφώτατ' and γλαφυρώτατε). Indeed, it could have been many more if the herald himself had not asked Peisetairos to be quiet as he was offering his compliments.

Then, obediently, Peisetairos interrupts him and the κῆρυξ gives him the much desired piece of news: "I've brought this golden garland to crown your head: All humankind desires to honour your wisdom" (Ar., *Av.* 1275). Bursting with pride, Peisetairos accepts the gift and asks the herald to expand on the information by means of a *Π-question*, typical of the tragic messenger scene (Ar., *Av.* 1276), thus leading in to the messenger speech, the ἀγγελικὴ ῥῆσις.

Once Peisetairos gives the floor to the κῆρυξ he expands on the issue with a speech (27 lines, 1277–1303) in which he refers to how many lovers there are in the city in the air and, as a result, he also refers to Peisetairos, its founder. The herald does not declare himself to be an eyewitness, although he need not do so, as everyone expected him to return with news. In any case, while he describes the humans' behaviour and explains how they imitate the birds, he compares their ways with those who, like them (ὥσπερ ἡμεῖς, v. 1287), inhabit the city in the sky. His description of the situation is so detailed that it is inconceivable that anyone could think he was lying.

Finally, at the end of the report, the herald utters a few final words by way of an epilogue. Firstly, he summarizes: "So that's the news from earth" (v. 1304). Then, he gives Peisetairos some advice: as far as he is aware, more than ten thousand individuals are coming to ask for wings and claws, so he had better get ready and equip himself as best he can.

After his performance, the κῆρυξ leaves the stage and Peisetairos is thoughtful. His words do not take long to come true — as soon as he leaves a string of characters expressing their love for birds arrive, keen to have their own wings so they too can live in the air. The first on stage is a parricide who approaches Peisetairos shouting that he wished he were an eagle to fly over the waves of the sea (vv. 1337–1339). Thus, the possible doubts that Peisetairos could have about the news that the κῆρυξ has brought him are completely dispelled, as he himself assures: "The messenger's warning is proving all too true! Here's someone coming along now, singing of eagles" (vv. 1340–1341). In his statement, Peisetairos refers to his informant as an ἄγγελος and celebrates his truthfulness by uttering the words οὐ ψευδαγγελήσειν.[5]

Ἄγγελοι: the parody of the tragic messenger

As we have already pointed out, the ἄγγελος is not as commonplace in Aristophanic comedy as in Greek tragedy. Evidence of this can be seen in the fact that manuscripts only indicate the entrance of ἄγγελοι in *Birds* and *Acharnians*. Aristophanes only uses the term ἄγγελος five times,[6] and it almost always refers to the messengers mentioned in the manuscripts, except in the case of *Women at the Thesmophoria*.

Regarding the role of the comic ἄγγελος, we can be certain that this character is analogous to the tragic messenger because it is the character in charge of reporting news. Unsurprisingly, the main difference lies in the kind of news given by the comic ἄγγελος, as a simple look at the examples shows.

The most interesting thing is, without a doubt, Aristophanes' use of these characters and the conventions of the tragic messenger scene as paratragic elements[7] in comedy to produce a comic effect. This is due to their contrast with the solemnity that is so characteristic of tragedy. In this regard, Rau (1967, 162–168) proposes that eight of the eleven Aristophanic comedies do indeed contain

---

5 See example (3) in chapter seven.
6 Cf. Ar., *Av.* 1119, Ar., *Av.* 1168, Ar., *Av.* 1340, Ar., *Plut.* 632 and Ar., *Thesm.* 768.
7 On paratragedy, see Rau (1967), Murray (1891), Delaney (1984), Bonanno (1987) or Mastromarco (2006). See also Taplin (1977, 81): "These speeches and their introductory dialogues collected many conventional features which were sufficiently stereotyped to supply material for Aristophanes and later comedy".

a messenger scene. Some of the plays even have two (*Assembly-Women*, *Wasps* and *Wealth*), three (*Acharnians*) and up to four (*Birds*).⁸

Let us first turn to *Birds*. In this play, besides a κῆρυξ, three ἄγγελοι are involved in the comic action. Let us start by examining the first one. Peisetairos seems to be despondent at the lack of news, but when he is about to lose his temper he notices that an ἄγγελος has arrived:

(7) Ar., *Av.* 1118–1121

> Τὰ μὲν ἱέρ' ἡμῖν ἐστιν, ὤρνιθες, καλά.
> Ἀλλ' ὡς ἀπὸ τοῦ τείχους πάρεστιν **ἄγγελος**
> οὐδείς, ὅτου πευσόμεθα τἀκεῖ πράγματα.
> Ἀλλ' οὑτοσὶ τρέχει τις Ἀλφειὸν πνέων.⁹

> That's taken care, my birds, of the sacrifice. But it's strange we've had no **messenger** from the wall to bring us up-to-date with progress there. Oh, here's one running—a right Olympic sprinter!

The parody could surely not be more obvious. What comes immediately afterwards is a messenger scene in which the comic poet mocks typical tragic messenger scenes. The entrance of this character is a clear parody. Whilst the tragic ἄγγελος usually utters expressions like "Alas!" that evoke drama, this solemnity is ridiculed in the speech of the comic messenger:

(8) Ar., *Av.* 1122–1124

> {ΑΓΓΕΛΟΣ Α}
>   Ποῦ ποῦ 'στι, ποῦ ποῦ ποῦ 'στι, ποῦ ποῦ ποῦ 'στι, ποῦ,
>   ποῦ Πισθέταιρός ἐστιν ἄρχων;
> {ΠΙ.}   Οὑτοσί.

---

8 According to Rau (1967, 162–168), paratragedy only occurs when the most typical conventions of the tragic ἄγγελος are parodied. Rau gives some examples, as the comic entrance performed by the comic ἄγγελοι in contrast to the seriousness and solemnity with which the entrance of tragic messengers occurs. A complete catalogue of the paratragic messenger scenes listed by Rau can be seen in the table 7 in Fornieles Sánchez (2015). My proposal agrees with that list, but I add the lexicon as an element to be taken into account for the recognition of such parody.

9 By means of πνέων, Peisetairos alludes to the gasping of the ἄγγελος, who arrives in a hurry. In Eur., *Med.* 1119, Medea refers to the agitated breathing (πνεῦμα δ' ἠρεθισμένον) of one of Jason's servants, who is coming to report some news. In Soph., *Ant.* 223–224, the guardian who alerts Creon that someone has buried the Polynices' corpse apologizes for not coming in panting because of the haste of his feet. Cf. Rau (1967, 164).

{ΑΓ. Α} Ἐξῳκοδόμηταί σοι τὸ τεῖχος.
{ΠΙ.} Εὖ λέγεις.[10]

MESSENGER. — Whe-whe, whe-whe, whe-whe, whe-whe, whe-whe, whe-where's our leader, Peisetairos?
Peisetairos. — Here!
MESSENGER. — Your wall's been built—it's finished!
PEISETAIROS. — That's splendid news!

In example (7) Peisetairos' lament preludes the immediate entrance of the ἄγγελος, who comes in haste, as illustrated in (8), repeating ad nauseam the adverb ποῦ to ask for the city's founder, thus showing passion in his expression (López Eire 1996, 160).[11]

The structure of the scene is also reminiscent of the typical tragic messenger scene, starting with the ἄγγελος giving the piece of news (the wall is built), just as messengers of the drama do. This news is a very brief piece of information, as if it were just a headline. It appears within a *stichomythic prologue* (vv. 1121–1132) that ends with the expected question that leads to the ἀγγελικὴ ῥῆσις, divided this time into two speeches[12] (vv. 1133–1141 and 1154–1163). The twelve lines separating these two brief ῥήσεις (vv. 1142–1153) are occupied by an also brief stichomythic dialogue in which Peisetairos asks the messenger for specific details. There is also an epilogue in which, after telling Peisetairos that he is going to leave, the messenger urges him to take care of everything (v. 1163). Just like the tragic ἄγγελοι, in the prologue the comic ἄγγελος is also keen to mention that he is an eyewitness, since he claims to have personally measured the great wall (v. 1130).

When the messenger leaves the stage, Peisetairos remains thoughtful, and the chorus leader asks him if the man could have lied to them. After answering that he is certain that the messenger was telling the truth, he announces the arrival of the second ἄγγελος from *Birds,* who has come to report that one of the gods of Zeus — who will turn out to be Iris — has entered the city of the birds:

---

10 An expression similar to this (εὖ ἀγγέλλεις) is found in Eur., *Supp.* 640, Pl., *Tht.* 144b or Pl., *Resp.* 432d. Cf. also Hdt., 7.80 (εὖ ἤγγειλας).
11 See also Sommerstein 1987, 274.
12 Remember that most tragic messenger speeches are uninterrupted, but we can find some exceptions in *Seven against Thebes, Agamemnon,* and *Persians.*

(9) Ar., *Av.* 1166–1174

{ΠΙ.}   Νὴ τοὺς θεοὺς ἔγωγε· καὶ γὰρ ἄξιον·
ἴσα γὰρ ἀληθῶς φαίνεταί μοι ψεύδεσιν.
Ἀλλ' ὅδε φύλαξ γὰρ τῶν ἐκεῖθεν **ἄγγελος**
εἰσθεῖ πρὸς ἡμᾶς δεῦρο πυρρίχην βλέπων.
{ΑΓΓΕΛΟΣ Β}
Ἰοὺ ἰού, ἰοὺ ἰού, ἰοὺ ἰού.[13]
{ΠΙ.}   Τί τὸ πρᾶγμα τουτί;
{ΑΓ. Β} Δεινότατα πεπόνθαμεν.
Τῶν γὰρ θεῶν τις ἄρτι τῶν παρὰ τοῦ Διὸς
διὰ τῶν πυλῶν εἰσέπτετ' εἰς τὸν ἀέρα,
λαθὼν κολοιοὺς φύλακας ἡμεροσκόπους.

PEISETAIROS. — I certainly am! How else could one react? It truly seems a work of first-rate fiction! [*Pointing*] But here's a guard from the wall: he's bringing a message and running towards us wearing a frenzied look.
MESSENGER. — Alarm! Alarm! Alarm!
PEISETAIROS. — What on earth is wrong?
MESSENGER. — There's terrible trouble afoot! Some god who comes from Zeus' palace above flew through the gates, invading our tract of air, unnoticed by jackdaw guards on daytime duty.

Immediately afterwards, Peisetairos asks him why no reinforcements have been sent to prevent the winged goddess from crossing the wall and the ἄγγελος assures him that they have. On this occasion, he delivers a very brief ῥῆσις (vv. 1178–1185), in which he explains that they sent a mass of mounted archer hawks and depicts how every bird with crooked talons had come: the kestrels, buzzards, vultures and eagles.

This ἄγγελος performs an identical function here to the previous messenger. He comes on stage as the bearer of apparently ridiculous news. However, the news turns out to be real, since right afterwards the winged goddess Iris makes her appearance.

This is not the only example of a 'paratragic' piece of news that comes true (Brioso Sánchez 2006, 114). The same effect is produced by the news announced by the third ἄγγελος in *Birds*, a town crier who loudly tells of Peisetairos' triumphant return along with a beautiful woman (vv. 1706–1719).

---

[13] The tragic ἄγγελος's haste is again parodied. Furthermore, the great emotion with which he charges his words is exaggerated (see Rau 1967, 167). Sommerstein (1987, 277) and Dunbar (1995, 608) point out that the scream of the messenger can be understood as a call to the birds, which would further increase the comic effect of the scene.

Three ἄγγελοι also appear in *Acharnians*. The arrival of the first is announced by the chorus leader and his intervention is very brief:

(10) Ar., *Ach.* 1069–1077

> {ΧΟ.}   Καὶ μὴν ὁδί τις τὰς ὀφρῦς ἀνεσπακὼς
> ὥσπερ τι δεινὸν **ἀγγελῶν** ἐπείγεται.
> {ΑΓΓΕΛΟΣ Α}
> Ἰὼ πόνοι τε καὶ μάχαι καὶ Λάμαχοι.
> {ΛΑ.}   Τίς ἀμφὶ χαλκοφάλαρα δώματα κτυπεῖ;
> {ΑΓ. Α} Ἰέναι σ' ἐκέλευον οἱ στρατηγοὶ τήμερον
> ταχέως λαβόντα τοὺς λόχους καὶ τοὺς λόφους·
> κἄπειτα τηρεῖν νειφόμενον τὰς εἰσβολάς.
> Ὑπὸ τοὺς Χοᾶς γὰρ καὶ Χύτρους αὐτοῖσί τις
> ἤγγειλε λῃστὰς ἐμβαλεῖν Βοιωτίους.

CHORUS LEADER. — But look, here comes someone in a hurry — **bringing** bad **news** by the frown of his face.[14]
MESSENGER A. — O War! O Battle! O Lamachus!
LAMACHUS. — Who is it knocks without these brazen halls?
MESSENGER A. — Orders from the Generals, sir. You're to go immediately, with all your troops and all your crests, take up position in the snow and keep a look-out for enemy raiders. There's been a report that the Boeotians may take advantage of the Pitcher and Pot Feasts to do a spot of rustling.[15]

A priori, this ἄγγελος behaves as we would expect a herald to, giving Lamachus an order (Longo 1978, 72) from the generals. Furthermore, Lamachus himself refers later to him as a κῆρυξ:[16]

(11) Ar., *Ach.* 1082–1083

> Αἰαῖ,
> οἵαν **ὁ κῆρυξ** ἀγγελίαν ἤγγειλέ μοι.

Alack, what news has **the herald** announced to me?

---

14 Another gesture that betrays the bearer of negative news. See Olson (2002, 331): "The herald enters from a wing. For the tragic trope of the entrance of a grim-faced messenger bearing disturbing news, e.g. Eur., *Med.* 1118–1120; *Hipp.* 1151–1152; *Tro.* 707–708; *Phoen.* 1332–1334".
15 Translations of *Acharnians* are borrowed from Sommerstein (1998).
16 This is more proof that the functions that differentiate the ἄγγελος from the κῆρυξ are not always so clear.

As we can see, derivatives of ἄγγελος are very much present in passages like these. In example (10) the chorus leader is afraid that the messenger is going to make a terrible announcement (τι δεινὸν ἀγγελῶν). Likewise, in (11) Lamachus refers to the piece of news by uttering the noun ἀγγελία and the verb ἀγγέλλω. His task here is not only to deliver an order to Lamachus but also to report the item of news that is forcing him to leave immediately. As soon as he has performed the task, he leaves the stage. From my point of view, examples like these reinforce the hypothesis that ἄγγελος and its derivatives have become specialized technical terms for the transmission of news and can be considered as terms coined to denote the informative role of the tragic ἄγγελος. As suggested in the previous chapter, clear evidence of this specialization is the fact that when news is not reported by an ἄγγελος, the characters in charge of doing it (even the heralds) adopt both the lexicon and the conventions of ἄγγελοι. The fact that Aristophanes uses the same vocabulary when he mocks the tragic messenger scene gives, in my view, strong evidence of this mentioned specialization.

A moment later, the second ἄγγελος comes on stage. On this occasion there is no doubt about what he has come to do. His task is not to transmit news but issue orders:

(12) Ar., *Ach.* 1084–1094

{ΔΙ.}   Αἰαῖ, τίνα δ' αὖ 'μοὶ προστρέχει τις **ἀγγελῶν**;
{ΑΓ.}   Δικαιόπολι.
{ΔΙ.}   Τί ἐστιν;
{ΑΓ.}   Ἐπὶ δεῖπνον ταχὺ
        βάδιζε τὴν κίστην λαβὼν καὶ τὸν χοᾶ.
        Ὁ τοῦ Διονύσου γάρ σ' ἱερεὺς μεταπέμπεται.
        Ἀλλ' ἐγκόνει· δειπνεῖν κατακωλύεις πάλαι.
        Τὰ δ' ἄλλα πάντ' ἐστὶν παρεσκευασμένα,
        κλῖναι, τράπεζαι, προσκεφάλαια, στρώματα,
        στέφανοι, μύρον, τραγήμαθ', — αἱ πόρναι πάρα, —
        ἄμυλοι, πλακοῦντες, σησαμοῦντες, ἴτρια,
        ὀρχηστρίδες, τὸ φίλταθ' Ἁρμοδίου, καλαί.
        Ἀλλ' ὡς τάχιστα σπεῦδε.

DIKAIOPOLIS. — Alack! What's this fellow coming **to tell me**?
MESSENGER B. — Dikaiopolis!
Dikaiopolis. — Yes?
MESSENGER B. — Message from the Priest of Dionysus, sir. You're to come to dinner as quickly as possible. Bring a boxful of food, and your pitcher. Hurry up, you're keeping everyone else waiting. He's got everything ready: couches, tables, cushions, covers, garlands, unguents; the nuts and raisins are there, so the tarts, and sponge-cakes and flat-

cakes and sesame-cakes and wafer-cakes and — oh yes, and lovely dancing-girls. 'Harmodius beloved', so to speak. Come on, hurry!

The third messenger of *Acharnians*, however, does have news to deliver. No one notices his arrival, but he appears in a hurry and expresses himself as follows:[17]

(13) Ar., *Ach.* 1174–1189

> Ὦ δμῶες οἳ κατ' οἶκόν ἐστε Λαμάχου,
> ὕδωρ, ὕδωρ ἐν χυτριδίῳ θερμαίνετε·
> ὀθόνια, κηρωτὴν παρασκευάζετε,
> ἔρι' οἰσυπηρά, λαμπάδιον περὶ τὸ σφυρόν.
> Ἀνὴρ τέτρωται χάρακι διαπηδῶν τάφρον,
> καὶ τὸ σφυρὸν παλίνορρον ἐξεκόκκισεν,
> καὶ τῆς κεφαλῆς κατέαγε περὶ λίθῳ πεσών,
> καὶ Γοργόν' ἐξήγειρεν ἐκ τῆς ἀσπίδος·
> πτίλον δὲ τὸ μέγα κομπολακύθου κλάσας
> πρὸς ταῖς πέτραισι δεινὸν ἐξηύδα μέλος·
> 'Ὦ κλεινὸν ὄμμα νῦν πανύστατόν σ' ἰδὼν
> λείπω φάος τόδ'. Οὐκέτ' οὐδέν εἰμ' ἐγώ'.
> Τοσαῦτα λέξας εἰς ὑδρορρόαν πεσὼν
> ἀνίσταταί τε καὶ ξυναντᾷ δραπέτας
> λῃστὰς ἐλαύνων καὶ κατασπέρχων δορί.
> Ὁδὶ δὲ καὐτός. Ἀλλ' ἄνοιγε τὴν θύραν.

Ye varlets in the house of Lamachus, heat water, water, in a little pipkin! Get lint and wax-salve and some greasy wool, to make a bandage for his injured ankle! The man's been wounded by a pointed stake when crossing o'er a ditch; he dislocated his ankle, broke his head upon a stone, and wakened up the Gorgon on his shield, and dropped the boastard-plume from off his helm upon the rocks, which seeing, he lamented: 'My glorious treasure, now I leave thee, never to see thee more, O light of all my life! I am no more!'. So said he, having fallen into the ditch; then to his feet he rose, and stayed his fleeing troops, and then pursued the fleeing raiders with this trusty spear. Now here he comes: open wide the door!

This scene lacks a *stichomythic prologue*. The ἄγγελος utters the news and he immediately begins a brief (but very expressive) ἀγγελικὴ ῥῆσις in which he makes use of another resource typical of the drama's messengers. He does not introduce himself as an eyewitness of the events, but he makes that position

---

17 Cf. Rennie (1909, 262): "1174–1189. A parody of the Euripidean ῥῆσις. The passage is even more significant if we assume that Lamachus was using the wounds he had received in Aetolia in order to further his candidature for the Generalship of 425–424". Cf. also Sommerstein (1980, 212) and Olson (2002, 352).

clear by reinforcing his speech with Lamachus' *verbatim* lament, which gives more reliability to his words. The 'paratragic' news — which seems to be ridiculous — turns out to be true, as we see a moment later: Lamachus, assisted by two soldiers and really upset because of the bad luck he has suffered, comes on stage.

Finally, the lexicon also allows us to identify another messenger in *Wealth*. This character is not mentioned as an ἄγγελος in the manuscripts, but like most of the tragic ἄγγελοι he is a servant.[18] I am referring to Karion, Chremylos' servant, whose arrival as a news-bearer is announced by the chorus leader as follows:

(14) Ar., *Plut.* 631–632

> Τί δ' ἐστίν, ὦ βέλτιστε, τῶν σαυτοῦ φίλων;
> Φαίνει γὰρ ἥκειν **ἄγγελος** χρηστοῦ τινος.
>
> My good fellow, what has happened to your friends?
> You seem **the messenger** bearer of good tidings.

The piece of news that Karion has come to report is a real miracle:

(15) Ar., *Plut.* 633–636

> Ὁ δεσπότης πέπραγεν εὐτυχέστατα,
> μᾶλλον δ' ὁ Πλοῦτος αὐτός· ἀντὶ γὰρ τυφλοῦ
> ἐξωμμάτωται καὶ λελάμπρυνται κόρας,
> Ἀσκληπιοῦ παιῶνος εὐμενοῦς τυχών.
>
> My master's now won perfect happiness! Yet Plutus is happier still: no longer blind. His sight has been restored, his eyes made clear thanks to Asklepios' kindly healing art.

What comes next is a typical messenger scene. After a short dialogue between the slave and the chorus leader (vv. 637–640), Chremylos' wife leaves the house and asks Karion if someone has brought good news?[19] She insists she wants to

---

18 Remember that even though most of the tragic ἄγγελοι are anonymous, we know that many of them are servants. In *Wasps* there is a slave, Xanthias, who is one of Bdelycleon's servants and who stars in a paratragic messenger scene to report the consequences of a ridiculous banquet in which everyone became drunk, and he was beaten.
19 Ar., *Plut.* 641–642: Ἆρ' ἀγγέλλεται | χρηστόν τι; The complete passage is given in the example (28). The use of ἀγγέλλω is not accidental, since (as shown in the previous chapter) it is a technical term closely associated with the ἄγγελος. The presence of the same vocabulary is also

find out about everything and Karion, after promising to give her all the details (vv. 644–658), keeps his word and delivers an extensive report of the events in eight short ῥήσεις (vv. 659–663, 666–683, 685–695, 707–711, 714–725, 727–733, 735–747 and 749–763), interrupted again and again by the woman as she asks questions and proclaims her astonishment.

As with many of the tragic ἄγγελοι, Karion's purpose is to report a prodigy, in this case Plutus' miraculous healing. Once again, despite the fact that the slave only seems to speak nonsense, his words will be proven to be true immediately afterwards, when Chremylos and Plutus burst onto the stage, giving evidence that the latter is indeed no longer blind.

Finally, it should be remembered that other characters perform messenger scenes in Greek tragedy despite not being explicitly labelled as ἄγγελοι. This can be said of two of Aristophanes' comedies in which, unsurprisingly, the situation depicted on stage is ridiculous. In *Women at the Thesmophoria*,[20] the female leader of the chorus notices the arrival of a woman who — in the manner of a tragic ἄγγελος — rushes on stage to deliver news. However, this person turns out not to be a woman, but a man. Cleisthenes has a 'crucial' piece of news to announce: Euripides has sent an elderly relative — disguised as a woman — to spy on the women and find out about their plans.[21]

In *Knights*, on the other hand, the sausage-seller reports the grotesque situation he has experienced in the Council, where he claims to have won his fierce debate with the Paphlagonian.

Both scenes include quite a few terms from the lexical family of ἄγγελος, which are uttered precisely to transmit news. I will go into more detail about these terms in the examples presented below.[22]

---

a paratragic feature. See Tordoff (2012, 147): "Again there is a metatheatrical reference to the relationship between this scene and the tragic messenger speech in the pointed use of the verb meaning to bring news (ἀγγέλλειν) in line 641, which is cognate with the word for a messenger (ἄγγελος)".
20 Cf. Ar., *Thesm.* 517–597.
21 See example (21).
22 On comic messenger scenes, and according to Rau (1967), see Fornieles Sánchez (2015, 308–312). Besides the three ἄγγελοι in *Acharnians* and the three ἄγγελοι of *Birds*, I have labelled as such the sausage-seller in *Knights* (vv. 61–682), the slave Xanthias in *Wasps* (vv. 1291–1325 and 1474–1481), the herald in *Birds* (vv. 1270–1307), the herald in *Lysistrata* (vv. 980–1013), Cleisthenes in *Women at the Thesmophoria* (vv. 517–597), the female herald (vv. 834–852) and the θεράπαινα (vv. 1112–1182) in *Assembly-Women* and Karion in *Wealth* (vv. 631–770 and 802–822).

Absurd announcements: the mockery of tragic news

Aristophanes, as he does with the ἄγγελος and the messenger scene, uses the transmission of news as a means of mockery. The analysis of the comic ἄγγελος has provided some information on how this character — just like the tragic ἄγγελος — uses terms from the lexical family of ἄγγελος. Up to this point, we have seen examples of the words ἄγγελος, ἀγγελία and ἀγγέλλω. The figure below shows all the derivatives of ἄγγελος that appear in the Aristophanic comedies.

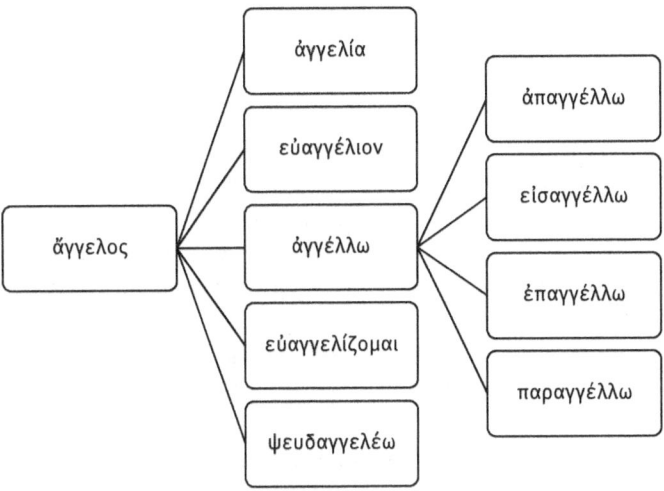

Fig. 9: Ἄγγελος and its derivatives in Aristophanes' comedies.

The noun ἀγγελία cannot be said to be particularly productive in Aristophanes' comedies as it only occurs twice. The syntactic constructions in which the term appears do make it possible, however, to establish some distinctions.

In the passage given in example (11), ἀγγελία is the complement in the accusative of ἀγγέλλω, its internal object. Let us remember that in *Acharnians* an ἄγγελος has make this announcement: "The Boetians may take advantage of the Pitcher and Pot Feasts to do a spot of rustling" (Ar., *Ach.* 1076–1077). After finding out, Lamachus complains about the bad news he just received: "What news has the herald announced to me! (οἵαν ὁ κῆρυξ ἀγγελίαν ἤγγειλέ μοι)". Ἀγγελία is in this case the second argument in the accusative (result) of ἀγγέλλω, which also takes the third argument in the dative (μοι).

In the following example ἀγγελία is the complement of the verb φέρω. In *Women at the Thesmophoria*, the female chorus leader is uttering an oath that the rest of women must repeat. The oath provides for a punishment in case there is a tattletale female slave:

(16) Ar., *Thesm.* 340–342

> (...) ἢ δούλη τινὸς
> προαγωγὸς οὖσ' ἐνετρύλισεν τῷ δεσπότῃ,
> ἢ πεμπομένη τις **ἀγγελίας** ψευδεῖς φέρει (...).
>
> Or if a slave-girl acts as a go-between but then tells the master or falsifies **a message** she's sent to deliver (...).

In this excerpt ἀγγελία is the object of the verb φέρω and, unlike what happens in Greek tragedy — where it is possible to interpret the reference to news — the term alludes here to messages that are likely to be manipulated by a servant.[23]

In Aristophanic comedy we come across three instances of the term εὐαγγέλιον, which is absent both in Greek tragedy and in Greek lyric poetry but documented in the *Odyssey* in reference to the return of Odysseus. Setting the Homeric poems aside,[24] Dickson (2005, 213–214) states that in the ancient world the root εὐαγγελ- is commonly used in relation to reports about military victories. One exception occurs, however, in the case of Aristophanes, in whose comedies the terminology may also be used of 'mundane' announcements not necessarily associated with the state.

The examples given in (17) and (18) are similar in that εὐαγγέλιον is in the accusative plural. It is not an argument, but an adjunct (expressing cause) not inherent to verbs that denote the action of crowning the bearer of the tidings in gratitude for having reported them.

In *Knights* the reporter is the sausage-seller who, as stated above, stars in a paratragic messenger scene. I shall refer to the news transmitted by him later on, since he utters the verb εὐαγγελίζομαι to fulfill his task. For now, it is enough to mention that the announcement has to do with the price of anchovies and that his audience — as pointed out by himself in the ἀγγελικὴ ῥῆσις — was so enthusiastic that it reacted in this way:

---

[23] The same applies to the works of Greek historians, as we shall see.

[24] Dickson (2005, 213) excludes understanding the term εὐαγγέλιον in the *Odyssey* as 'reward/offering for news' because he considers it to have little significance for his purpose, except to note that the message which prompts the reward or offering is always 'news' to the hearer.

(17) Ar., *Eq.* 646–647

> Ἡ δ' εὐθέως τὰ πρόσωπα διεγαλήνισεν·
> εἶτ' ἐστεφάνουν μ' **εὐαγγέλια**· (...)

> All faces brightened at once and I was voted a chaplet for my **good tidings**.[25]

The second passage brings us back to a messenger scene that we have also discussed. On this occasion, the man in charge of bearing news is Karion in *Wealth* and the information he transmits has already been introduced in examples (14) and (15). Plutus' eyesight is restored, and Chremylos' wife expresses her gratitude in this way:

(18) Ar., *Plut.* 764–766

> Νὴ τὴν Ἑκάτην, κἀγὼ δ' ἀναδῆσαι βούλομαι
> **εὐαγγέλιά**[26] σε κριβανιτῶν ὁρμαθῷ
> τοιαῦτ' ἀπαγγείλαντα.

> In Hekate's name, this **good news** of yours deserves a special reward: I'll hang around your neck a string of fresh-baked loaves.

In both cases, the bearer of the news is rewarded and εὐαγγέλια is the cause of this reciprocating gratitude.[27] The example given in (18) is also interesting because of the presence of the verb ἀπαγγέλλω, to which I will refer below.

Let us now turn to the messenger speech in *Knights*. After reporting the good news about the anchovies' price — example (20) —, the sausage-seller goes on to describe his debate with the Paphlagonian and explains that his rival made the following proposition in order to gain favor with the Council:

---

25 Translations of *Knights* and *Wasps* are taken from O'Neill (1938) with (sometimes) slight modifications.
26 See Mitchell (1836, 133): "**εὐαγγέλια** ἀνάδειν τινά: to bind a chaplet on a person's brow for the good news he brings".
27 Cf. *LSJ* or Bailly in general and *LfgrE* for the Homeric poems. Both passages from Aristophanes are mentioned in *LSJ*: εὐ. ἐστεφάνουν, ἀναδῆσαί τινα, "to crown one for good new brought". Ar., *Eq.* 647, Ar., *Pl.* 765. See also Neil (1901, 96): "The reward of the bringer of good news was in Athens a garland or crown, as here".

(19) Ar., *Eq.* 654–656

> (...) "Ἄνδρες, ἤδη μοι δοκεῖ
> ἐπὶ συμφοραῖς ἀγαθαῖσιν εἰσηγγελμέναις
> **εὐαγγέλια** θύειν ἑκατὸν βοῦς τῇ θεῷ".
>
> Friends, I am resolved to make a thanks-offering of one hundred oxen to the goddess for **the good tidings** announced.

I translate εὐαγγέλια θύειν as 'make a thanks-offering for good-tidings' following the *LSJ*'s proposal. The comic effect is evident. With the presence of the verb θύω, which implies the action of celebrating with offerings or sacrifices, the scene seems to become solemn.[28] Nevertheless, the implicit parody is unquestionable given the absurdity of the piece of news. The presence of the verb εἰσαγγέλλω in this excerpt as an allusion to the good news must be also noted. Now let us pay attention to the wonderful news for which the sausage-seller has been crowned and sacrifices are going to be made:

(20) Ar., *Eq.* 642–645

> (...) "Ὦ βουλή, λόγους ἀγαθοὺς φέρων
> **εὐαγγελίσασθαι** πρῶτον ὑμῖν βούλομαι·
> ἐξ οὗ γὰρ ἡμῖν ὁ πόλεμος κατερράγη,
> οὐπώποτ' ἀφύας εἶδον ἀξιωτέρας".
>
> "Senators, I wanted you to be the first to hear **the good news**; since the war broke out, I have never seen anchovies at a lower price!".

The word uttered by the sausage-seller to emphasize that he is going to report good news is εὐαγγελίζομαι, a term not documented in Homer, in Greek lyric poetry or in Greek tragedy[29] which only appears on this occasion in Aristophanes' comedies. On the other hand, we are facing an example of paratragedy taken to the extreme, since the sausage-seller has come before the chorus as an ἄγγελος and is performing a comic message scene.[30]

---

28 See Sommerstein (1981, 179): "Sacrificed... in honour of these good tidings: as if news had come of a victorious battle or some similar occasion for national rejoicing". As will be discussed in the corresponding chatter, Xenophon also takes advantage of the solemnity that emerges from the presence of the verb when he uses the term εὐαγγέλιον.
29 The term does not appear in the works of Greek historians either, but it does in Greek oratory, as we shall see in the corresponding chapter.
30 See Rogers (1930, 184): "This passage parodies the style of a tragic messenger speech".

This passage is included in the ἀγγελικὴ ῥῆσις, vulgar and hilarious (Dover 1972, 90–91), and now he is reporting how his bursting into the Council took place, behaving exactly like a tragic messenger. First, he captures the attention of his interlocutors with a solemn exclamation (Ὦ βουλή). Then, he imitates several *formulae* used by the tragic ἄγγελοι in the *stichomythic prologues*. First of all, he utters the verb φέρω accompanied with a complement in the accusative to refer to the news. Let us recall the example in Aesch., *Cho.* 659: ἥκω καὶ φέρω καινοὺς λόγους.

In addition to this, as we would expect from a tragic messenger, he pronounces one of the derivative terms of ἄγγελος (εὐαγγελίζομαι). In this case, this comes as an infinitive with the verb βούλομαι, in a construction very similar to those found in passages like example (20) from the previous chapter, in which the messenger claims to be the first to deliver the news (τὸ πρῶτον ἀγγεῖλαι θέλω). The presence of the adverb πρῶτον, which is very common in the transmission of news in Greek tragedy, should also be noted. The scene will immediately make the audience laugh when, in contrast to the serious situation previously witnessed, the sausage-seller reports the news that anchovies have never been so cheap.

Now my aim will be to focus on the study of the derivatives of ἄγγελος by examining the verb ἀγγέλλω and its derivatives documented in the Aristophanic comedies: ἀπαγγέλλω, εἰσαγγέλλω, ἐπαγγέλλω and παραγγέλλω.

Aristophanes gives us three instances of ἀγγέλλω, and its presence always involves the announcement of news. The expected construction of ἀγγέλλω with an argument in the accusative expressing result and a second argument in the dative (recipient) is highly productive. I will here focus on the paratragic messenger scene in *Women at the Thesmophoria* referred to earlier:

(21) Ar., *Thesm.* 571–591

{ΧΟ.} Παύσασθε λοιδορούμεναι· καὶ γὰρ γυνή τις ἡμῖν
ἐσπουδακυῖα προστρέχει. Πρὶν οὖν ὁμοῦ γενέσθαι,
σιγᾶθ', ἵν' αὐτῆς κοσμίως πυθώμεθ' ἅττα λέξει.
{ΚΛΕΙΣΘΕΝΗΣ}
Φίλαι γυναῖκες, ξυγγενεῖς τοὐμοῦ τρόπου,
ὅτι μὲν φίλος εἴμ' ὑμῖν, ἐπίδηλος ταῖς γνάθοις.
Γυναικομανῶ γὰρ προξενῶ θ' ὑμῶν ἀεί.
Καὶ νῦν ἀκούσας πρᾶγμα περὶ ὑμῶν μέγα
ὀλίγῳ τι πρότερον κατ' ἀγορὰν λαλούμενον,
ἥκω φράσων τοῦτ' **ἀγγελῶν** θ' ὑμῖν, ἵνα
σκοπῆτε καὶ τηρῆτε μὴ καὶ προσπέσῃ
ὑμῖν ἀφράκτοις πρᾶγμα δεινὸν καὶ μέγα.
{ΧΟ.} Τί δ' ἐστίν, ὦ παῖ; Παῖδα γάρ σ' εἰκὸς καλεῖν,

{ΚΛ.}   ἕως ἂν οὕτως τὰς γνάθους ψιλὰς ἔχῃς.
{ΚΛ.}   Εὐριπίδην φάσ' ἄνδρα κηδεστήν τινα
        αὑτοῦ γέροντα δεῦρ' ἀναπέμψαι τήμερον.
{ΧΟ.}   Πρὸς ποῖον ἔργον ἢ τίνος γνώμης χάριν;
{ΚΛ.}   Ἵν' ἄττα βουλεύοισθε καὶ μέλλοιτε δρᾶν,
        ἐκεῖνος εἴη τῶν λόγων κατάσκοπος.
{ΧΟ.}   Καὶ πῶς λέληθεν ἐν γυναιξὶν ὢν ἀνήρ;
{ΚΛ.}   Ἀφηῦσεν αὐτὸν κἀπέτιλ' Εὐριπίδης
        καὶ τἆλλ' ἅπανθ' ὥσπερ γυναῖκ' ἐσκεύασεν.

CHORUS LEADER. — You must both stop slanging each other like this. I can see there's a woman approaching. She's running this way with an urgent look. Before she enters our midst, please stop the noise: we need decorum to hear what her message will be.
CLEISTHENES. — Dear women, my kith and kin, who share my bent, my cheeks make it easy to see that I'm one of your friends. I'm besotted with women's affairs and I'm always your spokesman. Now I've heard about something important that matters to you: it was all the talk in the Agora just this morning. So I've come here **to bring you the news** and help make sure you're vigilant, on your mettle, and don't allow something great and awful to catch you all off your guard.
LEADER. — What is it, boy? It's right to call you a boy so long as your cheeks are all smooth and hairless like this.
CLEISTHENES. — Euripides, word has it, has sent a kinsman, an old male inlaw, to come to this place today.
LEADER. — With what end in view, what purpose behind the deed?
CLEISTHENES. — So that all your deliberations and plans today can be reported back. This man is a spy!
LEADER. — But how could a man have infiltrated the women?
CLEISTHENES. — Euripides singed and removed his pubic hair and dressed him to look like a woman in all respects!

We are faced with another ridiculous scene here. Cleisthenes comes on stage dressed as a woman and reports an all-important piece of news — something great and awful (πρᾶγμα δεινὸν καὶ μέγα): Euripides has sent one of his relatives to spy on the women posing as a woman. Parody is back on stage.

Cleisthenes secures the female chorus' interest with an exclamation that emulates the tragic solemnity but which could not be more ridiculous (Φίλαι γυναῖκες, ξυγγενεῖς τοὐμοῦ τρόπου). Besides, line 579, which contains the verb ἀγγέλλω and its complements in the accusative (τοῦτ') and the dative (ὑμῖν), is a replica of the typical entrance of the tragic ἄγγελοι. Next, Euripides' relative, who is effectively disguised as a woman amongst the other females in the chorus, tries to sneak away unsuccessfully but is caught. Then Cleisthenes asks the others to hold the mole while he tries to leave to tell whoever he is working for what happened:

(22) Ar., *Thesm.* 652–654

> Τουτονὶ φυλάττετε
> καλῶς, ὅπως μὴ διαφυγὼν οἰχήσεται·
> ἐγὼ δὲ ταῦτα τοῖς πρυτάνεσιν **ἀγγελῶ**.

> Make sure he can't wriggle away and make his escape. Meanwhile **I'll report** to the Prytaneis all about it.

Here, the arguments of ἀγγέλλω in the accusative (ταῦτα) and the dative (τοῖς πρυτάνεσιν) are explicitly referred to as well. I will return to this scene later, since it provides an example of ἀγγέλλω and Cleisthenes utters the verb εἰσαγγέλλω. Let us for now turn our attention to *Wasps*, however. The chorus has the floor:

(23) Ar., *Vesp.* 405–414

> νῦν ἐκεῖνο νῦν ἐκεῖνο
> τοὐξύθυμον, ᾧ κολαζό-
> μεσθα, κέντρον ἐντέτατ' ὀξύ.
> ἀλλὰ θαἰμάτια λαβόντες ὡς τάχιστα, παιδία,
> θεῖτε καὶ βοᾶτε, καὶ Κλέωνι ταῦτ' **ἀγγέλλετε**,
> καὶ κελεύετ' αὐτὸν ἥκειν
> ὡς ἐπ' ἄνδρα μισόπολιν
> ὄντα κἀπολούμενον, ὅτι
> τόνδε λόγον εἰσφέρει,
> μὴ δικάζειν δίκας.

> I feel my angry sting is stiffening, that sharp sting, with which we punish our enemies. Come, children, cast your cloaks to the winds, run, shout, **tell** Cleon what is happening, that he may march against this foe of our city, who deserves death, since he proposes to prevent the trial of lawsuits.

What the chorus claims should be reported to Cleon is the absurd situation that is taking place on the stage: Philocleon is addicted to the law court and his son Bdelycleon tries to prevent his father from going to trials day after day. To achieve his goal, Bdelycleon locks Philocleon in his home and the latter tries in vain to escape. The chorus members are surprised at Philocleon's absence, but he manages to peek out and tell them that his son has locked him up.

The argument in the dative is omitted in three contexts in which ἀγγέλλω is only accompanied by the complement in the accusative (result). One of the passages is the one given in the example (10), a parody of a tragic messenger scene (Ar., *Ach*. 1070: ὥσπερ τι δεινὸν ἀγγελῶν ἐπείγεται).[31] In (24) the chorus complains that Karion, one of Chremylos' servants, has just revealed that his master has brought home a wretched man dressed in rags:

(24) Ar., *Plut*. 268–269

> Ὦ χρυσὸν **ἀγγείλας** ἐπῶν, πῶς φῄς; πάλιν φράσον μοι.
> Δηλοῖς γὰρ αὐτὸν σωρὸν ἥκειν χρημάτων ἔχοντα.

> **This news** is worth its weight in gold! What are you saying? The asset which you've just announced seems ready for a coffin!

The man who arrives home with Chremylos is none other than Plutus. As the spectators know, thanks to the informative prologue of the play, Chremylos has gone to Delphi to consult the oracle. The oracle responded to him with a piece of advice: if he wanted his son to do well, he should leave with the first person he meets as soon as he left the oracle. That person turns out to be a ragged and blind man who introduces himself as Plutus (Wealth incarnate).

In (25) the recipient in the dative is referred to and the result is not expressed by means of an accusative but by a ὡς substantive clause.[32] A woman has just asked Karion where Plutus is. The servant replies that he is about to arrive and invites those present to enter their home:

(25) Ar., *Plut*. 760–763

> Ἀλλ' εἶ', ἀπαξάπαντες ἐξ ἑνὸς λόγου
> ὀρχεῖσθε καὶ σκιρτᾶτε καὶ χορεύετε·
> οὐδεὶς γὰρ ὑμῖν εἰσιοῦσιν **ἀγγελεῖ**,
> ὡς ἄλφιτ' οὐκ ἔνεστιν ἐν τῷ θυλάκῳ.

> So come, let everyone with one accord lift up their legs and join the happy dance! You'll never again come home to **hear the news** that all your grain's used up, your sacks are empty.

According to Macía Aparicio (2006, 478) this is a fake invitation — a joke that is recurrent throughout Greek comedy.

---

[31] The third one is in Ar., *Lys*. 1235: ἀγγέλλομεν δ' οὐ ταὐτὰ τῶν αὐτῶν πέρι.
[32] The construction of ἀγγέλλω + AcI + dative occurs only once. The complete passage is given in example (10).

In (26) the result is not referred to by means of a substantive but by an indirect interrogative clause. Let us turn again to the paratragic scene performed in *Knights* by the sausage-seller, who is going to report the hilarious debate he held with a Paphlagonian. The chorus urges him to begin the speech by uttering the imperative of ἀγγέλλω:

(26) Ar., *Eq.* 610–613

Ὦ φίλτατ' ἀνδρῶν καὶ νεανικώτατε,
ὅσην ἀπὼν παρέσχες ἡμῖν φροντίδα·
καὶ νῦν ἐπειδὴ σῶς ἐλήλυθας πάλιν,
ἄγγειλον ἡμῖν πῶς τὸ πρᾶγμ' ἠγωνίσω.

Welcome, oh, dearest and bravest of men! How distracted I have been during your absence! But here you are back, safe and sound. **Tell** us about the fight you have had.

Let us finally focus on those contexts in which ἀγγέλλω displays an absolute use. The first example is found in *Women at the Thesmophoria*. As we explain below, Cleisthenes has informed the female chorus that Euripides has sent one of his relatives to act as a spy amongst the women. Euripides' relative, trying not to be discovered, rebukes this curious ἄγγελος:

(27) Ar., *Thesm.* 592–596

{ΚΗ.}   Πείθεσθε τούτῳ ταῦτα; Τίς δ' οὕτως ἀνὴρ
         ἠλίθιος ὅστις τιλλόμενος ἠνείχετο;
         Οὐκ οἴομαι 'γωγ', ὦ πολυτιμήτω θεώ.
{ΚΛ.}   Ληρεῖς. Ἐγὼ γὰρ οὐκ ἂν ἦλθον **ἀγγελῶν**,
         εἰ μὴ 'πεπύσμην ταῦτα τῶν σάφ' εἰδότων.

KINSMAN. — Do you find these claims believable? What man's so stupid he'd let his pubic hair be plucked? I don't believe it, by the venerable goddesses two!
CLEISTHENES. — You're talking nonsense. I wouldn't have come here **to announce** it if I hadn't found out from people who know it for certain.

Once again, the mocking allusion to the typical tragic messenger scene is evident. As stated in the previous chapter, the reliability of the news reported by an ἄγγελος is a given as the character has eye witnessed the events. Cleisthenes indeed boasts that he has been an eyewitness.

Our final example also appears in a messenger scene. Let us go back to Karion's performance in *Wealth*. As if he were a real ἄγγελος, there he has the task of reporting the miraculous recovery of Plutus' eyesight. Chremylos' wife, who is listening to the noise outside, leaves the house to take an interest in what is happening:

(28) Ar., *Plut.* 641–643

> Τίς ἡ βοή ποτ' ἐστίν; Ἆρ' **ἀγγέλλεται**
> χρηστόν τι; Τοῦτο γὰρ ποθοῦσ' ἐγὼ πάλαι
> ἔνδον κάθημαι περιμένουσα τουτονί.
>
> What's all the shouting here? **Has someone brought** good **news**? That's what I've long been hoping for, sitting indoors and waiting for him to come.

Ἀπαγγέλλω is documented only once in Aristophanic comedy. The passage, also from *Wealth*, is given in example (18). Let us remember that when Karion finishes reporting Plutus' miracle, Chremylos' wife expresses her intention to give him a crown as a reward for the good news (εὐαγγέλια) he has announced (ἀπαγγείλαντα).

Aristophanes gives us two examples of the use of εἰσαγγέλλω. One of the passages in which this verb occurs has also been discussed above – see example (19). Above, we note that the good news (εὐαγγέλια) reported by the sausage-seller (ἐπὶ συμφοραῖς ἀγαθαῖσιν εἰσηγγελμέναις) has led the Paphlagonian to suggest he should be crowned. The second example appears in *Women at the Thesmophoria*. Cleisthenes has already reported that Euripides was going to send one of his relatives to spy on the women and, when the spy is about to be discovered, he distrusts the words of the news-bearer. However, the female chorus leader is clear that Cleisthenes is not lying and is sorry for that:

(29) Ar., *Thesm.* 597

> Τὸ πρᾶγμα τουτὶ δεινὸν **εἰσαγγέλλεται**.
>
> A terrible matter **is being reported**.

There is only one example of ἐπαγγέλλω in Aristophanes' comedies. In *Lysistrata*, the chorus of men and the chorus of women join their voices to sing a song that includes these words:

(30) Ar., *Lys.* 1049–1053

> Ἀλλ' **ἐπαγγελλέτω** πᾶς ἀνὴρ καὶ γυνή,
> εἴ τις ἀργυρίδιον δεῖ-
> ται λαβεῖν, μνᾶς ἢ δύ' ἢ τρεῖς·

So let a man or a woman **ask for** a few mines if someone needs to take them, two or three.

Unsurprisingly, ἐπαγγέλλω refers to a request, hence the translation 'ask for'.

Παραγγέλλω — a technical term from military language to refer to the transmission of commands — appears just once. The verb offers the typical construction with an infinitive and a complement in the dative and makes reference to an order. The passage appears in Karion's speech:

(31) Ar., *Plut.* 667–670

> ἕτεροί τε πολλοὶ παντοδαπὰ νοσήματα
> ἔχοντες. Ὡς δὲ τοὺς λύχνους ἀποσβέσας
> ἡμῖν **παρήγγειλεν** καθεύδειν τοῦ θεοῦ
> ὁ πρόπολος. (…).

And many others suffered from all kinds of diseases. And after turning off the lights, God's servant **ordered** us to sleep.

Finally, in Aristophanes appears ψευδαγγελέω (just once in our entire corpus). Attention will be paid to this term in the last chapter of this volume.

Final remarks

The findings of the analysis of ἄγγελος and its derivatives in Aristophanes' comedies allows me to draw the following conclusions. Just as in Greek tragedy (and unlike in the Homeric poems), in the Aristophanic comedies both the ἄγγελος and the subject of ἀγγέλλω is no longer just anybody: the news bearer par excellence is the ἄγγελος, although it is much less significant than the tragic one.

Aristophanes uses both this character and the messenger scene he stars in as a means of creating parody. Strong evidence of this can be found in the fact that eight of the eleven comedies have a paratragic messenger scene, and in some there are three (*Acharnians*) or even four (*Birds*) messengers. The mockery of the typical solemnity with which a tragic ἄγγελος comes on stage to report the news is not limited only to form. In order to complete the parody, Aristophanes attributes the same language as tragedy does to the comic ἄγγελοι, that is, ἄγγελος and its derivatives. In more than seventy per cent of cases (most of these appear in paratragic messenger scenes) these terms are uttered by an ἄγγελος or another character alluding to the news reported by this ἄγγελος. I believe that this can only serve as to support my hypothesis that ἄγγελος and its derivatives are consolidated as technical terms for the transmission of news, since, if this was not the case, Aristophanes would not resort to them for his parody.

On the other hand, as I have noted throughout this chapter, in addition to other terms already attested in Homer, in Greek lyric poetry and in Greek tragedy, in Aristophanes we also find the verbs εὐαγγελίζομαι and ψευδαγγελέω. Obviously, they both refer to the news reported by an ἄγγελος. In this regard, the study of ἄγγελος and its derivatives in Aristophanes yields highly suggestive results. Besides the data concerning the use of the terms in paratragic messenger scenes, it should be noted that the noun ἀγγελία no longer seems to be commonplace. However, analysis of the constructions in which it appears shows that when it is the complement of φέρω it is not to be interpreted as a piece of news but as a message. Furthermore, the noun εὐαγγέλιον is uttered to refer to good news and the verb εὐαγγελίζομαι, used for the same purpose — to report good tidings — is documented for the first time in the works of the authors that comprise the corpus of this volume.

Likewise, in Aristophanes' comedies, ἀγγέλλω always refers to news, and the same applies to ἀπαγγέλλω and εἰσαγγέλλω. Ἐπαγγέλλω, meanwhile, is attested only once and refers to a request, not a news item. Παραγγέλλω — which presents a typical construction of verbs of commanding — is also attested only once and refers to a command. Finally, it is also interesting to note the occurrence of another term that has not yet appeared in this study: the verb ψευδαγγελέω, to which we return below.

5 Historians: Herodotus, Thucydides and Xenophon

Let us now turn to Thucydides' *History of the Peloponnesian War* Book 7, and 'The Letter of Nicias' in particular.[1] After defeating Gylippus in an initial combat in Syracuse, the Athenian army commanded by Nicias suffers a heavy blow and the general realizes that it is time to ask for help. He decides to write a letter explaining what has happened and confesses that he is not in a position to take charge of the situation. He goes on to request that his successor be chosen. Thucydides reports that Nicias reacted by sending emissaries to Athens to announce (ἀγγέλλων) what had happened. The text tells us an important piece of information about the task these messengers have before them: they will not be in charge of transmitting the news in a speech and will not ask for help orally either. Instead, they must deliver a letter:

(1) Thuc. 7.8–2

> φοβούμενος δὲ μὴ οἱ πεμπόμενοι ἢ κατὰ τὴν τοῦ λέγειν ἀδυνασίαν ἢ καὶ μνήμης ἐλλιπεῖς γιγνόμενοι ἢ τῷ ὄχλῳ πρὸς χάριν τι λέγοντες οὐ τὰ ὄντα **ἀπαγγέλλωσιν**, ἔγραψεν ἐπιστολήν,[2] νομίζων οὕτως ἂν μάλιστα τὴν αὐτοῦ γνώμην μηδὲν **ἐν τῷ ἀγγέλῳ** ἀφανισθεῖσαν μαθόντας τοὺς Ἀθηναίους βουλεύσασθαι περὶ τῆς ἀληθείας·

> But fearing that his messengers **might not report** the actual facts, either through inability to speak or from lapse of memory, or because they wanted to please the crowd, wrote a letter, thinking that in this way the Athenians would best learn his own view, obscured in no way by any fault **on the part of the messenger**, and could thus deliberate about the true situation.[3]

Nicias' behaviour is as we would expect. As I will show throughout this chapter, it is common to individuals referred to as ἄγγελοι to be dispatched to carry out this type of task. Thucydides alludes to the messenger (ἐν τῷ ἀγγέλῳ) and attributes to him one of the verbs associated both with this figure and with the

---

[1] This passage has been widely studied. See, for instance, Rosenmeyer (2004), Peignez (2006), Griffiths (2007), Ceccarelli (2013) or Luginbill (2015).
[2] See Gomme *et al.* (1970, 385), where it is pointed out that Thucydides makes it seem unusual that a general should send a written message, although there are other similar cases, such as, for instance, in Xen., *Hell.* 1.7.4 and other passages to which I refer below.
[3] The translation of the Greek passages from Thucydides is from the Loeb edition by Foster Smith (unless specified otherwise).

https://doi.org/10.1515/9783111022376-006

transmission of news (ἀπαγγέλλωσιν). However, Nicias does not fully trust these ἄγγελοι, for he fears that they will not be able to speak, that their memory will fail them, or that they will distort the truth. The general is questioning, therefore, the messenger's reliability (note Nicias' wish that the Athenians deliberate περὶ τῆς ἀληθείας, that is, about the true situation), which is unthinkable in Greek tragedy.

Due to this suspicion, the general makes the decision not to report the defeat suffered or ask for help. Instead, he writes a letter (ἔγραψεν ἐπιστολήν) in which he provides all the details.[4] This is not the first time that an ambassador writes a message,[5] and Nicias mentions some other similar situations, although it is not particularly common. As reflected in most of the passages that will be discussed throughout this chapter, the ἄγγελος and the κῆρυξ are in charge of oral announcements, with all the risks that this could entail in terms of effective and faithful transmission.[6]

The change in behaviour referred to here by Thucydides should not be linked, in my opinion, to the fact that the ἄγγελος has lost the reliability usually attributed to him. Although he imputes different functions to the tragic messenger, the ἄγγελος depicted in the works of historians is faithful and efficient and faces missions of great responsibility, especially at times of war.

Ἄγγελος and its derivatives have not ceased to be associated with the truth either. This point is further supported by the fact that when someone wishes to transmit false news, he/she does so uttering the terms from the ἄγγελος family of words. The same can be said of Greek tragedy, as we shall see in the final chapter. The reason for this is that the bearer of news is completely sure that if he utters these words related to the messenger and associated with the truth, he/she will guarantee that the interlocutors believe him/her.

From my point of view, here we are rather facing a direct consequence of the move from orality to writing. In this regard, it is worth noting that Greek tragedy — a genre in which the ἄγγελος orally reports the news in front of thousands of people — coexists with the works of historians. The tension between oral and written literature is palpable.[7]

---

4 The complete text is given later (Thuc. 7.11–15) and it is a text written by the historian in the form of a discourse (Ceccarelli 2013, 142).
5 Cf. Thuc. 7.11.1 or Hdt. 5.35.
6 My conclusions are consistent with those of Longo (1978, 68). See also Torres Esbarranch (1990, 30).
7 This is clearly seen in Thucydides' criticism of his predecessor Herodotus. On this issue, see the excellent studies by Rosalind Thomas (1992 and 1992b). See also Iriarte Goñi (1996, 31), Aly

Ἄγγελοι and κήρυκες: professionals in diplomatic missions

On the surface, it can seem like the lexicon serves to establish a distinction between the main individuals responsible for the successful flow of information, since historians also use the terms ἄγγελος and κῆρυξ. However, as we shall see throughout this chapter, this difference is not as obvious as one might think.

The term ἄγγελος occurs 100 times in Herodotus, only 17 times in Thucydides and 46 times in Xenophon, whilst κῆρυξ appears 63 times in Herodotus, 32 times Thucydides and also 32 times in Xenophon. In addition, Herodotus makes a single use of the terms συνάγγελος[8] — referring to a messenger who accompanies another when he is entrusted to carry messages outside the camp —, εἰσαγγελεύς and ἀγγελιηφόρος. The latter two, as I will show, appoint individuals who hold office as messengers in the service of the Persian king. In Thucydides we also have the nouns αὐτάγγελος,[9] ἐξάγγελος and διάγγελος as well as the verbal adjective κατάγγελτος.[10]

The second Persian invasion of Greece is coming. In Polymnia, Book 7 of the *Histories*, Herodotus depicts the Persians' preparations to undertake an expedition against Greece. After the death of Darius, Xerxes summons an assembly to deliberate and Mardonius, general of the Persians, alludes to their enemies in the following terms:

(2) Hdt. 7.9β 1–2

> Καίτοι γε ἐώθασι Ἕλληνες, ὡς πυνθάνομαι, ἀβουλότατα πολέμους ἵστασθαι ὑπό τε ἀγνωμοσύνης καὶ σκαιότητος· ἐπεὰν γὰρ ἀλλήλοισι πόλεμον προείπωσι, ἐξευρόντες τὸ κάλλιστον χωρίον καὶ λειότατον, ἐς τοῦτο κατιόντες μάχονται, ὥστε σὺν κακῷ μεγάλῳ οἱ νικῶντες ἀπαλλάσσονται· περὶ δὲ τῶν ἑσσουμένων οὐδὲ λέγω ἀρχήν· ἐξώλεες γὰρ δὴ γίνονται. Τοὺς χρῆν, ἐόντας ὁμογλώσσους, **κήρυξί** τε διαχρεωμένους καὶ **ἀγγέλοισι** καταλαμβάνειν τὰς διαφορὰς καὶ παντὶ μᾶλλον ἢ μάχῃσι.

(1921), Finley (1975) Moles (1993), Luce (1997), Marincola (2001), Schepens (2007), Cartledge/Greenwood (2012) and Hornblower (2012).

8 Cf. Hdt. 7.230.1: 'fellow messenger' (cf. *LSJ*).

9 Sophocles also shows the term αὐτάγγελος, used to refer to the character who brings news of what he himself (or herself) has seen as an eyewitness. In *History of the Peloponnesian War*, it appears only once and the messengers are two ships, the Salaminia and the Paralus (cf. Thuc. 3.33.2).

10 Cf. Thuc. 7.48. The term alludes to how Nicias does not want the votes for withdrawal to be kept from the enemies. For definitions cf. *LSJ*: "Denounced, betrayed", Bailly: "annoncé, denoncé" or Bétant (1961, 40): "is de quo aliquid nunciatur".

> Yet the Greeks are accustomed to wage wars, as I learn, and they do it most senselessly in their wrongheadedness and folly. When they have declared war against each other, they come down to the fairest and most level ground that they can find and fight there, so that the victors come off with great harm; of the vanquished I say not so much as a word, for they are utterly destroyed. Since they speak the same language, they should end their disputes by means of **heralds or messengers,** or by any way rather than fighting.[11]

Mardonius refers to a very specific context: the war. The mention he makes of heralds and messengers as mediators is proof that the figures of the κῆρυξ and the ἄγγελος are not so apparent either in the works of historians.

In his *Lexicon to Herodotus,* Powell (1960, 2) defines the ἄγγελος as "messenger; often ambassador"[12] and relies on passages such as those given in (2) or (3) to distinguish this figure from that of the κῆρυξ:

(3) Hdt. 7.152.1

> Εἰ μέν νυν Ξέρξης τε ἀπέπεμψε ταῦτα λέγοντα **κήρυκα** ἐς Ἄργος καὶ Ἀργείων **ἄγγελοι** ἀναβάντες ἐς Σοῦσα ἐπειρώτων Ἀρτοξέρξην περὶ φιλίης, οὐκ ἔχω ἀτρεκέως εἰπεῖν, οὐδὲ τινα γνώμην περὶ αὐτῶν ἀποφαίνομαι ἄλλην γε ἢ τήν περ αὐτοὶ Ἀργεῖοι λέγουσι.

> Now, whether it is true that Xerxes sent **a herald** with such a message[13] to Argos, and that **the** Argive **envoys** came up to Susa and questioned Artoxerxes about their friendship, I cannot say with exactness, nor do I now declare that I consider anything true except what the Argives themselves say.

Nonetheless, it is clear from the excerpt that, although the lexicon used by Herodotus suggests two different types of individuals, both carry out — *avant la lettre* — identical diplomatic functions.[14] It all becomes even more complicated if Macan's (1908) observation is considered. Based on example (4), the author maintains that Herodotus uses the word ἄγγελος as a synonym of πρεσβευτής or πρέσβυς:[15]

---

11 The translation of the Greek Herodotus' passages is from the edition of Godley (Loeb Classical Library).
12 Cf. also *DGE s.u.* ἄγγελος.
13 On this message, cf. Hdt. 7.150.
14 Mosley has devoted numerous works to the study of diplomacy and of envoys on diplomatic missions. See Mosley (1972), Mosley (1973), Adcock/Mosley (1995) and Mosley (1998). The studies by Ramsay (1927), Sealey (1976), Missiou-Ladi (1987), Cresci *et al.* (2002) or Buono-Core (2010) are also of interest here.
15 See Macan (1908): "ἄγγελος in Hdt. = πρεσβευτής (or πρέσβυς, an ἅπαξ λ. in 3.58". This figure has been very controversial. Cf., for instance, Asheri/Lloyd (2011, 452).

(4) Hdt. 3.58.1

Ἐπείτε γὰρ τάχιστα πρὸς τὴν Σίφνον προσῖσχον οἱ Σάμιοι, ἔπεμπον τῶν νεῶν μίαν πρέσβεας ἄγουσαν ἐς τὴν πόλιν.

As soon as the Samians put in at Siphnus, they sent ambassadors to the town in one of their ships.

The situation is similar in Thucydides[16] and, as illustrated in (5), also in Xenophon. After the death of Cyrus, the King sent heralds before Spartan general Clearchus, to negotiate a truce:

(5) Xen. *An.* 2.3.2

τότε δὲ ἅμα ἡλίῳ ἀνατέλλοντι **κήρυκας** ἔπεμψε περὶ σπονδῶν. οἱ δ' ἐπεὶ ἦλθον πρὸς τοὺς προφύλακας, ἐζήτουν τοὺς ἄρχοντας. ἐπειδὴ δὲ ἀπήγγελλον οἱ προφύλακες, Κλέαρχος τυχὼν τότε τὰς τάξεις ἐπισκοπῶν εἶπε τοῖς προφύλαξι κελεύειν **τοὺς κήρυκας** περιμένειν ἄχρι ἂν σχολάσῃ. ἐπεὶ δὲ κατέστησε τὸ στράτευμα ὡς καλῶς ἔχειν ὁρᾶσθαι πάντῃ φάλαγγα πυκνήν, ἐκ τῶν ὅπλων δὲ μηδένα καταφανῆ εἶναι, ἐκάλεσε **τοὺς ἀγγέλους**, καὶ αὐτός τε προῆλθε τούς τε εὐοπλοτάτους ἔχων καὶ εὐειδεστάτους τῶν αὑτοῦ στρατιωτῶν καὶ τοῖς ἄλλοις στρατηγοῖς ταὐτὰ ἔφρασεν. ἐπεὶ δὲ ἦν πρὸς **τοῖς ἀγγέλοις**, ἀνηρώτα [πρῶτα] τί βούλοιντο. οἱ δ' ἔλεγον ὅτι περὶ σπονδῶν ἥκοιεν ἄνδρες οἵτινες ἱκανοὶ ἔσονται τά τε παρὰ βασιλέως τοῖς Ἕλλησιν ἀπαγγεῖλαι καὶ τὰ παρὰ τῶν Ἑλλήνων βασιλεῖ.

He now, at sunrise, sent **heralds** to negotiate a truce. When these heralds reached the outposts, they asked for the commanders. And when the outposts reported, Clearchus, who chanced at the time to be inspecting the ranks, told the outposts to direct **the heralds** to wait till he should be at leisure. Then after he had arranged the army so that it should present a fine appearance from every side as a compact phalanx, with no one to be seen outside the lines of the hoplites, he summoned **the messengers**; and he himself came forward with the best armed and best looking of his own troops and told the other generals to do likewise. Once face to face with **the messengers**, he inquired what they wanted. They replied that they had come to negotiate for a truce and were empowered to report the King's proposals to the Greeks and the Greeks' proposals to the King.[17]

Xenophon mentions some heralds (κήρυκας) at the beginning, but then he refers to them with the accusative ἀγγέλους and the dative ἀγγέλοις, and they themselves claim to be empowered to carry out one of the tasks entrusted to heralds: to negotiate in war.

---

16 Cf. Thuc. 4.118.13.
17 The translation of the *Anabasis* and *Hellenica*'s passages is from the edition of the Loeb Classical Library (Brownson).

Dictionaries do not do much to clear up the confusion either, since it is common for the term ἄγγελος to be defined as 'envoy', just like the κῆρυξ. This observation is not surprising, especially if attention is paid to the lexicon, since in more than half of the examples in which the terms appear, both the ἄγγελος and the κῆρυξ are the complement in the accusative of the verb πέμπω,[18] of its derivatives or of ἀποστέλλω.[19] On other occasions, as in example (6), it is as a predicative complement:

(6) Thuc. 8.106.4

> στήσαντες δὲ τροπαῖον ἐπὶ τῇ ἄκρᾳ οὗ τὸ Κυνὸς σῆμα καὶ τὰ ναυάγια προσαγαγόμενοι καὶ νεκροὺς τοῖς ἐναντίοις ὑποσπόνδους ἀποδόντες ἀπέστειλαν καὶ ἐς τὰς Ἀθήνας **τριήρη ἄγγελον** τῆς νίκης.
>
> So they set up a trophy on the headland where the Cynossema stands, brought in the wreckage, restored to the enemy their dead under a truce, and sent a **trireme as a messenger** to Athens to announce their victory.

The piece of news that this ἄγγελος has to transmit is very positive. The Athenian fleet commanded by Thrasybulus and Thrasyllus has just won the Battle of Cynossema and a trireme has been dispatched to announce the triumph.[20]

In most other contexts, the ἄγγελος and the κῆρυξ are the subjects of verbs of movement — ἀφικνέομαι (Hdt. 3.9.1), ἔρχομαι (Thuc. 1.27.1), etc. — that indicate they have reached their destination to successfully fulfill their task. When it appears with this type of verb, it is also common for ἄγγελος to function as a predicative complement in the nominative, as in (7). After the Battle of Pteria,

---

18 In the case of ἄγγελος, in Herodotus it is the complement of πέμπω (Cf., for instance, 1.3.2), περιπέμπω (4.83.1), ἀποπέμπω (4.94.2), μεταπέμπω (6.42.1) and εἰσπέμπω (ἐσπέμπω, as in 8.112.1); in Thucydides, of πέμπω (2.6.1), προπέμπω (4.30.4) and ἀποστέλλω (3.105.3) and, in Xenophon, of πέμπω (Xen., *An.* 1.3.8), προπέμπω (Xen., *Cyr.* 2.4.31), ἀποπέμπω (Xen., *Hell.* 2.1.7), μεταπέμπω (Xen., *Hell.* 2.1.9), διαπέμπω (Xen., *Hell.* 3.4.3) and ἀποστέλλω (Xen., *An.* 2.1.5). In Herodotus it is common for the κῆρυξ to be the complement in the accusative of πέμπω (Hdt. 1.21.1), διαπέμπω (Hdt. 3.61.3), εἰσπέμπω (Hdt. 6.133.2) and ἀποπέμπω (Hdt. 7.32.1); in Thucydides, of πέμπω (Thuc. 2.6.2), προπέμπω (Thuc. 1.29.1), ἐκπέμπω (Thuc. 2.5.5), προσπέμπω (Thuc. 7.3.1) and προπέμπω (Thuc. 1.29.1) and, in Xenophon, only of πέμπω.
19 Cf. Thuc. 3.105.3 or Xen., *An.* 1.3.8.
20 In this case, ἄγγελον modifies an accusative with an inanimate referent (the trireme), but the referent can be animate, as in Hdt. 8.136.1, where Herodotus reads the prediction of an oracle in a tablet that had been given to him and sent (ἔπεμψε) Alexandros (Ἀλέξανδρον) as a messenger (ἄγγελον) to Athens. The arrival of a ship as news-bearer also occurs in Pl., *Cri.* 43c–d, where a very important item of news is announced: Socrates' imminent death.

Croesus tried to return to Sardis by sea, but he failed and was captured. Cyrus, on his behalf, was informed that Croesus, after his withdrawal, was to discharge the army and decided that the best thing to do would be to march immediately against Sardis before the Lydian forces regrouped:

(7) Hdt. 1.79.2

Ὡς δέ οἱ ταῦτα ἔδοξε, καὶ ἐποίεε κατὰ τάχος· ἐλάσας γὰρ τὸν στρατὸν ἐς τὴν Λυδίην **αὐτὸς ἄγγελος** Κροίσῳ ἐληλύθεε. Ἐνθαῦτα Κροῖσος ἐς ἀπορίην πολλὴν ἀπιγμένος, ὥς οἱ παρὰ δόξαν ἔσχε τὰ πρήγματα ἢ ὡς αὐτὸς κατεδόκεε, ὅμως τοὺς Λυδοὺς ἐξῆγε ἐς μάχην.

This he decided, and this he did immediately; he marched his army into Lydia and so came **himself to bring the news** of it to Croesus. All had turned out contrary to Croesus' expectation, and he was in a great quandary; nevertheless, he led out the Lydians to battle.

As we can see, the arrival of Cyrus as a messenger is enough to announce that the war is not over.

I will now focus on the functions shared by ἄγγελοι and κήρυκες in the corpora covered in this chapter.[21] As I pointed out at the beginning, these individuals play an important role in carrying out diplomatic tasks. They are sent to intercede in negotiations at times of war with various purposes: to ask for help (Thuc. 4.78.1), ask for money (Xen., *Cyr.* 3.2.29) and establish military alliances and conclude treaties (Hdt. 7.152). They are also tasked to issue orders (Hdt. 3.138), demand compensation (Hdt. 5.17) or surrender (Hdt. 3.13), break the bonds of hospitality (Hdt. 3.43) or negotiate to arrange a truce (Hdt. 1.21). They are also sent as spies for information from the enemy, as we shall explore later (§ 2.3).

In addition to all these competencies, which are assigned equally to ἄγγελοι and κήρυκες, Thucydides and Xenophon attribute other tasks exclusively to heralds (this is not the case in the Herodotus' *Histories*), such as declaring war (Thuc. 1.29.1), making official proclamations (Xen., *An.* 2.20), summoning soldiers and commanders (Xen., *An.* 5.7.2), indicating tactical movements (Xen., [*Ath. pol.*] 11.6) and picking up bodies for burial[22] (Thuc. 3.113.1).

On the other hand, some 5th century BC inscriptions mention that the usual procedure followed by Athenians to collect the tribute (φόρος) of defaulting

---

21 On both figures, see Sealey (1976), Lateiner (1977), Longo (1978), Crowther (1994), Wolicki (2002) or Griffith (2008).
22 On this function, see Anderson (1970, 3 ff.).

allies was to send four supervisors (ἐπίσκοποι),[23] one to each of the predefined geographical areas (the islands, Ionia, the Hellespont, and Thrace), to demand payment.

Sometimes, the term with which these supervisors are appointed is not ἐπίσκοπος but κῆρυξ, as in IG³ 1453, B–G. Here, it is established that some heralds (κήρυκας) will be chosen and sent to proclaim the decrees (ἀπαγγελοῦντας τὰ ἐψηφισμ]ένα), and these heralds will compel them to make use of the Athenian currency and the same system of weight and measure.[24]

Heralds were 'inviolable' and could circulate freely even during wars, travelling anywhere without their lives being in danger (Lateiner 1977, 99). They were known for generally carrying a caduceus (if they did not, they lost their inviolability). Furthermore, just like in the Homeric poems, loyalty is one of their distinctive features, so they enjoy the full trust of those who give them their missions.[25] Even so, in Herodotus we see a reference to a snitch herald (Hdt. 3.63).[26]

Whilst most of the ἄγγελοι are anonymous, the names of some κήρυκες are made known, such as Tolmides (Xen., *An.* 2.2.20), Demoteles (Xen., *Hell.* 7.1.32), Philippides, an Athenian citizen who was sent to ask Sparta for help (Hdt. 6.105.1), and Phalinus (Xen., *An.* 2.1.7), a Greek who was with Tissaphernes and professed to be an expert in tactics and the handling of heavy infantry. Thanks to Herodotus (Hdt. 6.60.1) we also know that, at least in Sparta, being a κῆρυξ was a trade inherited from a character's father, as was the case with flute-players and cooks.

Bearers of news

The pertinent question now is what the real role played by both ἄγγελοι and κήρυκες was in the transmission of news. According to Lewis (1996, 51–73), the herald is one of the figures that should be given the most attention when dis-

---

[23] Cf., for example, the Clinias Decree (*IG*³ 34), number 46 in Meiggs/Lewis (1969, 117–121), 98 in Fornara (1983, 107–108) and 23 in Bertrand (1992, 58). See also Cortés Copete (1999, 259 ff).

[24] Number 45 in Meiggs & Lewis (1969, 111–117), 31 in Bertrand (1992, 72–55) and 97 in Fornara (1983, 106). See also Austin/Vidal-Naquet (1972, 98) and Cortés Copete (1999, 267 ff).

[25] Sometimes they were commissioned to carry secret messages, which shows how trusted they were. To fulfill this task, the heralds used a scytale. Cf. Thuc. 1.131.1.

[26] Thucydides also mentions a betrayer ἄγγελος (Thuc. 1.132.5) who had to deliver to Artabazos a letter from Pausanias, who was supposed to be his friend and whom he betrayed for fear of his life.

cussing the news in ancient Greece, since the mere existence of a herald used as a formal channel for the flow of information meant that his superiors could control all that information and use it to exercise and increase their power. However, the terms ἄγγελος and κῆρυξ seem to be synonymous in the works of the historians, so both must be taken into consideration.

As I have just highlighted, historians also present some specialized individuals in their works, but in a different sense to the specialization of the tragic ἄγγελοι, since those that appear Greek tragedy do not carry out diplomatic tasks. The ἄγγελοι and the κήρυκες that figure in the works of Herodotus, Thucydides, and Xenophon, on the other hand, also play an important role in the transmission of news. This is, in my opinion, because both characters are first and foremost emissaries.

Once again, the lexicon provides us with clear evidence, as has been illustrated by the examples (3) and (4) and as evidenced by the passages to be discussed below. These passages have two points in common: in all of them both the ἄγγελος and the κῆρυξ are in charge of transmitting news and their tasks are referred to by ἀγγέλλω, the verb most commonly used in conjunction with tragic ἄγγελοι to report the news. Although ἀγγέλλω will be dealt with later, in what follows I offer some examples that help us to define these figures.

The following passages have to do, without doubt, with some of the most important news in Herodotus' *Histories*. In the first one, Xerxes and his troops have reached Athens and were ransacking it, having passed through Boeotia, where they burned Thespiae and Plataea. They only ran into some resistance on the Acropolis, but they finally managed to set it on fire too. After succeeding, Xerxes wanted to inform Artabanus, whom he had appointed regent while he was away:

(8) Hdt. 8.54.1

Σχὼν δὲ παντελέως τὰς Ἀθήνας Ξέρξης ἀπέπεμψε ἐς Σοῦσα **ἄγγελον** ἱππέα Ἀρταβάνῳ **ἀγγελέοντα** τὴν παρεοῦσάν σφι εὐπρηξίην. Ἀπὸ δὲ τῆς πέμψιος **τοῦ κήρυκος** δευτέρῃ ἡμέρῃ συγκαλέσας Ἀθηναίων τοὺς φυγάδας, ἑωυτῷ δὲ ἐπομένους, ἐκέλευε τρόπῳ τῷ σφετέρῳ θῦσαι τὰ ἱρὰ ἀναβάντας ἐς τὴν ἀκρόπολιν, εἴτε δὴ ὦν ὄψιν τινὰ ἰδὼν ἐνυπνίου ἐνετέλλετο ταῦτα εἴτε καὶ ἐνθύμιόν οἱ ἐγένετο ἐμπρήσαντι τὸ ἱρόν·

So it was that Xerxes took complete possession of Athens, and he sent **a messenger** on horseback to Susa **to announce** his present success to Artabanus. On the day after **the herald** was sent, he called together the Athenian exiles who accompanied him and asked them go up to the acropolis and perform sacrifices in their customary way, an order given because he had been inspired by a dream or because he felt remorse after burning the sacred precinct.

Herodotus mentions an ἄγγελος whose mission is to go to Artabanus to report (ἀγγελέοντα) a good piece of news to him: the victory over Athens. However, the sending of a herald (πέμψιος τοῦ κήρυκος), not an ἄγγελος, is referred to just below.

The news that Xerxes must report is not always so favourable. In (9), the ἄγγελος leaves with fateful news:

(9) Hdt. 8.98.1

Ταῦτά τε ἅμα Ξέρξης ἐποίεε καὶ ἔπεμπε ἐς Πέρσας **ἄγγελον ἀγγελέοντα** τὴν παρεοῦσάν σφι συμφορήν. **Τούτων** δὲ **τῶν ἀγγέλων** ἔστι οὐδὲν ὅ τι θᾶσσον παραγίνεται θνητὸν ἐόν·

While Xerxes did thus, he sent **a messenger** to Persia **with news** of his present misfortune. Now there is nothing mortal that accomplishes a course more swiftly than do **these messengers**, by the Persians' skilfull contrivance.

The misfortune to which Herodotus alludes is the Persian's defeat in the Battle of Salamis. Xerxes dispatches an ἄγγελος to announce (ἀγγελέοντα) the unfortunate news. What follows is a detailed description of the system of Persian royal mounted couriers:

(10) Hdt. 8.98.2-3

Λέγουσι γὰρ ὡς ὁσέων ἂν ἡμερέων ᾖ ἡ πᾶσα ὁδός, τοσοῦτοι ἵπποι τε καὶ ἄνδρες διεστᾶσι, κατὰ ἡμερησίην ὁδὸν ἑκάστην ἵππος τε καὶ ἀνὴρ τεταγμένος· τοὺς οὔτε νιφετός, οὐκ ὄμβρος, οὐ καῦμα, οὐ νὺξ ἔργει μὴ οὐ κατανύσαι τὸν προκείμενον αὐτῷ δρόμον τὴν ταχίστην. Ὁ μὲν δὴ πρῶτος δραμὼν παραδιδοῖ τὰ ἐντεταλμένα τῷ δευτέρῳ, ὁ δὲ δεύτερος τῷ τρίτῳ· τὸ δὲ ἐνθεῦτεν ἤδη κατ' ἄλλον καὶ ἄλλον διεξέρχεται παραδιδόμενα, κατά περ παρ' Ἕλλησι ἡ λαμπαδηφορίη τὴν τῷ Ἡφαίστῳ ἐπιτελέουσι. Τοῦτο τὸ δράμημα τῶν ἵππων καλέουσι Πέρσαι **ἀγγαρήιον.**[27]

It is said that as many days as there are in the whole journey, so many are the men and horses that stand along the road, each horse and man at the interval of a day's journey. These are stopped neither by snow nor rain nor heat nor darkness from accomplishing their appointed course with all speed. The first rider delivers his charge to the second, the second to the third, and thence it passes on from hand to hand, even as in the Greek torch-bearers' race in honor of Hephaestus. This riding-post is called in Persia, ***angareion.***

---

[27] On ἄγγελος and ἀγγαρήιον (Ionic variant of ἄγγαρος), see Bowie (2007, 188).

The context is completely different in (11). Cambyses has a strange dream in which an ἄγγελος arrives to report something miraculous to him:[28]

(11) Hdt. 3.30.2–3

> Ἀποιχομένου ὦν ἐς Πέρσας τοῦ Σμέρδιος ὄψιν εἶδε ὁ Καμβύσης ἐν τῷ ὕπνῳ τοιήνδε· ἐδόκεέ οἱ **ἄγγελον** ἐλθόντα ἐκ Περσέων **ἀγγέλλειν** ὡς ἐν τῷ θρόνῳ τῷ βασιληίῳ ἱζόμενος Σμέρδις τῇ κεφαλῇ τοῦ οὐρανοῦ ψαύσειε. Πρὸς ὦν ταῦτα δείσας περὶ ἑωυτῷ μή μιν ἀποκτείνας ὁ ἀδελφεὸς ἄρχῃ, πέμπει Πρηξάσπεα ἐς Πέρσας, ὅς ἦν οἱ ἀνὴρ Περσέων πιστότατος, ἀποκτενέοντά μιν.

> Smerdis having gone to Persia, Cambyses saw in a dream a vision, in which it seemed to him that **a messenger** came from Persia and **told** him that Smerdis sitting on the royal throne touched heaven with his head. Fearing therefore for himself, lest his brother might slay him and so be king, he sent Prexaspes, the most trusted of his Persians, to Persia to kill him.

This murder is a direct consequence of the madness suffered by Cambyses. The king himself repents shortly after the atrocity he has committed and tells this to the most notable Persians. Before these men of power, he justifies his behaviour by alluding again to the ἄγγελος who announces that Smerdis touched heaven with his head (Hdt. 3.65).

In the following passage Thucydides tells us that Plataea has been besieged by the Thebans with dire consequences and the Athenians had sent messengers[29] to Plataea, but these men had not yet returned:

(12) Thuc. 2.6.3

> οὐ γὰρ **ἠγγέλθη** αὐτοῖς ὅτι τεθνηκότες εἶεν. ἅμα γὰρ τῇ ἐσόδῳ γιγνομένῃ τῶν Θηβαίων ὁ πρῶτος **ἄγγελος** ἐξῄει, ὁ δὲ δεύτερος ἄρτι νενικημένων τε καὶ ξυνειλημμένων· καὶ τῶν ὕστερον οὐδὲν ᾔδεσαν.

> For **the news had not arrived** that the men had been put to death. For **the** first **messenger** had set out at the time the Thebans were entering the city, the second immediately after their defeat and capture, and the Athenians knew nothing of later events.

---

28 Remember that some of the news transmitted by the tragic ἄγγελοι are, precisely, miracles.
29 Thucydides states previously that the Athenians had sent a herald to Plataea (Thuc. 2.6.2: ἔπεμψαν κήρυκα). However, he makes reference later to two envoys and does not refer to them as κήρυκες but as ἄγγελοι. Here we can see again how difficult it is to differentiate between these two figures.

In (13), Xenophon refers to the announcement of a triumph. The informant is not appointed as an ἄγγελος but a κῆρυξ. Archidamus, after achieving an important triumph in the second Syracusan expedition, sent him to report the news to his family:

(13) Xen., *Hell.* 7.1.32

> ὡς δὲ ληξάσης τῆς μάχης τροπαῖον ἐστήσατο, εὐθὺς ἔπεμψεν οἴκαδε **ἀγγελοῦντα** Δημοτέλη **τὸν κήρυκα** τῆς τε νίκης τὸ μέγεθος καὶ ὅτι Λακεδαιμονίων μὲν οὐδὲ εἷς τεθναίη, τῶν δὲ πολεμίων παμπλήθεις.

> Then as soon as the battle had ended and he had set up a trophy, he immediately sent home Demoteles, **the herald, to report** the greatness of his victory and the fact that not so much as one of the Lacedaemonians had been slain, while vast numbers of the enemy had fallen.

Sometimes the transmission of the news is not referred to with ἀγγέλλω but another verb of saying, usually λέγω. This is accompanied by a ὅτι or ὡς substantive clause expressing result which specifies the content of the announcement made by the ἄγγελος.[30] An example is given in (14). An ἄγγελος reports news related to the enemies:[31]

(14) Xen., *An.* 1.2.21

> τῇ δ' ὑστεραίᾳ ἧκεν **ἄγγελος** λέγων ὅτι λελοιπὼς εἴη Συέννεσις τὰ ἄκρα, ἐπεὶ ᾔσθετο ὅτι τὸ Μένωνος στράτευμα ἤδη ἐν Κιλικίᾳ ἦν εἴσω τῶν ὀρέων, καὶ ὅτι τριήρεις ἤκουε περιπλεούσας ἀπ' Ἰωνίας εἰς Κιλικίαν Ταμὼν ἔχοντα τὰς Λακεδαιμονίων καὶ αὐτοῦ Κύρου.

> On the following day, however, **a messenger** came with word that Syennesis had abandoned the heights, because he had learned that Menon's army was already in Cilicia, on his own side of the mountains, and because, further, he was getting reports that triremes belonging to the Lacedaemonians and to Cyrus himself were sailing around from Ionia to Cilicia under the command of Tamos.

---

30 Cf. also, for instance, Xen., *Cyr.* 2.4.1. or Xen., *Hell.* 1.4.2. Sometimes the result is expressed by a substantive clause but in direct style, as in Hdt. 1.36.2. or 7.172.1. When the ἄγγελος or the κῆρυξ announce the conditions of a negotiation, we often find an εἰ conditional clause (cf. Thuc. 3.5.2 or 7.3.1).

31 On other occasions the verb is omitted, but it is easy to understand within the context, as in Xen., *Cyr.* 5.3.26).

In (15) Thucydides describes the general Phrynichus as an ἐξάγγελος[32] when he betrays Alcibiades:

(15) Thuc. 8.51.1

> καὶ ὡς προῄσθετο αὐτὸν ὁ Φρύνιχος ἀδικοῦντα καὶ ὅσον οὐ παροῦσαν ἀπὸ τοῦ Ἀλκιβιάδου περὶ τούτων ἐπιστολήν, αὐτὸς προφθάσας τῷ στρατεύματι **ἐξάγγελος** γίγνεται ὡς οἱ πολέμιοι μέλλουσιν ἀτειχίστου οὔσης τῆς Σάμου καὶ ἅμα τῶν νεῶν οὐ πασῶν ἔνδον ὁρμουσῶν ἐπιθήσεσθαι τῷ στρατοπέδῳ, καὶ ταῦτα σαφῶς πεπυσμένος εἴη, καὶ χρῆναι τειχίζειν τε Σάμον ὡς τάχιστα καὶ τἆλλα ἐν φυλακῇ ἔχειν·

> And when Phrynichus learned betimes that Astyochus was working to injure him and that a letter from Alcibiades about these matters had all but come, he anticipated it by himself as a **messenger who brings out news** informing the army that the enemy intended, seeing that Samos had no walls and that not all the ships were anchored inside the harbour, to attack the camp; he said that he had certain information of this, and that they ought to fortify Samos as quickly as possible and keep a watch upon everything.

Tucker (1982) emphasizes the presence of ἐξάγγελος with its ordinary sense of betraying a secret to those not in it. Let us remember that in Greek tragedy the ἐξάγγελος is the messenger who reports events that occur within the palace or off stage. In contexts like this, in the middle of the war, he is also a man who reports news from within and, therefore, he is revealing a secret and committing treason.

Spies looking for information from the enemy

We must not forget that most of the contexts we are examining are related to war. Very little is known about espionage in times of peace, but we do have evidence of the role played by many secret agents in times of war (Richmond 1998, 1). In this regard, the dispatch of men on a spy mission to learn about the enemy's situation and plans is also a constant in Greek literature.[33]

---

32 Cf. *LSJ*: "Informer, messenger who brings out news, one who betrays a secret". See also *LSJ*, Bétant (1961) and Von Essen (1964). Thucydides also shows the adjective ἐξάγγελτος ('told of'). Cf. Thuc. 8.14.1.

33 Remember, for example, the Doloneia in the *Iliad*. On espionage, see Wedeck (1946), Starr (1974, 8–18), Gerolymatos (1986), Richmond (1998), Russell (1999), Hutchinson (2000, 143–149, 198–200 and 232–234), Sheldon (2003) or Crowdy (2006).

Although the Greek language has a specific term — κατάσκοπος — to designate spies and the κῆρυξ is never mentioned as involved in this type of tasks,[34] this is not the case for the ἄγγελος. An example is given in (16).[35] Descendants of the Argonauts who had been expelled from Lemnos go to Sparta and light a fire. The Lacedaemonians reacted as follows:

(16) Hdt. 4.145.3-4

Λακεδαιμόνιοι δὲ ἰδόντες **ἄγγελον** ἔπεμπον πευσόμενοι τίνες τε καὶ ὁκόθεν εἰσί· οἱ δὲ τῷ ἀγγέλῳ εἰρωτῶντι ἔλεγον ὡς εἴησαν μὲν Μινύαι, παῖδες δὲ εἶεν τῶν ἐν τῇ Ἀργοῖ πλεόντων ἡρώων· προσσχόντας γὰρ τούτους ἐς Λῆμνον φυτεῦσαι σφέας. Οἱ δὲ Λακεδαιμόνιοι ἀκηκοότες τὸν λόγον τῆς γενεῆς τῶν Μινυέων, πέμψαντες τὸ δεύτερον εἰρώτων τί θέλοντες ἥκοιέν τε ἐς τὴν χώρην καὶ πῦρ αἴθοιεν. Οἱ δὲ ἔφασαν ὑπὸ Πελασγῶν ἐκβληθέντες ἥκειν ἐς τοὺς πατέρας· δικαιότατον γὰρ εἶναι οὕτω τοῦτο γίνεσθαι· δέεσθαι δὲ οἰκέειν ἅμα τούτοισι μοῖράν τε τιμέων μετέχοντες καὶ τῆς γῆς ἀπολαχόντες. Λακεδαιμονίοισι δὲ ἕαδε δέκεσθαι τοὺς Μινύας ἐπ' οἷσι θέλουσι αὐτοί·

Seeing it, the Lacedaemonians sent **a messenger** to inquire who they were and where they came from. They answered the messenger that they were Minyae, descendants of the heroes who had sailed in the Argo and put in at Lemnos and there begot their race. Hearing the story of the lineage of the Minyae, the Lacedaemonians sent a second time and asked why they had come into Laconia and kindled a fire. They replied that, having been expelled by the Pelasgians, they had come to the land of their fathers, as was most just; and their wish was to live with their fathers' people, sharing in their rights and receiving allotted pieces of land. The Lacedaemonians were happy to receive the Minyae on the terms which their guests desired.

Sometimes they are informants who are inside the cities. Thucydides mentions some who worked for Nicias and who, in this case, are appointed as διάγγελοι:[36]

---

[34] We only know that he is sometimes commissioned to deliver secret messages. Pritchett (1974, 130) deals with the term κατάσκοπος and highlights the differences between this figure in Herodotus ("usually has the idea of a spy") and Thucydides ("In Thuc. κατάσκοπος is always — except perhaps in 6.63.3 — a man sent out to verify reports by personal observation").
[35] Cf. also Hdt. 4.151.
[36] The term διάγγελος does not occur in Herodotus, Xenophon, Homer, Greek lyric poetry, Greek tragedy or Aristophanic comedy. Dictionaries refer to it as a military term (cf. *LSJ*: "messenger, negotiator, esp. secret informant, go-between"; *DGE* or Bailly). See also Smith (1886), Von Essen (1964) or Bétant (1961): "διάγγελος: *internuntius*".

(17) Thuc. 7.73.3

πέμπει τῶν ἑταίρων τινὰς τῶν ἑαυτοῦ μετὰ ἱππέων πρὸς τὸ τῶν Ἀθηναίων στρατόπεδον, ἡνίκα ξυνεσκόταζεν· οἳ προσελάσαντες ἐξ ὅσου τις ἔμελλεν ἀκούσεσθαι καὶ ἀνακαλεσάμενοί τινας ὡς ὄντες τῶν Ἀθηναίων ἐπιτήδειοι (ἦσαν γάρ τινες τῷ Νικίᾳ **διάγγελοι**[37] τῶν ἔνδοθεν) ἐκέλευον φράζειν Νικίᾳ μὴ ἀπάγειν τῆς νυκτὸς τὸ στράτευμα ὡς Συρακοσίων τὰς ὁδοὺς φυλασσόντων, ἀλλὰ καθ' ἡσυχίαν τῆς ἡμέρας παρασκευασάμενον ἀποχωρεῖν·

He sent certain of his own friends with some horsemen to the Athenian camp when it was growing dark. These rode up close enough to be heard and called upon certain persons by name, as though they were friends of the Athenians — for there were **some who regularly reported** to Nicias all that went on in Syracuse — and bade them tell Nicias not to lead his army away that night, since the Syracusans were guarding the roads, but to withdraw at his leisure, in the daytime, after having made full preparations.

Losada (1972, 20) explains this passage as a stratagem to foil the Athenian retreat. He supports the idea that messengers are associated with the 'fifth column', a modern term to designate a group or faction in a state which acts traitorously or subversively in cooperation with the enemy.

However, if someone was skilled in the art of espionage and did not hesitate to put it into practice it was Cyrus, as Xenophon explains. In (18), (19) and (20) no mention is made of an ἄγγελος, but two verbs from the family of words studied here do appear:

(18) Xen., *Cyr.* 8.2.10

κατεμάθομεν δὲ ὡς καὶ τοὺς βασιλέως καλουμένους ὀφθαλμοὺς καὶ τὰ βασιλέως ὦτα οὐκ ἄλλως ἐκτήσατο ἢ τῷ δωρεῖσθαί τε καὶ τιμᾶν· τοὺς γὰρ **ἀπαγγείλαντας** ὅσα καιρὸς αὐτῷ εἴη πεπύσθαι μεγάλως εὐεργετῶν πολλοὺς ἐποίησεν ἀνθρώπους καὶ ὠτακουστεῖν καὶ διοπτεύειν τί ἂν **ἀγγείλαντες** ὠφελήσειαν βασιλέα·

Moreover, we have discovered that he acquired the so-called "king's eyes" and "king's ears" in no other way than by bestowing presents and honours; for by rewarding liberally those who **reported** to him whatever it was to his interest to hear, he prompted many men to make it their business to use their eyes and ears to spy out what **they could report** to the king to his advantage.[38]

---

[37] See Gomme (1956b, 450): "Certain men, among those in the city, who brought him news".
[38] The translation of the *Cyropedia*'s passages is from the digital edition of the Loeb Classical Library (Miller).

Cyrus' concern for espionage that is carried out well is evident in extracts of text such as the following, in which he addresses the Indian spies he intends to send as infiltrators to find out the intentions of the enemy:

(19) Xen., *Cyr.* 6.2.2

> κἂν ταῦτά μοι καλῶς ὑπηρετήσητε, ἔτι μᾶλλον ὑμῖν χάριν εἴσομαι τούτου ἢ ὅτι χρήματα πάρεστε ἄγοντες. καὶ γὰρ οἱ μὲν δούλοις ἐοικότες κατάσκοποι οὐδὲν ἄλλο δύνανται εἰδότες **ἀπαγγέλλειν** ἢ ὅσα πάντες ἴσασιν· οἱ δὲ οἷοίπερ ὑμεῖς ἄνδρες πολλάκις καὶ τὰ βουλευόμενα καταμανθάνουσιν.

> And if you perform this service acceptably, I shall be even more grateful to you for that than I am for your bringing the money with which you have come. And this is service which you are eminently fitted to perform; for spies disguised as slaves can **give information** of nothing more in their reports than what everyone knows; whereas men in your capacity often discover even what is being planned.

The Greek word for these spies is κατάσκοπος. Xenophon himself highlights the importance of these men, but also warns about them in *On the Cavalry Commander*:

(20) Xen., *Eq. mag.* 4.8

> οὐ μέντοι τοῖς γε κατασκόποις δεῖ ποτε πιστεύοντα φυλακῆς ἀμελεῖν, ἀλλ' ἀεὶ οὕτως κατεσκευάσθαι χρή, ὥσπερ ἂν ἥξοντες **εἰσηγγελμένοι** ὦσιν οἱ πολέμιοι. καὶ γὰρ ἢν πάνυ πιστοὶ ὦσιν οἱ κατάσκοποι, χαλεπὸν ἐν καιρῷ **ἀπαγγέλλειν**· πολλὰ γὰρ ἐν πολέμῳ τὰ ἐμπόδια συμπίπτει.

> Still, you must never neglect to post guards through reliance on spies; on the contrary, your precautions must at all times be as complete as when you **have information** that the enemy is approaching. For even if the spies are entirely reliable, it is difficult **to report** at the critical moment since many things happen in war to hinder them.

All of these passages include some of the terms belonging to the family of words that I am examining: ἄγγελος, διάγγελος, ἀγγέλλω, εἰσαγγέλλω and ἀπαγγέλλω. They are not the only ones, however, since as illustrated below, ἐξαγγέλλω is also used in espionage or to allude to news related to the enemies in times of war. From my point of view, these examples provide evidence that the lexicon derived from ἄγγελος has also become specialized as military terminology in this regard in the works of historians.

Royal messengers

Finally, attention should be paid to two derivatives of ἄγγελος that are only documented in Herodotus' *Histories*. I am referring to ἀγγελιηφόρος and εἰσαγγελεύς, which refer to two professionals.

Herodotus points out the existence of the royal messenger (the chamberlain) in Persia, the ἀγγελιηφόρος. This compound term (ἀγγελίη + φορός, an adjective derived from φέρω that is very common in compounds formation)[39] occurs 4 times (Hdt. 1.120.2, 3.118.2, 3.126.2 and 4.71.4). We are told the name of one of these royal messengers, Prexaspes,[40] who worked for Cambyses and was "the man who brought him all his messages". The ἀγγελιηφόρος was something like the king's private secretary, the individual charged with arranging the king's audiences.

The functions performed by the εἰσαγγελεύς are the same as those of the ἀγγελιηφόρος. The term occurs only once in Herodotus' *Histories* (3.84.2). During the enthronement of Darius, some extraordinary prerogatives are established for the conspirators, including the fact that all members of the group could enter the king's palace if they so wished without announcing their arrival through one of these introducers of messages (ἄνευ ἐσαγγελέος), unless at that moment the king was sleeping with a woman.

From news of war to legal terms

Now I have offered an initial approach to the concept of news in the works of historians through some relevant figures, I will now analyse the derivatives of ἄγγελος. The figures below show the terms that appear in the plays of Herodotus, Thucydides, and Xenophon.

---

39 His presence is already significant in Greek tragedy, specifically in the Euripides' *Rhesus*. The term is not documented in Homer, Sophocles, or Aeschylus — although manuscripts do mention the entrance of an ἄγγελος κατάσκοπος in *Seven against Thebes*. In Euripides, the term occurs 13 times: 3 in *Bacchae* and 10 in *Rhesus*. The term also appears once in Aristophanes (Ar., *Thesm.* 588), 22 times in Herodotus, 7 in Thucydides and 10 in Xenophon. Cf. Chantraine (1974, 1189) and Powell (1960): "Persian *usher*". In a scholium to the verb in 969 of Aeschylus' *Prometheus Bound* the verb ἀγγελιαφορέω occurs (cf. *LSJ*). On ἀγγελία (ἀγγελίη) as the complement of φέρω in other authors, see previous chapters.
40 Cf. Hdt. 3.34.

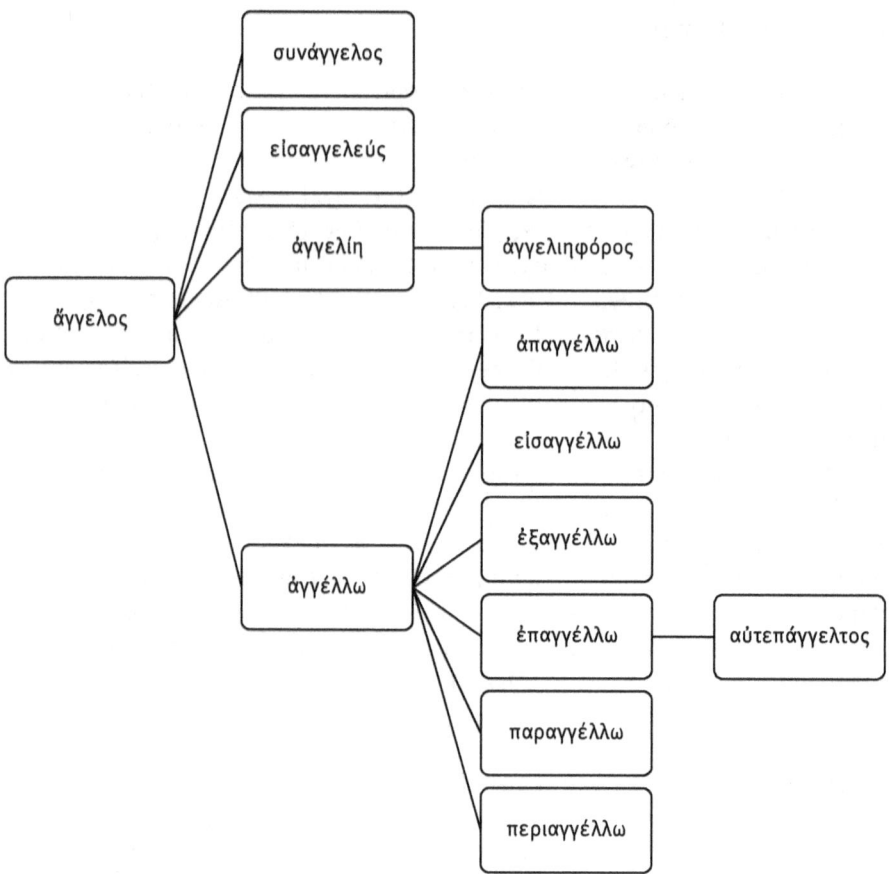

Fig. 10: Ἄγγελος and its derivatives in Herodotus.

From news of war to legal terms — 145

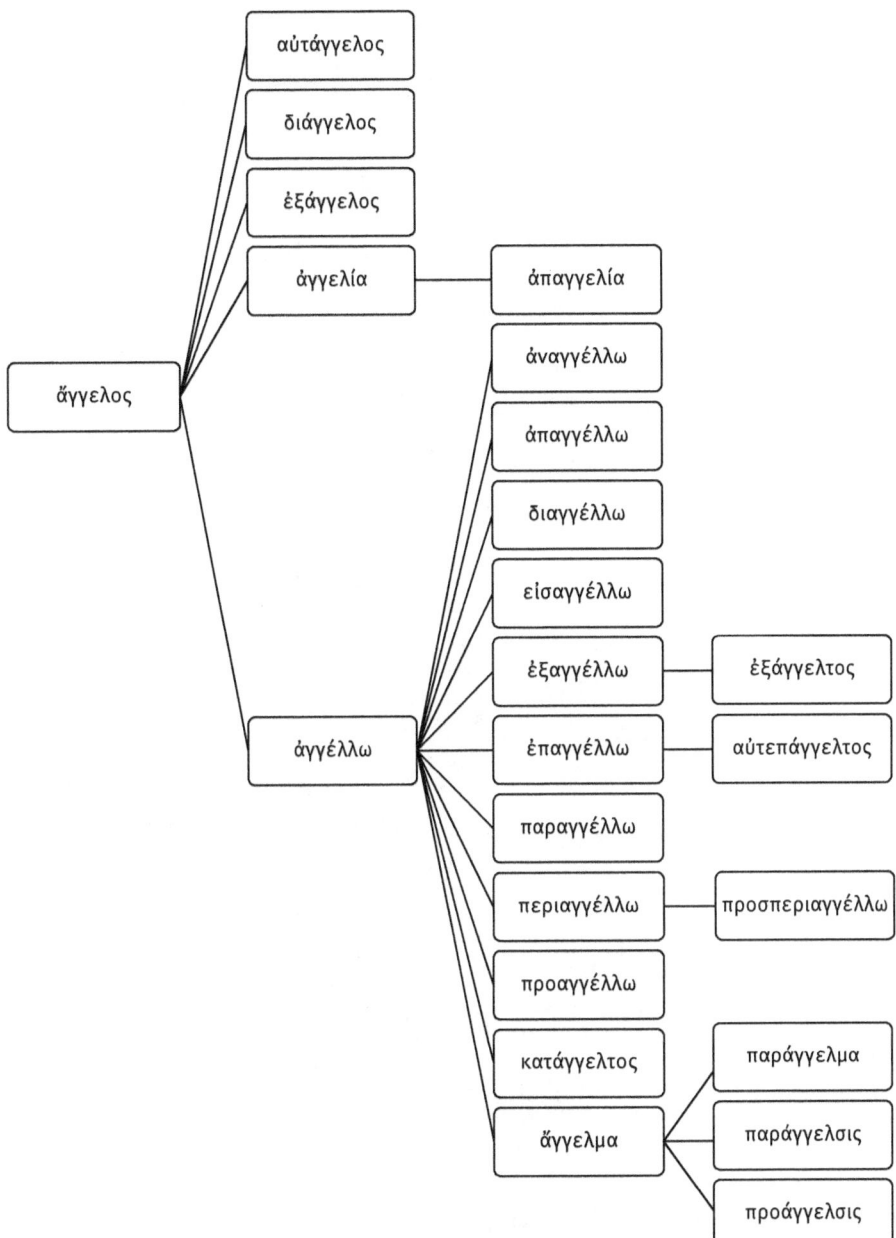

Fig. 11: Ἄγγελος and its derivatives in Thucydides.

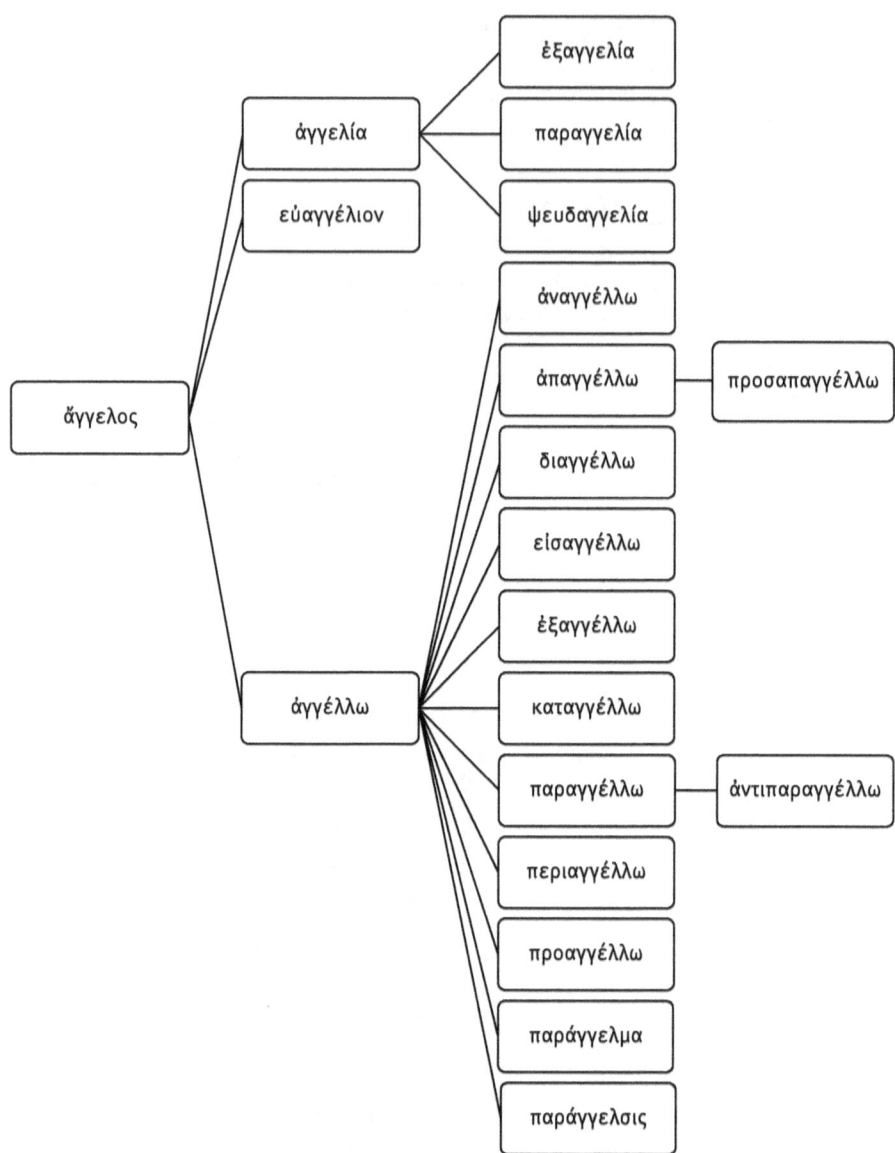

Fig. 12: Ἄγγελος and its derivatives in Xenophon.

In addition to ἀγγελία, the derivative ἀπαγγελία is documented in Thucydides' *History of the Peloponnesian War*. In Xenophon's works ἐξαγγελία, παραγγελία and ψευδαγγελία are also documented.

There are 43 instances of the noun ἀγγελία (ἀγγελίη in Herodotus' *Histories*) in the works of historians: 25 in Herodotus, 14 in Thucydides and only 4 in Xenophon. Ἀγγελία only appears once as the subject of a verb of saying, in a genitive absolute construction. The excerpt is taken from Thucydides and the news item referred to by ἀγγελία is the defeat suffered by the Thebans in Plataea — reported in Thuc. 2.3 and 2.4 — received by countrymen who had to break in at night if the former were in trouble:

(21) Thuc. 2.5.1

> οἱ δ' ἄλλοι Θηβαῖοι, οὓς ἔδει ἔτι τῆς νυκτὸς παραγενέσθαι πανστρατιᾷ, εἴ τι ἄρα μὴ προχωροίη τοῖς ἐσεληλυθόσι, **τῆς ἀγγελίας** ἅμα καθ' ὁδὸν αὐτοῖς ῥηθείσης περὶ τῶν γεγενημένων ἐπεβοήθουν.

> But the main body of the Thebans, who were to have come in full force while it was still night, on the chance that things might not go well with those who had entered the city, received while on the way **news** of what had happened and were now hastening to the rescue.

In other contexts, ἀγγελία is the complement of a verb of perception. In (22) the verb is πυνθάνομαι, and ἀγγελία clearly alludes to a piece of news. Herodotus explains that the Persian Mardonius sent Alexander as an ambassador to enter into peace negotiations with the Athenians. However, they rejected them and advised the Spartans to act as follows:

(22) Hdt. 8.144.5

> Ὡς γὰρ ἡμεῖς εἰκάζομεν, οὐκ ἑκὰς χρόνου παρέσται ὁ βάρβαρος ἐσβαλὼν ἐς τὴν ἡμετέρην, ἀλλ' ἐπειδὰν τάχιστα πύθηται **τὴν ἀγγελίην** ὅτι οὐδὲν ποιήσομεν τῶν ἐκεῖνος ἡμέων προσεδέετο.

> For as we guess, the barbarian will be upon us and invade our country in no long time as soon as he finds out **the news** that we will do nothing that he requires of us.

In (23), ἀγγελία is the complement in the genitive of the verb of hearing ἀκούω and is only likely to be interpreted in allusion to an order:

(23) Thuc. 5.44.1

> Οἱ δὲ Ἀργεῖοι ἀκούσαντες **τῆς** τε **ἀγγελίας** καὶ ἐπειδὴ ἔγνωσαν οὐ μετ' Ἀθηναίων πραχθεῖσαν τὴν τῶν Βοιωτῶν ξυμμαχίαν, ἀλλ' ἐς διαφορὰν μεγάλην καθεστῶτας αὐτοὺς πρὸς τοὺς Λακεδαιμονίους, τῶν μὲν ἐν Λακεδαίμονι πρέσβεων, οἵ σφίσι περὶ τῶν σπονδῶν ἔτυχον ἀπόντες, ἠμέλουν, πρὸς δὲ τοὺς Ἀθηναίους μᾶλλον τὴν γνώμην εἶχον (...).

When the Argives heard **the order** and realized that the alliance with the Boeotians had been made without the consent of the Athenians, but that these were involved in a serious quarrel with the Lacedaemonians, they took no further thought about their envoys at Lacedaemon, who had gone thither on the matter of the treaty and gave their attention rather to the Athenians (...).

The command received by the Argives came from Alcibiades who, according to Thucydides (Thuc. 5.43.3), had sent an ambassador to order them (κελεύων) to appear as quickly as possible before the Athenians to propose an alliance. The presence of the verb of commanding κελεύω shows that what the Argives have heard could only be the order given by Alcibiades.

Ἀγγελία also functions as the complement of πέμπω and its derivatives (4 times in Herodotus and once in Thucydides).[41] Let us place ourselves first in the *Histories*' Book 2, in Egypt. There, when Thonis — the guardian of the Canobic Mouth of the Nile — finds out that Paris and Helen have just arrived, he decides to inform Proteus, the Egyptian king:

(24) Hdt. 2.114.1

> Ἀκούσας δὲ τούτων ὁ Θῶνις πέμπει τὴν ταχίστην ἐς Μέμφιν παρὰ Πρωτέα **ἀγγελίην** λέγουσαν τάδε· "Ἥκει ξεῖνος, γένος μὲν Τευκρός, ἔργον δὲ ἀνόσιον ἐν τῇ Ἑλλάδι ἐξεργασμένος· ξείνου γὰρ τοῦ ἑωυτοῦ ἐξαπατήσας τὴν γυναῖκα αὐτήν τε ταύτην ἄγων ἥκει καὶ πολλὰ κάρτα χρήματα, ὑπὸ ἀνέμων ἐς γῆν τὴν σὴν ἀπενειχθείς. Κότερα δῆτα τοῦτον ἐῶμεν ἀσινέα ἐκπλέειν ἢ ἀπελώμεθα τὰ ἔχων ἦλθε;"

When Thonis heard it, he sent **this message** the quickest way to Proteus at Memphis: "A stranger has come, a Trojan, who has committed an impiety in Hellas. After defrauding his guest-friend, he has come bringing the man's wife and a very great deal of wealth, driven to your country by the wind. Are we to let him sail away untouched, or are we to take away what he has come with?"

When faced with such doubts, Proteus responds firmly: they must arrest Paris and bring him to him so that he can explain why he has acted in this way. But what interests us most is the fact that in this context ἀγγελία can be understood as the piece of news that a guardian who watches over the place must report.[42] I

---

[41] Cf. Thuc. 8.39.4. A Peloponnesian fleet has just landed in Cauno and the crew, fearing being discovered by the Athenians, decides to send a message (ἀγγελίαν ἔπεμπον) to ask for help.

[42] This is not the case in Hdt. 3.122.3–4, where ἀγγελία does not refer to a new item but to Oroetes' proposal to Polycrates, which he sends through an emissary.

have kept the translation of ἀγγελία as 'message' because Herodotus repeats the ἀγγελιηφόρος Thonis' words *verbatim*.

In (25) the verb that ἀγγελία complements is not πέμπω but ἐπιπέμπω:

(25) Hdt. 1.160.2

> Οἱ δὲ Μυτιληναῖοι ἐπιπέμποντος τοῦ Μαζάρεος **ἀγγελίας** ἐκδιδόναι τὸν Πακτύην παρεσκευάζοντο ἐπὶ μισθῷ ὅσῳ δή·
>
> Then Mazares sent **a message** to Mytilene demanding the surrender of Pactyes, and the Mytilenaeans prepared to give him, for a price.

The message sent by Mazares implies an order. The verb ἐπιπέμπω itself provides us with some clues, since the preverb ἐπί- can lead us us think of a complement in the dative expressing the beneficiary or maleficiary (as in this case) that is elided but is easily recovered from context. Likewise, it is common for verbs of sending to be accompanied by an infinitive that expresses purpose (here, ἐκδιδόναι). Hence, the most logical thing to do is to interpret that Mazares sends orders (ἀγγελίας) to the Mytilenaeans to force them. Besides, shortly beforehand (Hdt. 1.157.9) Herodotus had anticipated that Mazares had sent messengers (ἔπεμπε ἀγγέλους) demanding (κελεύων) that Pactyes be surrendered (ἐκδιδόναι Πακτύην).[43]

In Herodotus' *Histories*, ἀγγελίη appears as the object of φέρω, εἰσφέρω or φορέω six times. In such contexts, ἀγγελίη never refers to a piece of news. In most of the cases the noun is associated with the figures of the ἀγγελιηφόρος and the εἰσαγγελεύς.[44] On other occasions, the ἀγγελία is a proposal[45] or an order.[46]

On the other hand, in more than fifty percent of the excerpts in which it appears — 22 of the total of 43 instances — ἀγγελία is the subject of a verb of movement, especially ἔρχομαι,[47] as in (26). When Cyrus is already established as sovereign in Babylon, Artabazus, looking to get in the king's good books, addresses him in this way:

---

43 In Hdt. 3.69.1. the verb is εἰσπέμπω, and we can infer that these are orders from the use of imperatives (ποίησον, ἄφασον, νόμιζε).
44 Cf. Hdt. 1.114.1–2 (with εἰσφέρω), Hdt. 3.34.1 (with φορέω) and Hdt. 3.77.2 (with εἰσφέρω).
45 Cf. Hdt. 3.122., Hdt. 3.53.2.
46 Cf. Hdt. 5.14.2.
47 Also with ἐπεισέρχομαι (only once, cf. Hdt. 8.99.5).

(26) Xen., *Cyr.* 7.5.52

> ὥς γε μέντοι ἦλθεν **ἡ δεινὴ ἀγγελία** τὸ πάντας ἀνθρώπους ἐφ' ἡμᾶς συλλέγεσθαι, ἐγίγνωσκον ὅτι ταῦτα μέγιστα εἴη· εἰ δὲ ταῦτα καλῶς γένοιτο, εὖ ἤδη ἐδόκουν εἰδέναι ὅτι πολλὴ ἔσοιτο ἀφθονία τῆς ἐμῆς καὶ τῆς σῆς συνουσίας.

> Still, when **the terrible news** came that the whole world was assembling against us, I realized that that was a matter of paramount importance; but if it should turn out successfully, then at last I thought I might be sure that the intercourse between me and you would be unstinted.

The forms of ἔρχομαι are always the aorist active indicative (ἦλθε or ἦλθον)[48] or the aorist participle,[49] usually in a genitive absolute construction.[50]

Other verbs of movement used by Herodotus, Thucydides and Xenophon are ἀφικνέομαι,[51] ἄνειμι,[52] παραγίγνομαι,[53] ἥκω[54] and the frequentative φοιτάω.[55] When ἀγγελία appears with verbs of movement, the identity of the person in charge of making the announcement is almost always unknown.[56]

In (27) ἀγγελία is the subject of the verb δύναμαι. The Athenian landing in Sicily was imminent, but many Syracusans were reluctant to believe it. Several of them give speeches with different opinions on whether the news was true or false. The first man to speak was Hermocrates, who claimed to be informed by a very reliable source and to be able to assure, therefore, that it was true that the Athenians were advancing against them. According to him, the Athenians' sole purpose was to conquer Syracuse to then try to capture the rest of the cities in Sicily. Athenagoras, on the other hand, spoke in these terms:

---

48 Cf. Hdt. 1.83.1, Hdt. 5.117, Hdt. 6.28.1, Hdt. 9.14.1, Hdt. 9.15.1, Thuc. 1.61.1, Thuc. 3.33.2 and Xen., *Cyr.* 6.2.14.
49 Cf. Hdt. 8.14.2.
50 Cf. Thuc. 8.19.1 and Xen., *Ages.* 7.5.
51 Cf. Hdt. 7.1.1, Hdt. 6.10.1, Hdt. 8.99.1, Thuc. 5.64.1 and Thuc. 8.15.1.
52 Cf. Hdt. 5.108.1.
53 Cf. Thuc. 8.41.1.
54 Only once in Herodotus (Hdt. 8.140.1).
55 Cf. Thuc. 6.104.1.
56 In these contexts, the term always designates a piece of news except in Thuc. 8.19.1, a troublesome passage in which the term displays a construction with a ὅτι substantive clause and, in my opinion, should not be interpreted as a piece of news but as an order. On this excerpt, cf. Classen (1996) and Tucker (1892).

(27) Thuc. 6.36.1

> 'Τοὺς μὲν Ἀθηναίους ὅστις μὴ βούλεται οὕτω κακῶς φρονῆσαι καὶ ὑποχειρίους ἡμῖν γενέσθαι ἐνθάδε ἐλθόντας, ἢ δειλός ἐστιν ἢ τῇ πόλει οὐκ εὔνους· τοὺς δὲ ἀγγέλλοντας τὰ τοιαῦτα καὶ περιφόβους ὑμᾶς ποιοῦντας τῆς μὲν τόλμης οὐ θαυμάζω, τῆς δὲ ἀξυνεσίας, εἰ μὴ οἴονται ἔνδηλοι εἶναι. οἱ γὰρ δεδιότες ἰδίᾳ τι βούλονται τὴν πόλιν ἐς ἔκπληξιν καθιστάναι, ὅπως τῷ κοινῷ φόβῳ τὸν σφέτερον ἐπηλυγάζωνται. καὶ νῦν αὗται **αἱ ἀγγελίαι** τοῦτο δύνανται· οὐκ ἀπὸ ταὐτομάτου, ἐκ δὲ ἀνδρῶν οἵπερ αἰεὶ τάδε κινοῦσι ξύγκεινται.'

> 'As to the Athenians, whoever does not wish them to be so ill witted as to come here and fall into our hands, is either a coward or not loyal to the state; as to the men, however, who report such news and fill you with fear, I do not wonder at their audacity so much as at their simplicity, if they fancy we do not see through them. For men who have some private grounds of fear wish to plunge the city into consternation, in order that in the common fear their own may be overshadowed. So now this is the meaning of **this news**, which is not spontaneous, but have been concocted by men who are always stirring up trouble here.'

Athenagoras utters the verb ἀγγέλλω (ἀγγέλλοντας) to make mention of news that he considers false. This news — αὗται αἱ ἀγγελίαι — is the subject of δύναμαι and despite being an inanimate entity, the speaker is attributing to them the ability to fill people with panic through those who are spreading them. The news will turn out to be true this time. However, as we will see in the corresponding chapter, the spread of manipulating news (and the allusion made by means of the derivatives of ἄγγελος) is a resource frequently used in times of war.

The example (28) follows the excerpt given in (27), and ἀγγελία is the complement of the verb ἀπαλλάττω. Athenagoras accuses the Syracusans — especially Hermocrates — of wanting to instill panic and advises them to ride roughshod over:

(28) Thuc. 6.40.1

> καὶ **τῶν τοιῶνδε ἀγγελιῶν** ὡς πρὸς αἰσθανομένους καὶ μὴ ἐπιτρέψοντας ἀπαλλάγητε.

> 'So have done with such **reports**, understanding that you are dealing with men who are aware of your designs and will not put up with them.'

Finally, we should mention those contexts in which ἀγγελία displays uses as a non-inherent complement. It always appears in a prepositional phrase: μετά + accusative (Hdt. 5.92 η15: μετὰ τὴν ἀγγελίην),[57] κατά + accusative (Thuc. 3.110.1:

---

[57] It is not a piece of news, but a response.

κατὰ τὴν πρώτην ἐκ τῶν Ὀλπῶν ἀγγελίαν),[58] πρός + accusative (Thuc. 6.40.2: πρὸς τὰς ὑμετέρας ἀγγελίας)[59] or ἅμα + dative, as in (29). Tissaphernes, who is planning treachery after the death of Cyrus, meets with the Spartan Clearchus and reminds him of his past actions:

(29) Xen., *An.* 2.3.19

> ταῦτα δὲ γνοὺς ᾐτούμην βασιλέα, λέγων αὐτῷ ὅτι δικαίως ἄν μοι χαρίζοιτο, ὅτι αὐτῷ Κῦρόν τε ἐπιστρατεύοντα πρῶτος[60] ἤγγειλα καὶ βοήθειαν ἔχων **ἅμα τῇ ἀγγελίᾳ** ἀφικόμην.

> After reaching this conclusion I present my request to the King, saying to him that it would be fair for him to do me a favour, because I was the first to report to him that Cyrus was marching against him and because **along with the piece of news** I brought him aid also.

I have left for the end a passage that deserves, in my opinion, special mention as a matter of interest. Philippides, a professional Athenian running courier, was sent to ask Sparta for help when the Persians landed at Marathon. According to him, the god went forth to meet him near Mount Parthenion and commissioned him to ask the Athenians why they did not care about him. The term with which Herodotus refers to Pan's message is ἀγγελία (ἀπὸ ταύτης τῆς ἀγγελίης), but Philippides is also mentioned by Lucian in *Pro lapsu inter salutandum*. The author reflects on greeting with χαίρειν and alludes to Philippides as the man in charge of transmitting a crucial piece of news, the victory in the Battle of Marathon:

(30) Luc., *Laps.* 3.1

> Πρῶτος δ' αὐτὸ Φιλιππίδης ὁ ἡμεροδρομήσας λέγεται ἀπὸ Μαραθῶνος ἀγγέλλων τὴν νίκην εἰπεῖν πρὸς τοὺς ἄρχοντας καθημένους καὶ πεφροντικότας ὑπὲρ τοῦ τέλους τῆς μάχης, Χαίρετε, νικῶμεν, καὶ τοῦτο εἰπὼν συναποθανεῖν **τῇ ἀγγελίᾳ** καὶ τῷ χαίρειν συνεκπνεῦσαι.

> The modern use of the word dates back to Philippides, the dispatch-runner. Bringing the news of Marathon, he found the archons seated, in suspense regarding the issue of the battle. 'Joy, we win!' he said, and died upon **his piece of news**, breathing his last in the word Joy.[61]

---

58 A message to ask for help.
59 Again, this is the news about the Athenians' intentions to take Syracuse.
60 Note Tissaphernes' interest in making it clear that he was the first (πρῶτος) to report the news. This is reminiscent of tragic ἄγγελοι.
61 This translation is borrowed from Loeb's Classical Library (Fowler).

Ἀπαγγελία, the term that will allow us to later differentiate epic from tragedy in his *Poetics*[62] is documented only once in Thucydides when he hints at the need for brief accounts of events when delivering a speech: "If the facts are good, a short narration of them (βραχεῖα ἡ ἀπαγγελία) will serve the turn".[63]

Ἐξαγγελία also occurs only once, in *Cyropaedia*. The Persians prepare the expedition against the Armenians and Cyrus requests that the general Chrysantas head towards the mountains where the Armenian king usually takes refuge when he senses danger. Cyrus makes the following recommendation to Chrysantas:

(31) Xen., *Cyr.* 2.4.23

φασὶ μὲν οὖν καὶ δασέα τὰ ὄρη ταῦτα εἶναι, ὥστ' ἐλπὶς ὑμᾶς μὴ ὀφθῆναι· ὅμως δὲ εἰ προπέμποις πρὸ τοῦ στρατεύματος εὐζώνους ἄνδρας λῃσταῖς ἐοικότας καὶ τὸ πλῆθος καὶ τὰς στολάς, οὗτοι ἄν σοι, εἴ τινι ἐντυγχάνοιεν τῶν Ἀρμενίων, τοὺς μὲν ἂν συλλαμβάνοντες αὐτῶν κωλύοιεν **τῶν ἐξαγγελιῶν**, οὓς δὲ μὴ δύναιντο λαμβάνειν, ἀποσοβοῦντες ἂν ἐμποδὼν γίγνοιντο τοῦ μὴ ὁρᾶν αὐτοὺς τὸ ὅλον στράτευμά σου, ἀλλ' ὡς περὶ κλωπῶν βουλεύεσθαι.

'Now they say that these mountains are thickly wooded, and so I have hopes of your not being seen. Nevertheless, suppose you send ahead of your army some active men, in the guise of brigands both as to numbers and accoutrements; these, if they met any Armenians, would capture them and so prevent their spreading **any reports**; or, if they failed to capture them, they would frighten them away and so prevent their seeing the whole of your army, and would thus cause them to take precautions as against only a band of thieves.'

Dictionaries define ἐξαγγελία as 'secret information sent out to the enemy',[64] which fits perfectly in contexts such as those that concern this study, which are mostly warlike. Ἐξαγγελία is, therefore, another of the derivatives of ἄγγελος that make up a specific military terminology.

Let us now pay attention to παραγγελία, one of the terms that designate the order in military contexts. However, in the only passage in which it occurs, it is only likely to be interpreted as a public announcement or as response:[65]

---

[62] Cf. Arist., *Poet.* 1454b. On this passage, see Rhodes (1994, 227): "A short report. Defending the short question (52.4) to which the Plataeans objected (52.5–53.2)". For the function of this noun in the speeches of Greek orators, see the next chapter.
[63] Thuc. 7.67.3.
[64] Cf. Bailly and *LSJ*.
[65] See Sturz (1964).

(32) Xen., *Hell.* 2.1.4

> θορύβου δὲ γενομένου καὶ ἐρωτώντων τινῶν διὰ τί ἀπέθανεν ὁ ἄνθρωπος, παραγγέλλειν ἐκέλευεν ὁ Ἐτεόνικος, ὅτι τὸν κάλαμον εἶχε. Κατὰ δὲ **τὴν παραγγελίαν** ἐρρίπτουν πάντες ὅσοι εἶχον τοὺς καλάμους, ἀεὶ ὁ ἀκούων δεδιὼς μὴ ὀφθείη ἔχων.
> And when an uproar resulted and people asked why the man had been put to death, Eteonicus ordered his followers to give out word that it was because he had the reed. As a result of **this announcement** all those who were carrying reeds threw them away, each man as he heard the report being afraid that he might be seen with one.

Xenophon is the first to use παραγγέλλω, a military technicism to refer to the transmission of orders. In this passage, however, the order is not expressed by means of παραγγέλλω, but with ἐκέλευεν. From this we can deduce that παραγγέλλω refers to the reason why the blind citizen died. Thus, παραγγελία is not linked to a command, as suggested in *LSJ*.

It should be noted that Xenophon also documents the noun ψευδαγγελία (false report). It appears only once in a passage (Xen., *Eq. mag.* 5.8) which will be discussed in the chapter about *fake news*.

Furthermore, εὐαγγέλιον, which is only documented before now in the authors of our corpus in the *Odyssey* and in Aristophanic comedy, appears twice in the *Hellenica*. I will also present both passages in the last chapter of this volume, since in both cases news is manipulated.

Two concerns arise from the study of the verbs derived from ἄγγελος. On the one hand, the presence of up to six new verbs in addition to ἀγγέλλω, ἀναγγέλλω, ἀπαγγέλλω, διαγγέλλω, εἰσαγγέλλω, ἐξαγγέλλω, ἐπαγγέλλω and παραγγέλλω (present in previously examined authors): three other verbs derived from ἀγγέλλω (καταγγέλλω, περιαγγέλλω, προαγγέλλω), another from παραγγέλλω (ἀντιπαραγγέλλω), another from ἀπαγγέλλω (προσαπαγγέλλω) and another from περιαγγέλλω (προσπεριαγγέλλω) are documented. Besides, the noun ἄγγελμα, as well as παράγγελμα, παράγγελσις and προάγγελσις occur. Some of them — as will be illustrated throughout this chapter — become consolidated as military technical terms. Nonetheless, all are used at some point to refer to news.

On the other hand, although — as highlighted above — both the ἄγγελος and the κῆρυξ have some importance in the transmission of news (due, above all, to the role they play as mediators in diplomatic tasks), the truth is that news is not inextricably associated with them. Unlike in Greek tragedy and in Aristophanic comedy, where the subject of ἀγγέλλω is almost always the ἄγγελος himself, in the works of historians, like in Homer, anyone can be that subject. Strong evidence of this can be found in the fact that the identity of the person in charge of transmitting the news tends to remain unknown. We are simply told that someone (τις) reports (ἀγγέλλει, ἐξαγγέλλει, etc.) something or, much more frequently than in the texts of the authors previously studied, these verbs appear in the middle voice (ἀγγέλλεται, etc.) or in the passive voice (ἠγγέλθη, ἐξηγγέλθη, etc.) without the passive agent being expressed.

The main reason for this is the genre itself. Greek historiography, born in the heat of political events, does not have the same needs as tragedy — a show aimed at a very large audience gathered for a solemn occasion (Romilly 1970, 13). Herodotus, Thucydides and Xenophon did not face the same difficulties as tragic poets. Historians did not have to introduce information necessary for the development of the action that, for the aforementioned reasons, could not be staged. They did not need to create a character to transmit the news. The most important thing in the works of historians is for the news to be transmitted, whoever the person doing it is, and the fact that the news reaches its addressee is paramount. And, as we shall see in what follows, news spreads successfully.

There are 94 instances of ἀγγέλλω in the works of historians (24 in Herodotus, 43 in Thucydides and 27 in Xenophon). Like many other derivatives of ἄγγελος, it is a military term used to refer to orders but also to the news announced (nearly always) in war.

The expected construction of ἀγγέλλω with a direct object in the accusative and an indirect object in the dative is more common in Herodotus (six examples)[66] than in Thucydides and Xenophon (just one in each).

In (33), the piece of news is the death of Ayis, one of the sons of Croesus. His father had had a dream in which Atys would be killed by an iron spearhead. Although Atys was the leader of the Lydian troops, because of his dream his father did not let him return to his position and got rid of his weapons to avoid misfortune. According to Herodotus, however, a huge wild boar began to ravage the fields of Mysia and Atys begged and managed to convince Croesus to let him take part in the hunt organized to kill the boar. In this way Croesus' dream came true: Atys was killed by a spear thrown by Adrastus, whom Croesus had sent as one of his bodyguards.

(33) Hdt. 1.43.3

> ἔθεε δέ τις **ἀγγελέων** τῷ Κροίσῳ τὸ γεγονός, ἀπικόμενος δὲ ἐς τὰς Σάρδις τήν τε μάχην καὶ τὸν τοῦ παιδὸς μόρον ἐσήμηνέ οἱ. Ὁ δὲ Κροῖσος τῷ θανάτῳ τοῦ παιδὸς συντεταραγμένος μᾶλλόν τι ἐδεινολογέετο ὅτι μιν ἀπέκτεινε τὸν αὐτὸς φόνου ἐκάθηρε.

---

[66] In addition to the excerpts given in this paragraph, see the examples (8) and (9) and also Hdt. 3.140.2 or Hdt. 4.128.1.

One ran **to tell** Croesus what had happened and coming to Sardis told the king of the fight and the fate of his son. Distraught by the death of his son, Croesus cried out the more vehemently because the killer was one whom he himself had cleansed of blood.

In the *Cyropaedia*, Xenophon explains that in military campaigns it is customary to send scouts in advance to survey the land and inform the army of the situation:[67]

(34) Xen., *Cyr.* 6.3.5–6

Ὡς δ' οἱ προϊόντες σκοποὶ ἔδοξαν ἐν τῷ πεδίῳ ὁρᾶν ἀνθρώπους λαμβάνοντας καὶ χιλὸν καὶ ξύλα, καὶ ὑποζύγια δὲ ἑώρων ἕτερα τοιαῦτα ἄγοντα, τὰ δὲ καὶ νεμόμενα, καὶ τὰ πρόσω αὖ ἀφορῶντες ἐδόκουν καταμανθάνειν μετεωριζόμενον ἢ καπνὸν ἢ κονιορτόν, ἐκ τούτων πάντων σχεδὸν ἐγίγνωσκον ὅτι εἴη που πλησίον τὸ στράτευμα τῶν πολεμίων. εὐθὺς οὖν πέμπει τινὰ ὁ σκόπαρχος **ἀγγελοῦντα** ταῦτα τῷ Κύρῳ.

Now the scouts who went forward thought they saw men getting fodder and fuel on the plain; and they also saw beasts of burden, some loaded with other supplies of that sort and others grazing. Then, as they looked further on into the distance, they thought that they detected smoke or a cloud of dust rising up. From all these evidences they pretty well recognised that the army of the enemy was somewhere in the neighbourhood. Accordingly, the officer in command of the scouts at once sent a man **to report the news** to Cyrus.

When the third syntactic argument of ἀγγέλλω — the dative (recipient) — is omitted it is common for the result to be expressed by means of a neuter in the plural referring to something previously mentioned[68] and even more likely by an accusative with inanimate referent,[69] as in (35). The Persians are informed that, after their victory at Thermopylae, the Greeks have undertaken the retreat:[70]

---

67 Cf. also Xen., *An.* 1.7.13.
68 Cf. Thuc. 6.36.1 (τοιαῦτα) or Thuc. 7.17.3 (τὰ ἐν τῇ Σικελίᾳ).
69 Cf. also Thuc. 2.85.4: τήν τε παρασκευήν (the enemy's preparation), Thuc. 3.3.5: τὸν ἐπίπλουν (the coming of the fleet), Thuc. 7.25.9: τήν τε τοῦ Πλημμυρίου λῆψιν (the conquest of Plemmyrium), Thuc. 7.43.4: τὴν ἔφοδον (the enemy's approach) and Xen., *Hell.* 6.4.16: τὸ πάθος (the calamity).
70 According to Herodotus, the Persians, incredulous, kept the man who announced this news under close surveillance (Οἱ δ' ὑπ' ἀπιστίης τὸν μὲν ἀγγέλλοντα εἶχον ἐν φυλακῇ) and dispatched ships to verify it. Soon after, the same news was reported by the crew of these ships (Ἀπαγγειλάντων δὲ τούτων).

(35) Hdt. 8.23.1

Τοῖσι δὲ βαρβάροισι αὐτίκα μετὰ ταῦτα πλοίῳ ἦλθε ἀνὴρ Ἱστιαιεὺς **ἀγγέλλων** τὸν δρησμὸν τὸν ἀπ' Ἀρτεμισίου τῶν Ἑλλήνων.

Immediately after this there came to the barbarians a man of Histiaea in a boat, **telling** them of the flight of the Greeks from Artemisium.

On two occasions, the result is expressed by two elements connected by καί. The first is an accusative and the second a ὅτι substantive clause. In one of the passages — seen in (13) — the herald Demoteles must announce (ἀγγελοῦντα) the greatness of the victory (τῆς τε νίκης τὸ μέγεθος) and that not one Lacedaemonian has fallen, but many enemies (ὅτι Λακεδαιμονίων μὲν οὐδὲ εἷς τεθναίη, τῶν δὲ πολεμίων παμπλήθεις). In (36) the one who receives the news is Demosthenes:

(36) Thuc. 7.31.3

ὄντι δ' αὐτῷ περὶ ταῦτα ὁ Εὐρυμέδων ἀπαντᾷ ἐκ τῆς Σικελίας ἀποπλέων, ὃς τότε τοῦ χειμῶνος τὰ χρήματα ἄγων τῇ στρατιᾷ ἀπεπέμφθη, καὶ **ἀγγέλλει** τά τε ἄλλα καὶ ὅτι πύθοιτο κατὰ πλοῦν ἤδη ὢν τὸ Πλημμύριον ὑπὸ τῶν Συρακοσίων ἑαλωκός.

While he was attending to these matters, he was met by Eurymedon, who was returning from Sicily, whither he had been sent during the preceding winter with the money for the army; and **he reported**, among other things, that when he was already on his return voyage he had heard of the capture of Plemmyrium by the Syracusans.

In other passages only the syntactic argument in the dative (recipient) is explicitly referred to.[71] The argument in the accusative is omitted but can easily be recovered from context, as we see in the curious story that Herodotus heard about Aristeas of Proconnesus:[72]

(37) Hdt. 4.14.1

Ἀριστέην γὰρ λέγουσι, ἐόντα τῶν ἀστῶν οὐδενὸς γένος ὑποδεέστερον, ἐσελθόντα ἐς κναφήιον ἐν Προκοννήσῳ ἀποθανεῖν, καὶ τὸν κναφέα κατακληίσαντα τὸ ἐργαστήριον οἴχεσθαι **ἀγγελέοντα** τοῖσι προσήκουσι τῷ νεκρῷ.

---

71 Cf. also Hdt. 1.22.1, Hdt. 8.21.1, Hdt. 8.80.1, Thuc. 6.65.3 and Xen., *An.* 1.3.21.
72 Pausanias also mentions that Aristeas (cf. *Paus.* 1.24.6). On this character, see Phillips (1955) and Bolton (1962).

It is said that this Aristeas, who was as well-born as any of his townsfolk, went into a fuller's shop at Proconnesus and there died; the owner shut his shop and went away **to report** the dead to Aristeas' relatives.

In (38) ἀγγέλλω is in the passive voice and is only accompanied by the complement in the dative.[73] The news is about the enemy:[74]

(38) Thuc. 8.100.4

προαφιγμένος δὲ αὐτόσε ἦν καὶ ὁ Θρασύβουλος πέντε ναυσὶν ἐκ τῆς Σάμου, ὡς **ἠγγέλθη** αὐτοῖς ἡ τῶν φυγάδων αὕτη διάβασις.

Thrasybulus also had already arrived there from Samos with five ships, after **the news had been brought** to him of the crossing of the exiles.

On one occasion — seen in (39) —, ἀγγέλλω displays a construction with an infinitive and a third syntactic argument in the dative. Demosthenes needs reinforcements in the Battle of Pylos:

(39) Thuc. 4.8.3

Δημοσθένης δὲ προσπλεόντων ἔτι τῶν Πελοποννησίων ὑπεκπέμπει φθάσας δύο ναῦς **ἀγγεῖλαι** Εὐρυμέδοντι καὶ τοῖς ἐν ταῖς ναυσὶν ἐν Ζακύνθῳ Ἀθηναίοις παρεῖναι ὡς τοῦ χωρίου κινδυνεύοντος.

But before the Peloponnesian fleet had yet reached Pylos, Demosthenes managed to send out secretly ahead of them two ships which were **to order** Eurymedon and the Athenian fleet at Zacynthus to come at once to his aid, as the place was in danger.

As we have already demonstrated, in contexts like this the announcement inherent to the verb ἀγγέλλω is not a piece of news but an order.

Ἀγγέλλω appears frequently in the works of the three historians with a ὅτι substantive clause (result) and a complement in the dative (recipient), as in (40):

(40) Xen., *Ages.* 2.11

κἀνταῦθα οἱ μέν τινες τῶν ξένων ἐστεφάνουν ἤδη τὸν Ἀγησίλαον, **ἀγγέλλει** δέ τις αὐτῷ ὅτι Θηβαῖοι τοὺς Ὀρχομενίους διακόψαντες ἐν τοῖς σκευοφόροις εἰσί.

---

73 Cf. also Thuc. 2.6.1, Thuc. 6.65.3, Thuc. 8.94.3 and Xen., *Hell.* 2.1.20 (in the middle voice).
74 In Hdt. 6.69.4–5 the piece of news has nothing to do with war, since it is about the birth of Demaratus, king of Sparta. In Thuc. 6.58.1 the news is about the murder of Hipparchus at the hands of Harmodius and Aristogeiton.

And now some of the mercenaries were in the act of crowning Agesilaus with a wreath, when a man **reported** to him that the Thebans had cut their way through the Orchomenians and were among the baggage train.

In more than 75% of cases, the verb occurs in the middle[75] or passive voice,[76] as in (41), where the verb takes the dative and three ὅτι clauses connected with καί (subject):

(41) Thuc. 1.114.1

Μετὰ δὲ ταῦτα οὐ πολλῷ ὕστερον Εὔβοια ἀπέστη ἀπὸ Ἀθηναίων, καὶ ἐς αὐτὴν διαβεβηκότος ἤδη Περικλέους στρατιᾷ Ἀθηναίων **ἠγγέλθη** αὐτῷ ὅτι Μέγαρα ἀφέστηκε καὶ Πελοποννήσιοι μέλλουσιν ἐσβαλεῖν ἐς τὴν Ἀττικὴν καὶ οἱ φρουροὶ Ἀθηναίων διεφθαρμένοι εἰσὶν ὑπὸ Μεγαρέων, πλὴν ὅσοι ἐς Νίσαιαν ἀπέφυγον·

No longer after this Euboea revolted from Athens; and Pericles had just crossed over to the island with an Athenian army when **word was brought** to him that Megara had revolted, that the Peloponnesians were about to invade Attica, and that all the Athenian garrison had been destroyed by the Megarians except such as had escaped to Nisaea.

The construction of ἀγγέλλω with the ὅτι substantive clause only is also very common. With respect to this, in 70% of the examples ἀγγέλλω occurs in the active voice and the identity of the person who transmit the news is known, as in (42):[77]

(42) Thuc. 8.108.1

Κατέπλευσε δὲ ὑπὸ τοὺς αὐτοὺς χρόνους τούτους καὶ ὁ Ἀλκιβιάδης ταῖς τρισὶ καὶ δέκα ναυσὶν ἀπὸ τῆς Καύνου καὶ Φασήλιδος ἐς τὴν Σάμον, **ἀγγέλλων** ὅτι τάς τε Φοινίσσας ναῦς ἀποστρέψειε Πελοποννησίοις ὥστε μὴ ἐλθεῖν καὶ τὸν Τισσαφέρνην ὅτι φίλον πεποιήκοι μᾶλλον Ἀθηναίοις ἢ πρότερον.

At about this same time Alcibiades sailed back to Samos with the thirteen ships from Caunus and Phaselis, **reporting** that he had prevented the coming of the Phoenician ships to join the Peloponnesians and that he had made Tissaphernes more friendly to the Athenians than before.

---

75 Cf. Hdt. 9.69.1, Thuc. 5.10.2 and Thuc. 6.45.1.
76 Cf. also Thuc. 2.6.3, Thuc. 4.93.2, Thuc. 8.11.3, Xen., *Hell.* 1.1.27 and Xen., *Hell.* 4.3.18.
77 Cf. also Thuc. 6.46.1, Thuc. 7.31.4, Xen., *Hell.* 2.2.18, Xen., *Hell.* 4.3.1 and Xen., *Hell.* 4.5.8.

On the contrary, the verb does not appear very often in the passive voice. In these cases, the bearer of the news is almost never mentioned:[78]

(43) Thuc. 4.125.1

> καὶ ἐν τούτῳ διαφερομένων αὐτῶν **ἠγγέλθη** ὅτι οἱ Ἰλλυριοὶ μετ' Ἀρραβαίου προδόντες Περδίκκαν γεγένηνται·
>
> Meanwhile, as they were disputing, **it was announced** that the Illyrians had betrayed Perdiccas and taken sides with Arrhabaeus.

This construction of ἀγγέλλω alternates with those in which the verb is accompanied by a ὡς substantive clause[79] (44), by an AcI (45) or an AcP (46) construction. In (44) Herodotus tells the story of Psammetichus, who asked the oracle of Leto at Buto if there was any way to take revenge on those who had banished him. The answer was negative and surprising, since the oracle said that revenge would arrive by sea in the form of bronze men. Psammetichus, in disbelief, could not understand how this situation could occur. However, shortly afterwards, some Carians and some Ionians who were looking for loot landed in Egypt in their bronze armour:

(44) Hdt. 2.152.4

> ἐκβάντας δὲ ἐς γῆν καὶ ὁπλισθέντας χαλκῷ **ἀγγέλλει** τῶν τις Αἰγυπτίων ἐς τὰ ἕλεα ἀπικόμενος τῷ Ψαμμητίχῳ, ὡς οὐκ ἰδὼν πρότερον χαλκῷ ἄνδρας ὁπλισθέντας, ὡς χάλκεοι ἄνδρες ἀπιγμένοι ἀπὸ θαλάσσης λεηλατέουσι τὸ πεδίον.
>
> And when they disembarked in their armour of bronze, an Egyptian came into the marsh country and **brought news** to Psammetichus (for he had never seen armoured men) that men of bronze had come from the sea and were foraging in the plain.

In (45) we also find the noun ἀγγελία. However, in this context it does not refer to a piece of news, but to a request for help made by the Ambraciots, previously mentioned by Thucydides (Thuc. 3.105.4):

---

78 Cf. also Xen., *Hell.* 4.3.10 and Xen., *Hell.* 6.4.21.
79 Also ἀγγέλλω + ὡς substantive clause and the dative recipient omitted. Cf. Hdt. 3.30.2. and Hdt. 3.65.2.

(45) Thuc. 3.110.1

τῷ δὲ Δημοσθένει[80] καὶ τοῖς Ἀκαρνᾶσιν **ἀγγέλλεται** τοὺς Ἀμπρακιώτας τοὺς ἐκ τῆς πόλεως πανδημεὶ κατὰ τὴν πρώτην ἐκ τῶν Ὀλπῶν ἀγγελίαν ἐπιβοηθεῖν διὰ τῶν Ἀμφιλόχων.

Word was now brought to Demosthenes and the Acarnanians that the inhabitants of the city of Ambracia, in response to the first message that came from Olpae, were marching in full force through the Amphilochian territory.

Let us now examine the following excerpt from the beginning of a speech with which Cyrus intends to encourage the troops, who were frightened after hearing the news about their enemies (ἐπεὶ αἱ ἀγγελίαι ἦλθον ἐκ τῶν πολεμίων).[81] To raise the troops' spirits, Cyrus gives a fierce speech and appeals to the soldiers' pride with this rhetorical question:

(46) Xen., *Cyr.* 6.2.15

ὦ πρὸς θεῶν, ἔφη, τί δῆτα ἂν ἐποιήσατε οἱ νῦν δεδοικότες, εἰ **ἤγγελλόν** τινες τὰ παρ' ἡμῖν νῦν ὄντα ταῦτα ἀντίπαλα ἡμῖν προσιόντα (...).[82]

'What in the name of heaven, pray, would you who are now afraid have done, if the situation were reversed and someone **told** you that these forces that we have now were coming against us?'

Finally, I offer below an example in which ἀγγέλλω displays an absolute use. Teleutias has attacked the Piraeus and Xenophon has just referred all the actions he is carrying out. This is what happens next:[83]

---

[80] Cf. also Thuc. 8.26.1. Without the dative, cf. Hdt. 8.50.1 and Thuc. 1.91.3.
[81] In the preparations for the Battle of Sardis, Cyrus sent two spies to seek information from the enemies. On their return, they announced that Croesus had been appointed general of all the adversaries' troops and that the allied kings had made the decision to go to war with all their armies. They also reported that 120,000 armed Egyptians and a Cypriot army had arrived by sea and, in addition to some other movements made by Croesus, he had sent messengers to Sparta to try to make an alliance. In the face of such news Cyrus' soldiers could not help but panic.
[82] The recipient in the dative is omitted. The only documented example of ἀγγέλλω + AcP + dative is in Xen., *An.* 2.3.19, shown in the example (29) of this chapter.
[83] Cf. also Hdt. 3.126. 2, Hdt. 8.23.1, Hdt. 8.80.2, Thuc. 4.27.4, Thuc. 6.36.3, Thuc. 7.8.1, Xen., *Cyr.* 4.2.28 or Xen., *Hell.* 4.3.13.

(47) Xen., *Hell.* 5.1.22

ὧν δὲ Ἀθηναίων οἱ μὲν αἰσθόμενοι ἔνδοθεν ἔθεον ἔξω, σκεψόμενοι τίς ἡ κραυγή, ἱ δὲ ἔξωθεν οἴκαδε ἐπὶ τὰ ὅπλα, οἱ δὲ καὶ εἰς ἄστυ **ἀγγελοῦντες**

But as for the Athenians, some of them, upon hearing the uproar, ran from their houses into the streets to see what the shouting meant, others ran from the streets to their homes to get their weapons, and still others to the city to carry the news.

The verb ἀναγγέλλω is not documented in Herodotus, but it does appear in Thucydides (twice) and Xenophon (once).[84] The following excerpt contains an example of the expected construction of ἀναγγέλλω with the accusative and the dative. At the beginning of the ninth year of the Peloponnesian War, the Lacedaemonians and Athenians arranged an armistice for one year. Some ambassadors who had been present at the negotiations were to inform Brasidas:

(48) Thuc. 4.122.2

καὶ ἡ μὲν στρατιὰ πάλιν διέβη ἐς Τορώνην, οἱ δὲ τῷ Βρασίδᾳ **ἀνήγγελλον** τὴν ξυνθήκην, καὶ ἐδέξαντο πάντες οἱ ἐπὶ Θρᾴκης ξύμμαχοι Λακεδαιμονίων τὰ πεπραγμένα.

Whereupon his army crossed back to Torone, and the messengers formally **announced** the agreement to Brasidas, and all the Thracian allies of the Lacedaemonians acquiesced to what had been done.

Bailly and *LSJ* translate the verb in this passage as 'carry back tidings of', and this is also Classen's proposal (1966).[85]

In (49) the news has nothing to do with war but with gossip. According to Xenophon's account, Agesilaus fell in love with a certain Megabates, but he stopped the latter from kissing him. This is how Xenophon refers to this anecdote:

(49) Xen., *Ages.* 5.6.7

Ἀγησίλαον δέ τι πράξαντα μὲν τοιοῦτον οὔτε ἰδὼν πώποτε οὐδεὶς **ἀνήγγειλεν** οὔτε εἰκάζων πιστὰ ἂν ἔδοξε λέγειν. καὶ γὰρ εἰς οἰκίαν μὲν οὐδεμίαν ἰδίᾳ ἐν ἀποδημίᾳ κατήγετο, ἀεὶ δὲ ἦν ἢ ἐν ἱερῷ, ἔνθα δὴ ἀδύνατον τὰ τοιαῦτα πράττειν, ἢ ἐν φανερῷ, μάρτυρας τοὺς πάντων ὀφθαλμοὺς τῆς σωφροσύνης ποιούμενος.

---

[84] Up to now only Aeschylus has offered examples of ἀναγγέλλω.
[85] On this passage see also Graves (1884) or Mills (1909, 143).

We know too that no one ever **reported** that he had seen Agesilaus do any such thing, and that no scandal based on conjecture would have gained credence; for it was not his habit, when abroad, to lodge apart in a private house, but he was always either in a temple, where conduct of this sort is, of course, impossible, or else in a public place where all men's eyes became witnesses of his rectitude.

The last example — with ἀναγγέλλω in an absolute use — refers to Themistocles, who decided to go to Sparta and deceive the Lacedaemonians. Firstly, he asked them to ignore the rumours regarding the rebuilding of the walls of Athens. Then he lied and finally gave them this advice:

(50) Thuc. 1.91.2

γνοὺς δὲ ἐκεῖνος κελεύει αὐτοὺς μὴ λόγοις μᾶλλον παράγεσθαι ἢ πέμψαι σφῶν αὐτῶν ἄνδρας οἵτινες χρηστοὶ καὶ πιστῶς **ἀναγγελοῦσι** σκεψάμενοι.

When he (Themistocles) perceived this he bade them not to be misled by reports, but rather to send some trustworthy men of their own number who would see for themselves and **bring back a** faithful **report**.

Let us now examine the verb ἀπαγγέλλω and the derivative προσαπαγγέλλω. There are 123 instances of ἀπαγγέλλω in the works of historians: 22 in Herodotus, 19 in Thucydides and 82 in Xenophon, who also uses προσαπαγγέλλω (although only once). Ἀπαγγέλλω has a particular feature in these texts: in 95% of the examples the context in which it appears is an embassy and ambassadors, messengers or heralds have been sent to carry out diplomatic tasks. Given this circumstance, the announcement (always public) inherent to ἀπαγγέλλω is related to treaties of alliance, truces, the acceptance or rejection of proposals, requests for help from the allies in the face of the dangers of war, and so on. Therefore, a specialization of ἀπαγγέλλω in this sense should be noted.[86]

The foreseeable construction of ἀπαγγέλλω with a syntactic argument in the accusative (result) and another one in the dative (recipient)[87] turns out to be very productive in the works of historians. Most often the accusative is the neu-

---

86 For the few exceptions, cf. Xen., *An.* 1.6.5. and Xen., *An.* 1.7.2. As we shall see in the next chapter, specialization is consolidated in Greek oratory. Dictionaries make clear differences. Cf., e.g., *LSJ*: ἀπαγγέλλω: "Of a messenger, bring tidings, report, report in answer. Of a speaker or writer, report, relate".
87 The dative can alternate with a prepositional phrase. Cf., for example, Xen., *Hell.* 3.2.20 (εἰς Λακεδαίμονα and ἐπὶ βασιλέα). On some other occasions, as in Thuc. 4.122.4, both the result (περὶ αὐτῶν) and the recipient (ἐς τὰς Ἀθήνας) are expressed by prepositional phrases.

ter of the demonstrative pronouns in the plural (ταῦτα[88] or τάδε), as in (51), a passage that mentions an Indian embassy received by Cyrus. When the ambassadors came, they said that the king of India had sent them with orders to ask on what ground the Medes and Assyrians had declared war. Once he had heard the two versions, the king could decide which side he would support. Cyrus takes the floor and addresses the Indians:

(51) Xen., *Cyr.* 2.4.8

> Ὑμεῖς τοίνυν, ἔφη, **ἀπαγγείλατε** τῷ Ἰνδῶν βασιλεῖ τάδε, εἰ μή τι ἄλλο Κυαξάρῃ δοκεῖ, ὅτι φαμὲν ἡμεῖς, εἴ τί φησιν ὑφ' ἡμῶν ἀδικεῖσθαι ὁ Ἀσσύριος, αἱρεῖσθαι αὐτὸν τὸν Ἰνδῶν βασιλέα δικαστήν.
>
> 'Well then', said he, 'if Cyaxares has no objection, **tell** the king of India that we propose, in case the Assyrian says he has been wronged by us, to choose the king of India himself to be our arbitrator.'

It is also common for the dative (recipient) to be omitted and for the accusative to be ταῦτα[89] or a generic neuter in the plural.[90] It can also be a noun with inanimate referent,[91] however, as in Xen., *An.* 2.1.23, where the herald Phalinus asks: "Shall I report truce or war?" (Σπονδὰς ἢ πόλεμον ἀπαγγελῶ;) or in Hdt. 5.87.2, where a certain Phalerus makes his way to Athens and reports a misfortune (ἀπήγγελλε τὸ πάθος).[92]

In (52) the elided argument is the one in the accusative.[93] The announcement is linked to an oracle:

---

[88] Cf. also Hdt. 9.21.3, Xen., *An.* 1.4.13, Xen., *An.* 2.3.24, Xen., *An.* 7.1.34, Xen., *Cyr.* 3.3.56, Xen., *Cyr.* 6.2.19, Xen., *Hell.* 2.2.12, Xen., *Hell.* 5.1.32 and Xen., *Hell.* 5.4.33.
[89] Cf. Hdt. 3.25.1, Hdt. 3.53. 6, Xen., *An.* 1.4.12, Xen., *An.* 2.1.21, Xen., *Cyr.* 4.5.12 and Xen., *Hell.* 2.2.14.
[90] Cf. also Hdt. 8.23.1, Hdt. 8.80.1, Thuc. 3.4.1, Thuc. 5.46.4, Thuc. 7.8.2, Thuc. 8.74.1, Thuc. 8.89.1, Xen., *An.* 1.10.14, Xen., *An.* 2.5.27, Xen., *An.* 2.5.36, Xen., *Cyr.* 5.2.3, Xen., *Cyr.* 5.3.8, Xen., *Cyr.* 8.2.10, Xen., *Hell.* 2.1.29, Xen., *Hell.* 2.1.30, Xen., *Hell.* 4.3.2 and Xen., *Hell.* 7.1.37. Also τι (cf. Xen., *Hell.* 5.4.7).
[91] Cf. also Thuc. 1.29.4 (οὐδὲν εἰρηναῖον).
[92] A slaughter.
[93] See also Hdt. 1.78.2, Hdt. 3.123.2, Hdt. 4.151.3, Hdt. 6.105.2, Xen., *An.* 5.6.21, Xen., *An.* 7.3.1, Xen., *Cyr.* 8.6.16, Xen., *Cyr.* 8.7.28, Xen., *Hell.* 5.1.32, Xen., *Mem.* 1.2.33 and Xen., *Mem.* 1.2.38. The dative can also alternate with a prepositional phrase, as in Hdt 7.142.1, where Herodotus tells us that some θεοπρόποι (public messengers sent to enquire of an oracle) reported (ἀπήγγελλον) the oracle to the people (ἐς τὸν δῆμον). Cf. also Thuc. 5.37.1 (ἐπὶ τὰ κοινά) and Xen., *Hell.* 7.5.1 (πρός τε τὸ κοινὸν τῶν Ἀρκάδων).

(52) Hdt. 1.91.6

Ταῦτα μὲν ἡ Πυθίη ὑπεκρίνατο τοῖσι Λυδοῖσι, οἱ δὲ ἀνήνεικαν ἐς Σάρδις καὶ **ἀπήγγειλαν** Κροίσῳ.

This was the answer of the priestess to the Lydians. They carried it back to Sardis and **told** Croesus.

In (53), instead, the envoys are two Indian spies dispatched by Cyrus for the following purpose when he is preparing the Battle of Sardis:

(53) Xen., *Cyr.* 6.2.2

Κελεύω τοίνυν ὑμᾶς τοὺς μὲν ἄλλους μένοντας ἔνθα κατεσκηνώκατε φυλάττειν τὰ χρήματα καὶ ζῆν ὅπως ὑμῖν ἥδιστον· τρεῖς δέ μοι ἐλθόντες ὑμῶν ἐς τοὺς πολεμίους ὡς παρὰ τοῦ Ἰνδοῦ περὶ συμμαχίας, καὶ τὰ ἐκεῖ μαθόντες ὅ τι ἂν λέγωσί τε καὶ ποιῶσιν, ὡς τάχιστα **ἀπαγγείλατε** ἐμοί τε καὶ τῷ Ἰνδῷ·

'I ask some of you to remain where you have been assigned quarters and keep guard of this money and live as best pleases you, while three of you will please go to the enemy on pretence of having been sent by the king of India to make an alliance between them and him; and when you have learned how things stand there, what they are doing and proposing to do, **bring word of it** as soon as possible to me and to your king.'

Let us focus now on other cases in which the announcement inherent to the verb is expressed by a ὅτι — (54) and (55) — or a ὡς substantive clause (56). In (54) the news item is the death of Cyrus.[94] Clearchus addresses the generals in this way:

(54) Xen., *An.* 2.1.4

Ἀλλ' ὤφελε μὲν Κῦρος ζῆν· ἐπεὶ δὲ τετελεύτηκεν, **ἀπαγγέλλετε** Ἀριαίῳ ὅτι ἡμεῖς νικῶμέν τε βασιλέα καί, ὡς ὁρᾶτε, οὐδεὶς ἔτι ἡμῖν μάχεται.

'Well, would that Cyrus were alive! But since he is dead, **carry back word** to Ariaeus that, for our part, we have defeated the King, that we have no enemy left, as you see, to fight with.'

---

94 The dative is explicitly referred in this example and in (55). Xenophon is the historian in which this construction occurs the most. Cf. Xen., *An.* 2.3.5, Xen., *Cyr.* 5.2.4, Xen., *Cyr.* 6.2.1, *Cyr.* 6.2.19 (x2) and Xen., *Hell.* 5.4.21. The complement in the dative is omitted in Xen., *Hell.* 6.4.25. Xen., *An.* 1.10.15, Xen., *An.* 2.3.9., Xen., *An.* 4.5.20, Xen., *An.* 7.2.16, Xen., *Cyr.* 5.3.15, Xen., *Cyr.* 7.5.19, Xen., *Hell.* 2.2.17 and Xen., *Hell.* 5.3.25.

The example in (55) falls within the domain of the legal field. In the Battle of Arginusae, the Athenians lost twenty-five ships and a storm prevented them from recovering the corpses of the companions who were on board. On their return, six strategoi were brought to trial for failing to rescue the bodies. They defended themselves by blaming the storm, but when the Assembly was about to make a decision, the following occurred:

(55) Xen., *Hell.* 1.7.11

> παρῆλθε δέ τις εἰς τὴν ἐκκλησίαν φάσκων ἐπὶ τεύχους ἀλφίτων σωθῆναι· ἐπιστέλλειν δ' αὐτῷ τοὺς ἀπολλυμένους, ἐὰν σωθῇ, **ἀπαγγεῖλαι** τῷ δήμῳ ὅτι οἱ στρατηγοὶ οὐκ ἀνείλοντο τοὺς ἀρίστους ὑπὲρ τῆς πατρίδος γενομένους.
>
> And there came before the Assembly a man who said that he had been saved by floating upon a meal-tub, and that those who were perishing charged him **to report** to the people, if he were saved, that the generals did not pick up the men who had proved themselves most brave in the service of their country.

Thus, the strategoi were denounced by an eyewitness and convicted. According to MacDowell (1978, 187–188), although no ancient author calls it as such, the case closely resembles an *eisangelia* for treason (εἰσαγγελία), a legal procedure I will deal with in the next chapter. The public accusation is uttered by means of ἀπαγγέλλω, but the use of one of the derivatives of ἄγγελος in the context of a court does not occur only in this episode.

In the following pages, I will present other similar excerpts in which not only ἀπαγγέλλω but also other verbs of this family of words are uttered by someone who reports misconducts, both in a trial and publicly. We are facing, therefore, a case of denunciation and, as will be shown below, some derivatives of ἄγγελος (already coined as technical terms associated with the transmission of news) take on a special use in legal terminology.

In (56) the news announced has again to do with war:[95]

---

[95] In (55) the dative is elided. Cf. also Hdt. 3.64.1, Thuc. 8.86.3, Xen., *An.* 2.1.21 and Xen., *An.* 2.4.4. In these passages ἀπαγγέλλω always occurs in the active voice. The dative is expressed and ἀπαγγέλλω is in the active voice in Hdt. 5.20.4, Hdt. 8.143.2, Thuc. 3.24.3, Thuc. 8.6.4, Xen., *Ages.* 1.13, Xen., *Ages.* 8.3 and Xen., *Hell.* 3.4.11. In Xen., *Hell.* 7.1.38 the recipient is not expressed by the dative, but a prepositional phrase. The ὡς substantive clause is the subject of the verb in the passive voice in Xen., *Hell.* 6.4.7.

(56) Hdt. 4.153.1

Οἱ δὲ Θηραῖοι ἐπείτε τὸν Κορώβιον λιπόντες ἐν τῇ νήσῳ ἀπίκοντο ἐς τὴν Θήρην, **ἀπήγγελλον** ὥς σφι εἴη νῆσος ἐπὶ Λιβύῃ ἐκτισμένη.

As for the Theraeans, when they came to Thera after leaving Corobius on the island, they **brought word** that they had established a settlement on an island off Libya.

The presence of ἀπαγγέλλω in an absolute use is also very common in the works of Herodotus, Thucydides, and Xenophon.[96] The context of (57) is once again the imminent Athenian landing in Sicily. Remember that there are several speeches with different opinions on whether the news concerning that disembarkation were true or false. The first man to speak was Hermocrates:

(57) Thuc. 6.33.1

Ἄπιστα μὲν ἴσως, ὥσπερ καὶ ἄλλοι τινές, δόξω ὑμῖν περὶ τοῦ ἐπίπλου τῆς ἀληθείας λέγειν, καὶ γιγνώσκω ὅτι οἱ τὰ μὴ πιστὰ δοκοῦντα εἶναι ἢ λέγοντες ἢ **ἀπαγγέλλοντες** οὐ μόνον οὐ πείθουσιν, ἀλλὰ καὶ ἄφρονες δοκοῦσιν εἶναι.

'Possibly it will seem to you that what I and certain others say about the reality of the expedition against us is incredible, and I am aware that those who either make or **report news** that seem not credible not only do not carry conviction but are also regarded as foolish.'

Hermocrates then reveals the news he has heard: "The Athenians are coming against us with a great fleet army. They profess to be assisting their Egestaean allies and to be restoring the Leonties. But the truth is that they covet Sicily, and especially our city. They think that, if they can conquer us, they will easily conquer the rest".

Finally, the compound προσαπαγγέλλω[97] is documented once in Xenophon. The Lacedaemonians have just won in the Battle of Nemea and Agesilaus refers to the convenience of informing the allies:

(58) Xen., *Hell.* 4.3.2

Ἆρ' ἄν, ὦ Δερκυλίδα, ἐν καιρῷ γένοιτο, εἰ αἱ συμπέμπουσαι πόλεις ἡμῖν τοὺς στρατιώτας τὴν νίκην ὡς τάχιστα πύθοιντο; ἀπεκρίνατο δὴ ὁ Δερκυλίδας· Εὐθυμοτέρους γοῦν εἰκὸς

---

96 Cf. also Hdt. 2.121ε1, Thuc. 8.86.3, Xen., *Eq. Mag.* 4.8, Xen., *An.* 1.3.19, Xen., *An.* 2.3.9, Xen., *An.* 2.4.23, Xen., *An.* 7.1.4, Xen., *An.* 7.1.34, Xen., *An.* 7.2.36 and Xen., *Cyr.* 8.4.23.
97 Cf. *LSJ*: "announce besides". See also Sturz (1964): "praetera nunciare".

ταῦτ' ἀκούσαντας εἶναι. Οὐκοῦν σύ, ἐπεὶ παρεγένου, κάλλιστα ἂν **ἀπαγγείλαις**; ὁ δὲ ἄσμενος ἀκούσας, καὶ γὰρ ἀεὶ φιλαπόδημος ἦν, εἶπεν· Εἰ σὺ τάττοις. Ἀλλὰ τάττω, ἔφη, καὶ **προσαπαγγέλλειν** γε κελεύω ὅτι ἐὰν καὶ τάδε εὖ γένηται, πάλιν παρεσόμεθα, ὥσπερ καὶ ἔφαμεν.

'Would it not be advantageous, Dercylidas, if the cities which are sending their troops with us should learn of the victory as speedily as possible?'. Dercylidas replied: 'It is certainly likely that they would be in better spirits if they heard of this'. 'Then are not you the man who could **report** it best, since you were present at the battle?'. And Dercylidas, glad to hear this, for he was always fond of travel, replied: 'If you should so order'. 'Well, I do', said Agesilaus, 'and I bid you **announce**, further, that if the present undertaking also turns out well, we shall come back again, even as we said.'

Διαγγέλλω — documented so far in Pindar and Euripides — does not occur in Herodotus' *Histories*, but there are 10 instances in the works of Xenophon, and it does appear once in Thucydides. Διαγγέλλω is another verb from the analised family of words that refers to oracles. As shown in the chapter devoted to Greek tragedy, ἀγγέλλω[98] and ἀναγγέλλω[99] are also used with this purpose and this applies also to ἀπαγγέλλω[100] and ἐξαγγέλλω[101] in the works of historians.

The argument in the accusative (result) is only explicitly referred to in a passage from the *Apology of Socrates* and it is a generic neuter in the plural (τά) that alludes to the oracles: "Does not the very priestess who sits on the tripod at Delphi divulge (διαγγέλλει) the god's will through a 'voice'?".[102]

In (59) only the recipient in the dative appears.[103] Cyrus addresses some Assyrian soldiers taken prisoner by him to warn them he will retaliate if they rebel. After giving them the appropriate explanations, he says:

(59) Xen., *Cyr.* 4.4.12

ταῦτ' οὖν, ἔφη, αὐτοί τε ἴστε καὶ τοῖς ἄλλοις **διαγγέλλετε**.

'Accept these assurances for yourselves and **convey** them to the rest also.'

---

98 Cf. Eur., *Ion* 180.
99 Cf. Aesch., *PV.* 661.
100 Cf. Hdt. 1.91.6 (example (52) in this chapter).
101 Cf. example (69).
102 Cf. Xen., *Ap.* 91.
103 Cf. also Thuc. 7.73.4 and Xen., *An.* 2.3.7. In Xen., *An.* 7.1.14 the recipient is not expressed by the dative but by a prepositional phrase (εἰς τὸ στράτευμα).

Διαγγέλλω also displays uses with substantive clauses, as illustrated by the ὅτι clause[104] in (60), where the verb is involved in a harangue from Cyrus to the troops:

(60) Xen., *Cyr.* 6.2.20

> ἔπειτα δὲ **διαγγέλλεται** δήπου ὅτι αὐτοὶ μὲν οἱ πολέμιοι οὐχ ἱκανοὶ ἡγοῦνται ὑμῖν εἶναι μάχεσθαι, ἄλλους δὲ μισθοῦνται, ὡς ἄμεινον μαχουμένους ὑπὲρ σφῶν ἢ αὐτοί.
>
> 'And finally, you see, **the report is brought** that the enemy do not feel that they are strong enough to fight us by themselves but are hiring others in the hope that these will fight for them more valiantly than they can for themselves.'

Finally, we should make mention of διαγγέλλω in an absolute use. The example shown in (61) is the only one in which the verb appears in the middle voice. This use is mentioned in the lexicons as a military term to allude to the issue of commands.[105] The passage is about the movements of the Greek and Persian armies. The barbarians fear an attack in the middle of the night:

(61) Xen., *An.* 3.4.36

> ἐπεὶ δὲ ἐγίγνωσκον αὐτοὺς οἱ Ἕλληνες βουλομένους ἀπιέναι καὶ **διαγγελλομένους**, ἐκήρυξε[106] τοῖς Ἕλλησι συσκευάζεσθαι ἀκουόντων τῶν πολεμίων.
>
> When the Greeks became aware that they were desirous of withdrawing and **were passing the word along**, the order to pack up luggage was proclaimed to the Greek troops within hearing of the enemy.

When the verb is in the active voice the context provides us with the key to interpret the content of the announcement. In (62), for instance, we are told about a woman, Theodote. She was said to be so beautiful that her beauty could not be measured, and painters asked her again and again to show them her body to

---

104 There are no examples of ὡς substantive clauses or AcI constructions. With AcP + dative, only Xen., *An.* 1.6.2.
105 Cf. *LSJ*, *DGE*, Bailly and Sturz (1964). See also Boise (1870, 31): "διαγγελλομένους: that they were passing along the word". In Pindar and Euripides, it is always used in the active voice, and the same applies to the works of Thucydides and Xenophon, where it is only in the passive voice in Xen., *An.* 2.3.7 (a truce is announced). In the active voice and referring to orders, cf. Xen., *Cyr.* 8.3.19.
106 Note that, just like ἀγγέλλω, κηρύσσω can also be used as a verb of commanding when accompanied by a dative and an infinitive.

portray it. When Socrates himself verified it, he stated that if they spread the word, she could be highly favoured:[107]

(62) Xen., *Mem.* 3.11.3

> Οὐκοῦν, ἔφη, αὕτη μὲν ἤδη τε παρ' ἡμῶν ἔπαινον κερδαίνει καί, ἐπειδὰν εἰς πλείους **διαγγείλωμεν**, πλείω ὠφελήσεται.

> 'Well now', he went on, 'she already has our praise to her credit, and when **we spread the news**, she will profit yet more.'

Εἰσαγγέλλω — documented up to now only once in Euripides and twice in Aristophanes — occurs twice in Herodotus, 8 times Thucydides and 4 in Xenophon. This is perhaps one of the most interesting derivatives of ἄγγελος. In the works of historians, this verb is almost always linked to the transmission of news, although — as we will illustrate in the next chapter — it goes on to become specialized as a legal term. In fact, there is an example in Xenophon that indicates as much. Barely a year after Agesilaus seized power in Sparta, a man told him that someone was planning a conspiracy against him. Five days later, another man appeared before the ephors to confirm that the instigator of the plan was Cinadon:

(63) Xen., *Hell.* 3.3.5

> ἐρομένων δὲ τῶν ἐφόρων πῶς φαίη τὴν πρᾶξιν ἔσεσθαι, εἶπεν **ὁ εἰσαγγείλας** ὅτι ὁ Κινάδων ἀγαγὼν αὐτὸν ἐπὶ τὸ ἔσχατον τῆς ἀγορᾶς ἀριθμῆσαι κελεύοι ὁπόσοι εἶεν Σπαρτιᾶται ἐν τῇ ἀγορᾷ. καὶ ἐγώ, ἔφη, ἀριθμήσας βασιλέα τε καὶ ἐφόρους καὶ γέροντας καὶ ἄλλους ὡς τετταράκοντα, ἠρόμην· Τί δή με τούτους, ὦ Κινάδων, ἐκέλευσας ἀριθμῆσαι; ὁ δὲ εἶπε· Τούτους, ἔφη, νόμιζέ σοι πολεμίους εἶναι, τοὺς δ' ἄλλους πάντας συμμάχους πλέον ἢ τετρακισχιλίους ὄντας τοὺς ἐν τῇ ἀγορᾷ.

> And when the ephors asked how he had said that the plan would be carried out, **the informer (delator)** replied that Cinadon had taken him to the edge of the marketplace and directed him to count how many Spartiatae there were in the market-place. 'And I', he said, 'after counting king and ephors and senators and about forty others, asked 'Why, Cinadon, did you bid me count these men?'. And he replied: 'Believe', said he, 'that these men are your enemies, and that all the others who are in the market-place, more than four thousand in number, are your allies.'

---

107 Cf. also Xen., *Mem.* 2.6.36.

The translation of ὁ εἰσαγγείλας as 'the informer' or 'the delator' fits the context perfectly, since the scenario is clearly legal, and the accuser's only intention is to betray Cinadon. The excerpt is commented on in *DGE* and the verb is classified as a legal term.[108] In my opinion, this passage provides strong evidence that there are several derivatives of ἄγγελος — see the case of ἀπαγγέλλω in example (55) and καταγγέλλω below — that, in addition to being consolidated as technical terms associated with the transmission of news, begin to become part of legal terminology.

The following example is the continuation of the one provided in example (15), in which Phrynichus is called ἐξάγγελος when he reveals the plans of Alcibiades. The general had reported that the enemy's attack was imminent and warned of the need to protect Samos by building a wall as soon as possible. Shortly thereafter, a letter came from Alcibiades trying to discredit Phrynichus:

(64) Thuc. 8.51.3

δόξας δὲ ὁ Ἀλκιβιάδης οὐ πιστὸς εἶναι, ἀλλὰ τὰ ἀπὸ τῶν πολεμίων προειδὼς τῷ Φρυνίχῳ ὡς ξυνειδότι κατ' ἔχθραν ἀνατιθέναι, οὐδὲν ἔβλαψεν αὐτόν, ἀλλὰ καὶ ξυνεμαρτύρησε μᾶλλον ταὐτὰ **ἐσαγγείλας**.

But since Alcibiades was not regarded as a trustworthy man, but was believed, as he knew beforehand the plans of the enemy, to be actuated by personal enmity in attributing to Phrynicus a guilty knowledge of them, the accusation did Phrynicus no harm, but rather confirmed his statement **by giving** the same **information**.

In (65) we should also note the presence of an ἀγγελιηφόρος. The excerpt is about the recklessness of Intaphrenes, one of the seven men who revolted against the magician who had usurped Esmerdis' personality and who managed to get Darius to take the throne. Thereafter, the protocol was established for any of these seven men to have access to the king without having to be previously announced except at a specific moment:

---

108 Cf. *DGE ss. uu.* εἰσαγγέλλω II: "jur. rel. c. εἰσαγγελία [...] ὁ εἰσαγγείλας *el denunciante* Xen., *HG* 3.3.5." See also Sturz (1964). The same does not apply in Bailly or *LSJ*, where this passage is not mentioned, and the examples given of εἰσαγγέλλω as a legal technical term are from Greek oratory.

(65) Hdt. 3.118.2

Οὐκ ὦν δὴ ὁ Ἰνταφρένης ἐδικαίου οὐδένα οἱ **ἐσαγγεῖλαι**, ἀλλ', ὅτι ἦν τῶν ἑπτά, ἐσιέναι ἤθελε· ὁ δὲ πυλουρὸς καὶ ὁ ἀγγελιηφόρος οὐ περιώρων, φάμενοι τὸν βασιλέα γυναικὶ μίσγεσθαι.

Intaphrenes, as one of the seven, claimed his right to **enter unannounced**; but the gatekeeper and the messenger forbade him, telling him that the king was having intercourse with one of his wives.

In principle, it is in these types of context where the verb εἰσαγγέλλω might be expected to occur, since — as we have already seen — it is a term commonly used to announce someone's presence. Nevertheless, in many other cases, εἰσαγγέλλω clearly refers to the announcement of news related to the war. The main difference is usually given by the form of the verb itself, because it is usually in the middle or in the passive voice and the piece of news is then its subject, as in (66):

(66) Thuc. 8.79.1

αἰσθόμενοι δὲ οἱ ξύμμαχοι καὶ ὁ Ἀστύοχος τὸν θροῦν, καὶ δόξαν αὐτοῖς ἀπὸ ξυνόδου ὥστε διαναυμαχεῖν, ἐπειδὴ καὶ **ἐσηγγέλλετο** αὐτοῖς ἡ ἐν τῇ Σάμῳ ταραχή, ἄραντες ταῖς ναυσὶ πάσαις οὔσαις δώδεκα καὶ ἑκατὸν καὶ τοὺς Μιλησίους πεζῇ κελεύσαντες ἐπὶ τῆς Μυκάλης παριέναι ἔπλεον ὡς πρὸς τὴν Μυκάλην.

Astyochus and the allies were aware of their murmuring, and it was determined after a council to fight a decisive battle, so when the disturbance at Samos **was** also **reported** to them, they put to sea with their entire fleet, one hundred and twelve in all, and bidding the Milesians proceed by land towards Mycale they sailed in the direction of Mycale themselves.

In (67) the subject is a ὅτι substantive clause.[109] The recipient (in the dative) is omitted, and it is easily inferred that is Pericles:

(67) Thuc. 1.116.3

Περικλῆς δὲ λαβὼν ἑξήκοντα ναῦς ἀπὸ τῶν ἐφορμουσῶν ᾤχετο κατὰ τάχος ἐπὶ Καύνου καὶ Καρίας, **ἐσαγγελθέντων** ὅτι Φοίνισσαι νῆες ἐπ' αὐτοὺς πλέουσιν·

---

109 Cf. also Thuc. 3.3.3. In Thuc. 6.52.1, a ὡς and a ὅτι substantive clause connected by the conjunction καί. The news item is received by the Athenians: the Syracusans were manning a fleet. In Xen., *Symp*. 1.11 εἰσαγγέλλω is in the active voice, the result is expressed by a ὅστις interrogative clause and what is announced is the arrival of the buffoon Philip at Calias' house.

But Pericles took sixty ships away from the blockading fleet and departed in haste towards Caunus in Caria, **a report having come** that a Phoenician fleet was sailing against his forces.

Finally, εἰσαγγέλλω enjoys an absolute use on three occasions and it is usually linked to news of war, as in (68). According to Herodotus' account, Aristides, who was ostracized, has reported some news about the Persians to the Greeks:[110]

(68) Hdt. 8.81

> Καὶ ὁ μὲν ταῦτα εἴπας μετεστήκεε, τῶν δὲ αὖτις ἐγίνετο λόγων ἀμφισβασίη· οἱ γὰρ πλέονες τῶν στρατηγῶν οὐκ ἐπείθοντο **τὰ ἐσαγγελθέντα**.
>
> He said this and left, and again a dispute arose among them. The majority of the generals did not believe **the news**.

Ἐξαγγέλλω occurs in 51 passages (21 in Herodotus, only one in Thucydides and 29 in Xenophon). This verb acquires relevance in the works of historians when those in charge of reporting have been sent on espionage mission, hence one of the meanings given by dictionaries is that of 'betraying a secret'.[111] In addition to this, on occasions — as we shall see in the last chapter — ἐξαγγέλλω is used with very specific objectives.

The expected construction of ἐξαγγέλλω with a second syntactic argument in the accusative (result) and a third argument in the dative (recipient) occurs in Herodotus' *Histories* and in the works of Xenophon. The example shown in (69) is from the very beginning of the *Hellenica* when the author warns of Alcibiades' intentions:[112]

(69) Xen., *Hell.* 1.1.15

> τῇ δὲ προτεραίᾳ, ἐπειδὴ ὡρμίσαντο, τὰ πλοῖα πάντα καὶ τὰ μικρὰ συνήθροισε παρ' ἑαυτόν, ὅπως μηδεὶς **ἐξαγγείλαι** τοῖς πολεμίοις τὸ πλῆθος τῶν νεῶν.

---

110 Cf. also Thuc. 6.41.2 and Xen., *Eq. Mag.* 4.8.
111 See also Bailly: "Reveler, divulguer (un secret)" or Sturz (1964): "Enunciare clandestina consilia". Remember, besides, that Thucydides uses ἐξάγγελος and ἐξάγγελτος. In Xenophon the term ἐξαγγελία also appears.
112 Cf. also Hdt. 3.134.6. In Xen., *Cyr.* 7.5.49 (πρὸς Μήδους) the recipient is not expressed by the dative but by a prepositional phrase.

Now on the preceding day, when they had come to anchor, Alcibiades had taken into his custody all the vessels in the harbour, even the small ones, in order that no one should **report** to the enemy the size of his fleet.

Ἐξαγγέλλω also announces the content of the oracles:[113]

(70) Hdt. 7.178.2

Δελφοὶ δὲ δεξάμενοι τὸ μαντήιον πρῶτα μὲν Ἑλλήνων τοῖσι βουλομένοισι εἶναι ἐλευθέροισι **ἐξήγγειλαν** τὰ χρησθέντα αὐτοῖσι, καί σφι δεινῶς καταρρωδέουσι τὸν βάρβαρον **ἐξαγγείλαντες**[114] χάριν ἀθάνατον κατέθεντο·

When they had received the oracle, the Delphians first **sent word of it** to those Greeks who desired to be free; because of their dread of the barbarian, they were forever grateful.

In (71) ἐξαγγέλλω only takes the accusative (result), a noun with inanimate referent:[115]

(71) Xen., *Hell.* 1.6.22

ἡ δ' ἐπὶ τοῦ Ἑλλησπόντου φυγοῦσα ναῦς διέφυγε, καὶ ἀφικομένη εἰς τὰς Ἀθήνας **ἐξαγγέλλει** τὴν πολιορκίαν.

But the ship which fled toward the Hellespont escaped, and on its arrival at Athens **reported** the blockade.

The accusative is also often omitted when it is easily recoverable from context, as in (72),[116] where Xenophon recounts that Lysander wanted to observe the Athenians so as to be forewarned:

---

113 Cf. also Xen., *Ap.* 13.10.
114 Cf. How/Wells (1967): "The words ἐξαγγείλαντες χάριν ἀθάνατον κατέθεντο, making a hexameter, are probably a reminiscence of some poetical narrative of this event, or of a dedicatory inscription on a thank-offering at Delphi to the winds". See also Macan (1908): "ἐξαγγείλαντες ... κατέθεντο is a hexameter and suggests that this service of the Delphians had been recorded in poem, or epigram, before Hdt. came by it".
115 The accusative can also be a generic neuter in the plural. Cf. Xen., *Cyr.* 6.3.15 (τὰ ὄντα), Xen., *Ap.* 2.1 (τοιαῦτα), Xen., *Hell.* 1.1.8 (ταῦτα) and Xen., *Hell.* 1.6.36 (πάντα).
116 Cf. also Hdt. 7.239.2. In some other passages the verb is in the passive voice (cf. Hdt. 1.21.1, Hdt. 3.122.3, Hdt. 3.142.2, Hdt. 3.153.1, Hdt. 5.95.2 and Hdt. 5.118.1). In Hdt. 6.10.1 the recipient is expressed by a prepositional phrase (ἐς τοὺς ἑωυτοῦ) instead of by the dative.

(72) Xen., *Hell.* 2.1.24

Λύσανδρος δὲ τὰς ταχίστας τῶν νεῶν ἐκέλευσεν ἕπεσθαι τοῖς Ἀθηναίοις, ἐπειδὰν δὲ ἐκβῶσι, κατιδόντας ὅ τι ποιοῦσιν ἀποπλεῖν καὶ αὐτῷ **ἐξαγγεῖλαι**.

Thereupon Lysander ordered the swiftest of his ships to follow the Athenians and, when they had disembarked, to observe what they did, and then to sail back and **report** to him.

In this construction ἐξαγγέλλω almost always indicates the presence of news. The only exception is shown in (73), where it is linked to the issue of commands. The speaker is Cyrus, who is preparing a parade and addresses the Persians and allies who were to participate in it in these terms:

(73) Xen., *Cyr.* 8.3.2

πάρεστε οὖν, ἔφη, ἐπὶ τὰς θύρας κοσμηθέντες ταῖς στολαῖς ταύταις πρὶν ἥλιον ἀνατέλλειν, καὶ καθίστασθε ὡς ἂν ὑμῖν Φεραύλας ὁ Πέρσης **ἐξαγγείλῃ** παρ' ἐμοῦ· καὶ ἐπειδάν, ἔφη, ἐγὼ ἡγῶμαι, ἕπεσθε ἐν τῇ ῥηθείσῃ χώρᾳ.

'Come, therefore, to court before sunrise, dressed in these robes", said he, "and form in line as Pheraulas, the Persian, **shall direct** in my name; and when I lead the way, follow me in the order assigned to you.'[117]

Ἐξαγγέλλω also occurs with a ὅτι substantive clause. In these cases, the dative (recipient) tends to be explicitly expressed (74).[118] The Battle of Arginusae is about to begin and the Spartan Callicratidas is informed:

(74) Xen., *Hell.* 1.6.28

τῆς δὲ νυκτὸς ἰδὼν τὰ πυρά, καί τινων αὐτῷ **ἐξαγγειλάντων** ὅτι οἱ Ἀθηναῖοι εἶεν, ἀνήγετο περὶ μέσας νύκτας, ὡς ἐξαπιναίως προσπέσοι· ὕδωρ δ' ἐπιγενόμενον πολὺ καὶ βρονταὶ διεκώλυσαν τὴν ἀναγωγήν.

And when Callicratidas saw their fires during the night and people **reported** to him that it was the Athenians, he proposed to put to sea at about midnight, in order to attack them unexpectedly, but a heavy rain coming on, with thunder, prevented the setting out.

---

117 Cf. Watson/Dale (1893, 249): "And form yourselves as Pheraulas shall give you directions from me".
118 Cf. also Hdt. 5.33.3 and Xen., *An.* 7.2.14. Only in Xen., *Hell.* 5.2.18 the dative (recipient) is omitted.

In (75) the recipient does appear[119] and ἐξαγγέλλω is also accompanied by a ὡς substantive clause.[120] The excerpt is from a digression concerning Jason's successors:[121]

(75) Xen., *Hell.* 6.4.36

> τοῖς τε γὰρ ἀδελφοῖς **ἐξήγγειλεν** ὡς ὁ Ἀλέξανδρος ἐπιβουλεύοι αὐτοῖς καὶ ἔκρυψεν αὐτοὺς ἔνδον ὄντας ὅλην τὴν ἡμέραν.
>
> For she **reported** to her brothers that Alexander was plotting against them and concealed them within the house for the entire day.

Finally, in the only example in which Thucydides uses ἐξαγγέλλω it shows an absolute use,[122] but it refers to *fake* news. We will discuss it in the corresponding chapter.

Ἐπαγγέλλω[123] — absent in Homer, but present in Greek lyric poetry, Greek tragedy and Aristophanic comedy — appears 26 times in Herodotus, 15 in Thucydides and 18 in Xenophon. In the works of historians, this verb is consolidated as a military term to issue orders,[124] announce truces,[125] make promises,[126]

---

119 The dative is omitted in Hdt. 6.63.2, Xen., *An.* 2.4.24 and Xen., *Cyr.* 2.4.17.
120 Ὅτι and ὡς clauses alternate with AcI and AcP constructions. Cf. Hdt. 6.65.3., Xen., *Hell.* 4.4.8, Xen. *Hell.*, 7.5.10 and Xen., *Cyr.* 7.5.54 (in this case the announcement has not no do with news but with orders).
121 Cf. also Hdt. 5.105.1 and Hdt. 8.56.1.
122 Cf. also Xen., *Ages.* 1.6, Xen., *Cyr.* 5.3.17, Xen., *Cyr.* 6.1.42, Xen., *Cyr.* 6.2.21 and Xen., *Hell.* 5.4.56.
123 In Hdt. 7.29.1, Thuc. 1.33.2 and Thuc. 4.120.3 the verbal adjective αὐτεπάγγελτος ('offering of oneself, volunteer') occurs. Since this term is never related to news reporting, we will not study it under a separate heading.
124 On the three occasions on which the construction is ἐπαγγέλλω + dative + infinitive (cf. Hdt. 1.77.3, Xen., *Cyr.* 4.4.11 and Xen., *Mem.* 3.1.1). Also in Thuc. 3.16.3 (ἐπαγγέλλω + accusative), Hdt. 1.70.1, Hdt. 6.139.2, Thuc. 5.47.6, Thuc. 8.86.8 and Xen., *An.* 7.1.33 (ἐπαγγέλλω + dative) and Hdt. 3.142.5 and Thuc. 7.17.1 (ἐπαγγέλλω + accusative + dative), in Hdt. 4.200.1, Hdt. 7.150.3 and Hdt. 7.1.2 (ἐπαγγέλλω + infinitive) and Xen., *Cyr.* 3.1.10, Xen., *Cyr.* 7.4.9, Xen., *Cyr.* 8.5.25 and Xen., *Hell.* 3.4.28 (absolute use).
125 Only in Thucydides. Cf. Thuc. 5.49.2, Thuc. 5.49.4 or Thuc. 8.10.1 (absolute use) or Thuc. 5.49.3 (ἐπαγγέλλω + dative).
126 Cf. Hdt. 7.39.2, Hdt. 7.150.3 and Thuc. 8.32.3 (ἐπαγγέλλω + accusative), Hdt. 8.142.1 (ἐπαγγέλλω + dative), Xen., *Mem.* 1.2.8 (ἐπαγγέλλω + accusative + dative), Xen., *An.* 2.1.4 (ἐπαγγέλλω + AcI + dative) or Hdt. 6.9.3, Hdt. 7.130.3, Hdt. 8.25.1, Hdt. 8.30.2, Thuc. 5.47.4, Thuc. 6.88.6, Xen., *Hell.* 1.6.12 and Xen. *Hell.*, 7.4.38 (absolute use).

summon the troops,[127] make offers,[128] extend invitations[129] and offer or ask for help.[130]

The only instance in which ἐπαγγέλλω refers to the transmission of news is shown in (76). After having an argument with Croesus, Cambyses ordered his servants to kill him, but they decided to hide him, since they have reached the conclusion that if Cambyses regretted his decision, they could get a reward for saving his life. Sure enough, Cambyses changed his mind and then the servants removed Croesus from his hiding place:

(76) Hdt. 3.36.6

> Ἐπόθησέ τε δὴ ὁ Καμβύσης τὸν Κροῖσον οὐ πολλῷ μετέπειτα χρόνῳ ὕστερον, καὶ οἱ θεράποντες μαθόντες τοῦτο **ἐπηγγέλλοντο** αὐτῷ ὡς περιείη.
>
> Not long after this Cambyses did wish Croesus back, and the attendants, understanding this, **told** him that Croesus was still alive.

In this passage we cannot be sure if ἐπαγγέλλω refers to an order, an offering or a promise. In this regard, my interpretation is consistent with that of Powell (1960, 126), who proposes to translate the verb as 'announce'. In this case, therefore, ἐπαγγέλλω is used to report a piece of news.

The verb καταγγέλλω only appears once in Xenophon's *Anabasis*. Dictionaries offer several meanings,[131] including 'denounce', expressly referring to this passage in the speech of Ariaeus:

(77) Xen., *An.* 2.5.38

> Κλέαρχος μέν, ὦ ἄνδρες Ἕλληνες, ἐπεὶ ἐπιορκῶν τε ἐφάνη καὶ τὰς σπονδὰς λύων, ἔχει τὴν δίκην καὶ τέθνηκε, Πρόξενος δὲ καὶ Μένων, ὅτι **κατήγγειλαν** αὐτοῦ τὴν ἐπιβουλήν, ἐν μεγάλῃ τιμῇ εἰσιν.

---

127 Cf. Thuc. 8.108.4 (ἐπαγγέλλω + accusative + dative).
128 Cf. Hdt. 3.153.3 or Hdt. 8.30.1 (ἐπαγγέλλω + accusative + dative), Hdt. 8.29.1, Xen., *Hell.* 3.4.3 and Xen., *Mem.* 1.2.7 (ἐπαγγέλλω + accusative) or Hdt. 7.27.1, Xen., *An.* 4.7.20 and Xen., *Cyr.* 6.2.1 (ἐπαγγέλλω + dative).
129 In Thuc. 6.56.1. (ἐπαγγέλλω + accusative).
130 Cf. Xen., *Cyr.* 7.4.2 and Xen., *Cyr.* 8.4.33 (ἐπαγγέλλω + dative) or Hdt. 1.70.1, Hdt. 6.139.2, Thuc. 5.47.6, Thuc. 8.86.8 or Xen., *An.* 7.1.33 (absolute use).
131 Cf. *LSJ*: "Announce, proclaim, declare, recite, recount, denounce"; Bailly: "Annoncer contra, intenter un process à qqn., declarer una guerre || denouncer". On the case of Xenophon, see Sturz (1964, 671): "καταγγέλλειν, prodere, deferre".

Clearchus, men of Greece, inasmuch as he was shown to be perjuring himself and violating the truce, has received his deserts and is dead, but Proxenus and Menon, because they **denounced** his plotting, are held in high honour.

The excerpt is about the treachery of Tissaphernes, who broke the truce with Clearchus and imprisoned him along with other generals to be tried in Babylon. However, the Greek leaders refused to surrender and were executed. Thus, καταγγέλλω alludes to the public denouncement of an alleged plot (τὴν ἐπιβουλήν); the term, as well as other derivatives of ἄγγελος (ἀπαγγέλλω and εἰσαγγέλλω), is becoming specialized as a legal term.

Let us focus now on παραγγέλλω, a very prevalent verb in the works of historians (145 instances: 10 in Herodotus, 13 in Thucydides and 122 in Xenophon) and a military term used to refer to the issue of orders.[132] In fact, this verb always refers to a command except in the following passage:

(78) Xen., *Hell.* 2.2.3

Ἐν δὲ ταῖς Ἀθήναις τῆς Παράλου ἀφικομένης νυκτὸς ἐλέγετο ἡ συμφορά, καὶ οἰμωγὴ ἐκ τοῦ Πειραιῶς διὰ τῶν μακρῶν τειχῶν εἰς ἄστυ διῆκεν, ὁ ἕτερος τῷ ἑτέρῳ **παραγγέλλων**·

It was at night that the Paralus arrived at Athens with tidings of the disaster, and a sound of wailing ran from Piraeus through the long walls to the city, one man **passing on the news** to another.

The disaster reported in Athens was the defeat suffered in Aegospotami. The men were transmitting the painful pieces of news to each other, one by one. In this respect, we should note here a certain link with the use of this verb in the military context to give orders, since in many cases the soldiers themselves pass the instructions from row to row.

Xenophon also uses the derivate verb ἀντιπαραγγέλλω, another military term denoting the transmission of orders,[133] once. In the Battle of Nemea, the Lacedaemonians are unaware that danger is near, but soon realize that it is: "But when the latter struck up the paean, then at length they knew, and imme-

---

132 According to *LSJ*, the order is "not so strong as κελεύω". Remember that in the works of Thucydides and Xenophon we also see the nouns παραγγελία, παράγγελμα and παράγγελσις, all of which are synonyms that designate the order.

133 Cf. *LSJ*: "Give orders, command in turn"; *DGE*: "Dar órdenes a su vez"; Bailly: "Ordonner à son tour ou en retour" and Sturz (1964): "imperare".

diately gave orders (ἀντιπαρήγγειλαν) in their turn that all should make ready for battle".[134]

Historians also use περιαγγέλλω and the derivative προσπεριαγγέλλω. The former does not appear in any of the authors studied in previous chapters, and the works of historians show 13 examples of its use (3 in Herodotus, 9 in Thucydides and 1 in Xenophon). The preverb περί- gives the nuance of movement (its basic meaning is 'round about'). It denotes, therefore, an announcement that is made in a number of locations.[135] Περιαγγέλλω also become specialized as a military term referring the issue of orders,[136] but there are two passages in which it alludes to the dissemination of news. In (79) Herodotus explains the privileges of the kings in Sparta both in the military sphere and the private sphere (Hdt. 6.56–57). When a king dies, the news of the end of his life is made public:[137]

(79) Hdt. 6.58.1

> Ταῦτα μὲν ζώουσι τοῖσι βασιλεῦσι δέδοται ἐκ τοῦ κοινοῦ τῶν Σπαρτιητέων, ἀποθανοῦσι δὲ τάδε. Ἱππέες **περιαγγέλλουσι** τὸ γεγονὸς κατὰ πᾶσαν τὴν Λακωνικήν, κατὰ δὲ τὴν πόλιν γυναῖκες περιιοῦσαι λέβητας κροτέουσι.

> The kings are granted these rights from the Spartan commonwealth while they live; when they die, their rights are as follows: horsemen **proclaim** their death in all parts of Laconia, and in the city, women go about beating on cauldrons.

In (80) the public announcement is a truce when Brasidas was about to attack:[138]

(80) Thuc. 4.122.1

> Καὶ ὁ μὲν ἔμελλεν ἐγχειρήσειν ταῖς πόλεσι ταύταις, ἐν τούτῳ δὲ τριήρει οἱ τὴν ἐκεχειρίαν **περιαγγέλλοντες** ἀφικνοῦνται παρ' αὐτόν, Ἀθηναίων μὲν Ἀριστώνυμος, Λακεδαιμονίων δὲ Ἀθήναιος.

---

134 Xen., *Hell.* 4.2.19.
135 The first meaning given in *LSJ* is "Announce by messages sent round". Cf. also Bailly: "Fair annoncer tout autour, de tous côtes, publier".
136 Cf. Xen., *Hell.* 6.4.2, Thuc. 2.10.1, Thuc. 2.80.2 and Thuc. 6.88.6 (περιαγγέλλω + infinitive + dative); Thuc. 1.116.1, Thuc. 4.8.2 and Thuc. 5.54.2 (περιαγγέλλω + infinitive) or Hdt. 7.1.2, Hdt. 7.119.2 and Thuc. 5.17.2 (absolute use).
137 Powell (1960, 301) translates "take news round".
138 Hobbes (1843) offers this translation: "That carried about the news of the truce" and Jowett (1881) this one: "Who went round to proclaim the truce". On the same construction, cf. also Thuc. 7.18.4.

So he was about to attack these towns; but in the meantime those who **were carrying round the news** of the armistice arrived at his headquarters in a trireme, Aristonymus from Athens and Athenaeus from Lacedaemon.

On the other hand, the only excerpt in which we see προσπεριαγγέλλω belongs to Thucydides' *History of the Peloponnesian War*, where the term refers to commands: "They set to work with Cnemus to order forth around (προσπεριήγγειλαν)[139] ships from the different states".[140]

Προαγγέλλω occurs once in Thucydides and twice in Xenophon's *Cyropaedia*.[141] Due to the presence of the preverb προ-, dictionaries propose the translation 'announce beforehand'.[142] In the contexts in which προαγγέλλω appears, we should probably infer the anticipatory transmission of news.

In (81) the news reported is closely related to war. The verb is in the passive voice and the subject (patient) indicates the content of the announcement received by Gylippus and his men (dative recipient):

(81) Thuc. 7.65.1

τῷ δὲ Γυλίππῳ καὶ τοῖς Συρακοσίοις παρῆν μὲν αἰσθάνεσθαι, ὁρῶσι καὶ αὐτὴν τὴν παρασκευήν, ὅτι ναυμαχήσουσιν οἱ Ἀθηναῖοι, **προηγγέλθη** δ' αὐτοῖς καὶ ἡ ἐπιβολὴ τῶν σιδηρῶν χειρῶν, καὶ πρός τε τἆλλα ἐξηρτύσαντο ὡς ἕκαστα καὶ πρὸς τοῦτο·

Gylippus and the Syracusans, on the other hand, observing the actual preparations which they were making, could easily perceive that the Athenians were going to fight at sea, furthermore, the device of the grappling-irons **had** already **been** previously **reported**[143] to them, and while they were equiping their ships to meet every other contingency, they also took precautions against this.

---

139 See Rusten (1989, 230): "Sent around to cities for additional (πρόσ-) ships". The passage poses problems, since some manuscripts propose this verb, but others offer the verb περιαγγέλλω. Bétant (1961) does not include προσπεριαγγέλλω. Cf. Gomme (1956, 220): "Doubtless recent edd. are right to take from CG this doubled-compound verb".
140 Cf. Thuc. 2.85.3.
141 One of them (Xen., *Cyr.* 5.3.12) will be discussed in the last chapter.
142 Cf. *LSJ*: "Declare, announce beforehand", Bailly: "announcer d'avance". Cf. also Bétant (1961): "praenuntiari" or Sturz (1964): "praenunciare".
143 Smith (1886) surmises that the information could have come through spies.

In (82) the announcement inherent to προαγγέλλω is expressed by an AcI construction. Cyrus, having made sacrifices to win the favor of the gods, tells his men that the gods have made the following known to him:[144]

(82) Xen., *Cyr.* 3.3.34

> Ἄνδρες, οἱ μὲν θεοί, ὡς οἵ τε μάντεις φασὶ καὶ ἐμοὶ συνδοκεῖ, μάχην τ' ἔσεσθαι **προαγγέλλουσι** καὶ νίκην διδόασι καὶ σωτηρίαν ὑπισχνοῦνται ἐν τοῖς ἱεροῖς.
>
> 'Men, the gods **announce**, as the soothsayers say and also as I interpret it, that there is to be a battle; through the omens of the sacrifice, they grant us victory and promise us no loss.'

Let us now focus on the derivatives of ἄγγελμα. None of the terms presented below occur in Herodotus' *Histories*. They are used only by Thucydides and Xenophon. I am referring here to three derivatives of ἄγγελμα: παράγγελμα, παράγγελσις and προάγγελσις. The noun ἄγγελμα appears only once,[145] but it will be discussed later, since it implies the announcement of *fake* news.

Παράγγελμα[146] also occurs only once, in Thucydides, and is a military term denoting the issue of orders. The same applies to παράγγελσις, another military term to allude to commands.[147] Xenophon uses it on six occasions[148] and Thucydides uses it to describe the organization of the Lacedaemonian army and how the orders proceed in the same way and reach their destination quickly.[149]

Finally, προάγγελσις is documented only once, in this excerpt:[150]

---

144 The announcement implied in προαγγέλλω is a prophecy. Remember that some other cognates of ἄγγελος – ἀγγέλλω, ἀναγγέλλω, ἀπαγγέλλω, διαγγέλλω and ἐξαγγέλλω – are also used to make the public announcement of the responses of the oracles.
145 Cf. Thuc. 7.73.4.
146 Cf. Thuc. 8.99.1. Remember that it appears once in Greek tragedy (in Aeschylus' *Agamemnon*). On this example from Thucydides, see Bétant (1961): "Παράγγελμα, *imperatum*".
147 Cf. *LSJ*: "Transmission of orders in war", Bailly: "Commandement, ordre" and Bétant (1961): "Παράγγελσις, *imperatum*". See also Fowler (1888): "An order not given by the trumpet but passed along the ranks in such a way as not to attract the attention of the enemy", Graves (1891): "Orders 'passed along' the line, as opposed to those given by herald or sound of trumpet" and Gomme *et al.* (1970, 103): "Orders passed down the line, as opposed to those intended to be heard by all at once, given out by trumpet or herald; [or to the orders given in advance by the king through the polemarchs]".
148 Always ἀπὸ παραγγέλσεως. Cf. Xen., *An.* 4.1.5, Xen., *Eq. Mag.* 4.3. (x2), Xen., *Eq. Mag.* 4.9. (x2) and Xen., *Eq. Mag.* 8.18.
149 Cf. Thuc. 5.66.3.
150 Προάγγελσις does not appear in the works of the author examined up to now.

(83) Thuc. 1.137.4

> καί μοι εὐεργεσία ὀφείλεται (γράψας τήν τε ἐκ Σαλαμῖνος **προάγγελσιν** τῆς ἀναχωρήσεως καὶ τὴν τῶν γεφυρῶν, ἣν ψευδῶς προσεποιήσατο, τότε δι' αὐτὸν οὐ διάλυσιν), καὶ νῦν ἔχων σε μεγάλα ἀγαθὰ δρᾶσαι πάρειμι διωκόμενος ὑπὸ τῶν Ἑλλήνων διὰ τὴν σὴν φιλίαν.
>
> 'And there is a kindness due to me (here **he related** the timely warning to retreat given at Salamis, and the failure of the Hellenic fleet to destroy the bridges at that time, which he falsely claimed to have been due to his own efforts), and now I am here, having it in my power to do you great good, being pursued by the Hellenes on account of my friendship to you.'

The context is as follows: Themistocles lived in Argos and was continually travelling but had been ostracized. The Athenians sent some men before the Lacedaemonians with the order to pursue and arrest him. Themistocles then fled to Corcyra, but there he did not receive asylum and ended up arriving at the home of Admetus, king of the Molossians, who helped him to escape. Shortly afterwards, Themistocles wrote a letter to Artaxerxes asking him for help. The example given in (83) is a part of that letter, and the προάγγελσις that mentioned warning is linked to war operations.[151]

Final remarks

One of the most remarkable aspects of the study of the derivatives of ἄγγελος in the works of Herodotus, Thucydides and Xenophon is the sheer number of terms documented. Most of these terms are fully consolidated as technical terms associated with the transmission of news. In this respect, apart from ἀπαγγελία ('narration'), παράγγελμα, παράγγελσις, προάγγελσις, ἀντιπαραγγέλλω, προσπεριαγγέλλω (all of which indicate the presence of orders) and καταγγέλλω (used in a courtroom context to denounce a conspiracy), the rest of the words analysed can be linked to the transmission of news to a greater or lesser extent.

In the works of historians, the concept of news is strongly related to war and the study of the vocabulary used has given us some interesting results. On the one hand, the ἄγγελοι in the texts of Herodotus, Thucydides and Xenophon are also specialized, but in tasks of a diplomatic nature. On the other hand, it is practically impossible to distinguish the ἄγγελος from the κῆρυξ and, since both

---

[151] Cf. *LSJ*: "Forewarning, early intimation" and Bailly: "Annonce faite d'avance, prédiction". See also Bétant (1961): προάγγελσις: «praedictio». On the different interpretations of this passage, see Gomme (1945, 440–441).

are emissaries, both have important roles in the transmission of news, and both are responsible for the information circulating successfully, especially at times of war.

The ἄγγελος is again linked to the κῆρυξ because, just as in Homer, both act under the orders of public authorities or of ambassadors. As in Homer, the ἄγγελος and the subject of ἀγγέλλω can also be any character, and in historiography we are often unaware of the identity of the character giving the news. However, the fact that the ἄγγελος has an important role in contexts related to ambassadors and proves worthy for assuming responsibility for news arriving efficiently, is in my opinion sufficient reason to believe that when we are told that some news arrived or was given, it is quite probable that an ἄγγελος was responsible. Besides, Herodotus introduces us to two other figures: the ἀγγελιηφόρος and the εἰσαγγελεύς, royal messengers.

On the other hand, the analysis of ἄγγελος and its derivatives shows us that in the works of historians, the main news is public in nature since it affects the whole community. It is more often than not related to war and all things martial: victories, defeats, enemy movements, revolts, deaths whilst in combat, and the news given to ambassadors, that is, truces, proposals for peace, requests for help, etc. In this context, espionage acquires a very significant importance. Setting aside war, derivatives of ἄγγελος are also used to report other types of news, such as deaths and murders, the birth of Demaratus, responses of the oracles, miracles and (although rarely) gossip.

This analysis has also allowed me to demonstrate that derivatives of ἄγγελος are fully established as technical terms associated with the transmission of news. At the same time, it is also interesting that some of the derivatives of ἄγγελος also seem to indicate a specialization in two other senses: both in war and in legal contexts. Ἀγγελία, ἀγγέλλω, διαγγέλλω, ἐξαγγέλλω, ἐπαγγέλλω and περιαγγέλλω all indicate at certain points the transmission of orders, whilst παράγγελμα, παράγγελσις, προάγγελσις, ἀντιπαραγγέλλω, προσπεριαγγέλλω are always used for this purpose. Παραγγέλλω (the derivative of ἄγγελος associated with orders par excellence), on the other hand, always refers to the giving of orders, with one exception: when it is used to announce Athens' defeat in Aegospotami, although it is true that the soldiers themselves would have been telling each other from one line to the next, in a similar way to how orders are given in a chain.

In addition, ἀπαγγέλλω, εἰσαγγέλλω and καταγγέλλω begin to appear in legal contexts to refer to another kind of announcement: public denunciation – whose aim is to ensure that the denounced person is punished as is seen fit. Interestingly, denunciation can also be explained in a public context, since a citizen announces something that goes against the good of the community. This information is, in my opinion, of particular interest. In the texts of the historians, this only occurs in a small number of examples, but some derivatives of ἄγγελος do seem to be taking on a specialized nature as legal terms.

6 Greek Oratory: Isocrates, Lysias, Aeschines and Demosthenes

In this chapter, I will focus on the period of Attic eloquence, and the time of important orators such as Lysias, Isocrates, Demosthenes and Aeschines.[1] The study of the lexicon at this time yields an interesting initial finding: the term ἄγγελος is not documented in the speeches of Isocrates and Lysias and occurs only twice in Demosthenes and once in Aeschines. Isocrates does not use the word κῆρυξ either, but Lysias does, although only in one excerpt from his *Funeral Speech* (Lys. 2.7). The term is more productive in Demosthenes (occurs 27 times) and Aeschines (22 instances). The data is contrary to expectations, especially if we take into account that speeches often related the significant role played by embassies in times of war. As we have seen in the previous chapter, both the messenger and the herald are important in the works of historians. They behave as professionals specializing in diplomatic duties such as those involving embassies, on which I will focus much of my interest in the next few pages. In Greek oratory, as we will see, the κῆρυξ still continues to participate in this type of commission — although he carries out his main tasks in other areas –, but the ἄγγελος is barely seen at all.

No news from the messenger

The study of the works of historians has shown us the role played by κήρυκες mainly in times of war and far from the πόλις, but their presence in the speeches of Aeschines and Demosthenes allows us to link them much more to the public life of the city. Just as in Homer, the herald was a man in the public service.[2] He was a kind of official whose duties extended to both the Council and the Assembly: he announced that the sacred envoys and delegates should assemble (Aeschin., *In Ctes*.122) and asked them to withdraw (Aeschin., *Emb*. 35). He also ordered them to remain silent and gave the floor at each point of the agenda to whoever wanted to take it (Dem., *De cor*. 170, Aeschin., *In Tim*. 23). Likewise, in court cases he proclaimed out loud what the magistrates required him to do,

---

[1] There are, of course, other orators, such as Isaeus, Hyperides and so on, whose speeches are not included in the corpus analysed in this volume, but to which I refer (especially in the case of Hyperides) when necessary.
[2] The term used by Aeschines (*In Tim*. 20) to refer to the action carried out by the herald is κηρυκεύω (Cf. *LSJ*: "Perform the office of a herald").

dictated the processes to be held that day (Dem., *Emb.* 70) and called in the defendants and the witnesses (Aeschin., *Emb.* 86). In addition, a herald was the person in charge of announcing in the theatre the crowning of citizens recognized for their virtue and integrity (Aeschin., *In Ctes.* 49) and there was always a κῆρυξ among the members of an embassy (Aeschin., *In Ctes.* 62 or Dem., *Emb.* 185). However, he did not announce what had been discussed — that responsibility was given to one of the other ambassadors (the πρεσβευτής).[3]

In his speech *In Neaeram*, Demosthenes mentions another individual called ἱεροκῆρυξ ('attendant at a sacrifice'),[4] whilst Aeschines alludes to a δρομοκῆρυξ, a runner herald, a type of courier that we will see in example (26) below.

As stated above, there are only three instances of the term ἄγγελος in the analysed corpus. In *Against Ctesiphon*,[5] Aeschines remembers that Callias had decided to appear before the Assembly without using messengers (οὐκέτι δι' ἀγγέλων). The two other examples are from two Demosthenic speeches. In *Against Evergus and Mnesibulus*, the speaker is explaining the facts that led him to file legal actions and he tells us that a stone-cutter came before him as a messenger (ἄγγελος ἦλθε) to bring him word that Evergus had taken the rest of his furniture from his house.[6]

In (1), however, the news that the ἄγγελος is to announce is linked to war:

(1) Dem., *Neaer*.100

> καὶ ὡς ὑμᾶς πέμπουσιν εὐθὺς **ἄγγελον** τήν τε πρᾶξιν φράσοντα καὶ τὴν μάχην δηλώσοντα ὅτι νικῶσι, καὶ βοηθεῖν ἀξιοῦντες, ἂν οἱ Θηβαῖοι τὴν χώραν αὐτῶν δῃῶσιν·
>
> Then they immediately sent **a messenger** to you to report what has happened, announce their victory in the battle, and ask you to help them if the Thebans ravaged their land.[7]

As we can see, then, the figure of the ἄγγελος, the news 'reporter' par excellence in Greek tragedy, parodied by Aristophanes and present in the embassies mentioned by historians, seems to have blurred into the background. Obviously, this

---

[3] Demosthenes distinguishes the κῆρυξ from the πρεσβευτής ('ambassador') in *On the Dishonest Embassy* (cf. Dem., *Emb.* 338).
[4] Cf. Dem., *Neaer.* 78: "Βούλομαι δ' ὑμῖν καὶ τὸν ἱεροκήρυκα καλέσαι". See Colubí Falcó (1983b, 310).
[5] Cf. Aeschin., *In Ctes.* 95.
[6] Cf. Dem., *Evag.* 65.
[7] Translation taken from Bers (2003).

does not mean that there is no news to announce.⁸ Rather, the reason for this is, in my opinion, quite a simple one. The passages that I am going to present in what follows belong to legal contexts and usually take place in the Council and the Assembly. As Lewis (1996, 97) pointed out: "Assemblies did not act as neutral centers for the general transmission of news. The news they disseminated, and the audience that they reached, were limited by the nature of the assembly itself". Therefore, it is not surprising that ἄγγελος and its derivatives acquire great relevance in the speeches of ambassadors when they are accountable to the Assembly, because that is what really matters in this context.

The news that is of interest involves the threats that affect the entire community and is mainly related to enemies and defeats, because that is when the Assembly must make a decision that affects all citizens. Likewise, the ambassadors are aware of the responsibility that falls on them, and this motivates them to report good news (like a victory, for instance). They do not hesitate to claim popular recognition, as will be illustrated by example (12). And momentous decisions must also be made when it comes to legal procedures. In this regard, from my point of view, one of the most interesting findings from the analysis of ἄγγελος and its derivatives is that a large number of these terms become specialized as legal terms to allude to a public denunciation. After all, denouncing is nothing more than giving news to the judges of an act considered illegal.

Public matters and legal language

Let us pay attention to the lexicon to see how far the concept of news is closely linked to public matters in the speeches of orators. In addition to ἄγγελος, another 23 terms derived from ἄγγελος are documented in the speeches of Lysias, Isocrates, Demosthenes and Aeschines. Many of these are present in the authors previously examined, but others — specifically the nouns εἰσαγγελία, ἐπαγγελία and ἐπάγγελμα, the adjective εἰσαγγελτικός and the verbs κακαγγελέω, καταπαγγέλλομαι, προεξαγγέλλω and προσαγγέλλω — appear now for the first time. The figures below show all the analysed words.

---

8 According to Lewis (1996, 25), the reception of news in the *polis* is much more dependent on individual travels and personal experiences. Evidence of this can be seen in the introduction to Plato's *Phaedo*, which is referred to as a literary convention.

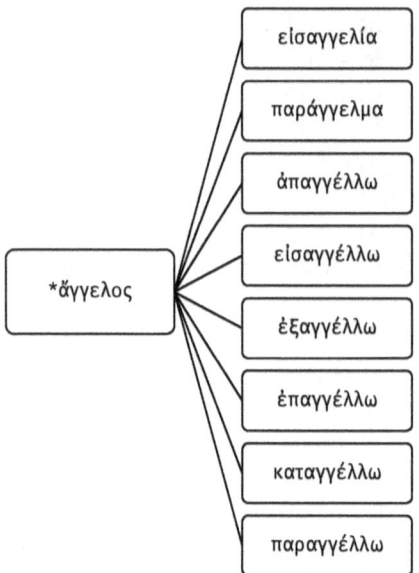

Fig. 13: Ἄγγελος and its derivatives in Lysias' speeches.

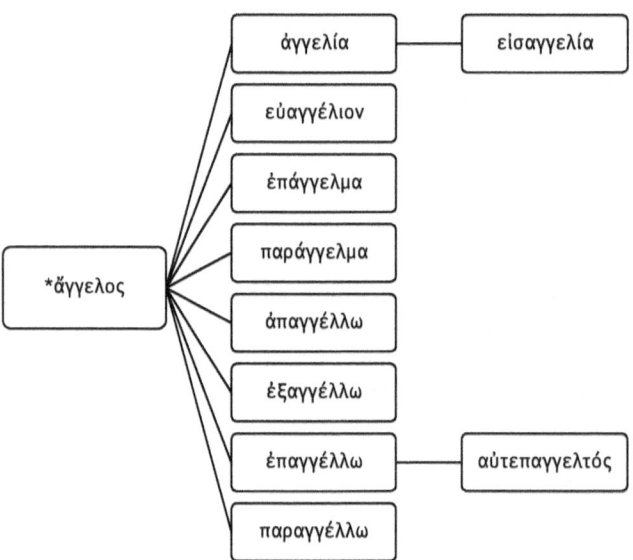

Fig. 14: Ἄγγελος and its derivatives in Isocrates' speeches.

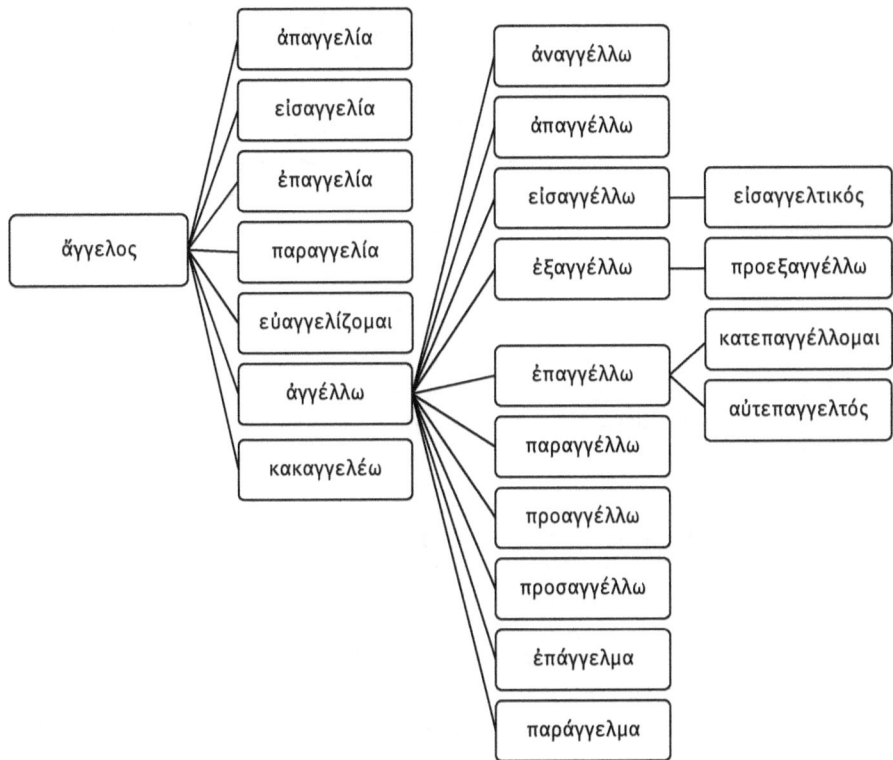

Fig. 15: Ἄγγελος and its derivatives in Demosthenes' speeches.

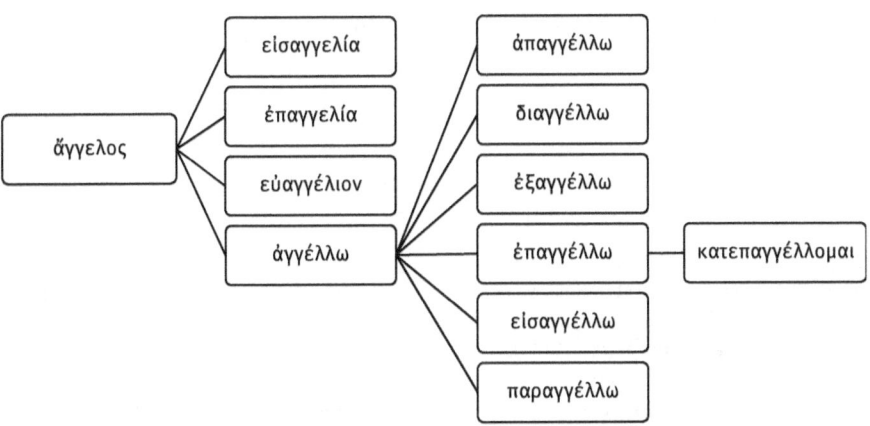

Fig. 16: Ἄγγελος and its derivatives in Aeschines' speeches.

The noun ἀγγελία occurs only once, specifically in Isocrates' *Aegineticus*, which deals with the claim to an inheritance. When he is about to die, a certain Thrasylochus (son of Thrasyllus), took as heir a nephew of his father's first wife and gave his sister in marriage to him. An illegitimate daughter of Thrasyllus claimed her right to the inheritance and the heir designated by Thrasylochus commissioned Isocrates with this defence speech. This is one of the arguments uttered by the accuser to attack the woman:

(2) Isoc., *Aegin*. 40

> Ἐπειδὴ τοίνυν εἰς Λυκίαν ἐκπλεύσας ἀπέθανεν, αὕτη μὲν οὐ πολλαῖς ἡμέραις ὕστερον **μετὰ τὴν ἀγγελίαν** ἔθυεν⁹ καὶ ἑώρταζεν καὶ οὐδὲ τὸν ἀδελφὸν ᾐσχύνετο τὸν ἔτι ζῶντα, οὕτως ὀλίγον φροντίζουσα τοῦ τεθνεῶτος, ἐγὼ δ' ἐπένθουν αὐτὸν ὥσπερ τοὺς οἰκείους νόμος ἐστίν·

> Moreover, when he had sailed to Lycia and died there, this woman, a few days **after the news** of his death, was sacrificing and holding festival, and had no shame before his surviving brother, so little regard did she have for the dead man, but I instituted mourning for him in the custom prescribed for relatives.¹⁰

The speaker is referring to the death of Sopolis, Thrasylochus' brother, who had been elected general with full power and who had appointed him secretary and treasurer, thereby showing his absolute trust. However, he repudiated the woman.

The term ἀπαγγελία is defined by dictionaries as a response or report brought by an ambassador who has been sent to carry out a certain task entrusted to him.¹¹ Only Demosthenes uses this noun (4 times). Let us now see an example from the speech *On the Dishonest Embassy*:¹²

---

9 Note the presence of the verb θύω, which has already been discussed in the chapter dedicated to Aristophanic comedy and which I will also discuss in the next chapter.
10 Translation taken from Norlin (1980).
11 Cf. *LSJ*: "Report, e.g. of an ambassador"; Bailly: "Réponse rapportée, rapport (d'un envoyé)". *DGE*: "Respuesta, noticia, informe traído por un embajador". Remember that ἀπαγγελία is also documented once in Thucydides (cf. Thuc. 7.67.3) and refers to a narration.
12 Cf. also Dem., *Emb*. 5 (ἐκ μὲν τῶν ἀπαγγελιῶν) and Dem., *Emb*. 31 (πρὸς τὴν ἐμὴν ἀπαγγελίαν ἐψηφίσαθ' ἡ βουλή).

(3) Dem., *Emb.* 53

οἱ μὲν τοίνυν Φωκεῖς, ὡς τὰ παρ' ὑμῶν ἐπύθοντ' ἐκ τῆς ἐκκλησίας καὶ τό τε ψήφισμα τοῦτ' ἔλαβον τὸ τοῦ Φιλοκράτους καὶ **τὴν ἀπαγγελίαν** ἐπύθοντο τὴν τούτου καὶ τὰς ὑποσχέσεις, κατὰ πάντας τοὺς τρόπους ἀπώλοντο.

Now, when the Phocians learned what transpired in the Assembly, when they received Philocrates' decree, when they learned **what the envoys reported** and what this man promised, their destruction was assured.[13]

The following example (4) is framed in a different context. The passage is from *Against Phormio*:

(4) Dem., *Phorm.* 16

Τοῦτο τὸ ἔγκλημα ἔγραφον ἐγώ, ὦ ἄνδρες Ἀθηναῖοι, οὐδαμόθεν ἄλλοθεν σκοπῶν ἀλλ' ἢ **ἐκ τῆς ἀπαγγελίας** τῆς Λάμπιδος, ὃς οὐκ ἔφασκεν οὔτε τὰ χρήματα ἐντεθεῖσθαι τοῦτον οὔτε τὸ χρυσίον ἀπειληφέναι·

This action I commenced, men of Athens, basing my complaint upon nothing else than **the report** of Lampis, who denied that Phormio had put the goods on board the ship or that he himself had received the money.[14]

Lampis' report, one of the accusers, is in this case a statement: an account of events used as an argument before the men of the jury.

The time has come to consider one of the most important legal terms in Athenian legislation, the εἰσαγγελία ('state prosecution', 'impeachment'). This word occurs 17 times in the examined speeches (twice in Isocrates' speeches, 3 in those of Lysias, 3 in those of Aeschines, and 9 in those of Demosthenes). According to Aristotle,[15] the εἰσαγγελία was a law (νόμον) introduced by Solon:

(5) Arist., *Ath. Pol.* 8.4

βουλὴν δ' ἐποίησε τετρακοσίους, ἑκατὸν ἐξ ἑκάστης φυλῆς, τὴν δὲ τῶν Ἀρεοπαγιτῶν ἔταξεν ἐπὶ τὸ νομοφυλακεῖν, ὥσπερ ὑπῆρχεν καὶ πρότερον ἐπίσκοπος οὖσα τῆς πολιτείας, καὶ τά τε ἄλλα τὰ πλεῖστα καὶ τὰ μέγιστα τῶν πολιτικῶν διετήρει, καὶ τοὺς ἁμαρτάνοντας ηὔθυνεν κυρία οὖσα καὶ ζημιοῦν καὶ κολάζειν, καὶ τὰς ἐκτίσεις ἀνέφερεν εἰς πόλιν, οὐκ

---

13 Translations of Demosthenes *On the Crown* and *On the Dishonest Embassy* are borrowed from Yunis (2005).
14 This translation is taken from Murray (1936).
15 The term appears also in Plato: "Then there ensue impeachments (εἰσαγγελίαι) and judgements and lawsuits on either side" (cf. Pl., *Resp.* 8.565e).

ἐπιγράφουσα τὴν πρόφασιν δι' ὃ τὸ ἐκτίνεσθαι, καὶ τοὺς ἐπὶ καταλύσει τοῦ δήμου συνισταμένους ἔκρινεν, Σόλωνος θέντος νόμον **εἰσαγγελίας**[16] περὶ αὐτῶν.

And he made a Council of four hundred members, a hundred from each tribe, but appointed the Council of the Areopagus to the duty of guarding the laws, just as it had existed even before as overseer of the constitution, and it was this Council that kept watch over the greatest and the most important of the affairs of state, in particular correcting offenders with sovereign powers both to fine and punish, and making returns of its expenditure to the Acropolis without adding a statement of the reason for the outlay, and trying persons that conspired to put down the democracy, Solon having laid down a law of **impeachment** in regard to them.[17]

The εἰσαγγελία implied a denunciation for major public offences[18] (Rhodes 1981, 156) and involved a summary trial (Thalheim 1905). Demosthenes and Hyperides[19] also mention a law of impeachment (εἰσαγγελτικὸς νόμος),[20] and Hyperides tells us that the εἰσαγγελία posed a permanent threat to Greek orators. Demosthenes, as he himself affirms in his speech *On the Crown*, had to face some of them:[21]

(6) Dem., *De cor.* 249

ἔπειθ' αἱρούμενος σιτώνην ἐκ πάντων ἔμ' ἐχειροτόνησεν ὁ δῆμος. καὶ μετὰ ταῦτα συστάντων οἷς ἦν ἐπιμελὲς κακῶς ἐμὲ ποιεῖν, καὶ γραφάς,[22] εὐθύνας, **εἰσαγγελίας** (...).

Following that, the persons intent on doing me harm joined forces and subjected me to indictments, audits, **trials for treason** (...).

---

16 See Ostwald (1986, 8–9): "The absence of an article before νόμον indicates that Solon enacted *a* law, not *the* law of *eisangelia* — in other words, legislation like, but not identical with, that which later come to regulate proceedings of *eisangelia*". See also Sandys (2000, 34–35).
17 Translation taken from Rackham (1952).
18 On the legal procedures and the distinct categories of εἰσαγγελία, see Ruschenbusch (1968), Harrison (1971, 50–59), Rhodes (1979), Carawan (1985) and (1987), Gagarin (1986), Sealey (1994, 130–134), Hansen (1980), (1998), (1999, 390) and Harris (2017).
19 In another of Hyperides' speeches (*In Defence of Lycophron*), the accusation is transferred to the private sphere.
20 Cf. Dem., *Tim.* 63 and the speech *In Defence of Euxenippus* of Hyperides, in which this law is mentioned up to 4 times. Cf. also Rhodes (2004, 320) and the commentaries of Wayte (1882, 140–141) to the Demosthenic speech *Against Timocrates*.
21 The term εἰσαγγελία also appears in Isoc., *De pace* 130, Isoc., *Antid.* 314, Lys. 12.58, Lys. 16.12, Lys. 30.22, Dem., *Chers.* 29, Dem., *De cor.* 13, Dem., *Emb.* 103 and 116, Dem., *Meid.* 121, Dem., *Tim.* 63 and Dem., *Aristog.* 1.47 (twice) and Aeschin., *Emb.* 52, 79 and 171.
22 See Goodwin (1979, 174): "γραφάς: here in the most restricted sense of ordinary public suits, excluding εἰσαγγελία, εὔθυναι, etc".

In *Brill's New Pauly* it is suggested that the term designates the statement of a claim as well as the proceedings it institutes. The charges would be presented in writing and they would be argued in detail during the process. A detailed study of the εἰσαγγελία is beyond the limits of this volume, but we cannot ignore that we are dealing with one of the derivatives of ἄγγελος here. I have no record of any text from antiquity in which the term εἰσαγγελία alludes to the transmission of a piece of news, but the reality is that both εἰσαγγελία and news do share a fundamental feature: its public character.[23]

Ἐπαγγελία is another of ἄγγελος' derivatives that becomes a technical term associated with legal language. This noun, which is absent from the previous corpora analysed in this volume, occurs 3 times in the speeches of Aeschines and 4 in those of Demosthenes, who tends to use it to designate a promise.[24]

In the case of Aeschines, however, it appears as a technical legal term almost without exception in the speech *Against Timarchus*. The legal action used by Aeschines against Timarchus was δοκιμασία τῶν ῥητόρων ('scrutiny of public speakers'), whose purpose is "to test the credentials of those whose sought to direct public policy in the Assembly and to remove from influence those deemed unworthy" (Carey 2000, 19).[25] The procedure began with the announcement of the submission of a *dokimasia* against a speaker who put forward a motion in the public assembly (ἐπαγγελία δοκιμασίας).[26] In such a context, Aeschines uses ἐπαγγελία as the complement of the verb ἐπαγγέλλω:[27]

(7) Aeschin., *In Tim.* 81

> Καὶ τὰ μὲν πολλὰ καὶ παλαιὰ ἐάσω, τὰ δὲ ἐν αὐτῇ τῇ ἐκκλησίᾳ γενόμενα, ὅτε ἐγὼ **τὴν ἐπαγγελίαν ταύτην** Τιμάρχῳ **ἐπήγγειλα**.

---

[23] See Harrison (1971, 51): "The verb εἰσαγγέλλειν (with its cognate εἰσαγγελία) has both a general sense 'report', 'give information about' and a technical sense of initiating the legal procedure of that name, for which the best translation is 'impeach'".
[24] Cf. Dem., *De cor.* 298, Dem., *Emb.* 26, Dem., *Meid.* 14 and Aeschin., *Emb.* 34.
[25] Cf. also Aeschin., *In Tim.* 28–32. Lysias also mentions a δοκιμασία τῶν στρατηγῶν. Cf. Lys. 15.2.
[26] On this scrutiny, cf. *Epangelia* (Thür) in *Brill's New Pauly*. See also Harrison (1971, 204), Hansen (1999, 390) and Lucas de Dios (2002, 138–139).
[27] Cf. also Aeschin., *In Tim.* 64 and Dem., *Andr.* 29. In the latter, ἐπαγγελία is not the complement of ἐπαγγέλλω, but the term is used in an identical sense. On the example given in (7) see Adams (1919, 68).

I shall leave out most of these occasions that occurred some time ago; but I do want to remind you of what happened in the actual Assembly when **I made formal declaration of this scrutiny** against Timarchus.[28]

As noted in the previous chapter, παραγγελία is one of the terms designating the order in military contexts. In the corpus studied here, this term is only documented in Demosthenes' *On the Dishonest Embassy*. It is noteworthy, however, that παραγγελία does not allude to commands in either of the two passages in which it appears. Instead, it is another technicism associated with legal language. This is how the speech begins:

(8) Dem., *Emb.* 1

Ὅση μέν, ὦ ἄνδρες Ἀθηναῖοι, σπουδὴ περὶ τουτονὶ τὸν ἀγῶνα καὶ **παραγγελία** γέγονε, σχεδὸν οἶμαι πάντας ὑμᾶς ᾐσθῆσθαι, ἑορακότας ἄρτι τοὺς ὅτ' ἐκληροῦσθ' ἐνοχλοῦντας καὶ προσιόντας ὑμῖν.

How much lobbying, Athenians, this trial has occasioned and how much **influence** has been **exerted** are evident, I think, to nearly all of you, for you saw the people badgering and accosting you just now as you were being chosen by allotment.

The translation given in *LSJ* for παραγγελία in this passage is 'exertion of influence'.[29] It seems to be used in the same sense in (9):

(9) Dem., *Emb.* 283

οὐκ ἀναμνησθήσεσθ' ὧν κατηγορῶν ἔλεγεν Τιμάρχου, ὡς οὐδέν ἐστ' ὄφελος πόλεως ἥτις μὴ νεῦρ' ἐπὶ τοὺς ἀδικοῦντας ἔχει, οὐδὲ πολιτείας ἐν ᾗ συγγνώμη καὶ **παραγγελία** τῶν νόμων μεῖζον ἰσχύουσιν·

Will you not recall what he said when he prosecuted Timarchus? — that a city that does not use muscle against criminals is of no use, nor is a state where clemency and **influence** outstrip the laws.

Εὐαγγέλιον, the word for good news, occurs only once, in the Isocrates' *Areopagiticus*. The orator reproaches his audience for having forgotten about the problems of the city in the following words, which are filled with irony:

---

[28] Translations of Aeschines are borrowed from Carey (2000).
[29] In the same sense, Bailly. On the procedure, cf. Arist., *Ath. Pol.* 63.

(10) Isoc., *Areop*. 9–10

Ἐοίκατε γὰρ οὕτω διακειμένοις ἀνθρώποις, οἵτινες ἁπάσας μὲν τὰς πόλεις τὰς ἐπὶ Θρᾴκης ἀπολωλεκότες, πλείω δ' ἢ χίλια τάλαντα μάτην εἰς τοὺς ξένους ἀνηλωκότες, πρὸς δὲ τοὺς Ἕλληνας διαβεβλημένοι καὶ τῷ βαρβάρῳ πολέμιοι γεγονότες, ἔτι δὲ τοὺς μὲν Θηβαίων φίλους σῴζειν ἠναγκασμένοι, τοὺς δ' ἡμετέρους αὐτῶν συμμάχους ἀπολωλεκότες, ἐπὶ τοιαύταις πράξεσιν **εὐαγγέλια** μὲν δὶς ἤδη τεθύκαμεν,³⁰ ῥᾳθυμότερον δὲ περὶ αὐτῶν ἐκκλησιάζομεν τῶν πάντα τὰ δέοντα πραττόντων.

You certainly seem to be in this condition, for you have lost all the cities in Thrace, have wasted more than a thousand talents to no avail on foreigners, have earned the scorn of the Greeks and the enmity of the barbarians, and moreover, were forced to save the friends of the Thebans, while you lost your own allies. In such conditions, we have twice made sacrifices celebrating the arrival of **good news**, but when we discuss these matters in the Assembly, we are less serious than men who have achieved all they want.

The verb εὐαγγελίζομαι expresses the action of reporting good news and until now has only appeared in Aristophanes' *Knights*. In Greek oratory εὐαγγελίζομαι appears only once, at the end of the speech *On the Crown*:

(11) Dem., *De cor.* 323

οὐκ ἐπὶ μὲν τοῖς ἑτέρων εὐτυχήμασι φαιδρὸς ἐγὼ καὶ γεγηθὼς κατὰ τὴν ἀγορὰν περιέρχομαι, τὴν δεξιὰν προτείνων καὶ **εὐαγγελιζόμενος** τούτοις οὓς ἂν ἐκεῖσ' ἀπαγγελεῖν οἴωμαι (...).

When others reap success, I do not go around the Agora beaming with joy, nor do I shake hands and **spread the good news** among people who will most likely report it there.

This Demosthenic assertion is found in the orator's own statement about his love for Athens and his fellow citizens.³¹

Now, I will focus on ἀγγέλλω and its derivatives. The verb ἀγγέλλω is scarcely present in Greek oratory and, as we will see, ἀπαγγέλλω is the most

---

30 Note again the presence of the verb θύω. As stated below, I will also discuss this context in the next chapter.
31 See Goodwin (1904): "εὐαγγελιζόμενος: Properly announcing good tidings (cf. εὐαγγέλιον, Gospel), but here congratulating on good news, e.g. saying "This is a great victory". He means any of those (a well-known class) who I ever think are likely to report thither (to Macedonia) such an event as my congratulating them on a victory of Alexander". See also Yunis (2001): "An especially caustic comment: this traitor makes a show of delight in Macedonian success in the hope of securing good standing with the masters in Macedon".

frequently used. In addition to this, two verbs that we have not discussed also appear: κατεπαγγέλομαι and προεξαγγέλλω.

Neither Isocrates nor Lysias use ἀγγέλλω in their speeches. Demosthenes and Aeschines, meanwhile, offer two examples each and in the four contexts the announcement inherent to the verb is related to news. In (12), where ἀγγέλλω shows the expected construction with a syntactic argument in the accusative (result) and another one in the dative (recipient), Aeschines asks to be favoured for reporting a victory:

(12) Aeschin., *Emb.* 171

> **Ἀγγείλας** τοίνυν πρῶτος[32] τὴν τῆς πόλεως νίκην ὑμῖν καὶ τὴν τῶν παίδων τῶν ὑμετέρων κατόρθωσιν, πρώτην ταύτην ὑμᾶς ἀπαιτῶ χάριν, τὴν τοῦ σώματος σωτηρίαν.
>
> So I was the first to **bring news** of the city's victory and your sons' success. And the first return I ask is that you spare my life.

The victory mentioned by Aeschines is that of the battle of Tamynae (348 BC) where — as Aeschines himself explains — he was crowned for having brought the news of the city's victory (τήν τε νίκην τῆς πόλεως ἀπαγγείλας).[33]

In (13) Demosthenes makes mention of Philip's capture of Elatea:

(13) Dem., *De cor.* 169

> Ἑσπέρα μὲν γὰρ ἦν, ἧκε δ' **ἀγγέλλων** τις ὡς τοὺς πρυτάνεις ὡς Ἐλάτεια κατείληπται.
>
> It was evening, and a messenger reached the Presiding Officers **with the news** that Elatea had been taken.

As in many of the contexts in which historians mention the transmission of a piece of news, Demosthenes does not specify the identity of the person(s) in charge of making the announcement either but refers only to someone (τις) who came to do so. The ὡς substantive clause makes the content of the news item clear. In (14) ἀγγέλλω is in the passive voice and the news is the subject:

---

[32] Note the importance given to being the first to break the news, which is reminiscent of the behaviour of tragic messengers.
[33] Cf. Aeschin., *Emb.* 169.

(14) Dem., *Olynth.* 1.5

> ὡς γὰρ **ἠγγέλθη** Φίλιππος ἀσθενῶν ἢ τεθνεώς (ἦλθε γὰρ ἀμφότερα), οὐκέτι καιρὸν οὐδένα τοῦ βοηθεῖν νομίσαντες ἀφεῖτ', ὦ ἄνδρες Ἀθηναῖοι, τὸν ἀπόστολον.

> When **news came** that Philip was ill or dead — both reports reached us — you, Athenians, thinking that help was no longer needed, abandoned the expedition.[34]

In the last passage, the announcement inherent to ἀγγέλλω is only likely to be interpreted from the context. Aeschines has previously alleged that Demosthenes wanted to convince a certain Aristophanes to testify against him and lie. However, this man refused to do so:

(15) Aeschin., *Emb.* 155

> Ὅτι δὲ ἀληθῆ λέγω, αὐτὸν Ἀριστοφάνην μαρτυροῦντα παρέξομαι. Κάλει μοι Ἀριστοφάνην Ὀλύνθιον, καὶ τὴν μαρτυρίαν ἀναγίγνωσκε, καὶ τοὺς ἀκηκοότας αὐτοῦ καὶ πρὸς ἐμὲ **ἀγγείλαντας**, Δερκύλον Αὐτοκλέους Ἁγνούσιον καὶ Ἀριστείδην Εὐφιλήτου Κηφισιέα.

> To prove I am telling the truth, I shall provide Aristophanes himself as my witness. Call Aristophanes of Olynthus and read out his deposition and call the people who heard him and **brought word to me**, Dercylus son of Autocles of Hagnus and Aristides son of Euphiletus of Cephisia.

Ἀναγγέλλω occurs only once in *Against Spudias*, a speech related to family law:

(16) Dem., *Spud.* 17

> ὅτε γὰρ Πολύευκτος διετίθετο ταῦτα, παρῆν μὲν ἡ τούτου γυνή, καὶ δῆλον ὅτι τὰς τοῦ πατρὸς διαθήκας **ἀνήγγειλεν**, ἄλλως τ' εἰ καὶ μηδὲν ἴσον εἶχεν ἀλλ' ἐν ἅπασιν ἠλαττοῦτο.

> For, when Polyeuctus gave these directions in his will, the defendant's wife was present, and you may be sure that she **reported** to him the will of her father, especially if he did not receive an equal share, but was at a disadvantage in all respects.[35]

Before tackling the analysis of ἀπαγγέλλω, we should first consider a few things Firstly, as I have pointed out above, there are only four instances of ἀγγέλλω in the speeches of the studied orators and ἀπαγγέλλω is the most frequently used verb. The reason, in my view, is linked to something I have already noticed in the works of historians, where ἀπαγγέλλω refers to reports made by ambassa-

---

34 Translation taken from Vince (1930).
35 Translation borrowed from Murray (1939).

dors at a rate of 95%. The specialization of ἀπαγγέλλω — documented 120 times (4 in the speeches of Isocrates, 11 in those of Lysias, 27 in those of Aeschines and 78 in those of Demosthenes) — as a specific term for the transmission of any kind of information that is dealt with in the context of an embassy is supported by an analysis of Greek oratory. As I shall show, this verb is almost always used for this purpose. On the other hand, in the rare contexts in which news is not transmitted as a result of an embassy, ἀπαγγέλλω is also used. This is proof that ἀγγέλλω has fallen into disuse in favour of this derivative.

The construction of ἀπαγγέλλω with the accusative and the dative appears in the speeches of the four orators, although in those of Isocrates it only appears once, when he refers to the most beautiful things that the poets tell us (τὰς καλλίστας ἡμῖν ἀπαγγέλλουσιν).[36]

In (17) the context is quite different. The example is taken from the Lysias' *Funeral Oration*,[37] delivered in honour of the Athenians who had died in combat. The excerpt is specifically framed in the part devoted to the praise of ancestors, their exploits in the Persian Wars:

(17) Lys. 2.26

> οὕτω δὲ διὰ ταχέων τὸν κίνδυνον ἐποιήσαντο, ὥστε οἱ αὐτοί[38] τοῖς ἄλλοις **ἀπήγγειλαν** τήν τ' ἐνθάδε ἄφιξιν τῶν βαρβάρων καὶ τὴν νίκην τῶν προγόνων.
>
> They responded to the danger so quickly that the same messengers **announced** to the rest of the Greeks both the arrival of the barbarians and the victory of our ancestors.[39]

In the cases of Demosthenes and Aeschines, it is common for the recipient not to be expressed by the dative but by a prepositional phrase πρός + accusative.[40] Furthermore, with the exception of one occasion,[41] the announcement inherent

---

36 Cf. Isoc., *Evag.* 36.
37 On the specific characteristics of this type of discourse, see the general introduction in Crespo (2012, 9–44). For the specific features of the Lysias' *Funeral Oration*, cf. ibid., 93–97.
38 See Todd (2007, 234): "[so quickly] that the same messengers announced to the others both the arrival here of barbarians and the victory won by our ancestors".
39 Translations of Lysias' speeches are borrowed from Todd (2000).
40 In addition to the example given in (18), cf. Dem., *De cor.* 33, Dem., *Emb.* 18, Dem., *Emb.* 20, Dem., *Emb.* 28, Dem., *Emb.* 53, Dem., *Emb.* 204, Dem., *Emb.* 253 and Dem., *Emb.* 304. The few exceptions are found in Dem., *Summ.* 28, Dem., *De cor.* 42, Aeschin., *Emb.* 60 and Aeschin., *Emb.* 80.
41 In a private speech, *Against Dionysodorus*, in which the defendant sends a man to Rhodes to inform (ἀπαγγελοῦντα) his partner Parmeniscus (τῷ Παρμενίσκῳ τῷ κοινωνῷ) of the state of

to ἀπαγγέλλω is reported by an ambassador. In this respect, it should be highlighted that in Aeschines the accusative is usually that of the term πρεσβεία ('embassy'), as in (18):[42]

(18) Aeschin., *Emb.* 45

> Ὡς γὰρ δεῦρ' ἤλθομεν καὶ πρὸς τὴν βουλὴν ἐπὶ κεφαλαίων τὴν πρεσβείαν **ἀπηγγείλαμεν**, καὶ τὴν ἐπιστολὴν ἀπέδομεν τὴν παρὰ Φιλίππου, ἐπαινέτης ἦν ἡμῶν Δημοσθένης, καὶ τὴν Ἑστίαν ἐπώμοσε τὴν βουλαίαν συγχαίρειν τῇ πόλει, ὅτι τοιούτους ἄνδρας ἐπὶ τὴν πρεσβείαν ἐξέπεμψεν, οἳ καὶ τοῖς λόγοις καὶ τῇ πίστει ἦσαν ἄξιοι τῆς πόλεως.

> We arrived back here and **gave a** summary **report** on our mission to the Council and handed over the letter from Philip. And Demosthenes was full of praise for us before the Council; he swore by Hestia of the Council that he shared the city's pleasure at sending men of this quality on the embassy, men whose speaking skill and honesty were a credit to the city.

The dative (recipient) tends to be omitted,[43] as in (19), referring to the Amazons:

(19) Lys. 2.6

> μόναις δ' αὐταῖς οὐκ ἐξεγένετο ἐκ τῶν ἡμαρτημένων μαθούσαις περὶ τῶν λοιπῶν ἄμεινον βουλεύσασθαι, οὐδ' οἴκαδε ἀπελθούσαις **ἀπαγγεῖλαι**[44] τήν τε σφετέραν αὐτῶν δυστυχίαν καὶ τὴν τῶν ἡμετέρων προγόνων ἀρετήν·

> They alone were given no chance to learn from their errors and make better plans for the future; nor could they return home and **tell** about their own disasters or about our ancestors' merits.

Aeschines and Demosthenes almost always use ἀπαγγέλλω in the speeches dealing with embassies. The complement in the accusative is usually a generic neuter like ταῦτα,[45] τι,[46] τοιαῦτα,[47] or τἀληθῆ[48] amongst others.[49] On some occa-

---

things (τὰ ἐνθένδε καθεστηκότα), that is, that his ship would be forced to stop over at Rhodes. Cf. Dem., *Dionys.* 9.
42 Cf. also Aeschin., *Emb.* 60 or Aeschin., *Emb.* 94.
43 Never in Isocrates' speeches.
44 Cf. Todd (2007, 217): "('nor [was it granted] to them to return home and report...')".
45 Cf. Dem., *De cor.* 32, Dem., *Emb.* 75 and Dem., *Emb.* 152, Dem., *Meid.* 72, Dem., *Epit.* 34 and Dem., *Erot.* 27. In Aeschin., *Emb.* 119 it is the singular τοῦτο.
46 Cf. Dem., *Emb.* 19. En Dem., *Emb.* 59 and 82 is the interrogative pronoun τί.
47 Cf. Dem., *Emb.* 324 and Aeschin., *In Ctes.* 63.

sions it is a noun[50] that allows us to easily recognize the content of the announcement. In Aeschines' speeches it is always the accusative of πρεσβεία[51] except in three examples, such as the one I present in (20), where the report given has also occurred in the context of an embassy:[52]

(20) Aeschin., *Emb.* 17

> εἷς δὲ τῶν βουλευτῶν ἦν Δημοσθένης ὁ ἐμὸς κατήγορος. Παρελθὼν δ' ὁ Ἀριστόδημος, πολλήν τινα εὔνοιαν **ἀπήγγειλε** τοῦ Φιλίππου πρὸς τὴν πόλιν.
>
> The Council members included my accuser Demosthenes. Aristodemus came forward and **reported** that Philip was very well disposed toward the city.

The complement in the accusative is also often omitted, as in (21), where the only referred syntactic argument is the one in the dative (recipient). The excerpt is from the *Accusation of Calumny* of Lysias. The accuser was a member of a private association (συνουσία) but, for some reason, he was not well regarded by his colleagues, who despised and mocked him. Fed up with the situation, the man decided to take action and finally left the association voluntarily. In this part, the main character admits that someone told him what the others thought about him:[53]

---

48 Cf. Dem., *Emb.* 76, Dem., *Emb.* 161, Dem., *Emb.* 223, Dem., *Emb.* 279 and Aeschin., *Emb.* 121. Also the plural ἀληθεῖς in Dem., *Emb.* 183, the negative μηδὲν ἀληθές in Dem., *Emb.* 8 and οὐδὲν ἀληθές in Dem., *Emb.* 177 or lies: τὰ ψευδῆ in Dem., *De cor.* 25 and Dem., *Emb.* 76.
49 οὐδ' ὁτιοῦν ὑγιές (Dem., *Emb.* 12), τἀναντία (Dem., *Emb.* 85), τἆλλα πάντα (Aeschin., *Emb.* 51) or τὰ προσηγγελμέν' (Dem., *De cor.* 170).
50 In Dem., *Emb.* 11 the accusative is τοὺς καλοὺς ἐκείνους καὶ μακροὺς λόγους. In one of Demosthenes' private speeches (*Against Timotheus* 13) it was reported before the Assembly the distress and need that existed (τὴν παροῦσαν ἔνδειαν καὶ ἀπορίαν) within the army in Calaureia.
51 Cf. Aeschin., *Emb.* 16, Aeschin., *Emb.* 47, Aeschin., *Emb.* 49 and Aeschin., *Emb.* 130.
52 The other exceptions are in Aeschin., *Emb.* 80 (τὴν εἰρήνην) and Aeschin., *Emb.* 169 (τήν τε νίκην τῆς πόλεως).
53 See Todd (2007, 572): "ἀπήγγειλε τοῖς ἐμοῖς ἀναγκαίοις ('passed it on [lit, "announced"] to my relatives". Cf. also Lys. 8.8. In Lys. 8.15 the recipient is expressed by a prepositional phrase πρός + accusative (πρὸς Εὐρυπτόλεμον). Cf. also Lys. 22.14.

(21) Lys. 8.9

οὐ γὰρ ἐπὶ τοῖς αὐτοῖς ἐκεῖνος ἡμῖν **ἀπήγγελλεν**, ἐφ' οἷσπερ ὑμεῖς ἐλέγετε πρὸς ἐκεῖνον. ἐκεῖνος μὲν γὰρ ἐμοὶ χαριζόμενος **ἀπήγγειλε** τοῖς ἐμοῖς ἀναγκαίοις, ὑμεῖς δὲ βλάπτειν ἐμὲ βουλόμενοι πρὸς ἐκεῖνον ἐλέγετε.

> He did not **pass on the information** to me with the same purpose that you spoke to him. He **passed it on** to my relatives as a favor to me, whereas you spoke to him because you wished to harm me.

In the speeches of Demosthenes and Aeschines, the announcement inherent to ἀπαγγέλλω is again mostly something that has happened in the context of an embassy or which an ambassador has negotiated,[54] although there are some exceptions.[55] In (22), for instance, reference is made to the intentions of Philip in the past:

(22) Dem., *Olynth.* 1.4

Μέμνησθ', ὦ ἄνδρες Ἀθηναῖοι, ὅτ' **ἀπηγγέλθη** Φίλιππος ὑμῖν ἐν Θρᾴκῃ τρίτον ἢ τέταρτον ἔτος τουτὶ Ἡραῖον τεῖχος πολιορκῶν.

> You remember, men of Athens, when **news came** three or four years ago that Philip was in Thrace besieging the fortress of Heraeum.

With this verb, the result is less likely to be expressed by a substantive clause, although there are some passages in which a ὅτι[56] (23) or a ὡς substantive clause (24) is used (never AcI or AcP constructions). In (23) the news is related to with Philip's behaviour:[57]

---

54 On these occasions the recipient is always expressed by a prepositional phrase πρός + accusative — as in Dem., *Emb.* 18, Dem., *Emb.* 37, Dem., *Emb.* 56, Dem., *Emb.* 111, Aeschin., *Emb.* 13, Aeschin., *Emb.* 25, Aeschin., *Emb.* 121 and Aeschin., *In Ctes.* 213 — or εἰς- + accusative, as in Dem., *Emb.* 23.
55 Cf. also Aeschin., *In Tim.* 135; Dem., *Meid.* 25, Dem., *Meid.* 37, Dem., *Meid.* 72 and Dem., *Meid.* 202; Dem., *Everg.* 57 and *Polyc.* 50.51.
56 The dative recipient tends to be explicitly referred to (this construction occurs only in the speeches of Demosthenes and Aeschines). Cf., e.g., Aeschin., *Emb.* 12. The recipient is omitted on three occasions (cf. Isoc., *Trapez.* 11, Dem., *De cor.* 32 and Aeschin., *Emb.* 119).
57 This same Dercylus is said to have reported (ἀπήγγειλεν) them (you, in the mouth of Demosthenes (ὑμῖν) that the Phocians were destroyed (ὅτι Φωκεῖς ἀπολώλασι). In *Against Lacritus* the context is different: a certain Antipater had lent money to another man for a voyage to Pontus on the ship commanded by Hyblesius. Shortly afterwards, his servants announced to

(23) Dem., *Emb.* 60

ἧκε δὲ Δερκύλος ἐκ Χαλκίδος καὶ **ἀπήγγελλεν** ὑμῖν ὅτι πάντα τὰ πράγματ' ἐγκεχείρικε Θηβαίοις ὁ Φίλιππος, καὶ πέμπτην εἶναι ταύτην ἡμέραν ἐλογίζετ' ἀφ' οὗ γεγόνασιν αἱ σπονδαί.

Dercylus returned from Chalcis **with the news** that Philip had handed everything over to the Thebans, and he reckoned that the truce had been made four days earlier.

The example (24) is taken from Lysias' speech *For the Soldier*.[58] Polyaenus, the defendant, explains himself as follows:

(24) Lys. 9.6

οἱ δὲ μετὰ Κτησικλέους τοῦ ἄρχοντος, **ἀπαγγείλαντός** τινος ὡς ἐγὼ λοιδοροῖμι, τοῦ νόμου ἀπαγορεύοντος ἐάν τις ἀρχὴν ἐν συνεδρίῳ λοιδορῇ, παρὰ τὸν νόμον ζημιῶσαι ἠξίωσαν.

Nevertheless, the supporters of Ctesicles the official claimed the right to punish me when somebody **reported** that I was slandering them: this was illegal, because the law forbids that someone should insult an official in the *sunedrion*.

Ἀπαγγέλλω could be translated as 'denounce' since, although he was not prosecuted for it, what someone reported was an infraction that the defendant had to pay.

Finally, the presence of ἀπαγγέλλω in an absolute use is well attested.[59] This is an example from the Isocrates' *Panathenaicus*:

(25) Isoc., *Panath.* 17

Ἕως μὲν οὖν τοὺς λόγους ἡμῶν ἐλυμαίνοντο, παραναγιγνώσκοντες ὡς δυνατὸν κάκιστα τοῖς αὑτῶν καὶ διαιροῦντες οὐκ ὀρθῶς καὶ κατακνίζοντες καὶ πάντα τρόπον διαφθείροντες, οὐδὲν ἐφρόντιζον **τῶν ἀπαγγελλομένων**, ἀλλὰ ῥᾳθύμως εἶχον·

As long as they confined themselves to abusing my discourses, reading them in the worst possible manner side by side with their own, dividing them at the wrong places, mutilat-

---

him (ἑαυτῷ) that the ship, with no one in charge, was wrecked while sailing along the coast (ὅτι ἡ ναῦς κενὴ διεφθάρη). Cf. Dem., *Lacr.* 33.
58 There are only four passages in which the recipient is omitted. In addition to (24), cf. also Lys. 8.10, Dem., *Emb.* 217 and Dem., *Lept.* 73.
59 In addition to (25) cf. Isoc., *Demon.* 33, Dem., *Halonn.* 21, Dem., *Symm.* 40, Dem., *Emb.* 124 Aeschin., *Emb.* 56 and Lys. 8.15.

ing them, and in every way spoiling their effect, I paid no heed **to the reports which were brought** to me, but possessed myself in patience.

We have only two occurrences of διαγγέλλω, both in the speeches of Aeschines. For now, I will discuss only one of them, since the other one is linked to rumours and will be discussed in the next chapter. The verb only takes the accusative:

(26) Aeschin., *Emb.* 130

οἱ δὲ Φαλαίκου τοῦ Φωκέων τυράννου δρομοκήρυκες τἀνθένδε ἐκεῖσε **διήγγελλον**, πιστεύσαντες δὲ οἱ Φωκεῖς ἐμοί, εἴσω Πυλῶν αὐτὸν παρεδέξαντο καὶ τὰς πόλεις τὰς αὑτῶν παρέδοσαν.

And the couriers of Phalaecus, the Phocian dictator (*tyrannos*), **took the news** there, and the Phocians on account of their trust in me allowed Philip to pass through Thermopylae and surrendered their cities to him.

In the speeches of orators, εἰσαγγέλλω is fully established as a legal term referring to a denunciation in the context of an εἰσαγγελία. The verb occurs 23 times (5 in the speeches of Lysias, 14 in those of Demosthenes and 4 in those of Aeschines) and it does not allude to a denunciation only twice.

Εἰσαγγέλλω is accompanied by a complement in the accusative with an animate referent in three of the six passages in which it appears.[60] In (27) the accuser, as explained by Demosthenes, is the orator Hyperides and the defendant is Philocrates, suspected of having received money from Philip when he was sent as ambassador to negotiate that which was later called the Peace of Philocrates:

(27) Dem., *Emb.* 116

ἴστε δήπου πρώην, ὅτ᾽ **εἰσήγγελλεν** Ὑπερείδης Φιλοκράτην, ὅτι παρελθὼν ἐγὼ δυσχεραίνειν ἔφην ἔν τι τῆς **εἰσαγγελίας**, εἰ μόνος Φιλοκράτης τοσούτων καὶ τοιούτων ἀδικημάτων αἴτιος γέγονεν, οἱ δ᾽ ἐννέα τῶν πρέσβεων μηδενός.

You are surely aware that recently, when Hyperides **indicted** Philocrates **for treason**, I stepped forward and said I was troubled by one aspect of **the indictment**, namely, that Philocrates should have committed so many serious crimes by himself while the nine other envoys did nothing.

---

60 Cf. also Aeschin., *Emb.* 139 and Dem., *Lept.* 79.

In some other excerpts,⁶¹ the accusative (in these cases with inanimate referent) is τἀληθῆ. Just as it appears in the speech *Against Agoratus* itself, Agoratus was an alleged informer of the Thirty. Now he is the man on trial:

(28) Lys. 13.50

> πρῶτον μὲν γὰρ τὰ ψηφίσματα αὐτοῦ τὰ ἐκ τῆς βουλῆς καὶ τὸ τοῦ δήμου καταμαρτυρεῖ, διαρρήδην ἀγορεύοντα «περὶ ὧν Ἀγόρατος κατείρηκεν». ἔπειτα ἡ κρίσις, ἣν ἐκρίθη ἐπὶ τῶν τριάκοντα καὶ ἀφείθη, διαρρήδην λέγει, «διότι» φησίν «ἔδοξε τἀληθῆ **εἰσαγγεῖλαι**».

> In the first place, the decrees of the Council and the one passed by the Assembly bear witness against him, because they explicitly say, 'concerning the people whom Agoratus has denounced'. Secondly, the verdict that was passed under the Thirty, and that acquitted him, explicitly states, 'because it appeared that **his information** is true.'⁶²

In (29), the verb is accompanied by a ὅτι substantive clause. This is one of the few examples in which εἰσαγγέλλω does not refer to a denouncement, but to a piece of news. The passage is from a private speech from Demosthenes' *Against Polycles* and the speaker is a litigant (Apollodorus), who explains the following:

(29) Dem., *Polyc.* 17

> τοιούτων τοίνυν μοι τῶν πραγμάτων συμβεβηκότων, καὶ τοῦ στρατηγοῦ ἅμα Τιμομάχου προστάξαντος πλεῖν ἐφ' Ἱερὸν ἐπὶ τὴν παραπομπὴν τοῦ σίτου καὶ μισθὸν οὐ διδόντος, **εἰσαγγελθέντων** δὲ ὅτι Βυζάντιοι καὶ Καλχηδόνιοι πάλιν κατάγουσι τὰ πλοῖα καὶ ἀναγκάζουσι τὸν σῖτον ἐξαιρεῖσθαι.

> This, then, was my situation when the general Timomachus ordered me to sail to Hieron to escort the grain transports, but he supplied no money. **Word also came** that the Byzantines and Chalcedonians were once again conducting the boats to shore and forcing them to unload their grain.⁶³

In (30) εἰσαγγέλλω appears with an AcP construction. The excerpt is taken from the beginning of Lysias' *Against Theomnestus*:

---

61 Cf. also Lys. 12.25 and Lys. 13.56.
62 Lamb translates: "In as much as his report has been approved as true".
63 Translation taken from Bers (2003).

(30) Lys. 10.1

> Μαρτύρων μὲν οὐκ ἀπορίαν μοι ἔσεσθαι δοκῶ, ὦ ἄνδρες δικασταί· πολλοὺς γὰρ ὑμῶν ὁρῶ δικάζοντας τῶν τότε παρόντων, ὅτε Λυσίθεος Θεόμνηστον **εἰσήγγελλε** τὰ ὅπλα ἀποβεβληκότα, οὐκ ἐξὸν αὐτῷ, δημηγορεῖν·
>
> I do not expect to have any difficulty finding witnesses, gentlemen of the jury. I can see that many of you who are judging the case were among those present when Lysitheus **denounced** Theomnestus, on the grounds that he was speaking in public when he was not permitted to do so because he had thrown away his shield.

This passage poses a problem. Theomnestus is faced with a prosecution for defamation but, apparently, he could have been on trial for other reasons. Based on Lamb's (1930) proposal (with which I fully agree), we cannot be sure what charges were brought against him then. If he was on trial for casting away his armour — which entailed the loss of rights of citizenship, including that of speaking in public — it would be a procedure of εἰσαγγελία. However, if the trial brought against him was for having spoken in public, it would be a procedure of ἐπαγγελία δοκιμασίας, which is why Gernet/Bizos (1924) propose ἐπήγγειλε[64] instead of εἰσήγγελλε.

Finally, I will turn to those passages in which εἰσαγγέλλω appears with an absolute use. In these cases, the term is always a legal technical term referring to a denunciation, with the only exception given in (31):

(31) Lys. 1.19–20

> καὶ τότε ἤδη πρὸς τὰ γόνατά μου πεσοῦσα, καὶ πίστιν παρ' ἐμοῦ λαβοῦσα μηδὲν πείσεσθαι κακόν, κατηγόρει πρῶτον μὲν ὡς μετὰ τὴν ἐκφορὰν αὐτῇ προσίοι, ἔπειτα ὡς αὐτὴ τελευτῶσα **εἰσαγγείλειε** καὶ ὡς ἐκείνη τῷ χρόνῳ πεισθείη.
>
> She immediately fell at my knees and made me promise she would suffer no harm. She admitted, first, how he had approached her after the funeral, and then how she had eventually **acted as his messenger**,[65] and how my wife had in the end been won over.

---

[64] See Todd (2000, 104): "According to the manuscript, the procedure was impeachment (*eisangelia*), which is not otherwise attested in such circumstances. I have therefore accepted the emendation *epangelia* (the preliminary denunciation necessary before bringing a *dokimasia* to scrutinize the qualifications of a public speaker)". See also Todd (2007, 662).

[65] Lamb (1930) translates "she became his messenger". See also Edwards (1999) and Carey (1989): "acted as a go-between".

As I have already pointed out, in the other the contexts εἰσαγγέλλω indicates the presence of a denunciation.[66] It is common for the verb to appear in the passive voice, as in (32):

(32) Aeschin., *In Ctes.* 223

> Οὐ τὸ τελευταῖον **εἰσαγγέλλεσθαι** μέλλων ὑπ' ἐμοῦ, τὴν Ἀναξίνου σύλληψιν τοῦ Ὠρείτου κατεσκεύασας, τοῦ τὰ ἀγοράσματα Ὀλυμπιάδι ἀγοράζοντος;

> And finally, when **you were about to be impeached** by me, did you not contrive the arrest of Anaxinus of Oreus, who was making purchases for Olympias?

There are only eight instances of ἐξαγγέλλω in the works of orators (one in Isocrates, one in Lysias, two in Demosthenes and four in Aeschines). As stated in the corresponding chapter, historians also used this verb to refer to information revealed by those who had been sent on a spy mission. In addition, as we will show in the next chapter, in the works of historians ἐξαγγέλλω is also used to transmit *fake news*. In the speeches of Isocrates, Lysias, Demosthenes and Aeschines this verb is not used to denote lying, although it does appear in the transmission of news and when strategic information is revealed. Moreover, on one occasion it is used as a legal technical term denoting a denunciation.

The expected construction of ἐξαγγέλλω with a second syntactic argument in the accusative (result) and a third argument in the dative (recipient)[67] occurs only twice. In Isoc., *Arch.* 72 the news is related to war after the Battle of Leuctra. In (33), however, Demosthenes warns of the presence of traitors among the Athenians:

(33) Dem., *Phil.* 1.17–18

> δεῖ γὰρ ἐκείνῳ τοῦτ' ἐν τῇ γνώμῃ παραστῆσαι, ὡς ὑμεῖς ἐκ τῆς ἀμελείας ταύτης τῆς ἄγαν, ὥσπερ εἰς Εὔβοιαν καὶ πρότερόν ποτέ φασιν εἰς Ἁλίαρτον καὶ τὰ τελευταῖα πρώην εἰς Πύλας, ἴσως ἂν ὁρμήσαιτε — οὗτοι παντελῶς, οὐδ' εἰ μὴ ποιήσαιτ' ἂν τοῦτο, ὥς ἔγωγέ φημι δεῖν, εὐκαταφρόνητόν ἐστιν — ἵν' ἢ διὰ τὸν φόβον εἰδὼς εὐτρεπεῖς ὑμᾶς (εἴσεται γὰρ ἀκριβῶς· εἰσὶ γάρ, εἰσὶν οἱ πάντ' **ἐξαγγέλλοντες** ἐκείνῳ παρ' ἡμῶν αὐτῶν πλείους τοῦ δέοντος) ἡσυχίαν ἔχῃ.

---

66 Cf. also Dem., *Chers.* 28, Dem., *De cor.* 13 and Dem., *De cor.* 250, Dem., *Aristog.* 1.47, Dem., *Phorm.* 50, Dem., *Polyc.* 4, Dem., *Everg.* 80, Aeschin., *In Ctes.* 3, Aeschin., *In Ctes.* 223 and Aeschin., *In Ctes.* 252.

67 The dative is omitted in Aeschin., *Emb.* 13. In Aeschin., *In Tim.* 43 ἐξαγγέλλω is in the passive voice and is accompanied only by the dative (recipient). Cf. also Aeschin., *Emb.* 34, where the recipient is expressed by a prepositional phrase (πρὸς τοὺς ἑταίρους).

You must present to his mind the consideration that you may possibly shake off your excessive apathy and strike out as you did at Euboea, and before that, as we are told, at Haliartus, and quite recently at Thermopylae. That, even if you should not act as I, personally, think you ought, is not an altogether trivial matter; for its purpose is that he may either hold his hand through fear, knowing that you are on the alert—he will know it sure enough, for there are some on our side, yes, too many, who **report** everything to him—or that he may overlook it and so be taken off his guard.[68]

The presence of ἐξαγγέλλω in this excerpt makes a lot of sense, since the preverb ἐξ- perfectly reflects that someone who is inside (in this case someone who is among the Athenians) comes out to take the information.[69] In this regard, as I have already stated,[70] ἐξαγγέλλω indicates the disclosure of secrets.

The announcement inherent to the verb can be also expressed by a ὅτι[71] substantive clause or an AcI construction, as in (34), where the transmitted news is linked, once again, to war:

(34) Dem., *Meid*.162

ἐπειδὴ δὲ πολιορκεῖσθαι τοὺς ἐν Ταμύναις στρατιώτας **ἐξηγγέλλετο**,[72] καὶ πάντας ἐξιέναι τοὺς ὑπολοίπους ἱππέας, ὧν εἷς οὗτος ἦν, προεβούλευσεν ἡ βουλή, τηνικαῦτα φοβηθεὶς τὴν στρατείαν ταύτην εἰς τὴν ἐπιοῦσαν ἐκκλησίαν, πρὶν καὶ προέδρους καθέζεσθαι, παρελθὼν ἐπέδωκεν.

But when **it was announced** that the troops at Tamynae were blockaded, and when the Council carried a preliminary decree to dispatch the rest of the cavalry, to which he belonged, then, alarmed at the prospect of this campaign, he came forward with a voluntary gift at the next meeting of the Assembly, even before the Committee could take their seats.[73]

Finally, in (35) ἐξαγγέλλω shows an absolute use. The passage is from the Lysias' speech *For Polystratus*, in which the son of Polystratus defends his father and compares him with those who had been disloyal to democracy:

---

68 Translation taken from Vince (1930).
69 Remember the figure of the tragic ἐξάγγελος, the messenger who is inside the palace and goes outside to report the events that have occurred on the inside.
70 Note that in Xenophon's *Cyropaedia* we also find the noun ἐξαγγελία.
71 Cf. Aeschin., *In Ctes*. 116.
72 See MacDowell (1990, 382): "ἐξηγγέλλετο: the imperfect implies that several reports arrived, perhaps over some days".
73 Translation taken from Murray (1939).

(35) Lys. 20.9

ὥστε οἱ πολλοὶ πάντα ἀπεγίγνωσκον αὐτῶν· τοὺς μὲν γὰρ ἐξήλαυνον αὐτῶν, τοὺς δὲ ἀπεκτίννυσαν. οἳ δὲ ἐκείνων ἔμελλον ἀκροᾶσθαι καὶ μηδὲν ἐπιβουλεύειν μηδὲ **ἐξαγγέλλειν**, τούτους ἂν καθίσταντο. ὥστε οὐκ ἂν ῥᾳδίως μετέστη ἂν ὑμῖν ἡ πολιτεία. οὔκουν δίκαιοί εἰσιν, ὧν ὑμῖν εὖνοι ἦσαν, τούτων δίκην διδόναι.

As a result, most of them gave up entirely, because the oligarchs were expelling some of them and executing others. They placed in power those who would obey them and not plot or **pass information**[74] **to the enemy**: so you could not easily change the constitution. It is not right that such people should be punished for the support they gave you.[75]

The derivative προεξαγγέλλω — not documented in any of the previously studied authors — occurs once in Demosthenes' speech *On the Dishonest Embassy*. A nuance of anteriority is given by the verbal prefix προ-:

(36) Dem., *Emb*. 248

Τούτων οὐδὲν Αἰσχίνης εἶπε πρὸς αὐτὸν ἐν τῇ πρεσβείᾳ, ἀλλ' ἀντὶ μὲν τῆς πόλεως τὴν Φιλίππου ξενίαν καὶ φιλίαν πολλῷ μεῖζον' ἡγήσαθ' αὑτῷ καὶ λυσιτελεστέραν, ἐρρῶσθαι πολλὰ φράσας τῷ σοφῷ Σοφοκλεῖ, τὴν δ' ἄτην ὁρῶν στείχουσαν ὁμοῦ, τὴν ἐπὶ Φωκέας στρατείαν, οὐ προεῖπεν οὐδὲ **προεξήγγειλεν**, ἀλλὰ τοὐναντίον συνέκρυψε καὶ συνέπραξε καὶ τοὺς βουλομένους εἰπεῖν διεκώλυσεν.

Aeschines recited none of these verses to himself during the embassy, but, bidding a fond farewell to sage Sophocles, he held Philip's hospitality and friendship far "above his" city and more profitable to himself, and as he "saw ruin advancing" close by — Philip's expedition against the Phocians — he uttered no warning and **gave no alert (*did not announce the expedition beforehand*)**, but, on the contrary, he kept it hidden, colluded, and obstructed those who wished to speak.

Unlike in the works of historians, in the speeches of Isocrates, Lysias, Aeschines and Demosthenes ἐπαγγέλλω is never used to indicate the transmission of a piece of news, but to make mention of promises,[76] orders,[77] requests,[78] offerings[79]

---

74 Cf. *DGE*: ἐξαγγέλλω II. abs.: "Revelar, delatar faltas".
75 Translation taken from Murray (1939).
76 Cf. Aeschin., *Emb*. 41, Dem., *De cor*. 19 and Dem., *De cor*. 38 (ἐπαγγέλλω + accusative + dative), Dem., *Phil*. 1.15, Dem., *Emb*. 44, Dem., *Emb*. 48, Dem., *Zenoth*. 8 (ἐπαγγέλλω + accusative), Lys. 12.70, Dem., *Emb*. 58 (ἐπαγγέλλω + dative), Dem., *Emb*. 175, Lys. 28.4, Aeschin., *Emb*. 133 and Aeschin., *In Ctes*. 103 (ἐπαγγέλλω + dative + infinitive), Cf. Isoc., *Demon*. 19, Isoc., *Soph*. 8, Dem., *De cor*. 178, Dem., *Emb*. 48, Dem., *Lept*.61, Dem., *Aristocr*. 121, Dem., *Everg*. 81, Aeschin., *In Tim*. 143, Aeschin., *Emb*. 21, Aeschin., *Emb*. 120 and Aeschin., *Emb*. 132 (ἐπαγ-

or invitations.⁸⁰ Ἐπαγγέλλω is documented 67 times (6 in Isocrates, 6 in Lysias, 14 in Aeschines and 41 in Demosthenes) and there are also five occurrences of κατεπαγγέλλομαι. From my point of view, it is interesting to note that ἐπαγγέλλω, as well as other derivatives of ἄγγελος, has become established legal term in certain contexts.

For example, when it appears in the expected construction with the accusative and the dative, the accusative is either ἐπαγγελία[81] or δοκιμασία — as in (37). Used alongside these two words, as well as other derivatives of ἄγγελος, the verb seems to form part of a specific legal terminology. In cases like these, the argument in the dative is not the recipient, but the beneficiary / maleficiary:

(37) Aeschin., *In Tim.* 2

> εἰδὼς δ' αὐτὸν ἔνοχον ὄντα οἷς ὀλίγῳ πρότερον ἠκούσατε ἀναγιγνώσκοντος τοῦ γραμματέως, **ἐπήγγειλα** αὐτῷ **τὴν δοκιμασίαν** ταυτηνί.
>
> And in the knowledge that he is guilty of the charges that you heard the clerk read out just now, I **declared this formal scrutiny** against him.

It is not surprising that the dative is omitted here. The noun in the accusative tends to have an inanimate reference and provides us with information on what is offered, promised or proclaimed (for example, the truces mentioned in Aeschin., *Emb.* 133 and 134). In (38) a δοκιμασία is referred to again:

γέλλω + infinitive), Isoc., *Hel.* 9, Dem., *De cor.* 122, Dem., *De cor.* 322 or Dem., *Emb.* 48 (absolute use).

77 Cf. Dem., *Macart.* 58 (ἐπαγγέλλω + dative), Dem., *Macart.* 57 or Dem., *Erot.* 101 (ἐπαγγέλλω + dative + infinitive).

78 Cf. Isoc., *Hel.* 57, Dem., *Emb.* 193 (twice) (ἐπαγγέλλω + accusative), Dem., *Everg.* 67 (ἐπαγγέλλω + dative + infinitive).

79 Cf. Aeschin., *Emb.* 156 (the recipient is expressed by a prepositional phrase πρός– + accusative), Isoc., *Soph.* 20, Lys. 12.52, Dem., *Emb.* 41, Dem., *Pantae.* 13 (ἐπαγγέλλω + accusative), Dem., *Everg.* 66 (ἐπαγγέλλω + dative), Lys. 12.68 and Lys. 31.15 (ἐπαγγέλλω + infinitive). In Isoc., *Demon.* 2 5 and Dem., *De cor.* 68 we find the verbal adjective αὐτεπάγγελτος ('offering of oneself, volunteer'), also present in the works of historians.

80 Cf. Lys. 2.1 (ἐπαγγέλλω + infinitive) and Dem., *Olymp.* 51 (ἐπαγγέλλω + dative + infinitive).

81 Cf. Aeschin., *In Ctes.* 64.

(38) Aeschin., *In Tim.* 32

Ἐὰν δέ τις παρὰ ταῦτα μὴ μόνον λέγῃ, ἀλλὰ καὶ συκοφαντῇ καὶ ἀσελγαίνῃ, καὶ μηκέτι τὸν τοιοῦτον ἄνθρωπον δύνηται φέρειν ἡ πόλις, «**δοκιμασίαν** μέν», φησίν, «**ἐπαγγειλάτω** Ἀθηναίων ὁ βουλόμενος, οἷς ἔξεστιν».

And if anyone in defiance of these rules does not just speak but plays the sykophant and behaves unscrupulously, and the city can no longer tolerate such a man, 'Let any Athenian who wishes and has the right', he says, '**declare a scrutiny**'.

The derivative κατεπαγγέλλομαι occurs four times in the speeches of Aeschines and once in those of Demosthenes, and it always denotes the announcement of a promise.[82]

Καταγγέλλω is found in Lysias' *Defence against a Charge of subverting the Democracy*. It is worthy of note here that this verb occurs once in Xenophon's *Anabasis* (2.5.38), and it is a legal term that alludes to the public denouncing of an alleged plot (τὴν ἐπιβουλήν). In the speech of Lysias, however, it refers to the proclamation of a war:

(39) Lys. 25.30

τούτων δ' ἄξιον θαυμάζειν, ὅ τι ἂν ἐποίησαν, εἴ τις αὐτοὺς εἴασε τῶν τριάκοντα γενέσθαι, οἳ νῦν δημοκρατίας οὔσης ταὐτὰ ἐκείνοις πράττουσι, καὶ ταχέως μὲν ἐκ πενήτων πλούσιοι γεγένηνται, πολλὰς δὲ ἀρχὰς ἄρχοντες οὐδεμιᾶς εὐθύνην διδόασιν, ἀλλ' ἀντὶ μὲν ὁμονοίας ὑποψίαν πρὸς ἀλλήλους πεποιήκασιν, ἀντὶ δὲ εἰρήνης πόλεμον **κατηγγέλκασι**, διὰ τούτους δὲ ἄπιστοι τοῖς Ἕλλησι γεγενήμεθα.

As for my opponents, it is legitimate to wonder what they would have done if someone had allowed them to become members of the Thirty, since under the democracy they are now doing the same things as the Thirty did. Out of poverty, they have rapidly become rich. They have held many public offices but have submitted no accounts (*euthinai*). They **have proclaimed** war instead of peace, and on their account we have lost the trust of the Greeks.

There are 13 instances of παραγγέλλω in the speeches of orators (one in Isocrates, 5 in Lysias, 4 in Aeschines and 3 in Demosthenes) and the verb is always related to the transmission of orders[83] or requests for help.[84]

---

82 Cf. *LSJ*: κατεπαγγέλλομαι: "Make promises or engagements" and Bailly: "Promettre expressément". It can be accompanied by an accusative (Aeschin., *In Tim.* 117), a prepositional phrase πρός- + accusative expressing recipient (Aeschin., *In Tim.* 173), an infinitive (Aeschin., *In Tim.* 117), a complement in the dative (Dem., *Zenoth.* 11) or a ὡς substantive clause (Aeschin., *In Ctes.* 205).

Προαγγέλλω — documented once in Thucydides and twice in Xenophon's *Cyropaedia* — appears once in Demosthenes and indicates the presence of news. It is noteworthy once again that the preverb πρό– is present here. In this example, the announcement inherent to the verb is linked to the failed mission of the ambassadors sent to negotiate with Philip:

(40) Dem., *Emb.* 35

ὥσθ' ὑμᾶς, ἐκπεπληγμένους τῇ παρουσίᾳ τὸ πρῶτον τῇ τοῦ Φιλίππου καὶ τούτοις ὀργιζομένους ἐπὶ τῷ μὴ **προηγγελκέναι**, πραοτέρους γενέσθαι τινός, πάνθ' ὅσ' ἐβούλεσθ' ὑμῖν ἔσεσθαι προσδοκήσαντας, καὶ μηδὲ φωνὴν ἐθέλειν ἀκούειν ἐμοῦ μηδ' ἄλλου μηδενός.

As a result, although you were shocked at first by Philip's arrival at Thermopylae and enraged at these men for failing **to inform** you in advance, after you were led to believe you would get everything you wished for, you became as mild as can be and would not give me or anyone else a chance to speak.

Προσαγγέλλω[85] is found only once, at the beginning of the Demosthenic *Fourth Philippic*. The verb is in the passive voice:

(41) Dem., *Phil.* 4.1

Οὐκ ὀλίγων δ' ὄντων ἁμαρτημάτων οὐδ' ἐκ μικροῦ χρόνου συνειλεγμένων, ἐξ ὧν φαύλως ταῦτ' ἔχει, οὐδέν ἐστιν, ὦ ἄνδρες Ἀθηναῖοι, τῶν πάντων δυσκολώτερον εἰς τὸ παρὸν ἢ ὅτι ταῖς γνώμαις ὑμεῖς ἀφεστήκατε τῶν πραγμάτων, καὶ τοσοῦτον χρόνον σπουδάζεθ' ὅσον ἂν κάθησθ' ἀκούοντες ἢ **προσαγγελθῇ** τι νεώτερον.

While the faults that have produced this unhappy state of things are neither few nor recently accumulated, there is nothing, men of Athens, more vexing at the present time than the way in which you detach your thoughts from affairs and display an interest only so long as you sit here listening, or when some fresh item of news **is announced**.[86]

---

83 Cf. Lys. 12.17 (παραγγέλλω + accusative + dative), Lys. 1.76, Dem., *Polyc.* 31 (παραγγέλλω + dative + infinitive), Aeschin., *Emb.* 77, Dem., *Polyc.* 19 (παραγγέλλω + infinitive), Lys. 12.44 (παραγγέλλω + relative clause), Aeschin., *In Ctes.* 98 (παραγγέλλω + AcI) and Isoc., *Bus.* 26 (absolute use).
84 Cf. Lys. 1.41 (x2), Lys. 1.42, Aeschin., *In Ctes.* 65 and Aeschin., *In Ctes.* 90 (παραγγέλλω + dative).
85 Cf. *LSJ*: προσαγγέλλω: "Announce, bring tidings" or Bailly: "Apporter une nouvelle".
86 Translation taken from Vince (1930).

The noun ἄγγελμα⁸⁷ is not documented in the speeches of Isocrates, Lysias, Aeschines and Demosthenes. The derivatives ἐπάγγελμα and παράγγελμα do appear, however.

Ἐπάγγελμα — which is used in four instances in the speeches of Isocrates[88] and once in those of Demosthenes[89] — is another of the derivatives of ἄγγελος that designates the promise. Παράγγελμα, meanwhile, designates the order and is used once by Isocrates,[90] once by Demosthenes[91] and once by Lysias.[92]

Finally, one of the most interesting findings of this research is that the lexical family of ἄγγελος offers hardly any specific terms to designate bad news. In the Homeric poems, the negative nuance of the news item is carried by the adjectives that describe it, such as λυγρός ('ghastly' or 'mournful') or ἀλεγεινός ('painful'), or the phrase κακὸν ἔπος functioning as the direct object of the verb ἀγγέλλω. Something similar applies to the other authors in the corpus of this volume, since only the terms κακάγγελος (Aesch., *Ag.* 636) and κακάγγελτος (Soph., *Ant.* 1286) appear. As far as the transmission is concerned, adversity tends to be depicted by means of negative adjectives or by uttering the plural κακά as the complement of the verb ἀγγέλλω. For all these reasons, there is one passage of particular interest from Demosthenes' speech *On the Crown* in which the orator asks that some verses of a tragedy be read, including this one, which contains the verb κακαγγελέω ('bring evil (bad) tidings'):

(42) Dem., *De cor.* 267

κακαγγελεῖν μὲν ἴσθι μὴ θέλοντά με.

Know that **I bring bad news**, though unwillingly.

It is not known from what tragedy this verse could have been drawn, although, according to López Eire (1980, 499), its presence should not be surprising, since it fits in with the literary character of the tragic messenger (ἄγγελος) as a bearer of bad news.[93]

---

87 Remember that this noun does occur in Euripides and Thucydides.
88 Cf. Isoc., *Soph.* 1, 5, 9 and 10.
89 Cf. Dem., *Emb.* 178.
90 Cf. Isoc., *Demon.* 44.
91 Cf. Dem., *Meid.* 168.
92 Cf. Lys. 12.17, in which is the direct object of παραγγέλλω.
93 See also Abbott/Mathenson (1899, 104): "The source of this verse is unknown" and Goodwin (1904): "This verse is otherwise unknown. κακαγγελεῖν must be pres. infin. of κακαγγελέω (otherwise unknown), depending on θέλοντα. The readings of the best MSS., κακαγγέλλειν or

Final remarks

In the speeches of Lysias, Isocrates, Demosthenes and Aeschines we have hardly seen any examples of the use of some of the most important words in the lexical family of ἄγγελος. However, despite the fact that the term ἄγγελος itself, the noun ἀγγελία and the verb ἀγγέλλω are barely used, the analysis of the rest of the terms is extremely fruitful.

The concept of news is strongly rooted in the Athens of the fourth century BC and the fact that the figure of the ἄγγελος had practically disappeared does not mean that there was no news to report. We now find ourselves in a mainly legal context, conditioning the frequency with which the concept of news is documented. The news that was given in the Council or in the Assembly is limited due to the very nature of both institutions and the audience for which it was destined. The πρεσβευτής, the ambassador sent to carry out diplomatic duties, must justify his actions before the Assembly. Among these emissaries, two orators stand out in particular: Demosthenes and Aeschines, who had to account for all that was related to these delegations sent as ambassadors and all that came from them. It is precisely in these speeches regarding embassies that we find most of the derivatives of ἄγγελος, especially the verb ἀπαγγέλλω, which in 95% of cases refers to the announcements given by ambassadors.

As in the works of Herodotus, Thucydides and Xenophon, the concept of news is also closely linked to public matters in the speeches of orators. It is in these speeches that war has an important role, both in the πόλις and on the battlefield. Evidence of this is that conflict itself is news, as is all that derives from it: death in combat, enemy movements, victories and defeats, treaties for alliances, and peace and truces. All of this is announced using derivatives of ἄγγελος.

On the other hand, the terms from the lexical family studied are now also established technical terms associated with the transmission of news, and there are still some (παράγγελμα, παραγγέλλω and, on some occasions, ἐπαγγέλλω) used to denote military language. Of even more importance is the fact that many others have become established legal terms. The study of the lexical family of ἄγγελος has brought us closer to one of the most important terms of Athenian legislation: the εἰσαγγελία or the complaint filed against a citizen accused of a matter of utmost seriousness: high treason or disloyalty to the State. In the entry

---

κἀκ' ἀγγέλλειν (Σ), are metrically impossible. The common reading is κἀκ' ἀγγελεῖν, an irregular fut. infin. with θέλοντα". See also Yunis (2000, 260) and Yunis (2005, 98): "With evident mockery, Demosthenes is himself the 'I' who brings bad news".

on εἰσαγγελία in Brill's *New Pauly* we are told that the term refers to both the written statement of claim and the proceedings themselves. In this way, the charges would be presented in writing and would be discussed in detail during the process. This word is not documented in any previous authors to refer to news and is a specific creation of legal terminology.

The same cannot be said, however, of the verb εἰσαγγέλλω, which is used to indicate the presence of news in the works of Euripides, Aristophanes and the historians, but not in oratory, where it has become a technical term to refer to the presentation of an accusation of high treason. Another derivative of ἄγγελος used as a legal term is ἐπαγγελία, which is used to announce the public summons of an individual that must be judged for competency. The nouns ἀπαγγελία and παραγγελία and the verbs ἐπαγγέλλω, ἀπαγγέλλω and ἐξαγγέλλω are also used in legal contexts. From this I can assert that I was not basing my beliefs on mere suspicions when I suggested that in the texts of historians the term took on a certain degree of specialization. In our analysis of the works of orators in this chapter, we have seen this confirmed.

The situation in which we find ourselves now is again a significant one. My research has allowed me to demonstrate that, ever since Homer's poems, announcements made using ἄγγελος and its derivatives are public and of public interest. The Council and the Assembly have to adopt measures and make decisions that affect the whole of society. For this reason, it makes sense that Greek vocabulary refers to denunciations using derivatives of ἄγγελος, a term that has denoted the transmission of news from the creation of the term itself, since a denunciation is also a public announcement (on this occasion of a crime or mistake made by somebody). In addition, the denunciations were issued in writing in the λευκώματα (white tablets used as a kind of public announcement board) under the statues of the heroes with the same names as on their monument in the Agora of Athens. This is once again proof that written communication is gaining strength over the spoken word in this period.

7 Fake News

Donald Trump popularized the term *fake news* during and after his presidential campaign and election in 2016. The term was soon admitted into the *Oxford English Dictionary*, defined as "news that conveys or incorporates false, fabricated, or deliberately misleading information, or that is characterized as or accused of doing so".[1] It is evident that this expression is applied to a very specific and current sociocultural context and cannot be understood without today's mass media. Social networks can spread hoaxes or false/pseudo-news aimed at generating disinformation across the globe in a matter of seconds. For this reason, it is obvious that the term *fake news* is used in this volume *avant la lettre*. This chapter aims to prove that in the societies represented in the texts of our corpus, *fake news* is spread for very specific purposes, as it is nowadays.

Given the constraints of my study, I will not focus on a discussion of the semantics of rumours and *fake news* and whether or not we are talking about essentially the same thing with these terms. The main difference between a rumour and a piece of news is traditionally considered to lie mainly in the identity of the source of information. In this sense, as Núñez Ladeveze (1991, 290) points out, when it comes to news, the speaker is not suspicious of the source and presents the piece of news as fact. Nonetheless, when it comes to a rumour, the source turns out to be unidentifiable or dubious. A rumour, therefore, does not reach the category of 'news' until it is verified[2] (Vázquez Bermúdez 2006, 58). However, this is not always possible, especially if we consider that the source of information may not be reliable and may not offer any guarantees. For that very reason, it is common for the person who spreads a rumour or refers to one to do so by means of expressions such as "it is said", "it is told" or "it is commented" (Scheinsohn 2009, 118). It is also for this reason that the αὐτοψία in tragic messenger scenes acquires so much importance when it comes to the transmission of news.

---

1 A significant amount of literature has been published since then. See, for instance, Amorós (2017), Alandete (2018), Illades (2018), Chiluwa, Samoilenko/Miller (2019), Levi (2019), Young-Brown (2019), Dalkir/Katz (2020), Zindar/McLeod (2020) or Safieddine/Ibrahim (2020). On *fake news* in Ancient Rome, see Marqués (2019).
2 In this respect, the term *fake news* is being reconsidered. See Ireton/Posetti (2018, 7): "News means verifiable information in the public interest, and information that does not meet these standards does not deserve the label of news. In this sense, *fake news* is an oxymoron which lends itself to undermining the credibility of information which does indeed meet the threshold of verifiability and public interest — i.e. real news".

There are numerous Greek terms that designate rumour (e.g. κληδών, φάτις or φήμη) but, as I have said, we will not analyse these in this chapter.³

From here on, I will focus only on certain passages of text containing derivatives of ἄγγελος that refer to the transmission of something that closely resembles *fake news* in its current sense: news designed and reported with the deliberate intention of deceiving, manipulating decisions, discrediting, and even gaining political or military profit.

Derivatives of ἄγγελος: truth and falsehood

The first thing to note from the study of derivatives of ἄγγελος is that only three of the 52 words documented in the entire analysed corpus — the adjective ψευδάγγελος, the verb ψευδαγγελλέω and the noun ψευδαγγελία — are terms specifically coined to refer to the transmission of *fake news*. Besides, these three terms are far from common since they only occur once each of them.

The adjective ψευδάγγελος does appear in the *Iliad*.⁴ Remember that Iris is the goddess in charge of passing on the messages, advice and orders from other gods and is especially linked to Zeus, who orders her in (1) to demand that Poseidon leave the battlefield:

(1) Hom., *Il.* 15.158–159

Βάσκ' ἴθι Ἶρι ταχεῖα, Ποσειδάωνι ἄνακτι
πάντα τάδ' ἀγγεῖλαι, μὴ δὲ **ψευδάγγελος** εἶναι.

'Go on your way now, swift Iris, to the lord Poseidon, and give him all this message nor be a **false messenger**.'

The presence of ψευδάγγελος in this passage has been interpreted as a play on words with μετάγγελος (Janko 1994, 245), a term with which Zeus describes the winged goddess fifteen lines beforehand (Hom., *Il.* 15.144: Ἶρίν θ', ἥ τε θεοῖσι μετάγγελος ἀθανάτοισι). It has also been suggested that it is an attenuation device, a litotes to show that it would also be unthinkable for Iris to dare to

---

3 On this subject, see the notes at the end of each of the chapters from Fornieles Sánchez (2015) and, especially, specialized works such as that of Hunter (1990), those of Larran (2010 and 2011) on the semantic field of rumour in Greek literature or that of Brioso Sánchez (2011), which focuses specifically on the study of the rumour as a literary motif in Greek tragedy.
4 This term also appears in Aristotle's *Poetics* alluding to the title of a lost tragedy of Sophocles: *Odysseus the False Messenger* (Arist., *Po.* 1455a: οἷον ἐν τῷ Ὀδυσσεῖ τῷ ψευδαγγέλῳ).

manipulate Zeus' words (Longo 1978, 176). In any case, the goddess herself behaves as a loyal subordinate and not even the presence of the word ψευδάγγελος implies the existence of deceit. Immediately afterwards, Zeus tells Iris the message to transmit and, far from being a false messenger, she obeys:

(2) Hom., *Il.* 15.174–183

> **ἀγγελίην τινά** τοι γαιήοχε κυανοχαῖτα
> ἦλθον δεῦρο φέρουσα παραὶ Διὸς αἰγιόχοιο.
> παυσάμενόν σ' ἐκέλευσε μάχης ἠδὲ πτολέμοιο
> ἔρχεσθαι μετὰ φῦλα θεῶν ἢ εἰς ἅλα δῖαν.
> εἰ δέ οἱ οὐκ ἐπέεσσ' ἐπιπείσεαι, ἀλλ' ἀλογήσεις,
> ἠπείλει καὶ κεῖνος ἐναντίβιον πολεμίξων
> ἐνθάδ' ἐλεύσεσθαι· σὲ δ' ὑπεξαλέασθαι ἄνωγε
> χεῖρας, ἐπεὶ σέο φησὶ βίῃ πολὺ φέρτερος εἶναι
> καὶ γενεῇ πρότερος· σὸν δ' οὐκ ὄθεται φίλον ἦτορ
> ἶσόν οἱ φάσθαι, τόν τε στυγέουσι καὶ ἄλλοι.
> Τὴν δὲ μέγ' ὀχθήσας προσέφη κλυτὸς ἐννοσίγαιος·

'I have **a certain message** for you, dark-haired, earth-encircler, and came here to bring it you from Zeus of the aegis. His order is that you quit the war and the fighting, and go back among the generations of gods, or into the bright sea. And if you will not obey his words, or think nothing of them, his threat is that he himself will come to fight with you here, strength against strength, but warns you to keep from under his hands, since he says he is far greater than you are in strength, and elder born. Yet your inward heart shrinks not from calling yourself the equal of him, though other shudder before him.'

Three derivatives of ἄγγελος are recognized in these two passages: ἀγγεῖλαι, ψευδάγγελος and ἀγγελίη, although we cannot be sure that a piece of news has been transmitted here.

As verified in previous chapters, ἀγγέλλω is a verb of saying, but can also be a verb of commanding when is accompanied by an infinitive and a dative complement, as in (1). Both the context and the speaker's intention (reflected in the uttered illocutionary speech act) as well as the social status of the speaker and the hearer will determine the semantic content of the announcement inherent to the verb. In this case, although Zeus, Iris and Poseidon are gods, they are differently positioned within their own social hierarchy. It is not surprising that Zeus uses Iris as a mediator to transmit an order from him to Poseidon, but it would be inconceivable for Iris to give that order and for Zeus and Poseidon to obey it. In this respect, here we see a very common aspect of Greek culture: human institutions — messengers on this occasion — are mirrored in the social organization of divinities and myths reflect the society in which gods appear or with which they coexist.

The verb ψευδαγγελέω, on the other hand, occurs only once, in Aristophanic comedy, specifically in *Birds*. The verb refers to a herald who Peisetairos calls an ἄγγελος:

(3) Ar., *Av.* 1340–1341

> Ἔοικεν οὐ **ψευδαγγελήσειν**⁵ ἄγγελος·
> ᾄδων γὰρ ὅδε τις αἰετοὺς προσέρχεται.
>
> The messenger does not seem to **have announced false news**! Here's someone coming along now, singing of eagles.

As for ψευδαγγελία, this noun denotes the false announcement. The compound term (ψεῦδος + ἀγγελία) is the only derivative of ἄγγελος that directly alludes to the transmission of false news in the works of historians. It also appears only once, in a very interesting passage in Xenophon's *On the Cavalry Commander*. Its presence in this single text is striking given the importance that Xenophon gives to lies as a perfect war strategy and as a means of intimidating the enemies:

(4) Xen., *Eq. mag.* 5.8

> φοβεῖν γε μὴν τοὺς πολεμίους καὶ ψευδενέδρας οἷόν τε καὶ ψευδοβοηθείας καὶ **ψευδαγγελίας** ποιοῦντα. θαρσοῦσι δὲ μάλιστα πολέμιοι, ὅταν ὄντα τοῖς ἐναντίοις πράγματα καὶ ἀσχολίας πυνθάνωνται.
>
> The means to employ for scaring the enemy are false ambuscades, false reliefs, and **false information**. An enemy's confidence is greatest when he is told that the other side is in difficulties and is preoccupied.

As I just mentioned, these are the only three derivatives of ἄγγελος expressly coined to designate false news. However, this does not mean that this kind of news does not exist in ancient Greek literature. The fact is, in my opinion, that — as has been stated on several occasions throughout this volume⁶ —

---

5 Cf. a conjecture proposed by Bentley and mostly accepted. See, for instance, Green (1894, 155): "ψευδαγγελὴς εἶν'] Bentley's ψευδαγγελήσειν is very neat: κακαγγελλεῖν quoted in Demosthenes from a tragic poet supports the verb; no adjective in -αγγελής is found. ψευδαγγελής is a doubtful form. Yet the future tense is not quite satisfactory". See also Dunbar (1995, 655).
6 Remember example (15) in the chapter devoted to the Homeric poems, in which we are told that Andromache was not aware of the fact that her husband had been killed by Achilles since,

ἄγγελος and its derivatives are associated with the truth, and no one doubts the words of the messenger. Therefore, when someone wants to transmit *fake news*, he/she does so by resorting both to the lexicon that a reliable ἄγγελος would utter and to certain conventions related to this figure.

My analysis of ἄγγελος and its derivatives provides clear evidence that false news acquires a more than remarkable importance related to that which is ψεῦδος in two genres in particular: tragedy and historiography. I will focus on these two genres in what follows.

Fake news in Greek tragedy

Let us first look at Aeschylus' *Libation-Bearers*. Seven years have passed since the murder of Agamemnon, and Orestes, together with his inseparable friend Pylades, has just returned to Argos. He explains to the chorus and his sister Electra his plan to avenge the death of his father: Pylades and he will pretend to be two men sent as messengers from Phocis to announce that Orestes has lost his life. They are confident that they will reveal their identity and kill them. In this example, then, Orestes stars in a perfect messenger scene.[7] He arrives at the palace with Pylades and asks a servant to report his arrival. Clytemnestra then goes out to meet them and asks Orestes to tell her his news. He prepares to deliver a messenger speech (Aesch., *Cho.* 674–690),[8] introduces himself as a foreigner (from Daulis) and tells her that, when he was on his way to Argos, he met the Phocian Strophius, who addressed him in this way:

---

as the poet points out, no sure messenger (ἐτήτυμος ἄγγελος) had come to announce it to her. Remember also that loyalty is a quality associated to the tragic ἄγγελοι, who are described as 'faithful' (Aesch., *PV*. 969: πιστόν) and 'true' (Aesch., *Sept.* 82: ἔτυμος).

7 According to Goldhill (1986, 15) Orestes pretends to be a messenger to gain the queen's trust.
8 This is not the only false speech in Greek tragedy. I will explain below the case of the pedagogue in Sophocles' *Electra*. Besides, in Soph., *Trach.* 249–290 the herald Lichas lies about the identity of the women who accompany him and a real ἄγγελος betrays him by alluding to him as οὐ δίκαιος ἄγγελος; in Soph. *Phil.* 319–390 Neoptolemus — who Philoctetes later calls ἄγγελος (Soph., *Phil.* 500) — reports the apparent death of Achilles and in Soph., *Phil.* 542–627 a merchant who introduces himself as a messenger (Soph., *Phil.* 564: ἀκούσας δ' ἄγγελος πάρειμί σοι) — also lies when informing Philoctetes. Marshall (2006) does not take into account the latter. On the messenger speech delivered by the pedagogue in Sophocles' *Electra*, see Sheppard (1918).

(5) Aesch., *Cho.* 680–682

> ἐπείπερ ἄλλως, ὦ ξέν', εἰς Ἄργος κίεις,
> πρὸς τοὺς τεκόντας πανδίκως μεμνημένος
> τεθνεῶτ' Ὀρέστην εἰπέ, μηδαμῶς λάθῃ.
>
> Since you're bound for Argos anyway, sir, please remember carefully to tell his parents that Orestes is dead; don't forget on any account.

Orestes does not use any derivatives of ἄγγελος, but Clytemnestra does when the false messenger regrets having had to communicate something so terrible to his hosts. The queen replies to him:

(6) Aesch., *Cho.* 707–709

> οὔτοι κυρήσεις μεῖον ἀξίως σέθεν,
> οὐδ' ἧσσον ἂν γένοιο δώμασιν φίλος.
> ἄλλος δ' ὁμοίως ἦλθεν ἂν **τάδ' ἀγγελῶν**.
>
> You will not receive less than you deserve, nor will you be any less a friend to this house. Someone else would have come anyway **to bring this news**.

Orestes' plan is working. He has managed to deceive his mother. The key to success is clearly to behave like an ἄγγελος, since he knows that no one will be suspicious of news reported by an ἄγγελος. The queen herself tells him that, if it had not been him, someone else would have announced the misfortune. She uses ἀγγέλλω, the verb used by the ἄγγελοι when they transmit news. In addition, after that scene a nurse cries before the chorus because of the news they have just announced (Aesch., *Cho.* 736: τὴν νεάγγελτον φάτιν) and explains that Clytemnestra has ordered her to go in search of Aegisthus and tell him about Orestes' death. The nurse adds that the queen pretended to be sad but was actually very pleased. This is how she sums it up:

(7) Aesch., *Cho.* 740–741

> (...) δόμοις δὲ τοῖσδε παγκάκως ἔχει,
> φήμης ὕφ', ἧς **ἤγγειλαν** οἱ ξένοι τορῶς.
>
> But for this house things are thoroughly bad, as a result of **the news** that the visitors have **reported** very plainly.

The nurse again refers to the bad news by means of ἀγγέλλω and she will do the same later, when the chorus advises her not to say anything to Aegisthus but simply to encourage him to come as soon as possible. The nurse asks then the chorus: "Are you gladdened at heart by the present news?",[9] and she gets this answer: "Why not if Zeus at last may cause our ill wind to change?".

Orestes' conspiracy is about to come to a successful end. The news of the alleged death of Agamemnon's son has reached Aegisthus, as he himself confirms:

(8) Aesch., *Cho.* 838–841

ἥκω μὲν οὐκ ἄκλητος, ἀλλ' **ὑπάγγελος**·[10]
νέαν φάτιν δὲ πεύθομαι λέγειν τινὰς
ξένους μολόντας οὐδαμῶς ἐφίμερον,
μόρον γ' Ὀρέστου. (...)

I have come after being **called here by a messenger**. I learn that some foreigners have come bearing word of news that is far from welcome, namely the death of Orestes.

The chorus leader replies that the chorus is also informed and urges him to enter the palace to verify the piece of news:

(9) Aesch., *Cho.* 848–853

{Χο.} ἠκούσαμεν μέν, πυνθάνου δὲ τῶν ξένων
       ἔσω παρελθών. οὐδὲν **ἀγγέλων** σθένος
       ὡς αὐτὸς' αὐτὸν ἄνδρα πεύθεσθαι πέρι.
{Αι.} ἰδεῖν ἐλέγξαι τ' εὖ θέλω **τὸν ἄγγελον**,
       εἴτ' αὐτὸς ἦν θνῄσκοντος ἐγγύθεν παρών,
       εἴτ' ἐξ ἀμαυρᾶς κληδόνος λέγει μαθών.

CHORUS LEADER. – We have heard the story, but you should go inside where the visitors are and inquire from them. The value of **a messenger's word** is nothing compared to inquiring directly, man from man.
AEGISTHUS. – I want to see **the messenger** and question him well as to whether he was himself present in the vicinity when the man died, or whether his story is based on an insubstantial rumour and amounts to nothing.

As we can see, both the chorus leader and Aegisthus view Orestes as an ἄγγελος and deduce that his news must be true. As Longo (1978, 76) rightly points out,

---

9 Cf. Aesch., *Cho.* 774: ἀλλ' ἦ φρονεῖς εὖ τοῖσι νῦν ἠγγελμένοις;

10 On ὑπάγγελος in this passage, see Garvie (1986, 276): "The tautological restatement of the negative οὐκ ἄκλητος in the positive ὑπάγγελος is a familiar feature of Greek style, but there is a particular point to it here, in that it reminds us more emphatically of Cilissa's mission, and that he has been told to come without his bodyguard".

the ἄγγελος is always associated with the truth because of the loyalty he constantly demonstrates. For this reason, it is inconceivable that a piece of news faithfully reported by an individual as loyal as an ἄγγελος not be considered true. To make sure, however, Aegisthus wishes to resort to the final test: the αὐτοψία, whether the messenger has been an eyewitness.[11] Then there would be no doubt. However, the lie will be discovered immediately: as soon as Aegisthus enters the palace, Orestes will kill him.

In Sophocles' *Electra* the purpose is identical, but the alleged death — a fictitious death that will mean a real salvation (Seale 1982, 56) — of Agamemnon's son and Clytemnestra will not be reported by Orestes himself, but by a pedagogue. Let us remember the prologue of the tragedy. Orestes is talking to the old man and tells him that, when he visited the Delphic oracle, Phoebus gave him this order: that alone and without the aid of arms he should kill the traitors. For this very reason, Orestes asks the pedagogue to enter the palace, find out what is happening inside, and come out to report it clearly (Soph., *El.* 41: ὅπως ἂν εἰδὼς ἡμὶν ἀγγείλῃς σαφῆ).[12] Before the servant leaves to carry out this task, Orestes gives him a series of instructions: he will introduce himself as a Phocian stranger sent by Phanoteus, since he is the greatest of their allies. This is the most important part of the plan:

(10) Soph., *El.* 47–50

ἄγγελλε[13] δ', ὅρκον προστιθείς, ὁθούνεκα
τέθνηκ' Ὀρέστης ἐξ ἀναγκαίας τύχης,
ἄθλοισι Πυθικοῖσιν ἐκ τροχηλάτων
δίφρων κυλισθείς· ὧδ' ὁ μῦθος ἑστάτω.

Tell them a sudden accident befell Orestes, and he's dead. Swear it on oath. Say in the Pythian games he was rolled out of his chariot at high speed. Let that be your story.

---

11 On information sources in Aeschylus, see Cesca (2017c).
12 Cf. example (39) in the chapter on Greek tragedy.
13 On the term uttered by the pedagogue, see Ringer (1998, 138): "Like an actor playing as a messenger (ἄγγελος), the Pedagogue must establish his playwright's *mythos* by announcing (ἄγγελλε, 47) a fictitious story. As in *Ajax* (719), *Trachiniae* (180–181) and *Philoctetes* (568), words relating to the messenger figure in tragedy — such as ἄγγελος (messenger) or ἀγγέλλειν (to announce) — are used to call attention to theatrical convention". On the false report and Orestes' strategy, see Kaibel (1967): "Auch der Inhalt der fiktiven Todesbotschaft wird in Kürze vereinbart, weil der Diener und Orest gesondert auftreten werden und natürlich in ihrem Bericht übereinstimmen müssen". See also Finglass (2007) and Hogan (1991).

The loyal pedagogue will obey. As soon as he enters the palace, he addresses Clytemnestra:

(11) Soph., *El.* 666–667

Ὦ χαῖρ', ἄνασσα· σοὶ **φέρων ἥκω λόγους**
ἡδεῖς φίλου παρ' ἀνδρὸς Αἰγίσθῳ θ' ὁμοῦ.

Greetings, royal lady! I **come with news** from a friend, **good news** for you and for Aegisthus.

The passage is in the *stichomythic prologue* of the messenger scene, and the queen therefore asks the old man for more information. He then briefly delivers the news:

(12) Soph., *El.* 673

Τέθνηκ' Ὀρέστης· ἐν βραχεῖ ξυνθεὶς λέγω.

Orestes is dead. There it is, in one short word.

Faced with the desperate cries of Electra, who is on the stage, and the disbelief expressed by Clytemnestra, the pedagogue is forced to repeat the news item: "What I said and say again is "Orestes is dead" (Soph., *El.* 676). Clytemnestra insists and asks him to give details of the events and then the old man shows off delivering a splendid messenger speech (Soph., *El.* 680–763) worthy of the best of the ἄγγελοι, despite being invented. According to Ringer (1996, 99), this speech could even serve as a model for real messenger speeches.

Later, Orestes is worried about the possibility of being discovered, but the pedagogue calms him down: "Well. There is no chance of your recognition", he says. "You have announced my death, I understand" (Soph., *El.* 1341: Ἤγγειλας, ὡς ἔοικεν, ὡς τεθνηκότα"), says the young man confidently. The servant then confirms this: "You are down in Hades, as far as they're concerned".

In the second part of the plan Orestes, pretending to be a foreigner, arrives before Electra with an urn containing his alleged ashes and tells her sister that he has been sent by a certain Strophius to announce something concerning Orestes (Soph., *El.* 1111: ἐφεῖτ' Ὀρέστου Στροφίος ἀγγεῖλαι πέρι): he brings with him the mortal remains of Agamemnon's son.

The plan works perfectly. Aegisthus wants the foreigners to tell him the piece of news in person and asks Electra where the strangers are who are said to have brought news to them of Orestes' death amidst the shipwrecked chariots

(Soph., *El.* 1442–1444: Τίς οἶδεν ὑμῶν ποῦ ποθ' οἱ Φωκῆς ξένοι | οὕς φασ' Ὀρέστην ἡμῖν ἀγγεῖλαι βίον | λελοιπόθ' ἱππικοῖσιν ἐν ναυαγίοις;). Clytemnestra's daughter claims to be unaware of this and he insists: "And do they genuinely report his death?" (Soph., *El.* 1452: Ἦ καὶ θανόντ' ὡς ἐτητύμως;). Finally, when Electra replies that they proved it with more than just words, her mother's lover is reassured.

Throughout this trick plotted by Orestes, the verb ἀγγέλλω occurs six times, four in the speech of the phonies and twice in that of Aegisthus, always in reference to the same piece of news: the alleged death of the son of Agamemnon. The plan, as we know, ends successfully: Orestes deceives everyone and fulfills his purpose of killing Clytemnestra and Aegisthus.

Euripides' *Helen* also contains *fake news* transmitted with derivatives of ἄγγελος. We now move to Egypt, where Theoclymenus, son of the king Proteus, wants to marry Helen. Menelaus, shipwrecked after the Trojan War, arrives in Egypt and plots an escape plan together with his wife. For the plan to work Helen must lie to Theoclymenus and make up the alleged death of the Atreus' son:[14]

(13) Eur., *Hel.* 1193–1196

{Ελ.} ὦ δέσποτ' – ἤδη γὰρ τόδ' ὀνομάζω σ' ἔπος –
       ὄλωλα· φροῦδα τἀμὰ κοὐδέν εἰμ' ἔτι.
{Θε.} ἐν τῶι δὲ κεῖσαι συμφορᾶς; τίς ἡ τύχη;
{Ελ.} Μενέλαος – οἴμοι, πῶς φράσω; – τέθνηκέ μοι.

HELEN. – My lord – for now at last I name you in such terms – my life is ruined. There is nothing left for me.
THEOCLYMENUS. – What has happened? What is the disaster that has struck you down?
HELEN. – My Menelaus —how shall I say it? He is dead.

Theoclymenus, aware that this would be great news for him, wishes to confirm it and therefore asks for the source of Helen's information:

(14) Eur., *Hel.* 1200

ἥκει γὰρ ὅστις καὶ τάδ' **ἀγγέλλει σαφῆ**;

There is someone here then, **with an authentic report**?

---

14 See Dale (1967, 144): "The lie direct is faintly shocking where it involves Theonoe, but in 1370–1373 we find the priestess herself preferring it to mere prevarication".

As we can see, Theoclymenus refers to the announcement by uttering ἀγγέλλω. Helen's answer is affirmative: a man who, according to her, eyewitnessed the misfortune has arrived. In addition, she points to a beggar — Menelaus disguised as such — who is curled up on the ground. The conspiracy devised by the son of Atreus and his wife will end successfully, as an ἄγγελος reveals:

(15) Eur., *Hel.* 1512–1518

{Αγ.}   ἄναξ, τὰ κάκιστ' ἐν δόμοις ηὑρήκαμεν·
        ὡς καίν' ἀκούσηι πήματ' ἐξ ἐμοῦ τάχα.
{Θε.}   τί δ ἔστιν; {Αγ.} ἄλλης ἐκπόνει μνηστεύματα
        γυναικός· Ἑλένη γὰρ βέβηκ' ἔξω χθονός.
{Θε.}   πτεροῖσιν ἀρθεῖσ' ἢ πεδοστιβεῖ ποδί;
{Αγ.}   Μενέλαος αὐτὴν ἐκπεπόρθμευται χθονός,
        ὃς αὐτὸς αὑτὸν ἦλθεν **ἀγγέλλων** θανεῖν.

MESSENGER. – My lord, the worst of news from our house. We have just learned. Fresh news, strange news and bad. Hear it from me at once.
THEOCLYMENUS. – What is it?
MESSENGER. – Your work is wasted for a wife who is not yours. Helen is gone away, out of our land.
THEOCLYMENUS. – How gone? On wings, or do her feet still tread the earth?[15]
MESSENGER. – Menelaus carried her away. For that was he. He came himself and **brought the news** of his own death.

The situation is striking because the ἄγγελος, after telling Proteus' son a real piece of news — in his speech he will expand on the details —, reveals to him that he has been deceived. Furthermore, the ἄγγελος himself utters ἀγγέλλων to refer to the false death of Menelaus (previously reported by Helen and ratified by the presence of Menelaus himself disguised as a beggar).

Fake news in the works of historians

As is inferred from many of the examples given in the corresponding chapter, the identity of the bearer of the news in the works of historians is very often unknown. On many occasions we are only told that the piece of news has arrived or that a certain fact or event has been announced to someone. Unlike tragedy, where the ἄγγελος is almost always introduced as an eyewitness, in the

---

15 Allan (2008, 329) interprets an ironic question that expresses Theoclymenus disbelief at the idea that Helen may have left Egypt.

texts of Herodotus, Thucydides and Xenophon the source of information does not seem so relevant. The veracity of the reported news is rarely questioned. However, in some of the examples we see exceptions of this, but in these cases αὐτοψία also plays an important role. That is, at least, the opinion of Xenophon, who warns of the relevance that spies have in war, but ensures that there is nothing better than informing yourself:[16]

(16) Xen., *Eq. mag.* 4.16

καὶ τὸ μὲν διὰ κατασκόπων πειρᾶσθαι εἰδέναι τὰ τῶν πολεμίων πάλαι εἴρηται ὡς ἀγαθόν ἐστιν· ἐγὼ δὲ πάντων ἄριστον νομίζω εἶναι τὸ αὐτὸν πειρᾶσθαι, ἢν ᾖ ποθεν ἐξ ἀσφαλοῦς, θεώμενον τοὺς πολεμίους ἀθρεῖν ἤν τι ἁμαρτάνωσι.

It is an old maxim that, in attempting to discover what the enemy is about, it is well to employ spies. But the best plan of all, in my opinion, is for the commander himself to watch the enemy from some safe coign of vantage, if possible, and take notice of his mistakes.

As I have already pointed out, this αὐτοψία gives credibility to the tragic ἄγγελος and means that the news he transmits – as well as the conventions he uses

---

16 Let us not forget, in addition, the role of information sources in the methods of historians. As Schepens (1980, 196 ff) points out, Herodotus was the first to grant to αὐτοψία the historical and methodological importance that it acquired over time. Αὐτοψία later became a τόπος of the historiographic genre (cf. Luc., *Hist. Conscr.* 47). On αὐτοψία in Greek historiography see, for instance, Nenci (1955), Marincola (1997, 63–117) or Petrovic (2004). Herodotus has been harshly criticized and it has been asked whether he saw everything he claims to have seen. In this respect, see Sayce (1885). Fehling (1989, 1–11), for example, suggests that he made up stories and put them in the words of his informants. Pritchett, in his book *The Liar School of Herodotus*, rejected the proposals of Fehling, Armayor (1978), (1980) and (1985) and Stephanie West (1985), whom he collectively dubbed *The Liar School*. In this 'school' he also included Hartog, who refers to Herodotus as "the father of lies" (see Hartog 1988, 300). Thordarson (1996, 43) maintains that Herodotus did not invent his stories and that the reference to fictitious authorities "[...] may be a part of a writer's or a storyteller's narrative technique". The case of Thucydides is quite different. He has been considered the perfect scientific historian. On Thucydides' objectivity, see Cochrane (1929), Romilly (1967), Adcock (1973) or Rood (2006). As far as Xenophon is concerned, he himself allows his methodology to be inferred from his own works (Marincola 1997, 69) and very often he refers to his information sources only with expressions of the type "someone says" (Xen., *Hell.* 6.4.7: τινες λέγουσιν) or 'it is said' (Xen., *An.* 1.2.9: λέγεται). However, due to his own participation in the war and the precision with which he narrates some specific events, there are those who have maintained that he wrote his works as an eyewitness (Delebecque 1957, 18 or Nickel 1979, 87). It had also been claimed that he may have had Spartan informants (Anderson 2001, 65–72) or that his were stories transmitted by oral tradition, especially regarding Cyrus and Persia (Hirsch 1985, 68).

to report the news (including use of derivatives of ἄγγελος) — gives strong evidence that these words are associated with the truth not only in Greek tragedy, but also in the works of historians. In this respect, although the term ψευδαγγελία (the only derivative of ἄγγελος that refers to false news in historiography) is found in Xenophon, there is evidence that supports this statement. Taking into consideration that no one doubts the authenticity of the words of an ἄγγελος, everyone who wishes to lie does so by resorting to the derivatives of ἄγγελος in the texts of Herodotus, Thucydides, and Xenophon too. Setting aside the noun ψευδαγγελία, the terms used are εὐαγγέλιον, ἀγγέλλω, ἄγγελμα, διαγγέλλω, ἐξαγγέλλω and προαγγέλλω.

The results of the examination of ἄγγελος and its derivatives reveal that the purpose of *fake news* is twofold: on the one hand, it is a strategy to deceive and intimidate the enemy; on the other hand, it is a resource used to encourage the troops by making the soldiers believe that everything is going well. The complete study on this type of practice has been conducted in Fornieles Sánchez (2021), so I shall limit myself to offering here only an example of each strategy.

The passages given in (17) and (18) show the intention with which Agesilaus — according to Hutchinson (2000, 149) a master of deception — manipulates the news concerning the defeat of the Lacedaemonians at the Battle of Cnidus. We are told that the fleet commanded by Peisander was defeated by the one led by the Athenian Conon. I present first in (17) the real news received by Agesilaus. Xenophon refers to them using the verb ἀγγέλλω:

(17) Xen., *Hell.* 4.3.10

Ὄντος δ' αὐτοῦ ἐπὶ τῇ ἐμβολῇ ὁ ἥλιος μηνοειδὴς ἔδοξε φανῆναι, καὶ **ἠγγέλθη** ὅτι ἡττημένοι εἶεν Λακεδαιμόνιοι τῇ ναυμαχίᾳ καὶ ὁ ναύαρχος Πείσανδρος τεθναίη.

When he was at the entrance to Boeotia, the sun seemed to appear crescent-shaped, and **word was brought** to him that the Lacedaemonians had been defeated in the naval battle and the admiral, Peisander, had been killed.

As I have just said, this is the real news. However, Agesilaus decides to distort it:

(18) Xen., *Hell.* 4.3.13–14

ὁ οὖν Ἀγησίλαος πυθόμενος ταῦτα τὸ μὲν πρῶτον χαλεπῶς ἤνεγκεν· ἐπεὶ μέντοι ἐνεθυμήθη ὅτι τοῦ στρατεύματος τὸ πλεῖστον εἴη αὐτῷ οἷον ἀγαθῶν μὲν γιγνομένων ἡδέως μετέχειν, εἰ δέ τι χαλεπὸν ὁρῷεν, οὐκ ἀνάγκην εἶναι κοινωνεῖν αὐτοῖς, ἐκ τούτου μεταβαλὼν ἔλεγεν ὡς **ἀγγέλλοιτο** ὁ μὲν Πείσανδρος τετελευτηκώς, νικῴη δὲ τῇ ναυμαχίᾳ. ἅμα δὲ ταῦτα λέγων καὶ ἐβουθύτει ὡς **εὐαγγέλια** καὶ πολλοῖς διέπεμπε τῶν τεθυμένων· ὥστε ἀκροβολισμοῦ ὄντος πρὸς τοὺς πολεμίους ἐκράτησαν οἱ τοῦ Ἀγησιλάου τῷ λόγῳ ὡς Λακεδαιμονίων νικώντων τῇ ναυμαχίᾳ.

Now Agesilaus, on learning these things, at first was overcome with sorrow; but when he had considered that the most of his troops were the sort of men to share gladly in good fortune if good fortune came, but that if they saw anything unpleasant, they were under no compulsion to share in it, thereupon, changing the report, he said that **word had come** that Peisander was dead, but victorious in the naval battle. And, at the moment of saying these things, he offered sacrifice as if **for good news** and sent around to many people portions of the victims which had been offered; so that when a skirmish with the enemy took place, the troops of Agesilaus won the day in consequence of the report that the Lacedaemonians were victorious in the naval battle.

Xenophon puts the verb ἀγγέλλω in the speech of Agesilaus — the same verb with which the real news had been announced to him — to report a fictitious victory to his men. This is not contrary to expectations because, as stated when dealing with Greek tragedy, it is exactly what some characters do in drama to lie without anyone questioning their words. The verb ἀγγέλλω and the other derivatives of ἄγγελος are associated with the truth and the presence of these terms lends credibility to the words of whoever utters them. As if that were not enough, on this occasion Agesilaus accompanies the lie with sacrifices, which gives the scene a great deal of solemnity.[17]

The purpose is quite different in (19). Cyrus prepares for the siege of Sardis and, taking advantage of Araspas' bad situation,[18] he tells him that he would do a great service to him if he pretended to go over to the enemies and lie to them. The term used this time is ἐξαγγέλλω:

(19) Xen., *Cyr.* 6.1.42

> **ἐξάγγελλέ** τε αὐτοῖς τὰ παρ' ἡμῶν, οὕτω τε **ἐξάγγελλε** ὡς ἂν αὐτοῖς τὰ παρὰ σοῦ λεγόμενα ἐμποδὼν μάλιστ' ἂν εἴη ὧν βούλονται πράττειν. εἴη δ' ἂν ἐμποδών, εἰ ἡμᾶς φαίης παρασκευάζεσθαι ἐμβαλεῖν ποι τῆς ἐκείνων χώρας· ταῦτα γὰρ ἀκούοντες ἧττον ἂν παντὶ σθένει ἀθροίζοιντο, ἕκαστός τις φοβούμενος καὶ περὶ τῶν οἴκοι.

> **Tell** them all about our affairs but frame your account in such a way that your information will be the greatest possible hindrance to the success of their plans. And it would be a

---

[17] Remember that εὐαγγέλιον, as the direct object of θύω (εὐαγγέλια θύειν), also appears in Aristophanic comedy (cf. Ar., *Eq.* 656). Εὐαγγέλιον is also found in Xen., *Hell.* 1.6.36–37. On this passage, see Manatt (1889, 53): "ἔθυε τὰ εὐαγγέλια: he made the (usual) thank-offerings for good news". On the relevance of sacrifices in war, see Hutchinson (2000, 47).

[18] His reputation was in tatters because he fell in love with a married woman and threatened to rape her if she did not have sex with him voluntarily (Cf. Xen., *Cyr* 6.1.31–37).

hindrance, if you should represent that we were making ready to invade their country at some point; for upon hearing this, they would be less likely to gather in full force, as each man would be afraid for his own possessions at home.

Cyrus is putting into practice what Xenophon himself explains in *On the Cavalry Commander*: a ψευδαγγελία as the perfect strategy to scare the enemy, to introduce hoaxes on the opposite side. It is, therefore, a military tactic against the rival.

Final remarks

In this chapter we have seen that there is strong evidence for the presence of false (*fake*) news in ancient Greek literature that is spread to generate disinformation to achieve specific objectives. Despite the fact that the lexical family derived from ἄγγελος contains only three terms (hardly productive) that refer to false news (ψευδάγγελος, ψευδαγγελλέω and ψευδαγγελία), the truth is that the analysed corpus gives evidence, especially in Greek tragedy and in the works of Thucydides and Xenophon, that this news — reminiscent to a certain extent of current *fake news* — was deliberately created and spread to deceive the enemy, mislead, manipulate decisions and even obtain personal, social or military advantage.

On the other hand, the study of ἄγγελος and its derivatives reveals that, ever since Homer, both the ἄγγελος and the news he transmits are associated with the truth. In Greek tragedy, some characters report *fake news* and, taking advantage of the reliability attributed to the ἄγγελος, play the role of an ἄγγελος, imitate his behaviour on stage and use the same vocabulary he would use: ἄγγελος and its derivatives.

The same applies to the works of historians. Evidence of this is the fact that, as no one doubts the reliability of an ἄγγελος or of someone who uses its derivatives to report the news concerning the war. Indeed, anyone who wants to lie does so by uttering the words derived from ἄγγελος (specifically ψευδαγγελία, εὐαγγέλιον, ἀγγέλλω, ἄγγελμα, διαγγέλλω, ἐξαγγέλλω and προαγγέλλω). The *fake news* reported in this context is used either as a strategy to intimidate the enemies or as a tactic to encourage the troops when a problem arises, making the soldiers believe that there is nothing to fear because everything is under control.

8 Conclusions

Throughout this volume, my aim has been to show that the concept of news that we have today is not a modern invention, but rather a social and cultural institution that has been passed down to us by the Ancient Greeks as a legacy. This concept is only modified by the social, political, and economic conditions that make our society different from theirs.

When we speak, we are continually forming concepts, and this is particularly the case when we are referring not to natural entities but to human institutions. This means that 'news' is not an entity that we refer to directly in our language. Rather, it is a conceptual construction that is fabricated by taking various things into account, such as its newness, its extraordinary nature, and its relevance or social repercussions. When it comes to the transmission of news, a series of pragmatic factors are all at play that allow us to understand how in order for a particular event to be considered a piece of news it must be new, that is, unknown until the specific moment when it is made known by somebody. This is true both in our own surroundings and in the world of the Ancient Greeks that we have studied in this book. But this is not all: the speaker must also assume that what he/she is announcing will be of interest to the receiver, will awaken feelings and emotions in them, and will have consequences.

Most of these aspects of news are already implicit in the etymology of the word (which, as we have seen, is related to English *news*, the Spanish learned term 'nueva' and the Latin term *notitia* from which the Spanish 'noticia' derives), and in the root of the family of terms that allude to them, as we have seen in the case of Greek. For this reason, when, in order to understand what was considered news by the Greeks in the period spanning from the second millennium BC to the end of the fourth BC, I asked myself how they represented their concept of news, it was the formation of the terms of this word family that led me to start not with ἀγγελία — the word used to designate news — but with ἄγγελος, from which ἀγγελία derives.

For this reason, it is not easy to find a definition of news. Indeed, the concept of news per se is most probably a social and cultural construction that does not necessarily have an equivalent in all languages. Let us look, for example, at the Latin term *nuntius*, which has no known etymological explanation and which we cannot even be sure is related to *nouus* (Ernout & Meillet 2001).[1] It is also

---

[1] It has been linked to **neu* – 'nod the head', although this is not a very plausible link according to De Vaan (2008).

significant that the Latin term *nuntiatio* is opposed to *spectatio*, as in tragedy. The German term *Nachricht* was coined in the sixteenth century and *Nachrichter* originally meant 'executioner', referring to a civil servant that was called 'he who rides behind' to use an euphemism in place of 'executioner' (Kluge 1999).

As I have mentioned, etymology has led me to examine ἄγγελος, the Greek word used to refer to the messenger in charge of transmitting news. From this term, I continued my study of all its derivatives, which make a total of fifty-two. This has also meant that I have also been able to elaborate a syntactic, semantic, and pragmatic description of a lexical family that had hardly been studied before. Working from the possible Indo-European etymology of the term and its oldest examples, which are most probably those found in the Mycenaean tablets from the second millennium BC, I have pinpointed the semantic content and the implications in the pragmatic use of ἄγγελος and its derivatives, by analysing examples of its use in the words of the different authors that make up my corpus.

The study of Greek literature has given us an insight into the concepts of messenger and news. In this way, we see how in Homer, for example, unlike in tragedy, the ἄγγελος is not a professional, and that the terms from the lexical family ἄγγελος are used to refer to good or bad news that affects important characters in the poems and which is therefore socially important or has important consequences. An example can be seen in the death of Patroclus: when Antilochus tells Achilles of his friend's death, the latter lays aside his anger and decides to take part in battle, a decision that will permanently change the course of the war.

On the other hand, with the study of the lexicon, my aim was to prove (especially with tragedy) that terms derived from ἄγγελος began to become technical terms associated with the transmission of news. Indeed, my analysis has been more fruitful than I first expected: as I have shown throughout the chapters of this volume, the specialization of this lexical family occurs not only in one sense but in three: in the communication of news, and in military and legal contexts.

In order to carry out my analysis, I did not take into consideration isolated examples of ἄγγελος and its derivatives, but have looked at other aspects, such as the verbal and extra-verbal contexts in which they are found. With regards to the former, I analysed the different terms considering the syntactic constructions in which they appeared. In this way, we were able to demonstrate, for example, that when ἀγγέλλω takes the accusative, it is the referent of this accusative that gives us the clues to interpret whether what is being announced is a piece of news, an order, or something else. On the other hand, if ἀγγέλλω appears in a construction with a dative and infinitive, it is much more plausible that we should infer the presence of an order as opposed to some news.

When it comes to extra-verbal context, the analysis of the figure of the ἄγγελος is very interesting. This role is essential, especially in tragedy, where the transmission of news is such an integral part of the ἄγγελος himself that the other characters in the drama take it as a given that if somebody should announce a piece of news, that person must be an ἄγγελος. The speakers have a series of shared pieces of knowledge with which they deduce immediately that when an ἄγγελος appears before them, they are about to receive news. This news can be good or bad, but nobody doubts whether it is true, since the ἄγγελος is associated with the truth. The analysis of the circumstances surrounding the use of the words that I have carried out is also relevant when the terms do not indicate the presence of news but rather orders. Let us remember, for example, what happens in the Homeric poems with the gods Zeus, Poseidon, and Iris. All of these are divinities but have different positions on their hierarchical scale. For this reason, it is no surprise that Zeus should use Iris as an intermediary to transmit an order for him to another god, such as Poseidon. It would, however, be unacceptable for Iris to issue the order and for Poseidon or Zeus to have to obey it. In this sense, it is clear once more (as occurs so often in Greek culture), how human institutions — in this case messengers — are reflected in the social organization of the gods and how myths reflect the society in which they appear or with which they coexist. This situation is the same with the writings on war by historians: no one would expect a general to obey the orders of a simple soldier.

In the same way, the source of information needs to be considered. When a receiver does not distrust the source, he or she assumes that they have been given some news. If the source is unidentifiable or doubtful, on the other hand, the receiver tends to interpret what he or she has heard as a rumour. For this reason, αὐτοψία, that is, the ability to announce something as a direct witness of the event, is of clear value when it comes to the transmission of news.

As I have shown, ever since Homer both the ἄγγελος and the news reported by him or her are associated with the truth. In this respect, my study also reveals an interesting point: the presence of false news — similar to current *fake news* — in ancient Greek literature, especially in tragedy and historiography when it comes to the use of the derivatives of ἄγγελος.

Considering all that I have presented in this book, I believe that this piece of research could provide new contributions both to studies in Classics (there are hardly any studies on the transmission of news in Antiquity) and in journalism, since I have given strong evidence that the concept of news, the backbone of as modern a discipline as journalism, also existed in Ancient Greece.

Bibliography

Abbott, Evelyn/Matheson, Percy Ewin (transl.) (1899), *Demosthenes: On the Crown*, Oxford.
Adams, Charles Darwin (transl.) (1919), *Aeschines*, Cambridge.
Adcock, Frank E. (1973), *Thucydides and his History*, North Haven.
Adcock, Frank E./Mosley, Derek J. (1975), *Diplomacy in Ancient Greece*, London.
Adler, Ada (1971 [1928–1938]), *Suidae Lexicon*, Stuttgart.
Alandete, David (2017), *Fake News: la nueva arma de destrucción masiva*, Vizcaya.
Amorós, Marc (2018), *Fake News: la verdad de las noticias falsas*, Barcelona.
Allan, William (transl.) (2008), *Euripides: Helen*, Cambridge.
Allan, Rutger J. (2009), "Towards a Typology of the Narrative Modes in Ancient Greek: Text Types and Narrative Structure in Euripidean Messenger Speeches", in: Stephanie Bakker/ Gerry C. Wakker (eds.), *Discourse Cohesion in Ancient Greek*, Leiden, 171–203.
Allen-Hornblower, Emily (2016), *From Agent to Spectator: Witnessing the Aftermath in Ancient Greek Epic and Tragedy*, Berlin/Boston.
Aly, Wolfgang (1921), *Volksmärchen, Sage und Novelle bei Herodot und seinen Zeitgenossen*, Göttingen.
Anderson, John Kinloch (1970), *Military Theory and Practice in the Age in Xenophon*, Berkeley/ Los Angeles.
Anderson, John Kinloch (2001), *Xenophon*, London.
Armayor, O. Kimball (1978), "Did Herodotus ever go to Egypt?", *Journal of the American Research Center in Egypt* 15, 59–73.
Arnott, Peter (1962), *Greek Scenic Conventions in the Fifth Century B.C.*, Oxford.
Arrowsmith, William (2013), "Orestes", in: David Grene/Richmond Lattimore (eds.), *Euripides IV: The Complete Greek Tragedies (third edition, edited by Mark Griffith/Glenn W. Most)*, Chicago/London.
Arrowsmith, William (2013), "The Bacchae", in: David Grene/Richmond Lattimore (eds.), *Euripides V: The Complete Greek Tragedies (third edition, edited by Mark Griffith/Glenn W. Most)*, Chicago/London.
Asheri, David/Lloyd, Alan (2011), *A Commentary on Herodotus. Books I–IV*, Oxford.
Austin, Michael/Vidal Naquet, Pierre (1972), *Économie et sociétés en Grèce ancienne*, Paris.
Bailly, Anatole (1973), *Abrège du dictionnaire grec-français*, Paris.
Barlow, Shirley (trans.) (1986), *Euripides: Trojan Women*, London.
Barrett, James (2002), *Staged Narrative: Poetics and the Messenger in Greek Tragedy*, Berkeley.
Barrett, William Spencer, (2001 [1964]), *Euripides: Hippolytus*, Oxford.
Bassi, Domenico (1899), "Il nunzio nella tragedia greca", *Rivista di Filologia e d'Istruzione Classica* 27, 50–89.
Bechter, Friedrich (1917), *Die historischen Personennamen des griechischen bis zur Kaiserzeit*, Halle.
Beekes, Robert (2010), *Etymological Dictionary of Greek*, Leiden.
Benedetto, V. di (1965), *Euripides: Orestes*, Firenze.
Benner, Allen Rogers (1903), *Selections from Homer's Iliad*, New York.
Bers, Victor (2003), *Demosthenes, Speeches 50–59*, Austin.
Bertrand, Jean-Marie (1992), *Inscriptions historiques grecques*, Paris.
Bétant, Élie-Ami (1961), *Lexicon Thucydideum (2 vol.)*, Hildesheim/New York.
Boise, James Robinson (1870), *Xenophon's Anabasis*, New York.

Bolton, J.D.P. (1962), *Aristeas of Proconnesus*, Oxford.
Bonanno, Maria G. (1987), "Παρατραγῳδία in Aristofane", *Dioniso. Rivista di studi sul teatro antico* 57.1, 135–167.
Borries de, Ioannes (1911), *Phrynichi Sophistae Praeparatio Sophistica*, Leipzig.
Bowie, Angus M. (2007), *Herodotus: Histories. Book VIII*, Cambridge.
Braswell, Bruce K. (1988), *A Commentary of the Fourth Pythian Ode of Pindar*, Berlin/New York.
Bremer, Jan Maarten (1976), "Why Messenger-Speeches?", in: Jan Maarten Bremer/Stephan Radt/C.J.Ruijgh (eds.), *Miscellanea tragica in honorem J. C. Kamerbeek*, Amsterdam, 29–48.
Brioso Sánchez, Máximo (2005), "Sobre las convenciones escénicas de la tragedia y la comedia clásicas", in: Máximo Brioso Sánchez/Antonio Villarrubia Medina (eds.), *Aspectos del teatro griego antiguo*, Sevilla, 173–263.
Brioso Sánchez, Máximo (2006), "Algunas observaciones sobre el mensajero en el teatro ático clásico", in: Esteban Calderón Dorda et al. (eds.), *Koinós lógos. Homenaje al profesor José García López (I)*, Murcia, 111–119.
Brioso Sánchez, Máximo (2011), "El rumor como motivo literario en la tragedia griega", in: Milagros Quijada Sagredo (ed.), *Eurípides, el teatro griego de finales del siglo V a. C. y su influencia posterior*, Madrid, 131–200.
Brioso Sánchez, Máximo (2013a), "De nuevo sobre los mensajeros trágicos: Un debate metodológico", in: Milagros Quijada Sagredo/María del Carmen Encinas Reguero (eds.), *Retórica y discurso en el teatro griego*, Madrid, 157–192.
Brioso Sánchez, Máximo (2013b). "Aspectos problemáticos del mensaje y el mensajero en la tragedia griega: El caso de Edipo en Colono", in: Luis Miguel Pino/German Santana (eds.), *Homenaje al profesor Juan Antonio López Férez. Καλὸς καὶ ἀγαθὸς ἀνήρ. διδασκάλου παράδειγμα*, Madrid, 121–126.
Broadhead, Henry Dan (transl.) (1960), *The Persae of Aeschylus*, Cambridge.
Brownson, Carleto L. (1922), *Xenophon in Seven Volumes*, Cambridge.
Buono-Core, Raúl (2010), "Embajadores griegos: ¿una diplomacia profesional?", *Intus-Legere-Historia* 4.2, 9–17.
Caminos Marcet, José María (1997), *Periodismo de investigación: Teoría y práctica*, Madrid.
Camp, John McK. (1986), *The Athenian Agora: Excavations in the Heart of Classical Athens*, London.
Camp, John McK. (2003), *The Athenian Agora: A Short Guide to the Excavation*, Princeton.
Campos Daroca, Francisco Javier (2014), "Mensajeros y escenas de anuncio. Esbozo de análisis dramático de una singularidad trágica", in: Francesco de Martino/Carmen Morenilla (eds.), *A la sombra de los héroes*, Bari, 69–102.
Carandell Robusté, Luis (1997), "El Periodismo, género literario", in: Annlies van Noortwijk (ed.), *Periodismo y literatura*, Amsterdam, 13–16.
Carawan, Edwin M. (1985), "Apophasis and Eisangelia: The Role of the Areopagus in Athenian Political Trials", *Roman and Byzantine Studies* 2.26, 115–140.
Carawan, Edwin M. (1987), "Eisangelia and Euthyna: The Trials of Miltiades, Themistocles, and Cimon", *Greek, Roman and Byzantine Studies* 2.28, 167–208.
Carey, Chris (transl.) (1989), *Lysias. Selected Speeches*, Cambridge.
Carey, Chris (transl.) (2000), *Aeschines*, Austin.
Carson, Anne (transl.) (2013), "Iphigenia among the Taurians", in: David Grene/Richmond Lattimore (eds.), *Euripides III: The Complete Greek Tragedies (third edition, edited by Mark Griffith/Glenn W. Most)*, Chicago/London.

Cartledge, Paul/Greenwood, Emily (2012), "Herodotus as a Critic: Truth, Fiction, Polarity", in: Hans van Wees, Irene de Jong/Egbert Bakker (eds.), *Brill's Companion to Herodotus*, Leiden, 351–372.
Cartledge, Paul (1997), "Deep plays: Theatre as Process in Greek Civic Life", in: P.E. Easterling, *The Cambridge Companion to Greek Tragedy*, Cambridge, 3–38.
Caverno, Julia (1917), "The Messenger in Greek Tragedy", *The Classical Journal* 12.4, 263–270.
Cazaux, Diana (2010), *El ADN del periodismo científico: El reportaje interpretativo*, Quito.
Ceccarelli, Paola (2013), *Ancient Greek Letter Writing. A Cultural History (600 – 150 B.C.)*, Oxford.
Cesca, Ombretta (2017), "Entre ambassades et 'messenger-scenes': enjeux narratologiques dans l'*Iliade*", in: A. Queryrel-Bottineau/M.R. Guelfucci (eds.), *Conseillers et Ambassadeurs dans l'Antiquité, supplément DHA 17*, Besançon, 721–744.
Cesca, Ombretta (2017b), "Which Limit for Speech Reporting? Messenger Scenes and Control of Repetition in the *Iliad*", in: Niall W. Slater (ed.), *Voice and Voices in Antiquity. Orality and Literacy in the Ancient World* (vol. 11), Leiden, 31–53.
Cesca, Ombretta (2017c), "About Information Sources in Aeschylus' *Agamemnon* and *Choephori*", *Skenè* 3.1, 28–56.
Cesca, Ombretta (2022), *Ripetizione e Riformulazione nell'Iliade*, Berlin.
Chantraine, Pierre (1933), *La formation des noms en grec ancien*, Paris.
Chantraine, Pierre (1958), *Grammaire homérique: Phonétique et morphologie (vol. I)*, Paris.
Chantraine, Pierre (1974), *Dictionnaire étymologique de la langue grecque*, Paris.
Chantraine, Pierre (1986), *Grammaire homérique: Syntaxe (vol. II)*, Paris.
Cherubin, Rose (2009), "Ἀλήθεια from Poetry into Philosophy: Homer to Parmenides", in: William Wians (ed.), *Logos and Muthos: Philosophical Essays in Greek Literature*, New York, 51–72.
Chiluwa, Innocent E./Samoilenko, Sergei A. (2019) (eds.), *Handbook of Research on Deception, Fake News, and Misinformation Online*, Hershey.
Clarke, Howard W. (1989), *The Art of the Odyssey*, Bristol.
Classen, Julius (1966 [1892–1922]), *Thukydides (I–VIII)*, Berlin.
Cochrane, Charles Norris (1929), *Thucydides and the Science of History*, London.
Coleridge, Edward P. (transl.) (1891–1938), "Orestes", "The Suppliants", in: Whitney J. Oates/ Eugene O'Neill (eds.), *Euripides. The Complete Greek Drama*, New York.
Collard, Christopher (1975), Euripides: *Supplices* (vol. II: Commentary), Groningen.
Collignon, Aurélien (2017), *Le rôle des messagers dans la tragédie grecque: le cas d'Eschyle*, PhD Diss., Toulouse.
Cortés Copete, Juan Manuel (1999), *Epigrafía griega*, Madrid.
Coseriu, Eugenio (1992), "Periodisme i historia", *Periodística* 5, 11–21.
Coseriu, Eugenio/Loureda Lamas, Óscar (2006), *Lenguaje y discurso*, Pamplona.
Coventry, Lucinda (1987), "Messenger Scenes in *Iliad* XXIII and XXIV (XXIII, 192–211, XXIV, 77–188)", *The Journal of Hellenic Studies* 107, 178–180.
Cresci, Lia Raffaella, Gazzano, Francesca/Orsi, Domenica Paola (2002), *La retorica della diplomazia nella Grecia Antica e a Bisanzio*, Rome.
Crespo, Emilio (1984), "On the System of Substantive Clauses in Ancient Greek. A Functional Approach", *Glotta* 62, 1–16.
Crespo, Emilio (1991), *Homero. Ilíada. Traducción, introducción y notas*, Madrid.
Crespo, Emilio/Conti Jiménez, Luz/Maquieira Rodríguez, Helena (2003), *Sintaxis del griego clásico*, Madrid.

Crespo, Emilio (coord) (2012), *Platón, Menéxeno. Discursos en honor de los caídos por Atenas.* Edición bilingüe, introducción, traducción española y notas de Emilio Crespo, Alberto Enrique Álvarez, Raquel Fornieles, María González, Mireia Movellán y Juan Muñoz, Madrid.
Cropp, Martin (transl.) (1988), *Euripides: Electra*, Warminster.
Cropp, Martin (transl.) (2000), *Iphigenia in Tauris: Electra*, Warminster.
Crowdy, Terry (2006), *The Enemy within: A History of Spies, Spymasters and Espionage*, Oxford/New York.
Crowther, Nigel B. (1994), "The Role of Heralds and Trumpeters at Greek Athletic Festivals", *Nikephoros* 7, 135–155.
Dale, Amy Marjorie (1967), *Euripides:* Helen, Oxford.
Dalkir, Kimiz/Katz, Rebecca (2020) (eds.), *Navigating Fake News, Alternative Facts, and Misinformation in a Post-Truth World*, Montreal.
Delaney, Christine A. (1984), *Studies in Greek Literary Parody, with Special Reference to Aristophanes and Plato*, Oxford.
Delebecque, Édouard, (1957), *Essai sur la vie de Xénophon*, Paris.
Delgado Jara, Inmaculada (2006), *Diccionario griego-español del Nuevo Testamento*, Salamanca.
Denniston, John Dewar (transl.) (1968), *Euripides: Electra*, Oxford.
Denniston, John Dewar/Page, Denys (1957), *Aeschylus: Agamemnon*, Oxford.
De Vaan, Michiel (2008), *Etymological Dictionary of Latin and the other Italic Languages*, Leiden.
DGE=Rodríguez Adrados, Francisco (dir.), *Diccionario Griego-Español*: http://dge.cchs.csic.es/xdge/
Di Gregorio, Lamberto (1967), *La scene d' annuncio nella tragedia greca*, Milan.
Dickin, Margaret (2009), *A Vehicle for Performance: Acting the Messenger in Greek Tragedy*, Lanham.
Dickson, John P. (2005), "Gospel as News: εὐαγγελ- from Aristophanes to the Apostle Paul", *New Testament Studies* 51, 212–230.
Dinter, Martin/Khoo, Astrid (2019), "Messenger scenes in Greek epic", in: *Christiane Reitz and Simone Finkmann, Structures of Epic Poetry* (vol. 2), Berlin, 481–500.
DMic.=Aura Jorro, Francisco (1985–1993), *Diccionario griego-español*, anejo I. *Diccionario Micénico*, Madrid.
Dodds, Eric Robertson (1966), *Euripides: Bacchae*, Oxford.
Dover, Kenneth James (1972), *The Aristophanic Comedy*, Berkeley.
Dunbar, Nan (transl.) (1995), *Aristophanes:* Birds, Oxford.
Durán López, María de los Ángeles (1999), "Bardos, heraldos y mensajeros en los poemas homéricos", in: Aurelio Pérez/Gonzalo Cruz (eds.), *Aladas palabras. Correos y comunicaciones en el Mediterráneo*, Madrid, 9–38.
Dyson, Michael/Lee, Kevin H. (2000), "Talthybius in Euripides' Troades", *Greek, Roman and Byzantine studies* 41.2, 141–173.
Easterling, Phillip E. (1982), *Sophocles: Trachiniae*, Cambridge.
Ebeling, Heinrich (1985), *Lexicon Homericum*, Leipzig.
Echevarría Llombart, Begoña (2011), *El reportaje periodístico*, Zamora.
Edo Bolós, Concha (2009), *Periodismo informativo e interpretativo. El impacto de internet en la noticia, las fuentes y los géneros*, Sevilla.
Edwards, Michael J. (transl.) (1999), *Lysias Five Speeches (1, 12, 19, 22, 30)*, London.
Ellendt, Friederich (1841), *A Lexicon to Sophocles*, Oxford.

Encinas Reguero, María del Carmen (2011), "El relato de mensajero en el Orestes de Eurípides", *Emerita LXXIX* 1, 131–154.
Encinas Reguero, Mª del Carmen (2014), "Los relatos de mensajero y la problematización de la visión en *Bacantes* de Eurípides", *Exemplaria Classica* 18, 5–21.
Ernout, Alfred/Meillet, Antoine (2001 [1980]), *Dictionnaire Étymologique de la Langue Latine*, Paris.
Fehling, Detlev (1989), *Herodotus and his 'Sources': Citation, Invention and Narrative Art*, Leeds.
Fernández Galiano, Manuel (1994), *Píndaro. Olímpicas*, Madrid.
Fernández Parrat, Sonia (2006), "Periodismo y literatura: una contribución a la delimitación de la frontera", *Estudios Sobre El Mensaje Periodístico* 12, 275–284.
Finglass, Patrick J. (2007), *Sophocles: Electra*, Cambridge.
Finglass, Patrick J. (2011), *Sophocles: Ajax*, Cambridge.
Finkelberg, Margalit (2011), "Dêmioergoi", in: Margalit Finkelberg (ed.), *Homer Encyclopedia*, Chichester, 203.
Finley, Moses I. (1975), *The Greek Historians. The Essence of Herodotus, Thucydides, Xenophon, Polybius*, New York.
Firth, Raymond (1956), "Rumor in a Primitive Society", *The Journal of Abnormal and Social Psychology* 53.1, 122–132.
Firth, Raymond (1996 [1936]), *We, the Tikopia. Kinship in Primitive Polynesia*, Boston.
Fischl, Johannes (1910), *De Nuntiis tragicis*, PhD Diss., Wien.
Fornara, Charles W. (1977), *Archaic Times to the End of the Peloponnesian War*, Cambridge.
Fornieles Sánchez, Raquel (2013b), "«Vengo con fieles noticias del campo enemigo»: Mensajeros reporteros en la tragedia griega", in: María Pilar Diezhandino Nieto/María Teresa Sandoval Martín (eds.), *Los Nuevos desafíos del oficio del Periodismo. Actas del XVIII Congreso Internacional de la Sociedad Española de Periodística*, Madrid, 858–871.
Fornieles Sánchez, Raquel (2015), *La transmisión de noticias en la literatura griega antigua*, PhD diss., Madrid.
Fornieles Sánchez, Raquel (2018), "El mensajero y la αὐτοψία en la tragedia griega", in: Luz Conti *et al.* (eds.), *Phílos hetaîros. Homenaje al profesor Luis M. Macía*, Madrid, 45–54.
Fornieles Sánchez, Raquel (2018b), "Sobre el mensajero trágico: propuesta de clasificación", *Euphrosyne* 46, 27–44.
Fornieles Sánchez, Raquel (2020), "Buenas y malas noticias en la literatura griega antigua: de Homero a la oratoria", *Byzantion Nea Hellás* 99, 37–58.
Fornieles Sánchez, Raquel (2021), *"Fake news* en Tucídides y Jenofonte como estrategia en la guerra", in: K. Lennartz (ed.), *Engaños e invenciones · Contribuciones multidisciplinares sobre pseudoepígrafos literarios y documentales (= De falsa et vera historia 4)*, Madrid, 49–59.
Forssman, Bernhard (1974), "Zu homerisch ἀγγελίης Bote", *Münchener Studien Zur Sprachwissenschaft* 32, 41–64.
Foster Smith, Charles (1919–1923), *Thucydides (in four volumes)*, Cambridge.
Foucault, Jules-Albert (1967), "Histiée de Milet et l'esclave tatoué", *Revue des Études Grecques* 80, 181–187.
Fowler, Henry Watson (1858–1933), *The Works of Lucian of Samosata*, Oxford.
Fraenkel, Eduard (1962 [1950]), *Aeschylus. Agamemnon* (3 vol.), Oxford.
Franklin, Bob/Carlson, Matt (eds.) (2011), *Journalists, Sources and Credibility. New Perspectives*, New York.

Frasca, Ralph (2003), "Newspapers in Europe before 1500", in: Shannon E. Martin/David A. Copeland (eds.), *The Function of Newspapers in Society: a global Perspective*, Westport, 79–87.
Frisk, Hjalmar (1960), *Griechisches etymologisches Wörterbuch*, Heidelberg.
Gagarin, Michael (1986), *Early Greek Law*, Berkeley.
Gagarin, Michael (2010), "Background and Origins: Oratory and Rhetoric before the Sophists", in: Ian Worthington (ed.), *A Companion to Greek Rhetoric*, London, 27–36.
Gaisford, Thomas (1972 [1836]), *Paroemiographi graeci quorum pars nunc primum ex codicibus manuscriptis vulgatur*, Osnabrück.
García Márquez, Gabriel (1997), "The best job in the world", *Index on Censorship*. 26.1, 77–80.
García Novo, E. (1981), *La entrada de los personajes y su anuncio en la tragedia griega*, Madrid.
García Novo, E. (1984), "Una entrada de personajes peculiar: *Ayante* 866 ss.", *Estudios Clásicos* 26, 225–228.
García Romero, Fernando (1992), *Los Juegos Olímpicos y el deporte en Grecia*, Sabadell.
García Santos, Amador (2011), *Diccionario del griego bíblico: Setenta y Nuevo Testamento*, Estella.
Gargurevich, Juan (1982), *Géneros periodísticos*, Quito.
Garvie, Alex (1986), *Aeschylus: Choephori*, Oxford.
Garvie, Alex (2009), *Aeschylus: Persae*, Oxford.
Gerolymatos, André (1986), *Espionage and Treason. A Study of the Proxenia in Political and Military Intelligence Gathering in Classical Greece*, Amsterdam.
Gil Fernández, Luis (1963), "Los demiurgos", in: Luis Gil Fernández (ed.), *Introducción a Homero*, Madrid, 414–415.
Gildersleeve, Basil L. (1885), *Pindar: The Olympian and Pythian Odes*, New York.
Godley, Alfred Denis (1920), *Herodotus, with an English translation*, Cambridge.
Goodwin, William Watson (1904), *Demosthenes: De Corona*, Cambridge.
Goodwin, William Watson (1906), *Demosthenes: Against Midias*, Cambridge.
Goodwin, William Watson (1979 [1831–1912]), *Demosthenes: On the Crown*, New York.
Goldhill, Simon (1986), *Reading Greek Tragedy*, Cambridge.
Gomme, Arnold Wycombe (1945), *A Historical Commentary on Thucydides*, vol. I, Oxford.
Gomme, Arnold Wycombe (1956), *A Historical Commentary on Thucydides*, vol. II. The ten Year's War, Books II–III, Oxford.
Gomme, Arnold Wycombe (1956b), *A Historical Commentary on Thucydides*, vol. III. The ten Year's War, Books IV–V 24, Oxford.
Gomme, Arnold Wycombe, Andrewes, A./Dover, K.J. (1970), *A Historical Commentary on Thucydides, vol. IV. Books V 25–VII*, Oxford.
Gomis, Lorenzo (1989), "Gèneres literaris i gèneres periodístics", *Periodística* 1, 129–141.
Goward, Barbara (1999), *Telling Tragedy*, London.
Graves, Charles Edward (1884), *Commentary on Thucydides: Book IV*, London.
Graves, Charles Edward (1891), *Commentary on Thucydides: Book V*, London.
Green, M.A. (1894), The Birds *of Aristophanes*, Cambridge.
Green, J. Richard (1996), *Messengers from the Tragic Stage, Bulletin of the Institute of Classical Studies* 41, 17–30.
Green, J. Richard (1999), "Tragedy and Spectacle of the Mind: Messenger Speeches, Actors, Narrative an Audience Imagination in Fourth-Century BCE Vase-Painting", in: Bettina/Christine Kondoleon (eds.), *Studies in the History of Art* 56, Washington DC, 36–63.

Grene, David (transl.) (2013), "Electra", in: David Grene/Richmond Lattimore (eds.), *Sophocles II: The Complete Greek Tragedies* (Third edition, edited by Mark Griffith/Glenn W. Most), Chicago/London.

Grene, David (transl.) (2013), "Oedipus the King", in: David Grene/Richmond Lattimore (eds.), *Sophocles I: The Complete Greek Tragedies* (Third edition, edited by Mark Griffith/Glenn W. Most), Chicago/London.

Griffith, Mark (1983), *Aeschylus: Prometheus Bound*, Cambridge.

Griffith, R. Drew (2008), "Heralds and the Beginning of the Peloponnesian War", *Classical Philology* 2.103, 182–184.

Griffiths, Emma M. (2007), "Fighting the Future: Euripidean Letters and Thucydides' Athens", in: Craig Cooper (ed.), *The Politics of Orality (Orality and Literacy in Ancient Greece) vol. 6*, Leiden, 277–292.

Grijelmo, Álex (2008 [1997]), *El estilo del periodista*, Madrid.

Guillamet Lloveras, Jaume (2008), "De las gacetas del siglo XVII a la libertad de imprenta del siglo XIX", in: Carlos Barrera (coord.), *Historia del Periodismo Universal*, Barcelona, 43–76.

Guzmán García, Helena (1999), "La escena del mensajero en la tragedia griega", in: Gonzalo Cruz Andreotti/Aurelio Pérez Jiménez (eds.), *Aladas palabras. Correos y comunicaciones en el Mediterráneo*, Madrid, 39–56.

Hamilton, R. (1978), "Announced entrances in Greek tragedy", *Harvard Studies in Classical Philology* 82, 63–82.

Halleran, Michael R. (2005), "Episodes", in: Justina Gregory (ed.), *A Companion to Greek Tragedy*, Malden, 167–182.

Halliwell, Stephen (transl.) (1998), *Aristophanes Birds, Lysistrata, Assembly-Women, Wealth*, Oxford.

Halliwell, Stephen (transl.) (2015), *Aristophanes Clouds, Women at the Thesmophoria, Frogs*, Oxford.

Hansen, Mogens Herman (1980), "Eisangelia in Athens: A Reply", *The Journal of Hellenic Studies* 100, 89–95.

Hansen, Mogens Herman (1998), *Eisangelia. La sovranità del tribunale popolare ad Atene nel IV secolo a. C. e l'accusa contro strateghi e politici*, Torino.

Hansen, Mogens Herman (1999), *The Athenian Democracy in the Age of Demosthenes: Structure, Principles, and Ideology*, Oxford.

Harris, Edward M. (2017), "The Athenian view of an Athenian trial", in: Emiliano J. Buis (coord.), *Derecho griego antiguo*, *Revista Jurídica de Buenos Aires* 94, 103–128.

Harrison, Jackie (1996), *News*, London.

Harrison, A.R.W. (1971), *The Law of Athens. Vol. 2: The Procedure*, Oxford.

Hartley, John (1982), *Understanding News*, Cambridge.

Hartog, François (1988), *The Mirror of Herodotus: The Representation of the other in the Writing of History*, Berkeley/Los Angeles.

Henning, E. (1910), *De tragiccorum atticorum narrationibus*, PhD Diss., Göttingen.

Hirsch, Steven W. (1985), *The Friendship of the Barbarians: Xenophon and the Persian Empire*, Cambridge.

Hobbes, Thomas (1843), *The English Works of Thomas Hobbes of Malmesbury, vols. VIII–IX: Thucydides, the History of the Grecian War*, London.

Hogan, James C. (1991), *A Commentary on the Plays of Sophocles*, Carbondale.

Hogan, James C. (1991), *A Commentary on The Complete Greek Tragedies. Aeschylus*, Chicago/London.
Hornblower, Simon (2012), "Herodotus and his Sources of Information", in: Hans van Wees/Irene de Jong/Egbert Bakker (eds.), *Brill's Companion to Herodotus*, Leiden, 373–286.
How, Walter Wybergh/Wells, Joseph (1967 [1912]), *A Commentary on Herodotus with Introduction and Appendixes*, Oxford.
Hunter, Virginia (1990), "Gossip and Politics of Reputation in Classical Athens", *Phoenix* 44.4, 299–325.
Hutchinson, Godfrey (1985), *Aeschylus: Septem contra Thebas*, Oxford.
Hutchinson, Godfrey (2000), *Xenophon and the Art of Command*, London.
HW=Leumann, Manu (1950), *Homerische Wörter*, Basilea.
Illades, Esteban (2018), *Fake News. La nueva realidad*, Madrid.
Ireton, Cherilyn/Posetti, Julie (2018) (eds.), *Journalism, Fake News and Disinformation*, Paris.
Iriarte Goñi, Ana (1996), *Democracia y tragedia: la era de Pericles*, Madrid.
Jaeger, Werner Wilhem (1962), *Paideia. Los ideales de la cultura griega*, Mexico.
Jameson, Michael (transl.) (2013), "The Women of Trachis", in: David Grene/Richmond Lattimore (eds.), *Sophocles II: The Complete Greek Tragedies* (Third edition, edited by Mark Griffith/Glenn W. Most), Chicago/London.
Janko, Richard (1994), *The Iliad: A Commentary*, vol. IV: Books XIII–XVI, Cambridge.
Jebb, Richard C. (1885), *Sophocles. The Plays and Fragments: Oedipus Tyrannus*, Cambridge.
Jebb, Richard C. (1894), *Sophocles. The Plays and Fragments: Electra*, Cambridge.
Jebb, Richard C. (1905), *Bacchylides: The Poems and Fragments*, Cambridge.
Jebb, Richard C. (1907), *Sophocles. The Plays and Fragments: Ajax*, Cambridge.
Jebb, Richard C. (1932), *Sophocles. The Plays and Fragments: Philoctetes*, Cambridge.
Jones, Peter (2001), *Homer's Odyssey. A Commentary based on the English Translation of Richmond Lattimore*, London.
Jones, Frank William (transl.) (2013), "The Suppliant Women", in: David Grene/Richmond Lattimore (eds.), *Euripides II: The Complete Greek Tragedies (third edition, edited by Mark Griffith/Glenn W. Most)*, Chicago.
Jong, Irene de (1989), *Narrators and Focalizers: The Presentation of the History in the Iliad*, Amsterdam.
Jong, Irene de (1991), *Narrative in Drama: The Art of the Euripidean Messenger-Speech*, Leiden.
Jong, Irene de (2001), *A Narratological Commentary on the Odyssey*, Cambridge.
Jowett, Benjamin (1881), *Thucydides*, vol. I, Oxford.
Kaibel, Georg (1967), *Sophokles. Electra*, Leipzig.
Kamerbeek, Jan Coenraad (1963), *The Plays of Sophocles. Commentaries. The Ajax*, Leiden.
Kamerbeek, Jan Coenraad (1963b), *The Plays of Sophocles. Commentaries. The Philoctetes*, Leiden.
Kamerbeek, Jan Coenraad (1967), *The Plays of Sophocles. Commentaries. The Oedipus Tyrannus*, Leiden.
Kamerbeek, Jan Coenraad (1970), *The Plays of Sophocles. Commentaries. The Trachiniae*, Leiden.
Kamerbeek, Jan Coenraad (1974), *The Plays of Sophocles. Commentaries. The Electra*, Leiden.
Kapferer, Jean Noël (1990), *Rumors. Uses, Interpretations & Images*, Princeton.
Kayser, Jacques (1996), *El periódico. Estudios de morfología, de metodología y de prensa comparada*, Quito.

Keller, Joachim (1959), *Struktur und dramatische Funktion des Botenberichtes bei Aischylos und Sophokles*, PhD Diss., Tübingen.
Kenyon, Frederic G. (1897), *The Poems of Bacchylides: from a Papyrus in the British Museum*, London.
Kirk, Geoffrey Stephen (1985), The Iliad: *A Commentary, vol. I: Books 1–4*, Cambridge.
Kirk, Geoffrey Stephen/Hainsworth, Bryan (1993), The Iliad: *A Commentary, vol. 3: Books 9–12*, Cambridge.
Kluge, Friedrich (1999 [1881–1883]), *Etymologisches Wörterbuch der deutschen Sprache* (23th ed.), Berlin.
Kovacks, David (transl.) (1994), *Euripides I: Cyclops, Alcestis, Medea*, Cambridge, MA.
Kyriakou, Poulheria (2006), *A Commentary on Euripides' Iphigenia in Tauris*, Berlin.
Lamb, Walter Rangeley Maitland (1930), *Lysias*, Cambridge.
Larran, Francis (2010), "De *kleos* a *pheme*, Approche historique de la rumeur et de la renommée dans la littérature grecque ancienne, d'Homère a Polybe", *Anabases* 11, 1–6.
Larran, Francis (2011), *Le bruit qui vole. Historie de la rumeur et de la renommée en Grèce ancienne*, Toulouse.
Lasswell, Harold D. (1948), "The Structure and Function of Communication in Society", in: Lyman Bryson (ed.), *The Communication of Ideas*, New York, 32–51.
Lateiner, Donald (1977), "Heralds and Corpses in Thucydides", *Classical World* 71.2, 97–105.
Lateiner, Donald (1989), *The Historical Method of Herodotus*, Toronto.
Latte, Kurt (1953), *Hesychii alexandrini lexicon*, Berlin.
Lattimore, Richmond (transl.) (1961), The Iliad *of Homer*, New York.
Lattimore, Richmond (transl.) (1967), The Odyssey *of Homer*, New York.
Lattimore, Richomnd (transl.) (2013), "The Trojan Women", in: David Grene/Richmond Lattimore (eds.), *Euripides III: The Complete Greek Tragedies (third edition, edited by Mark Griffith/Glenn W. Most)*, Chicago/London.
Lattimore, Richmond (transl.) (2013), "Rhesus", in: David Grene/Richmond Lattimore (eds.), *Euripides V: The Complete Greek Tragedies (third edition, edited by Mark Griffith/Glenn W. Most)*, Chicago/London.
Leaf, Walter (ed.) (1900), *The Iliad*, London.
Leaf, Walter/Bayfield, Matthew Albert (eds.) (1962), The Iliad *of Homer. Books XIII–XXIV*, London.
Leal Soares, Carmen (1999), *O discurso do extracénico: Quadros de guerra em Eurípides*, Lisboa.
Leal Soares, Carmen (2007), "Eurípides, reportero de guerra", in: Francisco Javier Campos Daroca *et al.* (eds.), *Las personas de Eurípides*, Amsterdam, 105–131.
Léon-Dufour, Xavier (1977), *Diccionario del Nuevo Testamento*, Madrid.
Létoublon, François (1987), "Le messager fidèle", in: Jan Maarten Bremer/Irene J. F. de Jong/J. Kalff (eds.), *Homer, Beyond Oral Poetry: Recent Trends in Homeric Interpretation*, Berlin, 123–144.
Leukart, Alex (1996), "Pylos vn 493.1: «a-‹ko›ro e-po a-ke-ra2-te»", in: Sacconi, A./De Miro, E./ Godart, L. (eds.), *Atti e memorie del secondo congresso internazionale di micenologia*, Roma, 311–314.
Levi, Simona (2019), *#Fake You: Fake News y Desinformación*, Barcelona.
Lewis, Sian (1992), "Public Information: News and Writing in Ancient Greece", *Hermathena* 152, 5–20.
Lewis, Sian (1996), *News and Society in the Greek Polis*, Chapel Hill.

LfgrE=Snell, Bruno (1979–2010), *Lexikon des frühgriechischen Epos*, Göttingen.
Lincoln, Bruce (1999), *Theorizing Myth: Narrative, Ideology and Scholarship*, Chicago.
Linwood, William (1843), *A Lexicon to Aeschylus*, London.
Longo, Odone (1978), "Tecniche della comunicazione e ideologie sociali nella Grecia antica", *Quaderni Urbinati di Cultura Classica* 27, 63–92.
López Eire, Antonio (transl.) (1980), *Demóstenes. Discursos políticos I*, Madrid.
López Eire, Antonio (transl.) (1985), *Demóstenes. Discursos políticos II*, Madrid.
López Eire, Antonio (transl.) (1985b), *Demóstenes. Discursos políticos III*, Madrid.
López Eire, Antonio (1987), "Sobre los orígenes de la oratoria (I)", *Minerva* 1, 13–32.
López Eire, Antonio (1988), "Sobre los orígenes de la oratoria (II)", *Minerva* 2, 117–132.
López Eire, Antonio (1996), *La lengua coloquial de la comedia aristofánica*, Murcia.
López Eire, Antonio (2000), "Homero", in: Juan Antonio López Férez (ed.), *Historia de la literatura griega*, Madrid, 33–65.
López Eire, Antonio (2000b), "La oratoria", in: Juan Antonio López Férez (ed.), *Historia de la literatura griega*, Madrid, 737–774.
Losada, Luis A. (1972), *The Fifth Column in the Peloponnesian War*, Leiden.
Loureda Lamas, Óscar (2001), *Análisis de las estructuras lexemáticas del metalenguaje de la lengua. Los nombres de los tipos de texto en el español actual*, PhD Diss., A Coruña.
LSJ= H.G. Liddell & R. Scott (1968), *A Greek – English Lexicon*, 9th ed. Revised by H.S. Jones, Oxford.
Lucas de Dios, José María (1982), *La estructura de la tragedia de Sófocles*, Madrid.
Lucas de Dios, José María (transl.) (2002), *Esquines. Discursos, testimonios y cartas*, Madrid.
Luce, Torrey James (1997), *The Greek Historians*, London.
Luginbill, Robert D. (2015), "The Letter of Nicias. Document or Fiction?", *Athenaeum: Studi di letteratura e Storia dell'antichità* 2, 390–416.
MacDowell, Douglas M. (1978), *The Law in Classical Athens*, London.
MacDowell, Douglas M. (2009), *Demosthenes the Orator*, Oxford.
Macan, Reginald Walter (1908), *Herodotus. The Seventh, Eighth & Ninth Books*, Oxford.
Macía Aparicio, Luis Miguel/García Blanco, José (1991), *Homero. Ilíada, vol. I: Cantos I–III*, Madrid.
Macía Aparicio, Luis Miguel (1989), *Tucídides. Historia de la guerra del Peloponeso*, Madrid.
Macía Aparicio, Luis Miguel (1998), *Homero. Ilíada, vol. II: Cantos IV–IX*, Madrid.
Macía Aparicio, Luis Miguel (2006), *Aristófanes. Comedias III*: Lisístrata, Las Tesmoforias, Las Ranas, La Asamblea de las mujeres, Pluto, Madrid.
Macía Aparicio, Luis Miguel (2007), *Aristófanes. Comedias II*: Las Nubes, Las Avispas, La Paz, Los Pájaros, Madrid.
Macía Aparicio, Luis Miguel (2009), *Homero. Ilíada, vol. III: Cantos X–XVII*, Madrid.
Macía Aparicio, Luis Miguel (2012), "El teatro y las representaciones dramáticas en la Atenas Clásica", in Emilio Crespo Güemes (coord), *Esquilo, Sófocles, Eurípides. Obras completas*, Madrid.
Macía Aparicio, Luis Miguel/De la Villa Polo, Jesús (2013), *Homero. Ilíada, vol. IV: Cantos XVII–XXIV*, Madrid.
Mannsperger, Brigitte (1971), "Die Rhesis", in: Walter Jens (ed.), *Die Bauformen der griechischen Tragödie*, München, 143–181.
Marchant, E.C. (1893), *Commentary on Thucydides: Book VII*, London.
Marchant, E.C. (1900–1920), *Xenophon in Seven Volumes*, Cambridge.
Marchant, E.C. (1905), *Commentary on Thucydides: Book I*, London.

Marchant, E.C. (1909), *Commentary on Thucydides: Book VI*, London.
Marcos Pérez, José María (1994), "El relato de mensajero en Eurípides: concepto y estructura", *Minerva* 9, 77–98.
Marincola, John (1997), *Authority and Tradition in Ancient Historiography*, Cambridge.
Marincola, John (2001), *Greek Historians*, Cambridge.
Marqués, Néstor F. (2019), *Fake News de la antigua Roma*, Madrid.
Marshall, C.W. (2006), "How to write a Messenger-Speech (Sophocles-*Elektra* 680–763)", *Bulletin of the Institute of Classical Studies* 87, 203–221.
Martin, Richard P. (1989), *The Language of Heroes: Speech and Performance in the 'Iliad'*, Ithaca/London.
Martín Vivaldi, Gonzalo (2006 [2000]), *Curso de redacción. Teoría y práctica de la composición y del estilo*, Madrid.
Martínez Albertos, José Luis (1972), *La información en una sociedad industrial: Función social de los mass media en un universo democrático*, Madrid.
Martínez Albertos, José Luis (2004), "Aproximación a la teoría de los géneros periodísticos", in: Juan Cantavella/José Francisco Serrano (coords.), *Redacción para periodistas: Informar e interpretar*, Barcelona, 51–75.
Martínez Albertos, José Luis (2007 [1984]), *Curso general de redacción periodística*, Madrid.
Martínez Hernando, Bernardino (2008), "Alicia en el país de los géneros. Géneros periodísticos y géneros literarios", *Comunicación y Estudios Universitarios* 8, 51–60.
Martínez Vázquez, Rafael/Ruiz Yamuza, Emilia/Fernández Garrido, María Regla (1999), *Gramática functional-cognitiva del griego antiguo I: Sintaxis y semántica de la predicación*, Sevilla.
Mastromarco, Giuseppe (2006), "La paratragodia, il libro, la memoria", in: Enrico Meda, Maria Serena Mirto/Maria Pia Pattoni (eds.), *KOMODOTRAGODIA. Seminari e convegni: Intersezioni del trágico e del comico nel teatro del V secolo a. C.*, Pisa, 137–191.
Mastronarde, Donald J. (1979), *Contact and Discontinuity: Some Conventions of Speech and Action on the Greek Tragic Stage*, Berkeley/Los Angeles/London.
Mastronarde, Donald J. (1994), *Euripides: Phoenissae*, Cambridge.
Mastronarde, Donald J. (2002), *Euripides: Medea*, Cambridge.
Meiggs, Russell/Lewis, David Malcom (1969), *A Selection of Greek Historical Inscriptions to the End of the Fifth Century BC*, Oxford.
Melero Bellido, Antonio (2000), "Comedia", in: Juan Antonio López Férez (ed.), *Historia de la literatura griega*, Madrid, 431–499.
Merry William Walter (1907), Homer. *Odyssey, Books XIII–XXIV*, Oxford.
Merry, William Walter/Monro, David B. (1886–1891), *Commentary on Odyssey*, Oxford.
Miller, Walter (1924), *Xenophon in Seven Volumes*, Cambridge.
Miller, Michael (2019), *Fake News: Separating Truth from Fiction*, Minneapolis.
Mills, T.R. (1909), *Thucydides Book IV*, Oxford.
Mills, S.P. (1981), "The Death of Ajax", *The Classical Journal* 76, 129–135.
Mireaux, Emile (1962), *La vida cotidiana en los tiempos de Homero*, Buenos Aires.
Mitchell, Thomas (transl.) (1836), *The Knights of Aristophanes*, London.
Missiou-Ladi, Anna (1987), "Coercive Diplomacy in Greek Interstate Relations", *Classical Quarterly* 37, 336–345.
Moles, J. (1993), "Truth and Untruth in Herodotus and Thucydides", in: Christopher Gill/Timothy Peter Wiseman (eds.), *Lies and Fiction in Ancient World*, Austin, 88–121.

Molotch, Harvey/Lester, Marilyn (1974), "News as Purposive Behavior: On the Strategic Use of Routine Events, Accidents and Scandals", *American Sociological Review* 39, 101–112.
Monaco, Giusto (2004), "La scena allargata in Eschilo, Sofocle, Plauto", *Dioniso* 3, 7–34.
Mondi, Robert (1978), *Function and Social Position of the Kerux in early Ancient Greece*, PhD Diss., Harvard.
Moore, John (transl.) (2013), "Ajax" and "The Women of Thrachis", in: David Grene/Richmond Lattimore (eds.), Sophocles II: The Complete Greek Tragedies (Third edition, edited by Mark Griffith/Glenn W. Most), Chicago/London.
Mosley, Derek J. (1973), *Envoys and Diplomacy in Ancient Greece*, Wiesbaden.
Mosley, Derek J. (1998), "Politics, Diplomacy and Disaster in Ancient Greece", in: Eckart Olshausen/Holger Sonnabend (eds.), *Naturkatastrophen in der antiken Welt*, Stuttgart, 67–77.
Mosley, Derek J. (1972), "Diplomacy in Classical Greece", *Ancient Society* 3, 1–16.
Murray, A.T. (1891), *On Parody and Paratragoedia in Aristophanes*, Berlin.
Murray, A.T. (1919), *The Odyssey* (2 vol.), Cambridge.
Murray, A.T. (1936), *Demosthenes. Vol. IV. Orations XXVII–XL*, Cambridge.
Murray, Gilbert (transl.) (1092), *Euripidis Fabulae, vol. I: Cyclops, Alcestis, Medea, Heraclidae, Hippolytus, Andromacha, Hecuba*, Oxford.
Murray, Gilbert (transl.) (1913), *Euripidis Fabulae, vol. II. Supplices, Hercules, Ion, Troiades, Electra, Iphigenia Taurica*, Oxford.
Murray, Gilbert (transl.) (1913b), *Euripidis Fabulae. vol. III. Phoenissae, Orestes, Bacchae, Iphigenia Aulidensis, Rhesus*, Oxford: Clarendon.
Nash, Laura L. (1990), *The Aggelia in Pindar*, New York/London.
Nenci, Giuseppe (1955), "Il motivo dell' autopsia nella storiografia greca", *Studi Classici e Orientali* 3, 14–46.
Nickel, Rainer (1979), *Xenophon*, Darmstadt.
Norlin, George (1980), *Isocrates* (with an English translation), London.
Núñez Ladeveze, Luis (1991), *Manual para Periodismo: Veinte lecciones sobre el contexto, el lenguaje y el texto de la información*, Barcelona.
O'Neill, Eugene (transl.), *The Complete Greek Drama*, vol. 2, New York.
Ober, Josiah (1989), *Mass and Elite in Democratic Athens: Rhetoric, Ideology and the Power of the People*, Princeton.
Oehler, J. (1958–1980), "Keryx", in: *Pauly-Wissowa (Paulys Realencyclopädie der klassischen Altertumswissenschaft neue Bearbeitung)*, Stuttgart.
Olson, S. Douglas (transl.) (2002), *Aristophanes: Acharnians*, Oxford.
Ostwald, Martin (1986), *From Popular Sovereignty to the Sovereignty of Law: Law, Society and Politics in Fifth Century Athens*, Berkeley/Los Angeles.
Owen, A.S. (transl.) (1963), *Euripides: Ion*, Oxford.
Padrón Barquín, Juan Nicolás (2004), *Géneros literarios y géneros periodísticos*, Nayarit.
Page, Denys (transl.) (1938), *Euripides: Medea*, Oxford.
Pallí Bonet, Julio (1956), "Los heraldos, Taltibio y Eurípides", *Helmántica* 7, 345–355.
Peignez, Jocelyne (2006), "Thucydide et la lettre de Nicias aux athéniens", in: Patrick Laurence/François Guillaumont (eds.), *Epistulae antiquae IV. Actes du IVe colloque international "L' épistolaire antique et ses prolongements européens"*, Louvain-Paris, 15–25.
Pena de Oliveira, Felipe (2006), *Teoría del Periodismo*, Sevilla.
Perea Morales, Bernardo (1993), *Esquilo. Tragedias*, Madrid.
Perris, Simon R. (2011), "What maketh the Messenger? Reportage in Greek Tragedy", in: Anne Mackay (ed.), *Australasian Society for Classical Studies 32 Proceedings*, 1–12.

Perris, Simon R. (2011), "Perspectives on violence in Euripides' Bacchae", *Mnemosyne* 64, 37–57.
Petrovic, Andrej (2004), "*Akoe e autopsia*. Zu den Quellen Herodots für die Thermopylai-Epigramme (Hdt. 7,228)" in: Angela Hornung/Christian Jäkel/Werner Schubert, (eds.), *Studia humanitatis ac litterarum trifolio heidelbergensi dedicata. Festschrift für E. Christmann, W. Edelmeier und R. Kettemann*, Frankfurt, 255–273.
Pfeijffer, Leonard (1999), *Three Aeginetan Odes of Pindar: A Commentary on Nemean V, Nemean III & Pythian VIII*, Leiden/Boston/Köln.
Phillips, E.D. (1955), "The Legend of Aristeas: Fact and Fancy in the early Greek Notions of East Russia, Siberia and Inner Asia", *Artibus Asiae* 18.2, 161–177.
Powell, J. Enoch (1960 [1938]), *A Lexicon to Herodotus*, Hildesheim.
Pritchett, William Kendrick (1974), *The Greek State at War (GSAW)*, vol. 1, Berkeley.
Pritchett, William Kendrick (1993), *The Liar School of Herodotos*, Amsterdam.
Quesada Pérez, Montse (2010), "Los sucesos como foco de atención informativa", in: Idoia Camacho Markina (ed.), *La especialización en el Periodismo: formarse para informar*, Sevilla, 61–77.
Quijada Sagredo, Milagros (1991), *La composición de la tragedia tardía de Eurípides*, Vitoria.
Quijada Sagredo, Milagros (2002), "Virtuosismo e innovación en la monodia trágica. Eurípides, *Or.* 1369–1502", *Veleia (Anejo XVII)*, 89–97.
Quijada Sagredo, Milagros (2012), "Intriga cómica versus intriga trágica en *Tesmoforiantes* de Aristófanes", *Emerita LXXX* (2), 257–274.
Rackham, Harris (transl.) (1952), *Aristotle in 23 volumes (vol. 20)*, London.
Ramsay, William (1927), "Diplomacy and Propaganda of the Peloponnesian War", *Abstracts of Theses, University of Chicago: Humanistic Series* 6, 305–310.
Rassow, Johannes (1883), *Questiones selectae de Euripideorum nuntiorum narrationibus*, PhD Diss., Greifswald.
Rau, Peter (1967), *Paratragodia: Untersuchung einer komischen Form des Aristophanes*, München.
Reece, Steve (2009), *Homer's Winged Words: The Evolution of early Greek Epic Diction in the Light of Oral Theory*, Leiden.
Rennie, W. (1909), The Acharnians *of Aristophanes*, London.
Richmond, James A. (1998), "Spies in Ancient Greece", *Greece and Rome* 45.1, 1–18.
Riedinger, J.C. (1995), "Technique du récit et technique dramatique dans le récit du messager d'Euripide", *Pallas* 42, 31–54.
Riepl, Wolfgang (1913), *Das Nachrichtenwesen des Altertums (mit besonderer Rücksicht auf die Römer)*, Leipzig.
Rijksbaron, Albert (1976), "How does a Messenger begin his Speech? Some Observations on the opening Lines of Euripidean Messenger Speeches", in: Jan Maarten Bremer/Stephan Radt/C.J. Ruijgh (eds.), *Miscellanea tragica in honorem J. C. Kamerbeek*, Amsterdam, 293–308.
Ringer, Mark (1996), "Reflections on an Empty Urn", in: Francis M. Dunn (ed.), *Sophocles'* Electra *in Performance*, Stuttgart, 93–100.
Ringer, Mark (1998), *Electra and the Empty Urn: Metatheater and Role Playing in Sophocles*, Columbia.
Rhodes, Peter John (1979), "ΕΙΣΑΓΓΕΛΙΑ in Athens", *The Journal of Hellenic Studies* 99, 103–114.
Rhodes, Peter John (1981), *A Commentary on the Aristotelian* Athenaion Politeia, Oxford.
Rhodes, Peter John (1994), *Thucydides History III*, Warminster.

Roberts, Deborah (transl.), "Andromache", in: David Grene/Richmond Lattimore (eds.), *Euripides II: The Complete Greek Tragedies (third edition, edited by Mark Griffith/Glenn W. Most)*, Chicago/London.
Rogers, Benjamin B. (transl.) (1902), The Ecclesiazusae *of Aristophanes*, London.
Rogers, Benjamin B. (transl.) (1927), *Aristophanes:* The Peace, The Birds, The Frogs, Cambridge, MA.
Rogers, Benjamin B. (transl.) (1930), *Aristophanes:* The Acharnians, The Knights, The Clouds, The Wasps, Cambridge, MA.
Romero Mariscal, Lucía P. (2014), "Mensajeros y escenas de mensajero en los fragmentos de Eurípides", in: Franceso de Martino/Carmen Morenilla (eds.), *A la sombra de los héroes*, Bari, 249–267.
Romilly, Jacqueline de (1967), *Histoire et raison chez Thucydide*, Paris.
Romilly, Jacqueline de (1970), *La Tragédie grecque*, Paris.
Romilly, Jacqueline de (1990), *La construction de la vérité chez Thucydide*, Paris.
Rood, Tim (2006), "Objectivity and authority", in: Antonios Rengakos/Antonios Tsakmakis (eds.), *Brill's Companion to Thucydides*, Leiden, 225–250.
Rosenmeyer, Patricia A. (2004), *Ancient Epistolary Fictions: The Letter in Greek Literature*, Cambridge.
Ross, Charles G. (1911), *The Writing of News. A Handbook*, New York.
Ruipérez, Martín S. (1972), "Le dialecte mycénien", *Minos: Revista De Filología Egea* 11, 136–166.
Rumpel, Johann (1883), *Lexicum Pindaricum*, Leipzig.
Ruschenbusch, Eberhard (1968), *Untersuchungen zur Geschichte des athenischen Strafrechts*, Graz.
Russell, Frank S. (1999), *Information Gathering in Classical Greece*, Ann Harbor.
Rusten, Jeffrey S. (1989), *Thucydides. The Peloponnesian War. Book II*, Cambridge.
Safieddine, Fadi/Ibrahim, Yasmin (2020) (eds.), *Fake News in an Era of Social Media: Tracking Viral Contagion*, London.
Sandys, John Edwin (2000 [1912]), *Aristotle's* Constitution of Athens, New Jersey.
Sanxay, James (1754), *Lexicon Aristophanicum Graeco-Anglicum*, London.
Sayce, Archibald Henry (1885), "The Season and Extent of the Travel of Herodotos in Egypt", *The Journal of Philology* 14, 257–286.
Schadewaldt, Wolfgang (1928), *Der Aufbau des pindarischen Epinikion*, Halle.
Scheinsohn, Daniel (2009), *Comunicación estratégica*, Buenos Aires.
Schepens, Guido (1980), *L'autopsie dans la méthode des historiens grecs du V⁰ siècle avant J.C.*, Bruxelles.
Schepens, Guido (2007), "History and Historia: Inquiry in the Greek Historians", in: John Marincola (ed.), *A Companion to Greek and Roman Historiography (vol. I)*, London, 39–55.
Schudson, Michael (1978), *Discovering the News. A Social History of American Newspapers*, New York.
Sheldon, Rose Mary (2003), *Espionage in the Ancient World: An Annotated Bibliography of Books and Articles in Western Languages*, Jefferson.
Seale, David (1982), *Vision and Stagecraft in Sophocles*, London.
Sealey, Raphael (1976), "The Pit and the Well: The persian Heralds of 491 BC", *The Classical Journal* 72.1, 13–20.
Sealey, Raphael (1993), *Demosthenes & his Time: A Study in Defeat*, New York.
Sealey, Raphael (1994), *The Justice of the Greeks*, Ann Arbor.

Segal, Charles (1998), *Aglaia. The Poetry of Alcman, Sappho, Pindar, Bacchylides and Corinna*, Oxford.
Seidensticker, Bernd (1971), "Die Stichomythie", in: Walter Jens (ed.), *Die Bauformen der griechischen Tragödie*, München, 183–200.
Seymour, Thomas Day (1891), *Homer's Iliad Books I–III*, Boston.
Seymour, Thomas Day (1891b), *Homer's Iliad Books IV–VI*, Boston.
Sheppard, J.F. (1918), "The Tragedy of Electra. According to Sophocles", *The Classical Quarterly* 12.2, 80–88.
Shoemaker, Pamela J. (2006), "News and Newsworthiness: A Commentary", *Communications* 31, 105–111.
Shoemaker, Pamela J./Cohen, Akiba A. (2006), *News Around the World*, New York.
Slater, William J. (1969), *Lexicon to Pindar*, Berlin.
Slater, Nial W. (2002), *Spectator Politics. Metatheatre and Performance in Aristophanes*, Philadelphia.
Smith, Charles F. (1886), *Commentary on Thucydides Book VII*, Boston.
Smith, Charles F. (1913), *Commentary on Thucydides book VI*, Boston.
Sommerstein, Alan H. (transl.) (1978), *Aristophanes*: The Knights, Peace, The Birds, The Assembly Women, Wealth, London.
Sommerstein, Alan H. (transl.) (1998), *The Comedies of Aristophanes*: Ecclesiazusae, Warminster.
Sommerstein, Alan H. (transl.) (1980), *The Comedies of Aristophanes*: Acharnians, Warminster.
Sommerstein, Alan H. (transl.) (1983), *The Comedies of Aristophanes*: Wasps, Warminster.
Sommerstein, Alan H. (transl.) (1987), The Comedies of Aristophanes: Birds, Warminster.
Sommerstein, Alan H. (transl.) (2003), *Lysistrata and other plays*, London.
Sommerstein, Alan H. (transl.) (2008), *Aeschylus: Oresteia*, Cambridge, MA.
Sommerstein, Alan H. (transl.) (2009), *Aeschylus: Persians, Seven Against Thebes, Suppliants, Prometheus Bound*, Cambridge, MA.
Stanford, W.B. (transl.) (1963), *Sophocles: Ajax*, New York.
Starr, Chester G. (1974), *Political Intelligence in Ancient Greece*, Leiden.
Stéfanis, Athanasios (1997), *Le messager dans la tragédie grecque: formes d'information et formes de falsification du message dans l'antiquité grecque*, Athens.
Steiner, Deborah (2010), *Homer. Odyssey, Books XVII and XVIII with commentary*, Cambridge.
Stephens, Michael (1988), *A History of News: From the Drum to the Satellite*, New York.
Strohm, Hans (1959), "Beobachtungen zum Rhesus", *Hermes* 87, 257–274.
Sturz, Friedrich Wilhelm (1964 [1801–1804]), *Lexicon Xenophonteum*, Hildesheim.
Suárez de la Torre, Emilio (1984), "El mito de Cirene y la victoria de Telesícrate (Pind. *Pyth.* 9)", *Estudios Clásicos* 87, 199–208.
Svarlien, Diane Arnson (1991), *The Odes of Pindar*, New Haven.
Svarlien, Diane Arnson (1991b), *Bacchylides' Odes*, New Haven.
Taplin, Oliver (1977), *The Stagecraft of Aeschylus: The Dramatic Use of Exits and Entrances in Greek Tragedy*, Oxford.
Taplin, Oliver (1978), *Greek Tragedy in Action*, London.
Taplin, Oliver (transl.) (2013), "Medea", in: David Grene/Richmond Lattimore (eds.), *Euripides I: The Complete Greek Tragedies (third edition, edited by Mark Griffith/Glenn W. Most)*, Chicago/London.
Thalheim, J. (1905), "Εἰσαγγελία", in: *Pauly-Wissowa (Paulys Realencyclopädie der klassischen Altertumswissenschaft neue Bearbeitung)*, Stuttgart.

Thalmann, William, G. (2011), "Heralds", in: Margalit Finkelberg (ed.), *Homer Encyclopedia*, Chichester.
Thordarson, Fridrik (1996), "Herodotus and the Iranians: ὄψις, ἀκοή, ψεῦδος", *Symbolae Osloenses* 71, 42–58.
Timoteo Álvarez, Jesús (2004), "Los medios y el desarrollo de la sociedad occidental", in: Carlos Barrera (coord.), *Historia del Periodismo Universal*, Barcelona, 25–42.
Thomas, Rosalind (1992), *Literacy and Orality in Ancient Greece*, Cambridge.
Thomas, Rosalind (1992b), *Oral Tradition and Written Record in Classical Athens*, Cambridge.
Thomas, Rosalind (2000), *Herodotus in Context. Ethnography, Science and the Art of Persuasion*, Cambridge.
Thür, Gerhard (2014), "Epangelia", in: Hubert Cancik/Helmut Schneider (eds.), *Brill's New Pauly. Antiquity Volumes* (Brill online).
Todd, Otis Johnson (1962), *Index Aristophaneus*, Hildesheim.
Todd, Stephen Charles (transl.) (2000), *Lysias*, Austin.
Todd, Stephen Charles (2007), *A Commentary on Lysias Speeches 1–11*, Oxford.
Tordoff, Robert (2012), "Carion down the Piraeus: The Tragic Messenger Speech in Aristophanes' Wealth", in: C.W. Marshall/George Kovacs (eds.), *No Laughing Matter: Studies in Athenian Comedy*, London, 141–158.
Torrance, Robert (1966), *The Women of Trachis and Philoctetes*, Boston.
Torres Esbarranch, Juan José (transl.) (1990), *Tucídides. Guerra del Peloponeso*, Madrid.
Tucker, Thomas George (1892), *Commentary on Thucydides Book VIII*, London.
Ussher, Robert G. (1973) (transl.), *Aristophanes*: Ecclesiazusae, Oxford.
Vázquez Bermúdez, M.Á. (2006), *Noticias a la carta*, Sevilla.
Van Hook, Laure (1945–1968), *Isocrates with an English Translation in three volumes*, London.
Van Leeuwen, Jan F. (1905), *Aristophanis*: Ecclesiazusae, London.
Verrall, Arthur Woollgar (transl.) (1889), *The Agamemnon of Aeschylus*, Londres.
Verdenius, Willem Jacob (1987), *Commentaries on Pindar, vol. I: Oympian Odes 3, 7, 12, 14*, Leiden.
Vermeule, Emily T. (2013), "The Trojan Women", in: David Grene/Richmond Lattimore (eds.), *Euripides III: The Complete Greek Tragedies (third edition, edited by Mark Griffith/Glenn W. Most)*, Chicago/London.
Vince, James Herbert (1930), *Demosthenes with an English translation*, Cambridge.
Von Essen, Martin Heinrich Nikolaus (1964), *Index Thucydideus ex Bekkeri Editione Stereotypa Confectus*, Darmstadt.
Walker, Charles R. (transl.) (2013), "Iphigenia in Aulis", in: David Grene/Richmond Lattimore (eds.), *Euripides V: The Complete Greek Tragedies (third edition, edited by Mark Griffith/Glenn W. Most)*, Chicago/London.
Warren, Carl Nelson (1934), *Modern News Reporting*, New York.
Watson, John Selby/Dale, Henry (1893), *Xenophons' Cyropaedia and* The Hellenics, London.
Wayte, William (1882), *Demosthenes*: Against Androtion and Against Timocrates, Cambridge.
Wedeck, Harry E. (1946), "Ancient spies", *The Classical World* XXXIX, 31–32.
Wells, James Bradley (2009), *Pindar's Verbal Art: An Ethnographic Study of Epinician Style*, Washington, DC.
West, Stephanie (1985), "Herodotus' Epigraphical Interests", *Classical Quarterly* 35, 278–305.
Wyckoff, Elizabeth (2013) (transl.), "The Phoenician Women", in: David Grene/Richmond Lattimore (eds.), *Euripides IV: The Complete Greek Tragedies (third edition, edited by Mark Griffith/Glenn W. Most)*, Chicago/London.

Willcock, Malcom M. (1970), *A Commentary on Homer's* Iliad. *Books I–IV*, London.
Willcock, Malcom M. (1995), *Pindar Victory Odes: Olympians 2, 7, 11; Nemean 4; Isthmians 3, 4, 7*, Cambridge.
Willetts, Ronald Frederick (2013) (transl.), "Ion", in: David Grene/Richmond Lattimore (eds.), *Euripides III: The Complete Greek Tragedies (third edition, edited by Mark Griffith/Glenn W. Most)*, Chicago/London.
Willink, Charles W. (1986), *Euripides: Orestes*, Oxford.
Willis, William James (1990), *Journalism. State of the Art*, New York.
Wilkins, John (transl.) (1993), *Euripides: Heraclidae*, Oxford.
Wolicki, Aleksander (2002), "The Heralds and the Games in Archaic and Classical Greece", *Nikephoros* 15, 69–97.
Yoon, Florence (2012), *The Use of Anonymous Characters in Greek Tragedy. The Shaping of Heroes*, Amsterdam.
Young-Brown, Fiona (2019), *Fake News and Propaganda*, New York.
Yunis, Harvey (2001), *Demosthenes. On the Crown*, Cambridge.
Yunis, Harvey (transl.) (2005), *Demosthenes Speeches 18 and 19*, Austin.
Zimdars, Melissa/McLeod, Kembrew (2020), *Fake News. Understanding Media and Misinformation in the Digital Age*, London.

General Index

accusation 166, 171, 192, 214
accusative XXII, 12, 14, 20, 22f., 26, 29, 44, 72, 78, 80–85, 88–98, 115f., 119–122, 131f., 151f., 155–157, 162–164, 168, 173f., 176f., 196, 198–201, 203f., 206, 208–211, 231
–internal 20
–AcI construction XXII, 28, 85, 91, 122, 160, 169, 176, 181, 201, 207, 211
–AcP construction XXII, 84, 91, 160f., 169, 176, 201, 204
accuser 171, 190, 200, 203
Achilles 6, 10f., 13, 15–17, 22, 28–30, 32f., 50, 78, 89, 218f., 231
addressee 29, 59, 67, 71, 102, 105, 155
Agamemnon 3, 12, 15, 17, 20, 28f., 32, 47, 49, 51f., 56, 58f., 63f., 69f., 79, 83–85, 88, 92f., 95, 98f., 104f., 108, 180, 217, 219–222
Ajax 10f., 15, 30, 61, 65, 71, 77, 80f., 84, 87, 96, 220
Alcibiades 139, 146, 158, 170, 172
alliance 133, 146, 160, 162, 164, 211
ambassador XX, XXI, 128, 130f., 146, 161f., 181, 184f., 188, 197, 199, 201, 209, 211
anger 11, 15, 28, 33f., 55, 68, 229
Antigone 12, 63, 69, 76
Antilochus 8–12, 22, 29, 32, 229
assembly 3, 35, 49, 60, 78, 102, 129
–Assembly XX, 164f., 183–185, 189, 191–193, 198, 202, 205, 211f.
Athena 1, 5, 8, 30, 94
athletic competitions XIX, 35, 38, 46, 50
audience XIIIf., 59, 61f., 66, 70, 101, 116, 119, 154, 185, 192, 211
battle 1, 8, 11, 15f., 19, 25, 31, 33, 39f., 60, 66, 87, 110, 118, 132f., 136, 138, 152, 158, 161, 164, 166–168, 172, 175, 179, 181, 186, 196, 206, 227f., 231
beneficiary 149, 209
Clytemnestra 52f., 80, 88, 91, 219–224

command 3, 15f., 27, 41f., 53, 58, 76, 80, 84, 88, 98f., 104, 125f., 132, 148, 154, 156, 169, 175, 178, 180f., 194
confidence 48, 90, 218
conflict XIII, XX, 213
consequences XIII, 11, 34, 38, 100, 113, 137, 230f.
conspiracy 170, 182, 221, 225
convention 34, 47, 51, 55–57, 69–71, 100, 106f., 111, 187, 219, 222, 226
Council XX, 103, 114, 117, 119, 185, 187, 192, 199f., 204, 207, 213f.
court 26, 121, 166, 175, 182, 185
dative XXII, 12, 22, 26f., 29f., 42, 78, 79–88, 91, 93–99, 115, 119–122, 125, 131, 149, 152, 155–180, 196, 198–201, 206, 208–211, 217, 231
death 10, 13, 15, 22, 29f., 32, 34, 58–63, 68, 70, 76, 80f., 83, 85, 90f., 96, 121, 129, 131f., 137, 152, 154–156, 165, 179, 183, 190, 213, 219–225, 231
deception speech 56, 69
decree 50, 55, 78, 102, 134, 191, 204, 207
defeat XIII, XX, 58, 128, 136f., 147, 178, 183, 187, 213, 227
defendant 186, 197f., 202f.
denunciation 166, 183, 187, 192, 203, 205f., 214
disinformation 215, 229
dream 8, 135, 137, 155
embassy 15, 20, 28, 49, 163f., 186, 198–201, 208
emissary 135, 148, 183, 213
emotion XII, XIII, 30, 109
enemy 3, 8, 24f., 68, 77, 84, 92, 110, 121, 129, 132f., 138, 139–142, 157, 161, 170, 187, 218, 228f.
envoy XXI, 21, 130, 132, 137, 148, 165, 185, 191, 203
espionage 26, 139, 141f., 173, 183
etymology XX–XI, 230f.
eyewitness 8, 13, 66–68, 90, 92, 100, 105, 108, 112, 123, 129, 166, 222, 225f.
faithful 64, 128, 163, 219

fake (news) XIII, 70, 79, 155, 176, 181, 206, 215–229
falsehood 216–219
– false messenger 6, 216f., 220
– false speech 219
features XII, 82, 106, 134, 198
gossip 162, 183
Hector 8, 10–13, 15, 20, 24, 28f., 32, 58, 64, 83, 87
Helen 4, 18, 61, 148, 224f.
Heracles 20, 38, 42f., 49, 55f., 60, 85, 87
Herald XIX, 1, 2–5, 9, 12, 19, 26, 32, 35f., 47–58, 64, 79, 84f., 88f., 92, 101–106, 110, 114f., 130, 134–137, 157, 164, 181, 185f., 218f.
Hermes XXI, 6, 9, 16, 31f., 35, 37, 42f., 47–49, 64, 75f., 101
impeachment 94, 191f., 205
indictment 192, 203
informative role 62, 65f., 68, 72, 80, 82, 100, 111
informer / informant 25, 71, 106, 138–140, 170f., 204, 226
Iris XXI, 6–8, 12, 17f., 22, 27f., 31f., 41, 108–f., 216f., 232
landing 150, 167
law 191f., 194, 197, 202
lawsuit 121, 191
legal language 187–211
legal term (terminology) 143–181, 187, 191, 193, 203, 209f., 213f.
lie XIV, 54, 56, 95, 197, 200, 215, 218, 222, 224, 226–229
loyalty 5, 48, 64, 134, 219, 222
maleficiary 149, 229
messenger scene 47, 55, 59, 62, 66, 69–71, 77, 82, 92, 100f., 103–108, 111, 113–126, 215, 219, 223
messenger speech 4, 52, 55, 59f., 62, 66–72, 78, 90, 105, 108, 114, 117f., 219, 223
military term (terminology) 53, 98f., 140, 142, 153, 155, 169, 176, 178f., 181
miracle 61, 66, 100, 113, 124, 137, 183
misfortune 76, 82, 97, 136, 155, 164, 220, 225

murder 17, 58, 89, 95, 100, 137, 158, 183, 219
negotiation 38, 133, 138, 147, 162
Odysseus 1f., 5, 9, 13–33, 84, 96, 116
Oracle 80f., 88, 95f., 122, 132, 160, 164, 168, 174, 181, 183, 222
order 75, 77, 84f., 88f., 93, 98, 100, 110f., 125, 135, 147–153, 158, 169, 177–182, 194, 212, 217, 222, 231f.
paratragedy 101, 106f., 118
parody 101, 104, 106–126
Patroclus 6, 8, 10f., 13–16, 22, 29–33, 35, 231
peace 8, 104, 139, 147, 183, 203, 210, 213
private sphere XX, 179, 192
promise 17, 38, 84, 94–97, 176f., 193, 205, 208, 210, 212
prophecy 42, 94, 181
prosecution 191, 205
public sphere XX, 3, 5
recipient XXII, 22, 26, 29f., 78, 80, 83–91, 94f., 119, 122, 156–168, 172–176, 180, 196, 198–202, 206, 209f.
relevance 11, 47, 173, 187, 226, 228, 230
reliability 56, 64, 100, 113, 123, 128, 229
request 125f., 160, 163, 208, 210
responsibility 128, 183, 186f.
result XXII, 80f., 84, 88, 92–95, 105, 115, 119, 121–123, 138, 156–158, 163, 168, 172f., 196, 198, 201, 206
return (home) 9, 13–33, 51, 53, 79, 92, 95, 99f., 116
reward 21f., 116f., 124, 177
royal messenger 143, 183
rumour XIII, XVI, XIX, 15, 163, 203, 215f., 221, 232
secret 134, 139f., 173
slaughter 17, 164
social hierarchy 7, 217
source (of information) 13, 52, 67, 150, 215, 222, 224, 226, 232
specialization 47, 50, 111, 135, 163, 183, 198, 214, 231
spy 63, 96, 120, 123f., 133, 139–142, 165, 180, 226
status (social) 3, 5, 7, 33, 41, 100, 217

strategy 218, 222, 227, 229
suicide 61, 72, 81, 100
tactic 134, 229
technical term XIX, 31, 36, 50, 55, 57, 72, 80, 94, 98, 100f., 113, 125f., 154, 166, 171, 182f., 193, 205f., 213f., 231
treason 192, 203, 213f.
trial 121, 166, 192, 194, 204f.
triumph XIII, 34–46
truce XX, 36f., 102, 131–133, 163f., 169, 176, 178f., 183, 202, 209, 213
truth 49, 56, 63, 66, 70, 75, 90, 103, 108, 128, 154, 197, 216–219, 222, 227–229
truthfulness XIII, 105
victory XIXf., 34, 36, 116, 132, 136, 138, 152, 156f., 168, 181, 183, 186f., 195f., 198, 213, 228

war XX, 7f., 11, 15, 24f., 32f., 40, 51f., 54, 56, 72, 79, 92, 99f., 110, 118, 128, 130f., 133f., 139, 142f., 151, 155, 158, 161–166, 172f., 180–183, 185f., 198, 206f., 210, 213, 217f., 224, 226, 228f., 231f.
warning 31, 42, 106, 182, 208
withdrawal 129, 133
witness 33, 61, 68, 163, 186, 197, 204f., 232
αὐτοψία 8, 66–68, 215, 222, 226, 232
ὅτι substantive clause XXII, 86, 93, 150, 157–159, 172, 175, 204
ὡς substantive clause 85, 122, 138, 160, 165f., 169, 176, 196, 201, 210

Index Locorum

Aeschines
Emb.
12	201 n56	103	208 n76
13	201 n54, 206 n67	116	207 n71
16	200 n51	122	185
17	200	205	210 n82
21	208 n76	213	201 n54
25	201 n54	223	206, 206 n66
34	193 n24, 206 n67	252	206 n66
35	185	*In Tim.*	
41	208 n76	2	209
47	200 n51	23	185
49	200 n51	28–32	193 n25
51	200 n49	32	210
52	192 n21	43	206 n67
56	202 n59	64	193 n27
60	198 n40, 199 n42	81	193
77	211 n83	117	210 n82
79	192 n21	135	201 n55
80	198 n40, 200 n52	143	208 n76
86	186	173	210 n82
94	199 n42		

Aeschylus
Ag.
119	199 n45, 201 n56	19	51
120	208 n76	21	63 n40
121	200 n48, 201 n54	26–30	52
130	200 n51, 203	40–257	52
132	208 n76	83–87	79
133	208 n76, 209	86	52
134	209	262	63 n40, 252
139	203 n60	264	63 n40
155	192 n21, 197	264–267	52
156	209 n79	280	52, 64
169	196 n33, 200 n52	281–283	53
171	196	282	XX n12
In Ctes.		285	64
3	206 n66	289	53, 98 n148
49	186	291	53, 64
62	186	294–295	53, 98
63	199 n47	315–316	53
64	209 n81	475	63 n40
65	212 n84	479–482	99
90	212 n84	493–494	51
95	186 n5	513–515	48
98	212 n83	522–526	51

587–589	54	1040–1041	75
588	64	*Sept.*	
604–605	89	40	72
624–625	53	40–41	67
632	53	66	69 n70
633	92 n133	82	64, 219 n6
636	12 n17, 63 n41, 64, 212	375–652	69
		634	49 n9
636–649	54	791–802	69
639	64	792–821	
646	63 n40	811	69
680	70 n72	848–850	70
Cho.		1005	50 n10, 90 n130
195		*Supp.*	
266	64	180	xxi, 64
658–659	90 n129	467–475	
659	83	727	50
674–690	70, 119	930–933	48
680–682	219	931	90 n130
707–709	220		
709	220	**Aristophanes**	
736	82 n105	*Ach.*	
740–741	63 n45, 220	135	102 n1
741	220	170	122
770	87 n119	623	101 n1
774	83 n107	748	101 n1
838	87 n121, 221 n9	1000–1004	102
838–841	63 n41	1069–1077	110
848–853	221	1076–1077	115
Eum.	221	1082–1083	110
566	40	1084–1094	111
Pers.		1174–1189	112
14	59 n26	*Av.*	
249–255	71	1119	107 n6
253	83 n108	1118–1121	107
265–266	66	1122–1124	107
290–531	60 n31	1166–1174	109
330	90 n130	1168	107 n6
468–470	98 n148	1269–1270	104
PV.		1271–1273	105
658–662	88	1275	105
661	88 n123, 168 n99	1276	105
941	64 n51	1340	107 n6
943	75	1340–1341	218
944	82 n103	*Eccl.*	
947–948	76 n84	684	101 n1
969	64, 219 n6	711–713	102

834–852	102	**Bacchylides**	
Eq.		*Dith.* 16.23–29	39
610–613	123	*Dith.* 15.40	35 n5
646–647	117	*Dith.* 18.17	35 n5
654–656	118	*Dith.* 19.30	37
642–645	118	*Ep.* 2.1–5	40
647	117 n27	*Ep.* 2.2–3	39
668–669	102	*Ep.* 5.19–20	37
Lys.		*Ep.* 13.98	37 n8
980–981	103		
983–984	102	**Demosthenes**	
992–1001	103	*Andr.*	
1002–1006	104	29	193 n27
1049–1053	125	*Aristocr.*	
1235	122 n31	121	208 n66
Plut.		*Aristog.1*	
268–269	122	47	192 n21
585	102 n1	*Chers.*	
631–632	113	28	206 n21
632	106 n6	29	192 n21
633–636	113	*De cor.*	
641–642	113 n19	13	192 n21, 206 n66
641–643	124	19	208 n76
667–670	125	25	200 n48
760–763	122	32	199 n45, 201 n56
764–766	117	33	198 n40
Ran.		38	208 n76
1172	102 n1	42	198 n40
Thesm.		122	209 n76
340–342	116	169	196
517–597	114 n20	170	185, 200 n49
571–591	119	178	208 n76
588	143 n39	249	193
592–596	123	250	206 n66
597	124	267	212, 12 n17
652–654	121	298	193 n24
768	106 n6	322	209 n76
780	101 n1	323	195
Vesp.		*Emb.*	
405–414	121	1	194
		4	
Aristotle		5	190 n12
Ath. Pol.		8	200 n48
8.4	191	9	
63	194 n29	11	200 n50
Poet.		12	200 n49
1454b	153	18	198 n40, 201 n54

19	199 n46	101	209 n79
20	198 n40	*Evag.*	
23	201 n54	65	186 n6
26	193 n24	*Everg.*	
28	198 n40	57	
31	190 n12	67	201 n51
35	211	80	206 n66
37	201 n54	81	208 n76
41	208 n79	*Halonn.*	
44	208 n76	21	202 n59
48	208 n76, 209 n76	*Lacr.*	
53	191, 198 n40	33	202 n57
56	201 n54	*Lept.*	
58	208 n76	61	208 n76
59	199 n46	73	202 n58
60	202	79	203 n60
70	186	*Macart.*	
75	199 n45	57	209 n77
76	200 n48	58	209 n77
82	199 n46	*Meid.*	
85	200 n49	14	193 n24
103	192 n21	25	201 n55
111	201 n54	37	201 n55
116	192 n21, 203	72	199 n45, 201 n55
124	202 n59	121	192 n21
152	199 n45	162	207
161	200 n48	168	212 n91
175	208 n76	202	201 n55
177	200 n48	*Neaer.*	
178	212 n89	78	186 n4
183	200 n48	100	186
185	186	*Olymp.*	
193	208 n78	51	209 n80
204	198 n40	*Olynth.1*	
217	202 n58	4	201
223	200 n48	5	197
248	208	*Pantae.*	
253	198 n40	13	209 n79
279	200 n48	*Phil. 1*	
283	194	15	208 n76
304	198 n40	17–18	206
324	199 n47	*Phil. 4*	
338	186 n3	1	211
Epit.		*Phorm.*	
34	199 n45	16	191
Erot.		50	206 n66
27	199 n45		

Polyc.		761–763	59, 105
4	206 n66	765–766	63
17	204	Hec.	
19	211 n83	104–109	78
31	211 n83	105–106	50
50.51	201 n55	187	82 n106
Spud.		146	49
17	197	423	87
Symm.		503–504	56
40	202 n59	508–510	56
Tim.		519–608	56
63	192 n20, 192 n21	530	49
Zenoth.		532–533	68 n64
8	208 n76	591	87 n119
11	210 n82	604–606	85
		671–673	92
Euripides		726–728	85
Alc.		734–735	68 n64
209	82 n104	Hel.	
731	72 n78	435–436	60
Andr.		447	83 n109
821	87 n121	448	82 n102
1070	82 n102	604	82 n106
1086–1166	60 n31	605–616	61 n32
1092–1095	69 n66	618–619	85 n117
1239–1242	89	736–738	86
Bacch.		1193–1196	224
173–174	94	1200	72, 224
604–641	61 n32	1487–1494	75
657	62 n79	1512–1518	225
657–658	66	1526–1619	60 n31
677–775	60 n31	1617	82 n105
680–860	61 n32	Heracl.	
1029	72 n77	49	49 n8
1085–1147	60 n31	54	83 n108
1109	89 n126	55	48 n5
El.		272	49
169–174	86	292–293	49
230	83 n108	530–532	96
303	80 n99	656	64
332	90 n129	658–660	99
418	83 n108	659	85
420–421	88 n124	751	59 n26, 77
461	64	784–792	77
650–652	91	798	82 n102
707	49	800–867	60 n31
757–760	58	824–825	98 n148

839–840	69 n65	856	64 n49
907–909	98 n148	866–957	60 n31
HF		875–876	99 n150
553	50	885	49
706	63 n44	895–897	49
1136	83 n108	1276–1278	78 n92
1185	98 n147	1395–1503	60 n31
Hipp.		1493–1498	61 n32
998	97 n145	1539	82 n105
1151–1152	1110 n14	1541	49 n9
IA.		1558	80 n99
352–353	93	*Phoen.*	
1447	81 n101	1072–1076	67
1301	64	1075	80 n99
Ion.		1090–1479	60 n31
180–181	81, 168 n98	1217	63 n40
769–775	76	1332–1334	69 n69
1122–1229	60 n31	1333	64
1605–1606	94	1334	82 n102
IT.		1546–1550	76
260–340	60 n31	1631	49
447–451	78 n91	*Rhes.*	
461	74 n80	34	82 n102
582	81 n101	39	82
588	87 n121	52	82 n102
639–642	89	70–71	98 n148
704	85 n117	91–92	84 n113
739–740	87 n119	267–268	85 n116
769–771	83	272	64 n50, 72
1182	81 n101	522	83 n109
1184	99 n149	754–755	72
1306	82 n103	*Supp.*	
Med.		121	49 n8
287–289	91	203	XXI, 64
719–721	98 n146	399	82 n102
975	63 n40	459–462	50
1007–1111	97	467–475	50
1009	82 n102	638	82 n102
1010	63 n40	640	108 n10
1011	82 n102	641	82 n102
1118–1120	40, 110 n14	643	82 n102
1119	107 n9	647–649	67
1137–1221	61 n31	650–730	60 n31
1149–1155	68	668	49, 49 n8
Or.		673	48 n9
360–367	95	849–852	92
618	82 n102	1169–1173	98 n148

Index Locorum — 261

Tro.		3.142.5	174 n116
55	82 n103	3.153.1	174 n116
235–238	57	3.153.3	177 n128
240	57	4.14.1	157
707–708	57, 110 n14	4.71.4	143
719	58	4.83.1	132 n18
1004	80 n99	4.94.2	132 n18
		4.128.1	155 n66
Herodotus		4.151	164 n93
1.21.1	132 n18, 174, n116	4.151.3	164 n93
1.22.1	157 n71	4.153.1	167
1.36.2	138 n30	4.200.1	176 n124
1.43.3	155	5.14.2	149 n46
1.70.1	176 n124, 177 n130	5.17	133
1.77.3	176 n124	5.20.4	168 n95
1.78.2	164 n93	5.33.3	175 n118
1.83.1	150 n48	5.35	128 n5
1.91.6	165, 168 n100	5.87.2	163
1.114.1–2	149 n44	5.92 η15	151
1.120.2	143	5.95	53 n15
1.157.9	149	5.95.2	174 n116
2.114.1	148	5.105.1	176 n121
2.121ε1	167 n96	5.108.1	150 n52
2.152.4	160	5.117	150 n48
3.9.1	132	5.118.1	174 n116
3.13	133	6.9.3	176 n126
3.30.2–3	137	6.10.1	150 n51, 174 n116
3.34	143 n40	6.28.1	150 n48
3.43	149 n44	6.42.1	132 n18
3.53.2	149 n45	6.58.1	158 n74, 179
3.58.1	131	6.60.1	134
3.61.3	132	6.63.2	176 n119
3.63	134	6.63.3	140 n34
3.64.1	166 n95	6.65.3	176 n120
3.65	137	6.105.1	134
3.65.2	160 n79	6.105.2	164 n93
3.69.1	149 n43	6.133.2	132 n18
3.77.2	149 n44	6.139.2	176 n124
3.84.2	143	7.1.1	150 n51
3.118.2	172	7.1.2	176 n124, 179 n136
3.122.3–4	148 n42	7.9β 1–2	129
3.123.2	164 n93	7.27.1	177 n128
3.126.2	143	7.29.1	176 n123
3.134.6	173 n112	7.32.1	132 n18
3.138	133	7.39.2	176 n126
3.140.2	155 n66	7.80	108 n10
3.142.2	174 n116	7.119.2	179 n136

262 — Index Locorum

7.130.3	176 n126	2.94	8
7.142.1	164 n93	2.97	3
7.150	176 n124	2.280	5 n10
7.150.3	176 n124, 176 n126	2.437–439	13
7.152.1	130	2.442	3, 5 n10
7.172.1	138 n30	2.786–787	7
7.178.2	174	2.790	12 n22
7.230.1	129 n8	2.795	12 n22
7.239.2	173 n116	2.796–806	8
8.14.2	150 n49	3.121	6 n13
8.21.1	157 n71	3.129	12 n22
8.23.1	157, 161 n83, 164 n90	3.205–206	18
8.25.1	176 n126	3.245	5
8.29.1	177 n128	3.265	5
8.30.1	177 n128	3.268	5
8.30.2	176 n126	3.271	5
8.50.1	161 n80	4.190	3
8.54.1	135	4.192	5
8.56.1	176 n121	4.382–384	20
8.80.1	157 n71	5.353	12 n21
8.80.2	161 n83	5.368	12 n21
8.81	173	5.388–391	32
8.98.1	136	7.183	3
8.98.2–3	136	7.274	2
8.99.1	150 n51	7.275–278	3
8.99.5	149 n47	7.345–378	4
8.112.1	132 n18	7.383–397	4
8.136.1	132 n20	7.413–424	7 n15
8.140.1	150 n54	8.397	29 n46
8.142.1	176 n126	8.398	12 n27
8.143.2	166 n95	8.409	12 n25, 19 n46
8.144.5	147	8.425	12 n22
9.14.1	150 n48	8.517–519	28
9.15.1	150 n48	9.10	5 n10
9.21.3	164 n88	9.85	27 n46
9.69.1	159 n75	9.170	3
		9.174	5
Hesiod		9.422	15
Theogony		9.617–618	29
781	18 n32	9.626–627	29 n48
		9.649–655	15, 29 n46
Homer		10.286	8
Iliad		10.315	3 n4, 5
1.321	5	10.405–411	24 n38
1.334	2	10.413–422	24
2.26	8	10.424–425	25
2.50	3, 5 n10	10.427–441	25

10.447–448	34	19.120	26 n40
11.138–142	20	19.337	12 n18, 15
11.185	12 n27	22.437–439	13
11.186	12 n24	23.39	5, 5 n10
11.195	12 n21	23.199	6
11.200–209	7 n15	23.205–210	7 n15
11.210	12 n22	23.567	3
11.652	8	23.896–897	35 n6
11.685	3, 5 n10	24.77	12 n25, 29 n46
11.715	8	24.87	12 n22
12.73	8	24.95	12 n21
12.342	3	24.133	8
12.343	5	24.144–148	12 n24
13.249–252	19	24.159	12 n25
14.355	14	24.169	6 n13
15.144	6, 216	24.171–187	7 n15
15.146–148	7 n15	24.188	12 n22
15.158–159	6, 12 n24, 216	24.173	6 n13
15.168	12 n21	24.282	3
15.172	12 n22	24.292	8, 12 n28
15.174–183	6, 217	24.296	8
15.200	12 n21	24.310	8, 12 n28
15.206	12 n26	24.561	8
15.207	6 n13, 37 n10	24.577	5 n10
15.636–640	20	24.701	5 n10
16.7–16	16	24.767	12 n20
16.21–29	16	*Odyssey*	
16.333–334	19	1.109	5
17.319–332	5	1.143	5
17.408–411	29	1.153	5
17.640–642	10	1.405–409	17
17.685–693	10	1.414	15
17.700–701	11	2.6	3, 5 n10
18.1–2	10	2.30	16
18.17	12 n19, 14	2.38	3
18.18–21	11, 15	2.42	16
18.82	12 n26	2.92	17
18.166	12 n21	2.255–256	15
18.182	6 n13	3.338	5
18.183	12 n21	4.24	27 n43
18.167	6 n13	4.301	3
18.170–180	6 n14, 7 n15	4.528	26 n41
18.196	21 n21	4.675–679	26
18.202	12 n22	4.697–702	27
18.502	3	4.774–775	30
18.503	3	5.29	9
18.505	5 n10	5.150	16

6.50	27 n43	18.424	3 n6, 5
7.163	5	19.134–135	2
7.178	5	19.244	3
7.263	16 n31	20.276	5
8.6–14	5 n11	21.270	5
8.62	5	22.431–434	27
8.69	5	22.496	27 n42
8.107	5	23.5–9	23
8.261	5	23.20–24	23
8.270	5	24.48	15, 32
8.399	5	24.354–355	17
8.418	5	24.405	9
8.471	5	24.413	9
9.90	3		
9.95	31	**Inscriptions**	
10.59	3	IG^3 34	124 n33
10.102	3	IG^3 1453, B–G	134
10.245	14		
12.374	9	**Isocrates**	
13.49	5	*Aegin.*	
13.64	3	40	190
13.93–95	23	*Antid.*	
13.381	17	314	192 n21
14.118–129	26	*Arch.*	
14.149–153	21	72	206
14.166–167	22	*Areop.*	
14.372–374	18	9–10	195
15.41	14	*Bus.*	
15.209–210	30	26	211 n83
15.314	14	*Demon.*	
15.447	18	2.5	210 n79
15.458	27 n43	19	208 n76
15.526	9, 12 n29	33	202 n59
16.130–134	31	44	212 n90
16.138	9	*De pace*	
16.150	29 n46	130	192 n21
16.153	30 n49	*Evag.*	
16.329	14	36	198 n36
16.333–337	19	*Hel.*	
16.355	17	9	209 n76
16.458–459	30	57	209 n768
16.465–469	9	*Panath.*	
17.335	5	17	202
17.382–385	2	*Soph.*	
18.1–7	31	1	212 n88
18.185–189	27 n42	5	212 n88
18.291	5	8	212 n88

9	212 n88	**Pindar**	
20	209 n79	*Isthm.*	
Trapez.		2.23	36 n9
11	201 n56	3.4–43	36 n8
		8.40–47	41
Lucian		*Nem.*	
Hist. Conscr.		1.59	37
47	226 n16	5.2–5	44
Laps.		6.56–61	37
3.1	152	*Ol.*	
		3.28	42
Lysias		4.5	34, 42, 46
1.19–20	205	5.8	36 n8
1.41	211 n84	6.78	35 n5
1.42	211 n84	6–90	37
1.76	211 n83	7.20–23	43
2.1	209 n80	8.48–51	
2.6	199	8.81–84	42
2.7	185	9.25	34
2.26	198	13.97–100	35
8.8	200 n53	14.20–25	40
8.9	201	14.21	34, 43 n16, 46
8.10	202 n58	*Pyth.*	
8.15	200 n53	1.28–33	36
9.6	202	2.4	40
10.1	205	2.40–41	41
12.17	211 n83	4.29–31	45
12.25	204 n61	4.170	35 n4
12.44	211 n83	4.277–278	37
12.52	209 n79	4.278	42
12.58	192 n21	6.14–17	44
12.68	209 n79	8.48–51	42
12.70	208 n76	9.1–4	44
13.56	204 n61		
15.2	193 n25	**Plato**	
16.12	192 n21	*Cri.*	
20.9	208	43c–d	132 n20
22.14	200 n53	*Resp.*	
25.30	210	432d	108 n10
28.4	209 n76	565e	191 n15
30.22	192 n21	*Tht.*	
31.15	209 n79	144b	108 n10
Pausanias		**Plutarch**	
1.24.6	157 n72	*Lys.*	
		23.4	47 n1

Sophocles
Aj.
221–223	77 n87
567	80 n99
718–721	65
719–732	60 n31
845–849	81
1240	50
1376	95 n138
1376–1377	84, 96 n141

Ant.
27	49 n9
34	49 n9
203	49 n9
223–224	107 n9
277	44
461	49 n9
1286	12 n17, 63 n43, 212

El.
38–41	81
41	222
47–50	222
149	64
168–172	79
68	449 n9
666–667	223
673	223
676	223
680–763	223
690	49 n9
1111	87 n121, 223
1341	85 n117, 223
1442–1444	85 n116, 224
1452	85, 224

OC
302	76 n85, 80 n99
333	62 n39
430	49 n9
1429	83 n108
1511	50, 83 n109
1587–1666	61 n32

OT
147–148	95
450	49 n9
604	80 n99
753	49
954–956	86
955–956	91
957–959	90

Phil.
319–390	219 n18
500	219 n18
542–627	219 n18
564	219 n18
568	62 n39
1178–1179	98 n148
1293	48 n5
1306	48

Trach.
73	87 n119
180–183	87
190	81 n100
232–235	55
249–290	219 n8
346–348	56
1109–1111	85

Thucydides
1.27.1	132
1.29.1	132 n18, 133
1.29.4	164 n91
1.33.2	176 n123
1.91.2	163
1.91.3	161 n80
1.114.1	149 n44, 159
1.116.1	179 n136
1.116.3	172
1.131.1	134 n25
1.132.5	134 n25
2.3	147
2.4	147
2.5.1	147
2.5.5	132 n18
2.6.1	132 n18
2.6.2	132 n18
2.6.3	137, 159 n56
2.10.1	179 n136
2.80.2	179 n136
2.85.3	180 n140
2.85.4	156 n69
3.3.3	172 n109
3.3.5	156 n69
3.4.1	164 n90
3.5.2	138 n30

Index Locorum — 267

3.16.3	176 n124	7.3.1	132 n18
3.24.3	166 n95	7.8.1	161 n83
3.33.2	129 n9, 150 n48	7.8.2	164 n90
3.105.3	132 n18, 132 n19	7.11.1	128 n5
3.105.4	160	7.11–15	128 n4
3.110.1	161	7.17.1	176 n124
3.113.1	133	7.17.3	156 n68
4.8.2	179 n136	7.18.4	179 n138
4.8.3	158	7.25.9	156 n69
4.27.4	161 n83	7.31.3	157
4.30.4	132 n18	7.31.4	159 n77
4.78.1	133	7.43.4	156 n68
4.93.2	159 n76	7.44.2	70 n71
4.118.13	131 n16	7.48	129 n10
4.120.3	176 n123	7.65.1	180
4.122.1	179	7.67.3	190 n11, 153 n63
4.122.2	162	7.73.3	141
4.122.4	163 n87	7.73.4	160 n103, 181 n145
4.125.1	160	8.6.4	166 n95
5.10.2	159 n75	8.10.1	176 n125
5.17.2	179 n136	8.11.3	159 n76
5.37.1	164 n93	8.14.1	139 n32
5.43.3	148	8.15.1	150 n51
5.44.1	147	8.19.1	150 n50
5.46.4	164 n90	8.26.1	161 n80
5.47.4	176 n126	8.32.3	176 n126
5.47.6	176 n124	8.39.4	148 n41
5.49.2	176 n125	8.41.1	150 n53
5.49.3	176 n125	8.51.1	139
5.49.4	176 n125	8.51.3	171
5.54.2	179 n136	8.74.1	164 n90
5.64.1	150 n51	8.79.1	172
5.66.3	180 n149	8.86.3	166 n95, 167 n96
6.33.1	167	8.86.8	176 n124, 177 n130
6.36.1	151	8.89.1	164 n90
6.36.3	161 n83	8.94.3	158 n73
6.40.1	151	8.99.1	181 n146
6.40.2	152	8.100.4	158
6.41.2	173 n110	8.106.4	132
6.45.1	159 n75	8.108.1	151
6.46.1	159 n77	8.108.4	177 n127
6.52.1	172 n109		
6.56.1	177 n129	**Xenophon**	
6.58.1	158 n74	*Ages.*	
6.65.3	157 n71	1.6	176 n122
6.88.6	176 n126, 179 n136	1.13	166 n95
6.104.1	150 n55	2.11	158

5.6.7	162	7.2.16	165 n94
7.5	150 n50	7.2.36	167 n96
8.3	166 n95	7.3.1	164 n93
An.		*Ap.*	
1.2.9	226 n16	2.1	174 n115
1.2.21	138	13.10	174 n113
1.3.8	132 n18, 132 n19	91	168 n102
1.3.19	167 n96	*[Ath. pol.]*	
1.3.21	157 n71	11.6	133
1.4.12	164 n89	*Cyr.*	
1.4.13	164 n88	2.4.1	138 n130
1.6.2	169 n104	2.4.8	164
1.6.5	163 n86	2.4.17	176 n119
1.7.2	163 n86	2.4.23	153
1.7.13	156 n67	2.4.31	132 n18
1.10.14	164 n90	3.1.10	176 n124
1.10.15	165 n94	3.2.29	133
2.1.4	165, 176 n126	3.3.34	181
2.1.5	132 n18	3.3.56	164 n88
2.1.7	134	4.2.28	161 n83
2.1.21	164 n89, 166 n95	4.4.11	176 n124
2.1.23	164	4.4.12	168
2.2.20	134	4.5.12	164 n89
2.3.2	131	5.2.3	164 n90
2.3.5	165 n94	5.2.4	165 n94
2.3.7	168 n103, 169 n105	5.3.8	164 n90
2.3.9	165 n94, 167 n96	5.3.12	180 n141
2.3.19	152, 161 n82	5.3.15	165 n94
2.4.23	167 n96	5.3.17	176 n122
2.3.24	164 n88	5.3.26	138 n131
2.4.4	166 n95	6.1.31–37	228 n18
2.4.23	167 n96	6.1.42	176 n122, 228
2.4.24	176 n119	6.2.1	165 n94, 177 n128
2.5.27	164 n90	6.2.2	142, 165
2.5.36	164 n90	6.2.14	150 n48
2.5.38	177	6.2.15	161
3.4.36	169	6.2.19	164 n88, 165 n94
4.1.5	181 n148	6.2.20	169
4.5.20	165 n94	6.2.21	176 n122
4.7.20	177 n128	6.3.5–6	156
5.6.21	164 n93	6.3.15	174 n115
5.7.2	133	7.4.2	177 n130
7.1.4	167 n96	7.4.9	176 n124
7.1.14	168 n103	7.5.19	165 n94
7.1.33	176 n124, 177 n130	7.5.49	173 n112
7.1.34	164 n88, 167 n96	7.5.52	150
7.2.14	175 n118	7.5.54	176 n120

8.2.10	141, 164 n90	3.4.11	166 n95
8.3.2	175	3.4.28	176 n124
8.3.19	169 n105	4.2.19	179 n134
8.4.23	167 n96	4.3.1	169 n77
8.4.33	177 n130	4.3.2	164 n90, 167
8.5.25	176 n124	4.3.10	227, 160 n78
8.6.16	164 n93	4.3.13	161 n83
8.7.28	164 n93	4.3.13–14	227
Eq. mag.		4.3.18	169 n76
4.3	173 n110, 181 n148	4.3.23	70 n71
4.8	142, 167 n96	4.4.8	176 n120
4.9	181 n148	4.5.8	169 n77
4.16	226	5.1.22	162
5.8	154, 218	5.1.32	164 n88, 164 n93
8.18	181 n148	5.2.18	175 n118
Hell.		5.3.25	165 n94
1.1.8	174 n115	5.4.7	164 n90
1.1.15	173	5.4.21	165 n94
1.1.27	169 n76	5.4.33	164 n88
1.4.2	138 n30	5.4.56	176 n122
1.6.12	176 n126	6.4.2	179 n136
1.6.22	174	6.4.7	166 n95, 226 n16
1.6.28	175	6.4.16	156 n69
1.6.36	174 n115	6.4.21	160 n78
1.6.36–37	228 n17	6.4.25	165 n94
1.7.4	127 n2	6.4.36	176
1.7.11	166	7.1.32	134, 138
2.1.4	154	7.1.37	164 n90
2.1.7	132 n18	7.1.38	166 n95
2.1.9	132 n18	7.4.38	176 n126
2.1.20	158 n73	7.5.1	164 n93
2.1.24	175	7.5.10	176 n120
2.1.29	164 n90	*Mem.*	
2.1.30	164 n90	1.2.7	177 n128
2.2.3	178	1.2.8	176 n126
2.2.12	164 n88	1.2.33	164 n93
2.2.14	164 n89	1.2.38	164 n93
2.2.17	165 n94	2.6.36	170 n107
2.2.18	169 n77	3.1.1	176 n124
3.2.20	163 n87	3.11.3	170
3.3.5	170	*Symp.*	
3.4.3	132 n18, 177 n128	1.11	172 n109

www.ingramcontent.com/pod-product-compliance
Lightning Source LLC
Chambersburg PA
CBHW020223170426
43201CB00007B/304